The Consumer's Practical Guide

to Funerals, Burials & Cremation

Scott D. Emmert

American Literary Press
Five Star Special Edition
Baltimore, Maryland

The Consumer's Practical Guide to Funerals, Burials & Cremation

Library of Congress
Cataloging-in-Publication Data
ISBN 1-56167-897-X

Library of Congress Card Catalog Number:
2005904873

Cover photo by Jeff Sherretz

Published by

American Literary Press
Five Star Special Edition
8019 Belair Road, Suite 10
Baltimore, Maryland 21236

Manufactured in the United States of America

Dedication

To all of those who have or will have to deal with the complex and difficult issues concerning the death of a loved one. May this book be a source of guidance and assistance.

Preface

WHY THIS BOOK

When I decided to go into funeral service back in 1996, I wanted to help people who were in a great time of need, and in need of professional guidance. After entering the funeral profession, I found that most people were totally unprepared and in the dark about what to do about making someone else's final arrangements.

I also learned that the time of death was one of the worst times to try to be making a lot of mostly major decisions.

And so, this book was written to help those who have the courage to face one of life's most feared and avoided subjects-death- by providing information and education about today's death care industry, what it can and cannot do, and to be able to be familiar with some of the language, terms and other information you will need to know when the time comes to have to go to the funeral home and/or cemetery to make those necessary arrangements.

My wish is that the following pages will be very resourceful and informative, if not interesting and insightful.

Scott D. Ernst

Table of Contents

Introduction

Statistics continue to indicate that the mortality rate among human beings is still 100%. What this means is that at some point in time everyone will pass away.

Because of this fact it is inevitable that regardless of how much one wants or does not want to be involved, that death will require everyone to arrange, help arrange or attend some event or be involved in some situation in connection to someone's death.

With this in mind, as a funeral director I want to use this opportunity to take you through the process of making final arrangements on a step-by-step basis from the time death occurs to the final disposition.

I want to show you how to choose a funeral director, funeral home and a cemetery or place for final disposition; what you can expect from a funeral director/funeral home; the difference between funeral expenses and burial expenses; what cremation is all about and why it is growing in popularity; how to personalize a funeral or memorial service and different ways of memorializing a departed loved one. I'm also going to share with you some of the available benefits, ways of paying for the continually high and increasing costs of dying and methods of dealing with grief after the services and disposition are over.

Knowing where we have been is vital in determining where we are going and so I am going to provide you with a little history and a description of different practices and customs for a culturally and sociologically diverse land.

Lastly, having resources available for where to get information that you'll need in various situations that may occur in different areas of the country will be invaluable.

Regarding the following pages and taking and acting upon the advise and information I am sharing, I believe can save you hundreds and even thousands of dollars, but as importantly save you headaches, stress and even more fatigue and grief than just losing a loved one by having this handbook of guidance and instruction.

My hope is that this practical guide to funerals, burials and cremation will be just that—a reference of direction, and information.

Scott D. Emmert

Chapter 1

Funeral Homes & Services

1. Introduction: What You Need To Know When You Need To Know It
2. Selecting A Funeral Home/Funeral Director
   Urban vs. Rural
   Corporate vs. Independent
   High Volume vs. Low Volume
   Reputation vs. Location
3. How Much Does A Funeral Cost?
4. What Does It Cost To Bury Someone?
5. The First Call: Contacting A Funeral Home
6. Etiquette At The Time Of Death And Preparing For The Arrangement Conference (What Has To Happen)
7. Right Of Disposition (Your Rights, Your Responsibilities)
8. Meeting With The Funeral Director, What To Expect
9. The Arrangement Conference (Arranging A Service)
10. Types Of Services (Funeral Home Chapel/Stateroom/Church/ Graveside/Other Facility/Location/Committal)
11. Types Of Disposition
12. Selecting A Casket: Types, Manufacturer, Size, Quality
    Casket Stores and Third Party Suppliers—What You Need To Know.
13. Selecting An Outer Burial Container—What You Need To Know
14. Embalming And Preparation: What Is Embalming And What's Its Purpose. Disinfection/Restoration/Preservation
15. Refrigeration
16. Cosmetology And Hairdressing/Dressing And Casketing
17. Professional Service Fees
18. Use Of Facilities And Staff Visitation/Viewing/Wake/Hosting And Receiving Family And Friends
19. Transportation: Rolling Stock Including First Call, Limousines, Coach, Flower Van/Lead Vehicle/Overland Transport Airlines/Other Delivery/Pickup Charges/Motor Escorts
20. Sundry Items: Register Book/Food Register/Service Folders/Programs/ Bulletins/Prayer Cards/Acknowledgment/Thank You Cards

21. Flowers: Fresh/Artificial
22. Clothing (Burial Garments or Deceased Clothing) Undergarments/Accessories/Jewelry
23. Ministers/Clergy/Officiants
24. Music: Live or Recorded
25. Pallbearers (Friends/Family/Guests/Funeral Home Staff Cemetery Staff/Military/Etc.
26. Honorariums: Officiants/Musicians/Pallbearers/Churches
27. Obituaries And Death Notices: Newspaper/Magazine/Periodical/ Trade or Hobby Journal/Internet
28. Death Certificates: Vital Statistics
29. Permits: Transport/Burial/Cremation/Etc.
30. Cash Advance Items: Third Party Charges
31. Miscellaneous Services: Picture Taking/Service Recording/House Cleaning/Food Preparation/Errand Running/Flower Placing/Marker Setting/Book, Card Typing/Security/Videographing/Catering/ Reception Hosting
32. Miscellaneous Products: Book Marks/Crucifixes/Picture Frames/ Candles/Paintings/Flag Cases
33. Other Charges: Director present/Per Day/Flower storage/Recording Fees/Holidays, Evenings, Weekends/Sender Fees/Overnight
34. Packaged Funeral Plans
35. Contracts And Agreements: Your Legal Rights
36. In Summary: Do I Have To Use A Funeral Home?

Funeral Homes And Services

What You Need To Know When You need To Know It

Next to purchasing a home and an automobile, buying the services and merchandise from a funeral home or mortuary are the largest expenditure that you will ever make. Ironically, most people will spend a great deal of time, some times years to find a good or best buy of a homestead or vehicle. However when it comes to death and what to do when the ultimate event takes place is not paramount on most peoples priority list despite its third place on the pyramid of major consumer expenditures.

Even more profound is the sad fact that most married couples will often make these big purchase decisions together both planning, saving and making the decision to trade big money for that house, car or whatever.

As a Funeral Director I've had the opportunity too many times to see a brand new widow or widower come to the funeral home maybe after 50 or 60 plus years of being together to make a large purchase decision alone - maybe and in many instances for the first time.

Confused, depressed and not always using good judgment, selecting items or services that one has not had to make alone before. And especially to make without any shopping, research, comparison or having time to make sure one is getting what they really want in the situation.

The purpose of this chapter is to help you understand what will happen and what you will need to do when the time comes for you to go make arrangements for a parent, spouse, brother, sister, etc., or perhaps even prearranging for yourself.

Selecting A Funeral Home/Funeral Director

There are many things to think about in choosing a Funeral Home that will serve you at your time of need. If you are looking around before a death has occurred in the family, you are at an advantage in a lot of ways. If a death has taken place and especially one that is sudden and unexpected you must act quickly and take action in picking a Funeral Home to handle the arrangements.

Some of the things that you will need to consider include convenience, reliability, facilities, the place of burial or disposition, and the integrity of the firm as a going concern, just to name several. Perhaps you have attended a funeral or memorial service where a particular funeral home was in charge of the arrangements. Was there anything in particular that impressed or displeased you about the way the services were handled? Maybe you know some families who have had a death in recent days. Finding out who they went to and how they were treated may help you make a good decision.

There are some important factors to ponder about choosing the right firm to meet you and your family's needs at such an important time, I want to talk about some of these as they can help you chose what your best options are.

Urban vs. Rural:

If you live in a small town or a rural area where there is only one funeral home you do not have a problem unless the one funeral home is not one that you do not respect or trust. In this case you do have a valid dilemma as to whether you want to travel some distance to use another funeral home or use the local one despite your lack of confidence.

If you are in a large city or metropolitan area or trade territory you will have many potential firms to choose from. Look in your city's yellow pages of the telephone directory. This will give you lots of information on what's available in your area.

Usually, the bigger the city the more options you have in selecting a funeral provider, however if the city that you live in has a predominately young population and a low death rate, there may not be as many funeral homes as other cities the same size or even smaller that have older populations, and as a result generally higher death rates.

High Volume vs. Low Volume:

Regardless of the size of the city or community in which it is located, some Funeral Homes perform thousands of services a year and others may handle only 50 or so calls in the same year. There can be a big difference in the way business is conducted at either place due to the size of the facility, staff availability to respond to your wishes, etc. Most high volume Funeral Homes (usually defined as those who handle over 400 calls per year) serve many families at the same time and may conduct 3-5 funerals per day on average. This does not necessarily mean that your family will receive less personal treatment, only that chances are at your time of need that the high volume Funeral Home may also be serving many others simultaneously. In the same respect, a smaller low volume Funeral Home may do no business for 2 or 3 weeks and all of a sudden get 6 calls in a 24-hour period. If the establishment only has one licensed Funeral Director available to serve the public, the case volume may stretch his or her ability to serve each family with equalized personal attention.

The question that you will need to address is what the needs are of your particular family and the type of services that will be required in relation to your desires. A larger high volume Funeral Home for instance may have a large Funeral Chapel that can seat 500 people at a service and smaller chapel for say 50-100 people also. A higher volume Funeral Home may be better equipped to accommodate a service requested for a particular time if it has more facilities, staff and flexibility to meet the demands. If you and your family desire a small intimate service in smaller room this could be handled as well be a low volume firm.

Corporate vs. Independent:

Many Funeral Homes, mortuaries, cemeteries and crematories today, especially in the bigger urban areas are owned by large

holding companies or corporations.

Led by Houston, Texas based Service Corporation International (SCI) who owned over 3,000 funeral and cemetery related facilities and generated over $2.2 billion dollars in revenue by the end of 2002, these funeral industry companies which also includes New Orleans, Louisiana based Stewart Enterprises as the second largest funeral and cemetery holding company in the U.S. at the end of 2002[1]. They focus primarily on efficiency and cutting the costs of doing business by sharing resources among commonly owned Funeral Homes in the same geographic area. Along with SCI and Stewart Enterprises are various smaller regional companies that also own primarily funeral homes and/or cemeteries. In past years and also currently on a much smaller scale, the funeral/cemetery corporations grew into large companies by acquiring previously owned independent funeral homes and cemeteries and retaining the businesses name to minimize the perception of change.

More recently however, the corporations have shifted strategy by employing a stronger marketing approach and growing its revenues from within its funeral providing locations through the use of brand names such as the Dignity Memorial Funeral Service packages introduced to the public by SCI in 2000[2]. This has allowed SCI, for instance, to increase its sales from the Funeral Homes it currently owns and operates without having to incur the burdensome debt of purchasing previously non-SCI firms to increase its revenues, profits and shareholder value.

Independent Funeral Homes are those that are usually owned by an individual's family, nonprofit group, etc. They tend to be single-owned businesses where the owner(s) has/have only one or two Funeral Homes usually in the same general area where staff can help work at either location.

From the consumer's standpoint there is not necessarily a big difference between an independent or corporately owned funeral or cemetery establishment. Both types are committed to furnishing the public with funeral goods and services and provide the consumer with an opportunity to gain their business.

Reputation

This can be critically important in finding the right Funeral Home to serve you at a crucial time. Regarding a particular firm that you may be interested in, consider such things as how long the funeral home has been in the community, whether it is an active part of the community it serves, and whether it has been recognized or cited with any awards, achievements or honors for outstanding service. If on the other hand you need guidance to a reputable Funeral Home in the area, a recommendation by a minister, priest or rabbi can be beneficial since

The Big Three

No, not General Motors, Ford and Chrysler, but the funeral and death care industry has its own Big Three which along with industry leader Service Corporation International includes New Orleans, Louisiana-based Stewart Enterprises and the Alderwoods Group which was formed in January, 2002 out of the formerly bankrupt Loewen Group Inc., which was based in Toronto, Ontario and now continues as Alderwoods, the second largest funeral home and cemetery operator in North America.

All three companies own and operate funeral homes, cemeteries and crematories and offer prearrangements that are transferable to other locations throughout their vast networks. The companies also focus on investing in resources that will allow them to better serve consumers in the future such as employee training, involvement in the communities they serve and improving their efficiencies in operating as funeral care providers.

these people are in a position to know all the Funeral Homes in the area as they usually have an opportunity to work with them on an ongoing basis. Also the considerate word of a close friend or relative can be helpful in deciding as can a referral from the chamber of commerce or local Better Business Bureau. Also the governing body over funeral service firms for the state in which the funeral homes you are considering are located in will keep records of any complaints or grievances filed against it (see chapter 12 for state regulatory boards).

Location

Along with price, location of the funeral establishment is the biggest factor that most consumers consider in choosing a funeral provider. How close is the Funeral Home from our residence? To or from the church or other place where the funeral will be held at? How close is the Funeral Home (if that is where the service will be held) from the cemetery or place of disposition? How convenient is the Funeral Home's location in proximity to where most of those coming to the visitation or funeral will be coming from? Will there be a lot of elderly people coming who are better off only traveling a short distance? Will you or others have to deal with traffic during rush hours to get there? Consider who is coming, when they will be coming and where they will be coming (and going) from.

How Much Does A Funeral Cost?

As a practicing Funeral Director, quite frequently I will receive phone calls from people asking the question how much does a funeral cost? The answer is: it depends. Depends on what you consider to be part of the funeral or funeral provider's service.

A traditional funeral can range from $3,500 to $12,000 or more contingent upon the service and merchandise items that you select at the time of making the arrangements, what area you are in, competition among funeral providers, etc. The national average for 2002 was $5,211.21 as noted by the Federated Funeral Directors of America[3].

There are basically three separate categories of charges that make up the cost of a funeral:

1) The professional services of the Funeral Director and staff which consists of making and procuring the arrangements that are made, embalming and the specialized preparation of the deceased, transportation charges provided by the funeral provider, and facilities and related staff charges for any viewing, visitation or funeral or memorial services.

2) Funeral goods and merchandise which would include the casket, outer burial container, alternative container (used for cremation), flowers sold by the Funeral Home, register book, funeral or memorial service programs/handouts, acknowledgment cards, etc.

3) Cash advances items or third party charges where the funeral home will pay for the expenses incurred to carry out the services you've arranged for on your behalf with outside providers such as newspaper notices, motor escorts, death certificate certified copies, cemetery burial fees, as examples. The costs

Typical Funeral Costs Include:

- Embalming
- Viewing or Visitation
- Ceremony (Cost of Funeral Home)
- Transportation to Funeral Home
- Register Book
- Flowers
- Thank you Cards

Typical Burial Costs Include:

- Cemetery Space or Crypt
- Open and Close the Space or Crypt
- Monument or Memorial

of these items are then placed on your contract as part of the total charges.

Beginning in 1984, the Federal Trade Commission of the United States Government began mandating that funeral providers itemize both their price lists and their contracts or sale/purchase agreements with the buyer. This means that funeral homes or funeral providers as defined by the FTC Funeral Trade Rule, must disclose written prices and descriptions of all the goods and services purchased from the Funeral Provider. More about this as we go through this chapter.

How Much Does It Cost To Bury Someone?

Why ask this question: I thought that was part of the cost of the Funeral? This is one of the biggest misconceptions on the part of consumers both today and in the past. Most people just automatically lump funeral and burial or disposition costs together. Of course the Funeral Home will and can handle the details of disposition of the decedent as part of their service,

Origin of the FTC Funeral Rule

In 1972 the U.S. Government through the Federal Trade Commission began an investigation into the trade practicees of the funeral industry. The study lasted 12 years and in 1984 the commission issued what has become known as the FTC Funeral Rule.

This rule is an effort to bring funeral providers into compliance with basic guidelines such as itemization of consumer purchase agreements, availability of price information and mandatory disclosures concerning services and merchandise offered on a funeral provider's price lists.

The FTC Funeral Rule is printed in its entirety in chapter 11 of this book.

however the placement of the deceased into a cemetery or other place of disposition is added for the purchaser's convenience to the Funeral Home's contract. In other words the two events are in a sense mutually exclusive activities.

Burial costs can consist of purchasing a space at a cemetery or memorial park, transportation to the place of burial, charges for opening and closing the grave space and possible perpetual care cost for future maintenance of the space. There can also be the cost of a permanent market or other memorial to be placed on the space. I will talk extensively about burial costs in chapter 2.

And so it is possible to hold a funeral or memorial service for someone and not have the disposition at that time. This can be the case when cremation or transporting the decedent is going to take place, as examples.

One other way to mentally separate funeral from burial is the fact the FTC's Funeral Rule does not cover cemeteries and memorial parks unless they sell both funeral goods and services also. Because the costs of burying a passed loved one can vary widely and depend on some largely material factors I will answer this section's question in detail in chapter 2.

The First Call: Contacting A Funeral Home

Once you have decided what Funeral Home you wish to call at the time of need, if you are preplanning (making this decision before death has actually occurred) be sure that you place the name, address and phone number of the Funeral Home in an easily accessible place where it can be retrieved. The reason that the address of the firm is important is because if you live in a large city and for example the funeral home may have four locations in town. You want to employ the services of the Smith Funeral Home a mile from your house, not one of Smith's locations in another part of town. This becomes important because some Funeral Homes will use an answering service after hours to receive its telephone calls. The answering service operator is probably taking calls for each Smith Funeral Home location and if the caller does not designate Smith's Funeral Home on Brown Avenue the south side of town the operator may take the call for one of the other Smith's Funeral Homes.

Although it is rare, there have been instances when the next morning when the family went to the Funeral Home to make the arrangements that the deceased was at one of the firm's other locations. So the point is to be as specific as possible. Another consideration when death occurs is whether a physician or other medical personnel have been in attendance at the time of death. If not, the medical examiner or coroner (in some states) or other designated authority must be contacted to determine the cause of death. This notification properly takes place before calling the Funeral Home.

Once the proper authorities have been notified and release the family or next of kin to call a Funeral Home the Funeral Director should be contacted as soon as possible. If the death takes place in a hospital, nursing home, retirement home, assisted living facility, etc., they will usually make the telephone call or you. Something very important to remember is to contact the Funeral Home in the town where you want to have the funeral. The reason is that it will save you time, effort, worry and money by letting one Funeral Home handle all the arrangements.

If death occurs unexpectedly out of town for example and you will want your loved one taken back home for the funeral and disposition, call the Funeral Home in that town, not a local one where the death occurs. It will save you a lot of headaches. By letting one funeral home handle all of or as many of the arrangements as possible, you will eliminate any duplication of costs by two different funeral homes. The destination Funeral Home can arrange for the local removal, preparation and transport for you without your having to call someone local and without unnecessary costs.

Upon placing the call or initial contact with the Funeral Home, there will be a series of questions that will be asked of the caller that include the following:

1. Who has died?
2. Where is that person now?
3. Where did the death take place?
4. Who pronounced the person dead and who is to sign the certificate of death?
5. Who is the deceased's next of kin
6. Will this next of kin be making the arrangements? How can they be contacted and when?

If the caller is a hospital or other representative, the Funeral Home may go ahead and ask for some more vital information such as time of death, whether any autopsy or organ donation is pending as well as statistical information that may be listed on the decedent's chart such as date of birth, social security number, etc.

If the next of kin or other family member is the caller, the funeral home may ask such questions as to what type of arrangements are desired, what type of disposition is wanted, whether any prearrangements have been made for either funeral or cemetery property and if so when and under whose name. The Funeral Director will also want to take the opportunity to secure permission for embalming at this time especially if the family will not be present at the time that the Funeral Director comes to pick up the decedent to take back to the Funeral Home. The Funeral Director may go ahead and set an appointment time for you to come to the Funeral Home to make arrangements or if it is later in the day or at night may ask to call you the next morning to set a time.

Etiquette At The Time Of Death
And Preparing For The Arrangements Conference
(What Has To Happen)

After contact has been made with your Funeral Home of choice and the Funeral Director goes into action to remove the decedent from the place of death back to the Funeral Home, there will be a good number of things that will need to be tended to before meeting with the Funeral Director.

Sometimes when the death has occurred at a hospital for example and they made the call to the Funeral Home for you, wait a reasonable length of time. If they have not been in contact with you, you call them. In situations where you are present at the time of death and then decide you want to go straight to the Funeral Home, I would advise against it.

Although it is only human nature to want to go there as quickly as possible, if the Funeral Home has not been notified or if you show up without an appointment you may be asked to come back or may have a long wait. One example that happened several years back was a family that came to the Funeral Home only minutes after a death had occurred at the local hospital which was across the street from the Funeral Home. When the Funeral Home receptionist told the family that there was no director available to wait on them and they would need to call later for an appointment they refused and decided to wait, and wait they did-for about 2 1/2 hours.

What this family did not take into account was that our Funeral Home had other families with appointments that were being waited on, other Funerals to work, other visitations to prepare for. In other words the staff was currently committed to planned activities. Most of the families that do just show up are usually in a large majority of the cases ill prepared to make and complete the arrangements when they do arrive unannounced.

The flip side is that when a Funeral Director has had a chance to talk with you first by telephone, he or she has had a chance to calculate several things from the conversation. He or she will have a general idea of how to prepare for the arrangements in such a way that will make the conference meeting with you as easy and efficient as possible. That way you will have to spend less time at the Funeral Home waiting on the director to put things together that he or she could do before your arrival.

If your Funeral is prearranged in advance and on file with your Funeral Home of choice, you will still need to meet with the Funeral Director, but your meeting time in most cases will be substantially lessened. Since prearrangement information can vary widely from one simple contract with only a few major items purchased such as a casket and burial vault all the way to every possible purchase item and wishes recorded in writing down to the smallest of details regarding all facets of the services chosen. Nevertheless, the preparation for the meeting with the Funeral Director or the arrangement conference will usually consist of gathering the following items and information:

1) Death Certificate Data (differs from State to State) usually includes a minimum of full legal name of decedent, place of birth, occupation, parents full names, level of education. You will be asked how many certified death certificate copies you'll need;

2) Clothing that decedent will be buried in including any jewelry, eyeglasses, dentures.

3) Obituary information usually consisting of surviving family members names and community of residence, and any biographical data you wish to be included. Names and cities of out of town papers. Also any memorial gifts you wish to designate.

4) A photograph for the obituary and for hairdressing and cosmetology.

5) Discharge papers for honorably discharged veterans from the armed forces.

6) Copies of any prearranged funeral or cemetery agreements as well as deed papers to burial or mausoleum property.

7) Any life insurance policies you would like to use for paying the funeral/burial expenses or for the Funeral Home to file for you.

8) Day/time/place desired for services.

9) Name and phone number of minister, priest, Rabbi or other officiant who will conduct the service(s).

10) If cremation is to be arranged you can expect to be asked what you would like the Funeral Home to do with the decedent's ashes.

11) Means of payment such as cash, check, credit card etc.

Even with prearrangements, there can be some items desired that are not on the pre-need contract such as newspapers charges, flowers, or death certificates.

Having these things in order before you go to the Funeral Home will make your experience easier and more productive.

Right Of Disposition
(Your Rights, Your Responsibility)

One of the other central issues that must be determined by the family before going to the arrangement conference is the question of who holds the right of disposition. Sometimes this is very clear cut and other times it is not. With an increase in divorce remarriage, cohabitation, availability in disposition options and splits among family members who, legally speaking, hold equal weight regarding right to arrange for disposition, it is in everyone's best interest to decide who will have and exercise the responsibility to make the arrangements with the Funeral Home. From a judicial point of view the general rule for who has the superior right to arrange and direct disposition of a decedent goes as follows:

1. Surviving spouse of the decedent
2. Adult children of the decedent
3. Surviving parents of decedent
4. Adult brothers and sisters of decedent

Another key party to making decisions is the decedent himself or herself through wishes that were recorded verbally or expressly when still living, as through a preplanned or prearranged funeral contract. There is however various differing court rulings concerning the weight given to a decedent's wishes.

There is a wide range of laws among the states on the issue of right to disposition and arranging for services with a Funeral Home. In other words, there is no single hard and fast definitive method uniformly among all the states as to who holds the supreme right to arrange for disposition. Court decisions throughout the country have stressed that each case must turn on its own particular facts and that courts will balance competing interests in deciding these issues[5].

Most of the time however this is not a major factor. If the decedent's spouse is living and capable, they are usually the ones that come to make the arrangements unless they chose to waive this right to someone else such as an adult child. What the Funeral Home is looking for is the legal next of kin to make the arrangements or to at least be present at the arrangement conference to consent to decisions and choices the arranging purchaser is making.

When there is more than one person who shares equal right (such as a brother and sister) what the Funeral Home wants is for there to be a unison of communication concerning the arrangements. The Funeral Home will oftentimes not act if the decedent's family (those holding equal rights to disposition) are not in agreement in making the arrangements in order to shield itself from any potential lawsuits. And so the bottom line is decide which family member will speak for the family as a unit. If more than one family member will be in charge of making the arrangements with the Funeral Home, be sure you are in agreement on what needs to be done before going to the Funeral Home.

Meeting With The Funeral Director
(What To Expect)

A very large majority of the time, arrangements will be made at the Funeral Home. It is easier for the family to go to the Funeral Director rather than the other way around for a lot of reasons. One for example is selecting a casket. If the Funeral Director is going to come to your home to make arrangements, the only way that you will be able to select will be from a picture book of the caskets available. This may be fine for some but most consumers want to actually see the item especially if it is a large dollar or high price item.

Even if you do not like Funeral Homes because you had a bad experience at one in the past, plan to have services at another location such as a church, or for whatever other reason, the arrangements should in most circumstances take place at the funeral home. This way the Funeral Director will have at a beck and call, the staff, resources and familiar environment and conditions to best help you and your family in the most efficient and beneficial way to meet your needs.

When you go into the Funeral Home check out the property, look over the facility; is the staff helpful and courteous? Are they neat and well groomed? Are the furniture and fixtures maintained and well kept? When you meet the Funeral Director, is he or she empathic and compassionate toward you and your family? Is there a sense and an atmosphere that this place knows it exists to serve you and other families that have had a death. Although first impressions are not everything they are important. It is imperative that you have confidence that the Funeral Director and his/her staff can adequately meet your family's needs.

Most career classifications place Funeral Directors (also called morticians or undertakers) under the helping or helper listings in occupation categories. A Funeral Director is someone who practices funeral directing and possesses a license to do so by whatever state he or she works. A mortician is one who can have two licenses-a Funeral Directors license and an embalmers license also. Sometimes the Funeral Director/Embalmer holds two separate licenses or a combination license to practice both trades. A licensed Funeral Director or mortician meets with families for the purpose of making arrangements.

Whatever the arrangements are that you desire, the funeral director is your helper. He or she is there to enter into a relationship with you to discuss service options and alternatives if no prearrangements have been made, to help you understand what needs to happen and to plan and then implement services that will be satisfactory to you and select merchandise for your loved one.

The Arrangement Conference
(Arranging A Service)

A death in any family is a burden for the survivors to bear. Grief and shock often portray those left to deal with the hardship of their normal schedule being interrupted to face the situation at hand as undesirable as it may seem. To many of us today in our highly competitive modern society, death can be just plain inconvenient.

Going in to make the arrangements for services and disposition (usually either burial or cremation) can be highly stressful over and above what tension the death itself has created. The purpose of this book and especially the rest of this chapter is to help you know and understand what needs to happen and to equip you with the knowledge and tools to assist you in the situation.

Basically the arrangement conference is the meeting between service provider (the Funeral Home) and service consumer (the

surviving family). Funeral Home staffs today are trained to help your family in not only arranging and carrying out the services but coping with the death as well. Funeral Directors have various styles in making arrangements. Some will sit around a table with the participants while others will sit behind a desk; others may sit in a chair with a clipboard and fill out information while visiting with the family. Sometimes a secretary or Funeral Director intern will come in first and take the vital statistic information and then turn the family over to a Funeral Director. Other times the Funeral Director will handle the entire conference himself or herself (this is what a majority of Funeral Homes prefer).

When the arranging Funeral Director comes in usually he or she will introduce himself or herself and greet the family and ask for each person's name depending on how many people are present and express their condolences. If you and the Director do not know one another or the director did not know the decedent, the Director may open the conversation asking about the circumstances of the death. This is the Director's way of learning information about both the decedent and the family that will help him or her know how to best serve you.

Most arrangement conferences follow a somewhat basic model that includes the following four categories:

1) Gathering information for the death certificate and for any newspaper obituary or death notices.

2) Making selections on which services and merchandise offered by the Funeral Home you desire and choose to be part of the Funeral and disposition you want.

3) Communication between the Director and the family concerning details about what services that will be carried out.

4) Procuring compliance with governmental and Funeral Home policies concerning arrangements between the two parties contractually and financially.

Once the family has decided what arrangements it desires in connection to the ceremony or rites and the burial or disposition every other question asked by the director for the most part will hinge upon these two decisions. Every family is different and every person who has died is unique, therefore not everyone wants the same type of funeral or ceremony. If the funeral has been prearranged and information has been recorded in a personal planning guide, be sure to take it with you to the arrangement conference (there is one at the back of this book). A lot of the questions that will be asked at the arrangements can be answered from it.

In order to give you a little more preparation for making the arrangements, I have developed an outline for you that can add more detail to the four major categories of what will usually be covered in an arrangement conference.

I. Information For Death Certificate And Obituary Or News Notice

- A) Full Legal Name
- B) Resident Address
- C) Date & Place of Birth
- D) Social Security Number
- E) Occupation (or Retired From)
- F) Marital Status
- G) Parents Full Legal Birth Names
- H) Veteran of Armed Forces
- I) Names of Surviving Family Members and Cities/State of Residence
- J) Schools Attended, Achievements Obtained
- K) Clubs, Organization Activities, Memberships
- L) Other accomplishments, Facts of Interest

II. Service And Merchandise Selections

- A) Day/Time/Place of Funeral or Memorial Ceremony
- B) Type of Disposition Desired
- C) Casket or Alternative Container (For Cremation)
- D) Burial Container or Vault (For Cemetery or memorial park)
- E) Clothing
- F) Flowers
- G) Register Book

H) Services Handouts or Bulletins
I) Thank You Cards
J) Transportation Provided by Funeral Home
K) Visitation or Viewing
L) Musicians, Hairdressers, Clergy Provided by Funeral Home

III. Service Detail Communication
A) Casket Open or Closed, When & Where
B) Days/Times/Place of Visitation
C) Names, Number of Pallbearers (Active & Honorary)
D) Any Jewelry for Decedent & Disposition of
E) Disposition of Flowers Received At Funeral Home
F) Names of Family Provided Musicians For Service or Ritual
G) Disposition of Clothing And Personal Effects that came to the Funeral Home w/ Decedent from place of death
H) Any other logistical information that needs to be communicated about services
I) Information that may or may not be given to callers by the Funeral Home on the family's behalf.

IV. Procurement of Compliance With Government And/Or Funeral Home Policies
A) Presentation and analysis of statement of goods and services selected agreement
B) Signing form for permission to embalm
C) Signing of claim forms for insurance or prearranged policies
D) Signing form for receipt of price lists
E) Signing statement of goods and services selected
F) Signing form authorizing Funeral Home to dispose of or return property or personal effects of deceased
G) Financial arrangements made
H) Payments or assignments to make funeral/Account paid or secured.

There is not really any set standard of time as to how long an arrangement conference will last. Generally I will tell a family if prearrangements have already been made to allow about an hour to come into the Funeral Home to finalize everything. If no prearrangements have been made and the situation is at need where the family has maybe never made funeral arrangements before, it could conceivably take 2-3 hours longer or shorter depending on many different variables such as how many family members come to the conference, how many questions there are, number of selections to make, etc. There are times when the arrangements cannot be completed in one meeting and the family will need to come back later the same day or the next day to finish.

If you will be having the funeral or visitation or other rites or ceremonies at the Funeral Home, if the Funeral Director does not offer, ask for a tour of the public areas of the Funeral Home that you and your family will be using such as the stateroom(s), reception coffee or vending machines, restrooms, kitchen or visitation area(s), chapel, etc. Usually the director will be glad to do this but may decline if the area(s) are currently being occupied or used by other families using them while you are there.

TYPES OF SERVICES
(What's Available)

There are basically three types of ceremonies used to ritualize and acknowledge death: funeral, memorial and committal. Within the framework of these three basic types of services however is a rather large range of latitude within parameters of what activities may compose which type of service that you may choose.

First however I want to present the reason of why we have funeral or other services whenever someone dies. The question has been asked publicly of why do we need funerals? Although some kind of ceremonies or rites connected with death have been held since ancient times, there is a very contemporary reason to have a funeral:

* Acknowledgment of a life lived

* Confirms the reality and finality of death

* Provides bereaved with a chance for closure

* Gives opportunity for family and friends to support one another physically and emotionally

* Allows mourners to initiate and process their grief in a safe atmosphere

* Helps survivors to better cope and adjust to their own life without the deceased

* Enables participants to honor the sanctity of life and move forward with their own lives

With these values in mind, lets look at what variables and factors need to be taken into account when deciding what type of ceremony you want to have for your loved one.

Things To Consider

To help you decide the when, where, and how of planning a service you and your family will need to consider many different aspects that affect the function, content and outcome of whatever service is selected. These things are listed as follows:

- Do you want the casket containing the decedent present for the ceremony

- How many attendees do you anticipate coming to the service

- Where will most of the attendees be coming/traveling from and back to

- What type of accommodations may be needed for any who are elderly, handicapped or impaired

- What activities do you wish to comprise the service such as songs, speakers, recorded or live music, visual presentation(s), etc.

- What type of time allowances or constraints are imposed?

- Will any type of special conditions or effects be needed regarding air, sound or lights?

- What needs to be considered regarding the display and arrangement of floral tributes and/or any other items such as pictures or personal belongings?

- Are the services going to be short enough that seating or standing of attendees is an issue?

- What personal, social or religious beliefs or traditions do you want to be part of the service?

- Will you want or need a special place to gather for prayer, for visiting, eating, serving refreshments, etc.

- What transportation needs will be required in connection to decedent, the family, attendees, etc. What needs to be considered concerning distance of transport, traffic or parking?

- What weather conditions are forecast for the area on day(s) of service(s)?

- Will there be more than one service? If so, when, where, what is desired?

Taking everything into consideration is perhaps the most important thing and that is what is the most fitting thing for the deceased? As we will see in a later chapter, personalizing services to fit the individual is a growing trend in funeral service today.

Traditional Funeral Or Memorial Service

A funeral is a service held where the decedent's body is present in either an open or closed casket. The ceremony is the most traditional and usually includes a display of floral arrangements, a clergy person or officiant and some form of live or recorded, music. The family of the deceased is usually seated together as a group in the area or seating space closest to the front with the best view of what will take place.

The job of the funeral director and the funeral home staff will be to set up the service with the casket, arrangement of flowers, passing out of service folders, register guests, open and close the casket, seat the family, greet and direct visitors, get the order of the service (outline of activities) to those participating in it such as musicians and speakers, and the funeral started on time. The Funeral Home's work will also include removing the flowers and casket to the place of burial or disposition as well as direct the family and visitors out as well.

A memorial service is similar to the Funeral in virtually every aspect except that it is held without the body of the deceased present. This can be the case if the death occurred somewhere else or in the case of direct cremation, or other disposition, or if burial has already taken place. As with the funeral, the funeral director and staff can be charged with the responsibility of carrying out the details of the memorial service in a timely and efficient manner, however it is not uncommon for families to hold a memorial service without the direction or supervision of a Funeral Home.

If attendance is expected to be large or if there are many details that need to be procured, I recommend the involvement of a Funeral Director to make sure that plans and wishes are properly carried out. If you do not wish or feel the need for a Funeral Director's services, I recommend putting a family member in charge of overseeing the coordination of the memorial service who is capable of handling the tasks at hand.

It is important to try to keep as many of the previous mentioned 13 points in mind in deciding where you would like the service to take place. Let's look at the alternatives.

Funeral Home Chapel

Of the various places where a funeral service can be held, as a rule of thumb, the Funeral Home's chapel in a majority of cases is the best place to have the service. This is because it is constructed and built just for that purpose. As mentioned earlier in this chapter, when you go to the Funeral Home to make the arrangements, ask for a tour of the Funeral Home's chapel. This will allow you to see the layout and evaluate it with the type of service that you have in mind.

If the chapel is well suited to accommodate your family and friends that will be attending, is large enough to comfortably seat those attending, I strongly recommend having the service at the Funeral Home's chapel. Since they are made for funerals, chapels are better able to display floral arrangements, get the casket in and out, usually have a private room for the family if desired and generally have parking that allow cars to park and leave in an orderly fashion after the service.

CHURCH

Along with the Funeral Home's chapel, if the decedent or the family has ties to a particular church, that is a popular choice to hold the service.

One of the key factors to consider in whether or not to have the funeral or memorial service at a church will be what the tradition of that particular church is concerning funeral customs. For example, it is customary in the Catholic Church for the casket to be closed at all times inside the church. If you are catholic and want to have the casket open for viewing then you will probably need to have the service elsewhere. Other churches such as the Presbyterian and the Episcopal Churches also have some restrictions (see chapter 8 for summary of customs and practices).

Again, you will need to consider some important factors along with the customs of that particular church such as whether it has the facilities to accommodate you and your family, whether it is large enough to comfortably seat those attending, whether it has conducive parking capacity; does it have the sound and equipment or capacity to play the type of music you will want? How close is the church from where you'll be coming from and to where you will be going for burial or disposition afterwards?

Although I have been in some wonderful and beautiful church buildings, I have never really seen one that was constructed for or with the idea in mind of facilitating a funeral service. Some churches are just not built to get a casket in and out without hardship. Others do not have a private room to gather the family in before seating for the start of the service or even an area conducive to gathering and instructing pallbearers.

Churches are built with a church service in mind, and so they should be. So think carefully about what you want to do in creating a service honorable to the decedent when considering a church as a place to hold the service.

Graveside

The graveside service is the ceremony that is held at the cemetery or memorial park where the burial or entombment is to take place. Although the term graveside is meant to convey the service will be held at the actual gravesite or exact place where the burial or entombment will be made, some cemeteries have permanent shelters or covered spots where all graveside or committal services are held. Afterwards the cemetery grounds crew will come and move the casket and flowers out to the actual grave for burial and do the grave closing. This has been designed and employed by some cemeteries to eliminate the task of setting up and taking down of the traditional tent, folding chairs, and artificial grass carpet for each and every service it has on its grounds. Most cemeteries however still do the plastic or fabric tent set up at the actual place of disposition.

The graveside service is a good alternative to consider when a small gathering is expected and you wish the service to be rather short. Usually if the decedent's family is small and there will be no recorded music or visual presentation requiring elec-

> Most Funeral homes charge less for the Graveside service than for the chapel or church funeral.

tric sound equipment, if there will be only one speaker or several with very short messages, the graveside may be your best option. Most cemeteries will/set up from 10-20 folding chairs to be used first by family and those who are not able to stand and then by others who are in attendance. All others who can stand for very long may stand. Also most Funeral Homes charge less for the graveside service than for a chapel or church funeral because many times they do not need to commit as many staff and other resources to carrying out the graveside as opposed to the others.

If a smaller gathering is expected, if there is no long order of service and weather conditions will be favorable or not extreme, you may want to consider a graveside as your choice.

Funeral Home Stateroom

Anytime that you anticipate the service to be very small attendance wise or do not desire the go out to the gravesite or place of disposition, a service at the Funeral Home in one of the state or visitation rooms may be appropriate.

This can be the chosen form of ceremony if bad weather is expected, if no more than a handful of people are going to attend or the family wishes to have a more casual, informal or intimate setting.

The stateroom service can consist of the same elements as a larger service with the decedent's casketed body present, flowers, and speaker or speakers and music without the awkwardness of having a rather small gathering in a chapel or church sanctuary that may seat 300 plus people.

One stateroom service that I conducted in past years that only had about 8-10 people total in attendance chose to simply have us arrange the chairs in an /informal circle with the service consisting of those present who wanted to talk and share their memories and stories about the decedent. We also served some refreshments and played some soft background music and this service meet the family's wishes and needs and to a tee.

One factor that you may want to consider in pondering the possibility of the stateroom service is if you run an obituary or death notice in the newspaper, if the decedent was a longtime resident, is the chance that many old friends and acquaintances that you did not count on showing up for the service. There have been several instances when a next-of-kin would arrange for a stateroom service with the assurance that no more than 15 people would come (usually 20 is the maximum for average stateroom). Nevertheless an obituary was run in the paper (the decedent had lived and worked in the town for over 60 years and as a result over 45 people showed up with about half those unable to squeeze into the room for the service.)

If you can without question know you'll have a small gathering of no more than 10-15 maximum, the stateroom service may be your best choice.

Other Location/Facility

One of the big changes taking place in funeral service today is the movement toward personalization of services. Chapter 4 of this book speaks directly to this concept. In past years it was highly unusual to hold funeral or memorials services anywhere other than the Funeral Home, church or graveside. There have always been however, some high profile community leader, politician, sports figure or other VIP whose services may have been held at a sports stadium, public building or other place where Funeral Services are not normally held.

Now with a trend in place to personalize services, one of the ways to do this is to hold the funeral or memorial service at a place that exemplifies the decedent for the individual that he or she was. Several places where funerals have been held before include skating rinks, lakes, football stadiums, school gyms, tour boats, public park pavilions, lodge or clubhouse of a private golf or country club.

Again there are many things that will need to be considered here and it is highly recommended that you rely largely on the Funeral Director to help you with this decision. Depending on what type of establishment and where it is located may determine whether a funeral can be held there subject to local laws or regulations (such as a public park).

There will probably also be at the minimum several logistical challenges to work out such as moving the casket in and out, seating, displaying flowers, etc.

Committal Service

The committal service is a brief optional ceremony held at the gravesite, tomb, crypt, crematory or in the case of a cremation that has already taken place the place where the ashes will be placed or scattered. It is often used in combination with the Funeral or memorial service where the family, close friends and loved ones gather to say good-bye to the deceased.

The committal is usually/held after the funeral ceremony and is traditionally preceded by a procession from the place of the funeral to the cemetery or crematory. Some committals are held prior to the memorial service that may be held. Committal rituals help us acknowledge the finality of the death and also give attendees peace of mind by physically going to and seeing the grave or place of final disposition.

Types of Disposition

In chapter 3 of this book I will discuss in detail about the alternative forms of the disposition of a deceased human being but here I want to very briefly mention the basic types of disposition because of its relevance to the remainder of this chapter which describes the various services and merchandise offered by Funeral Homes today.

Since 1984, the United States Federal Government has

established and enforced through the Federal Trade Commission what is called The Funeral Rule. In essence, the rule obligates Funeral Homes to follow certain laws in doing business with the public. It requires written itemized prices and descriptions of all the goods and services provided by the Funeral Home. It establishes that a person has the right to only choose the funeral goods and services desired, and that any specific item that is required by state or local law to be purchased must be stated so in writing. Full disclosure of the FTC Funeral Trade Rule composes chapter 11 of this book.

This relates to the manner of disposition chosen in that you as the consumer will not need to purchase or be required to purchase/any goods or services that you do not need for the type of Funeral and or method of disposition you choose (unless required by law or for a reason that must be given to you in writing).

With this in mind the five basic forms of disposition are:

1. Interment (or ground burial)
2. Entombment (or above ground burial)
3. Cremation
4. Burial At Sea
5. Donation (to medical science or research)

Choosing a particular form of disposition can affect what type of ceremony or ritual that you want as well as what items you will need or may want to supplement and add meaning to the services you select.

Choosing A Casket
(Return To Sender)

The casket plays an important part in the funeral rite or ceremony. Many times when you mention death, funeral or Funeral Home most people automatically register a mental image in their mind of a casket or coffin (which is now an outdated term in most places).

Oftentimes, for a lot of funeral purchases, the casket is the single most expensive item bought as part of the Funeral Home sales contract. Let's first look at what the casket is for. The purpose of a casket is to provide a reliable dignified way to move the deceased's body to and from the place of any ceremony or services to the place for disposition. There is no casket that will preserve or prevent the decomposition of the body over time. Some caskets however are made to keep or delay the entrance of any grave elements such as water.

Caskets made today vary more than ever before but the basic contents of the casket are essentially the same, consisting of some form of a durable exterior, type of fabric interior lining, a pillow, mattress that may (as strange as it may seem) or may not be adjustable (more about this shortly) and some type of handles or bars on each side of the exterior for carrying.

Since caskets do vary widely in style, material and price it will be important for you to understand the basics about the differing types before you make a decision on which casket you want to purchase.

Caskets are made of different materials that can be grouped into 3 general classifications, wood, metal, and plastic.

Woods

Wood caskets are subclassified as either soft woods (wood that is derived from a needle or cone bearing_tree) or hardwoods (woods that come from a leaf bearing tree). Softwood caskets usually include cedar, cypress, fur, pine and redwood; hardwood caskets are ash, birch, cherry, cottonwood, mahogany, maple, oak, poplar and walnut. A casket's cost is to some measure determined by the quality of the finished wood as well as the interior fabric quality.

With wood being the oldest material known to man, wood caskets are the most traditional and there are very few, if any, Funeral Homes that would not offer at least some type of wood casket as part of its selection.

Metals

Metal caskets also come in different types such as steel, stainless steel, cooper or bronze. Metals come in a variety of colors and interiors and also vary in cost due to type and durability.

Steel caskets are made with 20 gauge, 19-gauge, 18-gauge and 16-gauge steel. The lower the gauge the thicker the steel and the better the quality. They are also more expensive due to the heavier metal content.

Stainless steel caskets are made of an alloy available in various grades and protects against rust and corrosion also. Both steel and stainless steel are made from ferrous metals meaning it contains iron whereas the copper and bronze caskets do not contain iron and are therefore nonferrous.

Wood Caskets

Softwoods:	Hardwoods:
Cedar	Ash
Cypress	Birch
Fir	Cherry
Pine	Cottonwood
Redwood	Mahogony
	Maple
	Oak
	Poplar
	Walnut

Metal Caskets

Steel: Such as 16, 18, 20 Gauge
Stainless Steel: Does Not/Will Not Rust
Copper: High Quality
Bronze: Best

Protective: Air and Water tight and
Non Protective: Outside elements such as air and water may enter

Copper caskets are the next strongest to resistance to corrosion and will not rust. Bronze is the strongest and longest lasting and the most superior to all other casket materials in strength and durability.

Plastic

Finished in the same manner as metal caskets, plastic caskets come in the form of fiberglass as the most common type. There is no standard thickness for this type casket and fiberglass constitutes a small percentage of all caskets selected. As a result there is a good chance your Funeral Home may not even offer caskets in this material.

Interiors

Caskets will also feature along with the exterior material some type of interior make such as crepe, velvet or satin. The various kinds of fabric can also come in different colors and styles, such as ivory, pink, rose tan, beige, and drexel. As with the exterior material, the type of interior will add to the overall cost of the casket you are considering.

Colors

The metal caskets are made with a large variety of various colors and shades including but not limited to black, blue, gray, green, brown and silver and color mixes.

The competing makers of caskets are and probably will continue to feature caskets in as many differing colors as possible to appeal to a wider market of potential buyers who want individualization and personalization.

Sizes

A large majority of all caskets made and sold are what we call the adult standard size casket. It is made for the adult size of the population which compose a large number of the deaths that take place each year. Usually the Funeral Home will also keep on hand a small stock of infant caskets that range from one to three feet in length for the several families that must deal with the always sad event of an infant death. Also for the unfortunate event of a minor child's passing, these caskets are rarely kept at the Funeral Home and are usually special ordered when needed to show the family. The reason I mention this is because the Funeral Director may need to order these caskets and have them delivered to the Funeral Home resulting in a possible time delay in starting or completing the arrangements.

The area that is currently going through somewhat of a change concerning size is the growing demand for oversize caskets with a rise in problems with obesity and in more and more people being overweight, the funeral and casket manufacturing industries are now having to deal with ordering and delivering more oversize caskets. It is a fact today that there are some people who no longer fit in the standard size casket.

The Centers for Disease Control and Prevention estimates that 20 percent of Americans are obese up from 12.5 percent in 1991. Of those 70 and older about 17 percent are obese[6]. This can (and already has been) an embarrassing situation for all parties involved in arranging funerals. However as a growing trend I mention it here to make you aware of the situation that there will be a more limited number of choices available in oversized caskets and you can probably count on the price of the caskets being more than a standard size casket because of the added materials and labor costs to make the larger sized casket.

Other Features

Along with the materials, colors, and sizes, there are additional features that you need to be aware of including the protective vs. non-protective elements of the metal caskets. Protective means there is a rubber gasket built in as part of the casket's base where the lid and top of the casket body meet. This gasket when sealed is meant to hinder the entrance of air, water and other outside elements into the casket. Non-protective caskets do not have this gasket and are closed with a snap shut hinge in the lid of the casket.

Again, as you may guess, the protective casket will cost more than the non-protective and depending on the disposition you must make the highly personal decision of whether you want to protect the body from the elements.

Other casket features that are relevant include half-couch vs. full couch caskets. Half-couch caskets are where the lid is cut in half; with the head panel open if viewing is desired and the foot panel closed at all times; in other words the decedent is viewed from waist up. The full couch casket is where the entire lid is one piece and when the casket is open you can view the decedent from head to foot. There is also full couch casket with an inner foot panel. As stated earlier some caskets may include an adjustable mattress. This is because some adults "standard" do vary in height and weight. The adjustable mattress makes it possible for raising or lowering the decedent for viewing purposes. For example a 90-pound elderly woman may need to be "raised up" higher, whereas a 250-pound man may need to be lowered down. This way everyone will be at the same general level in caskets for viewing purposes.

Other features with caskets include personalized insertable cap panels that can be mounted inside the interior head panel of the casket during viewing. There is a large selection of panels

Casket Interior Head Panels

Personalization at its best:

- Military
- Sportsman
- Homemaker
- College Alma Mater
- Political Affiliations
- Bible
- Hobbies
- Flag
- Fraternal
- Job/Career
- Outdoors
- Cross

from Gone Fishing to Military to Going Home. Most Funeral Homes will be able to order these if none are displayed with the caskets. The Funeral Home may or may not keep a display of the head panels in the selection room with the caskets. If there is not, the director may keep a picture book or print display that shows pictures of head panels that can be ordered. Usually these personalized panels can be purchased as part of the cost of the casket or separately for an additional $40-125.

Keepsake or personal item drawers that are built into the foot panel of the casket are also available as an added feature to some caskets. This drawer opens outward toward the head of the decedent and is another way to allow families to display and hold items such as photos, jewelry, letters and other small memos during and after services.

For many years family members have placed cherished items into the casket of a loved one prior to closing and this practice led to the concept and development of building a drawer into the casket itself. Since the word "casket" is of French origin meaning a container for precious items, the keepsake drawer continues and upholds the casket's original meaning.

Another feature that can be an option with some caskets is corner designs. These ornamental pieces that can be attached to the four exterior corners of a casket that is made to accommodate such attachments, are another way to personalize the casket towards the individual tastes of the family.

Currently there are about 15 different corner designs that include such designs as a tree, deer, words mom or dad, a Christian cross, etc. This is a way to add more personalized value to the casket without having to necessarily add another separate item or good to consumer families along with the casket without having to greatly increase the Funeral Home's show space. The corner designs that a Funeral Home may offer with one or more of its compatible caskets may possibly be displayed on the casket or with the Funeral Home's cremation urn (container) selection.

Casket warranties

Along with various other types of merchandise that a Funeral Home may sell, certain types of warranties either expressed or implied usually attach to the sale. At first glance you may ask, why do I need a warranty for a casket, something that is permanently going into the ground? The reason is that as stated earlier in this section about caskets, I mentioned that the casket is usually the single most expensive item on any funeral sale contract. Because of this and also because of the fact that the casket with your loved one's body in it will be moved around from place to place depending on the services you're selecting, how transported, how it will be lifted carried etc.; whether the casket will be placed in the ground or entombment in a mausoleum or temporarily (such as winter ice thawing to the point of being able to procure a final burial place).

The term warranty generally describes the quality or title of the item being sold and that the manufacturer promises to ensure that certain variables will be as the seller represents them. Since laws vary state by state, you should consult with an attorney in whatever state you are considering your casket purchase in. The law does not require sellers to provide a written warranty, however when a manufacturer provides a written warranty, the seller is obligated to provide it to the consumer. This can be done by displaying it on the casket or nearby. The Funeral Home as seller may also post a prominently displayed sign indicating that any written warranty is available upon request.

The key idea for you as the consumer to know about is does the Funeral Home as seller warrant the caskets it offers and if so on what terms? If not, does the manufacturer have a warranty for the casket and if so read it and understand what it means. This is just a good idea for any smart consumer whether it relates to buying a casket or any other consumer product. Try to make a habit of knowing what and if there are warranties attached to what you are purchasing.

Third Party Sellers

A growing phenomenon in the retail side of funeral service the last several years is the emergence of third-party casket sellers into the marketplace. Since the Federal Trade Commission implemented a new rule in 1994 to forbid Funeral homes from charging a handling fee to families for buying their caskets from an outside supplier, casket retailers in the form of storefront proprietors, computer online sellers or factory direct retailers have come on the scene to sell caskets and sometimes other types of funeral-related merchandise to the public at large.

With some of these third party vendors offering caskets for sale at sometimes one-third to one-half less than what some Funeral

Homes offer, casket retailers can offer a viable alternative for consumers to consider. Some of the casket sellers are one-person operations that are mom-and-pop type retailers, while others may be a part of a larger company that owns and operates casket retail entities large scale. Since casket retailing is presently unlicensed and unregulated, it is somewhat unknown who owns and who is doing what in this segment of the industry.

Third party casket retailers have created more selection, more options and lower priced alternatives to some of the caskets sold by traditional Funeral Homes, but before seriously considering purchasing from a third party supplier ask yourself some important questions:

- Since the FTC does not regulate casket sellers, is the third party retailer regulated by any other authority that can hold it accountable by the public?

- How long has this third party been in business and is their merchandise recommended or endorsed by any legitimate or reputable persons or entities?

- What knowledge about the funeral or burial business does

Shopping around for prices on caskets can sometimes save a lot of money with the emergence of third party casket retailers.

the salesperson at the third party have? Do they know the difference between caskets?

- What happens if the casket delivered to the Funeral Home is not the one you ordered? What if it is damaged?

- Will the seller accept a form of payment that I can pay? Credit cards, insurance assignments, etc.

- Unlike most Funeral Homes, casket stores usually have set hours and days of operation. If you run into a problem on a weekend or holiday, etc. and cannot contact the retailer, what recourse do you have if it is say a casket ordered over the internet for instance; and does the third party retailer warrant what it is selling? If not, why not, and what if the supplier is across the country?

Since selecting a casket, getting it delivered safely, on time and in good condition oftentimes within a very compressed period of time because of imminent services having been set can be a risky venture to say the least.

If you and your family are already grieving because of the death that has taken place, be sure that your casket seller is available to help you with anything in connection to your casket purchase at the time you will need it.

In Summary

Decide what is important to you and your family regarding the casket selection. Take into consideration the various features of different caskets and that the one you want will do what it is intended to do. Whether the casket is to be transported across the street or across the world, buried in the ground or placed in an above ground mausoleum, be sure to ask about any warranties and get in writing a warranty copy of what you are buying. Be sure that when you walk away you are getting something that you are proud to see and for others to look at; that you have bought something you are within your means to pay for and that the seller is available to service your questions, concerns and feedback.

Selecting An Outer Burial Container
(What You Need To Know)

Commonly called the vault or burial vault, outer burial containers are the outside enclosures that a casket fits into as the casket is placed into the grave. The term outer burial container therefore applies to any container that is designed for placement around the casket when burial takes place.

There is basically a twofold purpose for an outer burial container.

The first purpose is to support the earth's load between the casket and the surface of the ground. Without a capable outer container the casket would at some point give way because of the weight of the earth and cause the grave to cave or sink.

The second purpose is to provide the casket additional protection by limiting the entrance of outside elements by possessing sealing qualities that prevent or delay the intrusion of air, water, insects, etc. Not all outer containers possess the capabilities of

Outer Burial Containers

Dome - air seal outer container where dome top lowers down over a base with casket sitting on the base.
Top Seal – box-like shell container houses the casket, then the lid or top is placed down to enclose it (metal and concrete).

Metal - Stainless Steel, Copper, Bronze
10 Gauge or 11 Gauge
Galvanized - coating process over metal to increase resistance to rust using zinc.
Concrete - Vault: Protective
Graveliner: Non Protective
Fiberglass/Plastic - The same way that plastics are being utilized in many aspects of our world today, outer containers for ground burial are being manufactured with plastic using a molding process that creates a solid form of durable strength and protection.

the second purpose.

There are two basic types of outer burial containers that you need to know about. Seal and non-seal.

Sealing containers are designed to perform just as the name implies-to keep the elements that could potentially come in contact with the casket housed inside of it out. Air seal vaults utilize a dome top and a base on the bottom. The casket is lowered down into the grave to rest on the base. The dome top is then lowered down over the casket and connects to the base on each side of the casket.

Top seal vaults seal using an epoxy compound in conjunction with and groove closure at the top of the vault. It is built with a shell-like body to encase the casket and a tope that is a solid, one-piece lid that fits on and attaches to the vault around the casket.

Among the sealer vaults or containers comes various levels of protection such as single, double or triple reinforced. As can be expected the more protection and preservation from the outside elements you want for the casket and deceased the more you can expect to pay.

The non-seal containers come in the form of grave liners. These containers simply serve the purpose of supporting the earth load above the buried casket. Grave liners do not provide any sealing qualities.

The grave liner comes in a grave box, which is a body and a one or two piece top, a sectional which consists of six or eight piece slabs of concrete that fit around the casket like a puzzle when the casket is lowered on top of the bottom slab, and the bell container which is shaped like a dome and placed over the casket without a base. It needs to be remembered that these grave liners do not protect the casket from water or other elements.

Also, as with the caskets, outer burial containers are made of different types of materials such as concrete, metal and polymers and fiberglass. Among the metals, steel, stainless steel, copper and bronze are used with 12 gauge steel as standard metal for the industry. 10 gauge and 11 gauge steels are also available and stainless steel and bronze offering better quality than the others. Copper made vaults also give excellent value.

It should also be mentioned that some of the vaults available might have an exterior with one material and an interior made with another. Some vaults have steel exterior and a fiberglass interior. A rigid concrete exterior may have a plastic inner lining, for example. Rely on your funeral professional to explain the differences in relation to disposition.

Several other points about outer containers are that some containers come in a variety of finishes. One type of finish that can be applied to metal vaults is galvanizing which is a process of coating the steel with zinc in order to increase resistance to rust. A spray paint can also be applied to increase a container's eye appeal. Some vault makers also can add the name and date of birth, date of death as well as a meaningful symbol or design on some vaults as a distinctive emblem such as the Christian cross, wreath, and pink rose or possibly a flag or military emblem for veterans.

Be sure to ask about any warranties that may come with a particular container that you are interested in. It will be important in case there is ever a disinterment that the container does what it is intended to do.

As far as outer container requirements are concerned, some cemeteries and memorial parks require some type of outer burial container and some do not. Even if you have burial property at a cemetery that a does not require one, if at all financially able I recommended at least a minimum grave liner that will maintain the ground and support the earth. There has been more than one instance where someone bought a burial space at a cem-

As with caskets, outer burial containers can also be purchased from third party sellers, and the consumer has the opportunity to possibly save money as a result.

etery that did not require outer burial containers for a deceased loved one without an outer container for the casket and later when the surviving family member went out to visit the gravesite were horrified to find the ground sunk in and the grave marker disheveled and tilted downward. Such a scenario could have been averted with an outer container purchased.

Embalming And Preparation

What Is Embalming And What's Its Purpose?

There is probably no one issue a part of funeral service that is as misunderstood as embalming. I want to try to explain what it is, why it is done and what the value is in it.

Embalming is the artificial preservation of a deceased human body using a chemical solution specially designed for such. It is an operation that consists of removing blood and other bodily fluids and injecting preservative solution through the body's circulatory system for the purpose of disinfection and retarding decomposition.

An untreated/not-embalmed body will start to decompose immediately after death. Because of this the longer the time lapse after death occurs the poorer the results are from embalming. In a nutshell, embalming provides a degree of sanitation, preservation and cosmetic benefit when skillfully performed.

There are also two types of embalming: autopsied and unautopsied. Autopsied is the more entailed of the two and usually consists of multiple injections at different points of the body due to prior examination by a medical pathologist. The autopsy performed may be cranial only or also involve an examination of the trunk and abdominal regions in an effort to learn about the cause and/or circumstances relating to the death. The unautopsied embalming operation is somewhat simpler in that the embalmer's main challenge is to initiate both drainage and injection without unduly altering the body's condition. As a general rule (each case varies) the autopsied embalming operation takes about 2 hours and the unautopsied about an hour.

If the decedent was involved in an accident or some other form of traumatic death where the body is disfigured or not completely intact; another dimension to the embalming process called restoration is also performed, if viewing is desired.

This may or may not be extensive depending on the cause and manner of death. It may include such methods as rebuilding sunken facial areas, using a specialized mortuary wax to restore viewable areas or replacing missing limbs or hair if desired. Usually restoration costs are included with the charge for embalming but may not be. If extra time, effort and skill is required there may be a per hour charge over and above the embalming charge.

Another part of the embalming process is bathing and shampooing. Sometimes this is part of the Funeral Home's embalming charge and sometimes it is separately itemized on the contract. Once the embalming task has been completed the embalmer will bathe the body with soap and water and shampoo and rinse the hair, if applicable.

Many times people do not understand if embalming is needed for the type of service or services that they desire to have. If you are planning to have any type of open casket viewing or visitation, then embalming should be done to protect the health of the public and those viewing. Most Funeral Homes do require embalming if you want to have any service with viewing.

Embalming usually is not required by law, and you should find out what your state does or does not mandate concerning embalming. It is generally not necessary or legally required if the deceased is to be cremated or buried immediately or shortly after death. Embalming is also not done sometimes for religious reasons.

Under the Federal Trade Commission's rule, the funeral provider:

* may not provide embalming without permission;

* may not falsely state that embalming is required by law;

* must expressly disclose in writing that embalming is not

required by law except in certain special cases;

* may not charge a fee for unauthorized embalming unless regulated by the state law;

* must disclose in writing that you usually have the right to choose the type of disposition such as direct cremation or immediate burial, that does not require embalming if you do not want it;

* must disclose in writing that some funeral arrangements, such as a funeral with viewing, may make embalming a practical necessity and if so, a required purchase.

The certain special cases refers to situations for example where the death resulted from a reportable contagious disease, if the deceased is to be transported from one state to another or transported by common carrier. (See chapter 11 for entire FTC Funeral Rules).

Insofar as the value of embalming is concerned there has been some disagreement and debate over the real worth that it has in Funeral service. Despite the fact that it has been ongoing and probably will continue to be discussed by lawmakers, consumer advocates, religious groups and others, if the time-honored tradition of viewing the deceased in a pleasant, blissful state is continued for the purposes of mourning, grieving and facing the reality of the death, then embalming will and should continue to be a part of providing reverence and dignity to the dead and sanitation and cleanliness for the living. I say this from the standpoint of seeing many bodies both before and after the embalming process and the results to the survivors who need and want to view can be priceless. Embalming prices usually range from $200 to $950 and are listed on the funeral home's general price list.

Refrigeration

When embalming is not required or chosen, refrigeration of the deceased is usually customary in order to slow the decomposition process until time of disposition.

In refrigeration, the deceased body is placed into a cooling unit that is usually kept around 35-36 degrees Fahrenheit. This keeps the body from decomposing too rapidly but also keeps the body from freezing. Some families can't decide at the time of death whether to embalm or not and need time to make a decision. The Funeral Director may go ahead and place the body into the refrigeration unit until notified. Also in situations where the Funeral Home cannot get in contact with a family member to secure permission to embalm when the death occurs may also prompt the use of refrigeration.

Since some states require a waiting period before a decedent can be cremated and there are also formalities to go through in procuring an immediate burial, refrigeration is more commonplace now than in years past with more and more Funeral Homes acquiring their own refrigeration units on the premises, while other usually smaller Funeral Homes use the refrigeration unit at a mortuary service that is used to serve other area mortuaries as well. Refrigeration is usually less than embalming, however the same amount may be charged for either. Also check with the Funeral Director to find out if there is a per day holding charge. Some Funeral Homes will have one set price to refrigerate for so many days and then add on a charge per day from then on. Usual refrigeration costs range from $150 to $850.

Cosmetology & Hairdressing

This service involves making the decedent look presentable for an open casket viewing for a visitation and or funeral. Usually the Funeral Home will have a local hairdresser or someone they can call on to come to the Funeral Home to fix and style

Money Saving Tip

Provide own family member to style deceased hair.

the hair and usually to also apply cosmetics as needed. The hairdresser may or may not be a licensed beautician depending on whether it is required by the state or not for cosmetizing and hairdressing the dead. The funeral director usually asks for a recent photograph that the hairdresser can use. Normally the hairdresser will also do the nail polish on ladies as part of the cosmetic application, if desired.

The charge for the services of a hairdresser or beautician provided by the Funeral Home usually ranges from $40-150, however if the family has someone else in mind that may do it as a service to the family or in gratitude to the decedent for less or at no charge, the Funeral Home will usually accommodate the stylist and be available to provide any needed assistance.

Dressing And Casketing

As the description states, this means the charge that the Funeral Home imposes for the service of dressing the decedent in the clothing that is either bought at the Funeral Home or that the family provides prior to placing the decedent into the casket. Casketing is then the placement, positioning and proper posturing of the decedent into the casket that the family has bought from or supplied to the Funeral Home. This is not quite as easy as it may sound going back to the prior discussion about caskets. Making a decedent that is smaller, bigger, taller, shorter, etc., than the average adult can take come maneuvering of the casket's underlying mattress, pillow and inner lining to give the decedent the best possible appearance and presentation.

Some families (usually for religious reasons) will do the dressing and/or casketing themselves, which is usually permissible under most circumstances, and as a result do not incur the charge for dressing and casketing, which together usually runs from $50-250.

Professional Services Fees

Also known as the minimum professional service fee or professional fee, this is the charge incurred for the basic services of the Funeral Director and staff.

Regardless of the type of arrangements you make with the funeral home, there is a cost for orchestrating the services and merchandise selected from beginning to end. The Funeral Home incurs many expenses in arranging for and then carrying out the arrangements made according to the family's wishes.

The professional minimum services of the Funeral Director and staff consists of:

1) The arrangement conference

2) Coordinating the arrangements with any and all parties involved in the procurement of the arrangements made and the final disposition of the deceased.

3) Staff assistance needed in the preparation, filing, documentation of, communication and completion of the various forms and administrative procedures associated with arrangements and final disposition.

4) Provision of personnel available 24 hours a day, every day to receive and respond to initial call.

5) Covering the costs associated with mandates such as insurance, taxes, equipment and compliance with local, state and Federal laws.

Every Funeral Home charges some form of professional minimum services fee and it can range widely anywhere from $500-2,500.00 depending on trade area, competition, size and volume of the Funeral Home, etc. There is a huge overhead burden associated with operating a Funeral Home entity in order to properly and effectively serve the public at large. As a result there is a cost for Funeral Homes to be able to render the services, merchandise and professional assistance needed to help grieving families at their time of need day or night, weekend, weekday or holiday.

Visitation And Use Of Facilities

A long held traditional custom in North America, the visitation, also called the viewing or wake by some, is the time set aside the day before or earlier in the day before the funeral when family members may meet and visit with friends, visitors and one another as a way of comfort, console and support one another, and accept the reality of the death. The deeper psychological benefit from the viewing helps the survivors began the grieving process also. There are also some families that wish to meet with, host and receive friends and well wishers after the Funeral or memorial service and this can also like the visitation be held at the Funeral Home.

The charge for visitation at the Funeral Home is normally on a per-day basis since some customs call for more than one day of viewing. Usually a stateroom or visitation/reception area is set aside for each family having calling hours. The charge may also be incurred on the basis of per hour or a half-day as opposed to a full day, depending on how the particular Funeral Home offers it.

If the situation happens to be a cremation with a memorial service (decedent's body not present) or a closed casket out of preference or necessity, a visitation may still be held so that others can pay respects to the family and loved ones of the deceased.

One way that this charge can be reduced or eliminated would be to have/the visitation at a private residence, place of worship or other facility, however you may incur a charge to have the Funeral Home transport the decedent's casket to the other place and to transport any flowers also. The other factors to consider is parking, hosting people at a place large enough, seating of and accommodating visitors and arranging and displaying of floral arrangements.

Transportation
(On the Beaten Path)

When we discuss transportation we are talking about getting from point A to point B. There is a potential for either a large or small amount of expense depending on the services chosen.

The two charges that are non-declinable are the transport of the deceased from the place of death to the Funeral Home and from the Funeral Home to the place of burial, cremation, etc.

One of the factors affecting either charge is the distance either to or from the Funeral Home Most Funeral Directors have a certain radius that they define as their locality or trade area. Any transportation exceeding the established radius will incur an additional mileage charge. For most Funeral Homes it is 20-50 miles depending on such things as how urban or rural the area they serve is. Any transport over the established boundary will incur a per mile charge (usually $1.00 - 2.00 per mile one way). This gives you as

The Horse Drawn Carriage

If you are taking your deceased loved one to burial and want to go in unique fashion, there are several funeral homes that, if requested, may be able to arrange for a horse drawn carriage to take the casket in procession.

A horse drawn carriage is something that will have to be specially arranged and may not be available if the funeral director does not have an agreement with someone locally to do it. Any extraordinary arrangement for acquiring one from a distance may delay the service day until the carriage can arrive and may also come at a great cost. The other factor will be distance and local ordinance that may restrict such activity if processing on the public streets.

If it can be arranged, the horse drawn carriage can be a very fitting and memorable tribute.

the consumer a real incentive to do as much of the funeral and disposition activities as local as possible.

The funeral coach (formerly know as a hearse, which is becoming an outdated term) is a specially constructed vehicle designed to hold and transport a standard adult size casket. If your arrangements express that you are paying for a funeral coach, be sure you get one, not a suburban, van or station wagon. You need this special vehicle to take the decedent to the church or cemetery. The charge is usually between $100-250 but is worth the charge.

Limousines

Limousines are used to transport the family and/or the pallbearers from their residence or place of meeting to the place of the service and then to the cemetery, funeral home or place of disposition. Some families opt to use their own cars however limos do provide a convenience to the families who do not wish to drive or bother with getting to and from on their own. Most limousines used for funerals come in 6, 8 or 10 passenger models. If the surviving family does not want to make use of a limo, if the Funeral will go in procession from the chapel or a church to the cemetery, it's often a good idea to have a limo provided for the pallbearers who will be carrying the casket. This way they will all stay together as a group and upon arriving at the cemetery there will be no time wasted waiting for all the bearers to meet at the coach. If money is an issue and you need to cut expenses as much as possible, limousines are an added value to serve the family, but are also a place to save some money if the vehicles you have are fine for the occasion. Several things regarding limo use for you to think about are any assistance that any elderly or handicapped individual(s) may need getting safely in and out of the vehicle in comfort, the relief of not having to be concerned about grieving family members driving, and the safety factor of having fewer personal vehicles involved in a procession. Typical limo charges range from $75-$250 per limo.

Other Vehicles

Several other vehicles that are commonly used for the traditional funeral are the "lead car" driven by the Funeral Director who is directing the service and a flower van used to take any floral arrangements to the place of burial or cremation.

The lead car or Funeral Director's car is also used in the Funeral to take the clergy or if there are any additional pallbearers or relatives to take. As stated, the lead car is also the first in the motor procession.

The flower car or van transports not only the flowers that were with the casket at the Funeral Home, but also is used to transport any other items or tributes such as picture boards or flower arrangement racks, register book stands, or other equipment the Funeral Home may need to carry out the arranged services.

Since Funeral Homes must dispose of the flowers in some way the flower van charge is hard to decline. Even if there is no burial after the service to take the flowers to, some hospitals, churches or nursing homes receive floral donations. However if the Funeral Home delivers them for you there will still be the charge for the transport.

One solution is that the family can take the flowers after the services themselves or ask for donations to charity instead of flowers being sent. Both the Funeral Director's car and flower van usually run between $40-$150 each.

Long Distances

Another area concerning transportation that is less frequent but you still need to be aware of is long distance transports. Anytime that the death takes place away from home or when the funeral takes place and there is a distance to the place of burial or disposition, the transportation will generally take one of two forms, either overland (taking by motor vehicle) or by air shipment, which is usually via one of the major airlines.

The two biggest factors in determining which mode the Funeral Director may use are the timing—how long it will take to get a decedent from point A to point B on an airline as opposed to the length of an overland trip—and the cost to do one or the other. This is where you come into play. Let's say for example that your relative who has died 400 miles away can be flown back to the place of the funeral for less than it would cost for the Funeral Director to drive out and bring the relative back by motor vehicle overland; however the earliest flight out of the nearest airport cannot happen for 3 days due to the airlines schedule. If you cannot wait 3 days, the Funeral Director may be able to get the relative back home overland in a day and a half. In this case, you must wait if you want to pay less to get the decedent back soon enough to have a funeral and burial instead of waiting a couple of extra days. Different factors can enter into the picture, so anytime there is the potential of transporting more than one way, find out the cost and timing of each alternative.

Another element that must be noted here is that your Funeral Director will be working with variables that will be outside his or her control such as airline schedules and regulations, the shipping Funeral home and what the laws are in the place where the death takes place. If the shipment is an overseas flight or to/from another country, the Funeral Home will have to make arrangements through the consulate for that country which can sometimes take two to three days (or longer). Also some states have more or less stringent requirements before a deceased human body can come into or leave the state.

Airline fares will vary greatly, but the Funeral Director usually has an established account with the airline and will simply put the airline charges directly onto your bill of sale as a cash advance item.

Regardless of coming or going, the Funeral Home also usually has a charge to drive the decedent to or from the airport to or from the Funeral Home, which often depends on the distance one way.

Very seldom anymore will long-distance transportation take place anyway other than motor vehicle or airplanes and remember, let the funeral director where the services and disposition will be held handle the travel details and arrangements when possible. The receiving director will know how to control the costs involved to the benefit of the client family.

Escorts: Anytime that there are more than two or three vehicles involved in going to or from the Funeral Home or other place connected with the funeral process, a procession is formed. Whenever you have the vehicles driving together as a form of unit or convoy with a need to have traffic yield, you will need a motor escort or escorts.

This is another way that has evolved in some aspects where in past years, many local cities would provide a free police escort, but many no longer do, especially in larger towns and cities. As a result some police departments will allow an off duty uniformed officer to act as an escort for a fee using a patrol car or motorcycle. Other times a private motor escort service can be arranged by the Funeral Director to take the funeral from the church to the cemetery or whatever the arrangements call for.

The motor escort's job is to allow the funeral procession to safely and uninterrupted by stop signs and traffic lights to go from place of service to place of disposition.

Because of the danger involved in stopping traffic for the procession there is or can be considerable risks for the escort. As a result of this, the escort fee can be as high as $200-250 per escort.

Depending on factors such as distance, anticipated traffic congestion, road construction, number of cars in procession, etc. will usually determine how many escorts the Funeral Director will arrange for. Escorts can be, as mentioned, one person such as the off-duty police officer or 3-4 motorcycle escorts (oftentimes the private escort company escorts dress comparable to the police).

Because of the risks, anytime you desire to have the funeral go in procession from one place to another you need motor escorts if possible. If money is an issue, the alternative is to have everyone leave after the funeral on their own and meet at the cemetery or crematory in (for example) 30 minutes, or a set time that's a reasonable amount of time to allow attendees to safely get there for the committal on their own.

Sundry Items
(Convenience And Costs)

Sundry merchandise are those products that are not necessarily required but add value to the funeral or memorial service. Such items include register book, thank you or acknowledgment cards, service bulletins or programs or prayer/mass cards for a rosary or funeral mass and food register.

Register Book

It is customary to have one of these available for visitors and guests to sign as they come to the viewing/visitation or to attend the service. Usually the Funeral Home will place it inside the door or foyer area so that it will be the first thing attendees will see and therefore sign their name.

The register book can be bought at the Funeral Home when arrangements are made, and some will include it with the purchase of the casket. You are also free to buy one somewhere else such as a retail store or gift shop that sells stationary products. The book will usually have some pages for typing information about the deceased such as date and place of birth, place and time of services, surviving family memos, etc.

When you buy a register book from the Funeral Home they will usually type the information for the book from the obituary and death certificate data at no extra charge. If you purchase it elsewhere they may not type it or may only do so at a charge. As a general rule, most register books costs $15-95, with some very simple and others more ornate and decorative.

The Funeral Home: Many times the Funeral Home will offer a selection of register books to choose from. They usually come in wood vinyl or leather and are custom made for the funeral occasion.

Acknowledgment Cards

Also known as "Thank You" cards, these are used after services are over and are sent to people who have sent donations, food, flowers, telegrams, or other forms of condolence. It is a way to show gratitude to those who have been thoughtful or helpful in some way. Acknowledgment cards are also usually offered by the Funeral Home and are usually preprinted and packaged together with so many cards and with envelopes for mailing. Like register books there is usually more than one kind to choose from and some can even be custom printed and are usually priced according to how many you think you'll need. They usually come 10-25 per box and the average cost is about $10-100 depending on how many come in a box. As a general rule if you are paying $1 or less per card, either standard (preprinted) or custom printed, you're getting a fair deal.

Thank You Cards

General (Standard):
- Pre-printed
- Can Be Used To Thank Any and All

Customized (Specific):
- Minister/Clergy Cards
- Pallbearer Cards
- Musician Cards
- Food Cards
- Gift or Letter Cards

Personalized (Engraved):
- Will Have Name of Deceased and/or Family Name

One other good thing about acknowledgment cards is since they generally are not used until after the service, if you run out you can get more. Also, since these cards are not sent until after services, there is not the "time pressure" element of having to get these before services at a higher price, but rather you may find a lower cost on cards by shopping around when you have more time after services when you are ready to use the cards.

Proper etiquette should be followed as sending out the acknowledgments following services. It is standard protocol to send thank yous to all those who partake including clergy, pallbearers, musicians, along with relatives who may have devoted time to help in some way. It is preferable to also write a short, handwritten note of thanks on the acknowledgment; if the funeral was large with hundreds or possibly even thousands of replies the handwritten notes may only be used for those nearest and dearest, which is quite understandable. Acknowledgments are generally sent 5 to 15 days following services. If you are unsure how to properly write some of the acknowledgments do not feel embarrassed to ask your Funeral Director or perhaps a friend who has already had a death in their family for help.

Service Folders

Also called service bulletins, programs or mass or prayer cards for catholic services, these are the "handouts" that are distributed by the Funeral Home staff to visitors who come to the funeral or memorial service.

Funeral Homes have become creative in recent years in offering more personalized service folders. The simplest most standard folders will have the name, date of birth, date of death of the decedent and the most elaborate which are called programs or bulletins, may have a picture of the deceased, have an order of service with names of service participants, an obituary or printed biographical sketch, poem or Bible verse and possibly the lyrics to any congregational hymns to be sung during the service.

Because of the wider range of options offered by more and more Funeral Homes in relation to service folders there is also a large price range connected to what is available. Like acknowledgments, service folders usually come in groups of l0s, 25s or 50s. Some Funeral Homes print the folders or programs themselves while others may have an outside printer who does the work for them.

When it comes to prices you may or may not be able to get a better deal on service folders yourself. Many times if the funeral is set you may not have time to shop around if you don't already have someone in mind who can do what you want at a reasonable price and have the reliability to get it done in time for the service. Having the Funeral Home do it saves you time and inconvenience of having to go someplace else.

Another advantage if you get the service folders at the Funeral Home with the other items (register book and thank you cards) is that some Funeral Homes offer these items together as a package which can be discounted, compared to if you bought them all separately. Many times the three products will match in color, style, design, etc. so that you can get a package whose parts complement one another. (Example: The outdoor scene that is chosen to go on the front of the service folders can also be printed on the acknowledgment cards and register book front covers also).

Money Saving Tip

If you are planning services at your church for example, the church may offer to provide service folders at no charge to the family.

This is a courtesy to the family that some churches extend to their members when one has passed away.

Food Register

This is a booklet like supplemental item that is given to the family at the arrangement conference or possibly at the time of the removal from the place of death if family members are present. It is primarily used to help you keep a record of those who have furnished food at your home and keep track of the containers in order to return them to the providers. It also is used as a register book for friends who called at home and for recording the names of those who may have called and left messages while you were out. Some of the food register books will also include data on how to prepare for the arrangement conference or with suggestions and tips on what needs to be done after services are over.

Flowers
(When Words Are Not Enough)

Since the early days of mankind, flowers have been used as a symbol of almost every aspect of the life cycle from birth through death. Flowers and funerals (like caskets and Funeral Homes) are normally associated together. Flowers serve the role of offsetting the imagery of the darkness of death and helps create a memory picture that stays in the minds of the bereaved long after the services are over. Western civilization expresses its respect for the deceased by sending flowers.

Money Saving Tip

Look at what the funeral home sells in the way of Sundry items and compare it to what the same or similar item(s) can be obtained for somewhere else.

Depending on time, money and effort as well as having to make another stop can all be factors as to where when and how you purchase these items if they are needed for services planned.

Along with the value and sympathetic expression it contributes to death and the Funeral, the symbolism connected to flowers can often be used to select floral tributes as a tribute to the decedent.

Since flowers can be selected in different colors, types and quantities, lets see how these variations help add meaning and sanctity to the funeral process. Colors are used to symbolize a trait or value. Examples:

Green: Freshness and Nature
Purple: Royalty
Red: Fire; Charity
White: Joy, Glory

Then there are types of flowers such as carnations, daises, lilies and roses. Some types of flowers are used quite often for funeral tributes while others seldom are.

The quantity usually is determined by the type of floral arrangement. Quite often for funerals, flowers are selected and ordered in the form of a basket, cut arrangement, spray, easel, or vase. Customarily the family will buy the flower arrangement that is placed on top of the casket and possibly one or two cut or basket arrangements or easel(s) to place at both ends of the casket.

It is quite easy to get creative with buying flowers in that

Flowers

(Always in Season)

Colors: Pink, White, Red, Purple
Types: Carnations, Lilies, Roses, Gladiolas
Arrangements: Cuts, Pot Plants, Wreaths, Baskets, Easels, Sprays
Added Value: Ribbons, Inscriptions, Stuffed Animals, Balloons, Streamers, Candy/Snacks
Sizes: Miniature to Large
Costs: $20-1,000 per piece

florists have become more competitive with one another and therefore found new and different ways to arrange and sell flowers. Some arrangements are offered with ribbons that can be inscribed with one name or message; others can come with ornamentation such as nick knack attachments, heart or bible shapes, even glitter, balloons and streamers for life celebrations.

As far as buying is concerned, many Funeral home have gotten into the flower sales business as a way to create another source of revenue, as an added convenience to its funeral arranging families and as a way to increase its exposure to the community.

Oftentimes the Funeral Director will go over floral options himself or herself or will have the family talk to the florist while at the arrangement conference. Other times if the Funeral Home does not have a flower shop on premises it may contract with one close by so when the family leaves the Funeral Home it is a matter of going a block or two down the street. For those Funeral Homes that do not have or are not affiliated with a flower shop, the director can usually give you a referral to a good florist since the Funeral Home sees and handles flowers from all of the local florists in the area.

The prices on flower arrangements vary greatly depending on whether the type of flower is in season or not, the supply and demand, the size and color, etc. It should be remembered that live flowers will generally stay fresh for 2-4 days depending on climate temperature, moisture, etc., while green plants will last much longer and are usually taken to the home of the family after services. Artificial flowers are usually not bought for the funeral services but generally are bought to place on the grave at the cemetery after services.

One of the big advantages to flower buying is that oftentimes when you are ordering an arrangement that is yet to be made you can decide how much you would like to spend and then order accordingly.

An example of this is if the florist shows you a picture of a yellow rose casket arrangement that can be made "as is" in the picture, at the retail price that would be $300. It would be made at this price with say hypothetically speaking 50 yellow roses. However, if you want to only spend say $225, the same arrangement would be made but with fewer flowers (say 30-35).

When ordering flowers for the funeral of a friend or relative you can generally do the same thing over the telephone using either a local florist or a florist in the town where the funeral will be held. If you call a local florist, normally they can FTD the order to a florist close to the funeral home because that way they will last longer at the area where services will be held and this is usually best if you know and trust your local florist. They may know who or who are not the reliable flower shops in that area. Vise-versa if you do not know any florist in your city but do know a good one in the area where services will be held then it is better to go ahead and call the out-of-town florist yourself directly. When you order over the telephone or by computer you will usually need to have either a debit or credit card ready to do the transaction. The other thing you will need to know at the time of ordering is what message you would like written on the card that will be sent with the arrangement or piece. Depending on your relationship to the next-of-kin or surviving family, it is usually okay to put, for example, "Deepest Sympathy From Joe and Mary."

Clothing And Apparel
(Going Out In Style)

This is an area that has seen some change from past traditions in that there is more informality in clothing used and away from the black color long associated with funerals.

Today more and more people are choosing to dress their deceased family members in their normal attire. Some hard-line religious groups still practice restrictions on clothing but usually the person in charge of making funeral arrangements decides.

The Funeral Home usually keeps clothing in stock for both adult size men and women, including both outer and undergarments. What the Funeral Home sells in clothing is usually displayed in the selection room with the caskets. The reason for this is that when people are going to buy something at the Funeral Home they want to pick out something that will be color complementary to the casket chosen.

The clothes at the Funeral Home are usually purchased from a supplier that only makes burial garments. They are somewhat different from regular made clothes in that the texture is different and they are made to be easily altered in the back to fit the deceased within the normal adult height and weight range. They are also tailored to be easily fitted unto the deceased without any cutting. The "normal" height/weight range is not necessarily standardly defined but generally is 150-225 lbs. and 5'7"-6'3" for men and 90-200 lbs. and 5'0"-5'8" for women.

Specialty burial garments are usually made of nylon print or polyester and consist of dresses, night gowns and shrouds for women that come in solid quiet colors and black, brown or dark blue single or double breasted suits for men.

If the deceased is a young girl, usually white is a customary color and for children whatever would be worn to Sunday School should be bought.

The most common practice today is to bring something from the decedent's existing wardrobe, which has the advantages of being clothing the deceased normally wore, it would be the right size and it is already bought. Items that may not be seen such as a belt or suspenders or pocket handkerchief for a man wearing a suit, or shoes when the casket selected is a half-couch (the foot end of the casket is closed) are not needed unless they are desired. Sometimes in cases where the deceased's hands are discolored or not sightly, gloves or a handkerchief may be needed for a woman. The Funeral Director will advise you as to any other special needs concerning clothing such as a garment with long sleeves, high neckline, a wig, scarf, bandanna, etc.

In normal cases, you as the funeral arranging family member should try as much as possible to stay with clothing that would best be associated with the decedent. If you do need to purchase some clothes, check the prices and selection at some retail stores that sell clothing and also look at the display and prices of what the Funeral Home offers in garments. This way you can make the most informed choice.

Ministers/Clergy/Officiants

There is not always a single definition to the title of the clergy or person who will officiate at a funeral or memorial service.

In past days it was oftentimes the pastor of the church that the decedent attended but today with a more secular society and fewer people affiliated with a particular church congregation, the person who speaks or presides over the service may not be a clergy member or church minister.

Still a large majority of the time, the family or person in charge of making funeral arrangements would like to have an officiant-someone who is the (main) speaker or leader of the funeral insofar as the actual conduction of the service for those in attendance.

In certain traditions such as the catholic funeral, it will be the church's priest. For the 'Jewish Funeral, it will be the Rabbi of the Synagogue and for the Lutheran Church for example, it will be the congregation's senior or associate pastor. Many times if a family does not have a relationship with a clergy member or an affiliation with a particular church, I will ask them if they have a religious or denominational preference and go from there.

If you are going in to make funeral arrangements and do not have a church or relationship with a minister, what you will need to do is to have a general idea of what kind of funeral service you would like to have and discuss this with your Funeral Director. It would be at this time to mention any concerns, qualifications or ideas you have about getting the right person.

At that point he or she can guide you and oftentimes can contact a clergy member about doing the service. Most Funeral Homes have an ongoing relationship with the churches and religious community in their trade area and using any preferences you have such as protestant, catholic or other, can contact someone in many cases who would be appropriate to officiate the funeral.

Regardless of the circumstances or the arrangements connected to the minister or clergy, once they have been contacted and agree to do the service, usually he or she will want to meet with you to talk about plans for the funeral or memorial service. The discussion will include gathering information about the deceased, what biographical activities you want included in the service and in what order you would like certain things done. Normally the only time that the order and activities of a funeral are predetermined is when the service is to be held in a liturgical church (more about this in chapter 8). It will then be the clergy/officiant's responsibility to give the Funeral Director the order of service, which is basically an outline of what happens in what order concerning music to be played, speaking, video presentation, etc. This way as facilitator, the Funeral Director and staff can assist with starting and ending the service according to the family's wishes.

Music
(Is it Live or, Is It Recorded)

There is little doubt about the important role that music plays in our culture both past and present. It has also in the past and continues now to play an important role in funeral and memorial services.

Although the presence and importance of music in funeral service has not changed, the type and flavor of selections definitely has. Along with the traditional church hymns and religious music that are still played at many services so is contemporary and secular tunes including but not limited to jazz, country and western, orchestra, pop, R&B, etc.

Using music can be one of the best practical ways to make a funeral or memorial service more personalized and meaningful. Many psychologists concur that music can set a mood or tone in certain situations and can soothe and lift the spirits of those who are going through a time of sorrow and mourning. There are basically two types of playing either recorded or live. Since each situation is different and there are various factors to consider such as time and place, the order of the funeral, the decedent's wishes or tastes for music in life, the family's desires, etc. Where is the funeral to be held? What type of sound or audio system does the place of the service have or will accommodate?

If the service is to take place in the funeral home chapel, I suggest that you let them arrange for the music. They have the staff who are familiar with the musical equipment and acoustics and know how services are conducted there. Most all Funeral Homes will house either a piano, organ or keyboard with microphones for live music and a wired sound system for playing either cassette tape or compact discs. If the service is to be at a church it is best to let their staff arrange for the music for the same reasons as the Funeral Home, but also because some churches want to only allow certain musical songs played that do not clash or contain lyrics that may not be conducive to that church's particular beliefs. As a general rule when having a church funeral it is best to stay with selections that are consistent with that church's doctrine and teachings. This can be an advantage

Money Saving Tip

Providing recorded music on tape or CD or having a family member(s) or friend(s) volunteer to perform the musical portion of the ceremony.

to having services at the Funeral Home in that a greater degree of freedom can usually be exercised in selecting music.

If the services are to be held at graveside, cryptside or other facility *you* will need to check and see what can be done as far as sound or equipment. Many times if the family would like to play a recorded song at a graveside, a portable battery powered cassette/CD player can be used for this setting or for a small gathering elsewhere. Most of the time the Funeral Director will have a hand carry portable player to take out for just this purpose. If the service is to be held at another indoor place and you are expecting a crowd large enough to require a speaker system, you will need to check on that first and then move forward with deciding what kind of music and by who.

In the case that you have a particular song or type of music you want played in a recorded mode, a lot of Funeral Homes keep a stock of some kind of music that can be played there. Usually there is a range of songs that come in different versions or background melodies such as piano, strings, orchestra, instrumental lyrical options like chorus, acapella or male or female soloist.

Pallbearers
(Honor Where Honor Is Due)

There are two types of pallbearers: active and honorary. Active pallbearers are the persons designated to carry the casket at the funeral service. This can include before and after depending on where the service is and where disposition will be. Honorary pallbearers are those who will do no actual carrying of the casket and have no actual duties to perform as such.

The Funeral Director, with the family's consent will usually advise as to how many active pallbearers will be needed and when and where they will be needed at. If the Funeral Home is also handling the family's order for flowers, the director usually will get the boutonnieres for the pallbearers to wear. As a general rule if the decedent is a woman the active bearers boutonnieres will be pink, if a man red. The honorary pallbearers bouts are usually white. If you want some different color be sure to mention it when ordering the flowers. If the family is getting their casket or family flowers at an outside florist the boutonnieres will usually come from there. Be sure to ask the director at the arrangements if he will order them or if you will need to. Don't assume anything. Unfortunately there have been services with no boutonnieres for the pallbearers because the family thought the Funeral Home would get them and the Funeral Home thought the family would.

As far as selecting who will serve as active pallbearers, the main qualification is that they can lift and help carry the casket.

Pallbearers For Hire?

Sometimes a family arranges a ceremony that includes moving the casket as part of the ceremony (such as out of a church with steps outside the building) as the final act of the formal ceremony.

If the family does not or cannot provide pallbearers to handle carrying the casket down the steps, this can create a problem if the casket and the deceased together weight over 400 lbs. combined and the funeral director who usually escorts and tends to the family has two or three assistants to help him with the ceremony?

It will take more than three gentlemen to handle carrying the casket from the church doors down the steps and/or over the curb and safely place the casket into the coach. Realistically it will take six able bodied bearers to carry the casket in such situations.

This is an issue that will have to be addressed with the individual funeral home that is handling the arrangements.

They may be either men or women and they should be reliable enough to be prompt and at the place of the service with time to spare before the funeral. Otherwise pallbearers may be anyone you would like to honor as such. They can be friends, close family, relatives, etc. Several things to consider in deciding who to ask can be those who the decedent had close ties with. Was the decedent a part of any groups clubs or organizations such as a church, sports group, civic or fraternal function; or perhaps former or current coworkers, school friends, etc. If you are in a situation of maybe having a large number of potential pallbearers, select 6 or 8 that you feel would make the best active bearers and have the others serve as honoraries.

At the service, the Funeral Director and staff will be in charge of instructing the pallbearers and seating them for the service. Usually the active pallbearers will sit on the front two rows across from the family with any honorary pallbearers seated on pews behind the active.

If you are unable to provide any pallbearers for the service, usually the Funeral Director can improvise depending on the place and order of service. Usually the director will bring more staff from the Funeral Home to help if the funeral is to be at the chapel or cemetery. If the service is held at a church with steps for example the director may call the church to see if they may be able to provide some help. At the cemetery or crematory if there are no pallbearers provided by the family then the workers at the cemetery/crematory will help with the casket. It should be noted that with the formality and dress up attire characteristic of most funerals, be aware of the fact that the cemetery/crematory crew will almost always be wearing the informal work clothes. The only other real alternatives are for the Funeral Director to hire pallbearers, which will add to the cost of the funeral, or if the decedent was a retired veteran who qualifies for full military honors. Even in this case, the military bearers may only be available to help carry the casket at one place, such as the cemetery, depending on arrangements and veterans policies.

Honorariums
(Paying The Piper)

An honorarium is an unsolicited gift that may be forwarded to those who provided some type of duty or professional service that was a part of the funeral or memorial service.

It is standard practice for the minister or officiating clergy to be given an honorarium for his/her participation in the services. The amount will vary depending on the family's relationship with the officiant, and anytime that the family does not know the clergy before making funeral arrangements and asks the Funeral Director to obtain an officiant, the honorarium is paid by the Funeral Director, who in turn places the amount on the purchase agreement. Several other factors will determine the amount, such as the time/day/place of the service, length of service/effort expended to perform the service, involvement in committal service and any transportation costs if driving a distance. Most clergy honorariums run between $50-250.

A separate honorarium may or may not be needed if the funeral service is to be held at a church. Some churches will customarily ask for or expect an honorarium in connection to the use of the church's facility, especially if there is a need to have the sexton or other church staff to ready the facility for the services, doing such tasks as unlocking doors, turning on lights, air conditioner or heat setting, and clean up and shut down af-

Honorariums may be considered for:

- Minister(s) and/or officiant(s)
- Musicians and/or singers
- Pallbearers and/or ushers
- Church or other facility that allows its building and staff to be used for service(s).

terwards. Also working and overseeing the sound system for any music can also be included as well as overseeing coordinating a large funeral with the Funeral Director and getting the church's musicians notified. Your Funeral Director can advise you if your arrangements include a service at a church whether or not an honorarium for the church will be needed.

Most anytime that a request is made for live music to be played regardless of singing or performing on a musical instrument, there will be a charge involved, regardless of the place of the service. The only real exception here is if a close friend or member of the family wishes to do so as their contribution or offering to help. Otherwise as with any other service performed in connection to carrying out the funeral, expect to pay anywhere from $35-250 for each musical participant. In the rare case of the use of a band or choir, consult with the clergy or the church pastor or your Funeral Director.

The other participants that honorariums should be considered or planned for are pallbearers and in the event of a large funeral with many attendees, anyone who volunteers to be or usher to seat guests. Usually the situation and circumstances will dictate whether to tip the pallbearers and/or ushers for their help. If honorariums are not given to those who serve the family in these capacities usually some expression of gratitude is appreciated such as a thank you card, an invitation to join the family for any luncheon, dinner or reception that may be held in connection to the funeral or offering one of the floral arrangements or plants as a token of gratitude.

Obituaries And Death Notices
(News Worth Reading)

The two types of written pieces used to help communicate the death to the outside world are obituaries and death notices. Obituaries are the write-ups that usually include information containing the history of the decedent's life along with survivors, any service or viewing time, day, place, etc., and any other details such as accomplishments, affiliations, activities, etc.

Death notices on the other hand tend to be shorter and very brief, usually notifying the public of the decedent's passing. Usually the name, address and phone number of the Funeral Home in charge of arrangements is also listed for those wishing to call for more information.

Most obituaries and death notices are published in newspapers however they can also many times be placed in magazines, journals or periodicals in which readers may have an interest such as the publication of a civic or fraternal organization that the decedent was a long time member of, for example. Also the information technology age has made it possible to place an obituary or notice on the internet. Many funeral homes now are or have plans to offer some type of obit notice on the internet, due to the increased mobility and likelihood of families being more scattered across the country, this is one way to allow out-of-state family or relatives a way to view an obituary with computer access.

The Funeral Director will usually prepare the obituary from data gathered on the funeral home's information sheet. Since information needs to be gathered anyway for the death certificate and services, writing the obituary is a natural extension for the Funeral Director. Many times the Funeral Director will ask you to bring to the arrangement conference a list of survivors and other facts you want as part of the obit. The director usually will jot down the information on his or her sheet and then hand it off to one of the Funeral Home staff to process the raw data into a polished looking obituary. Each publication or carrier usually has its own format and the staff member who is writing it is familiar with that format if it is a local publication that the funeral home is used to working with.

Depending on what publication(s) the obit will appear in depends on whether it will be transmitted by phone, fax, e-mail, teletype or even hand-delivered if a short distance from the

Funeral Home. Both the preparation and delivery of obituaries and death notices are part of the Funeral director's service charge and is usually not charged extra. Some families do and handle the obituary on their own which is fine if they know what they are doing. Since most newspapers have their own format, deadline and procedures, it is usually best to let the Funeral Home handle the obit/notice processing since they do it as a normal part of business, have the transmission capability and know the best ways of complying with the publications policies and procedures.

As a general rule you are allowed to include a large range of information about the decedent's life if you wish. Most obits and notices will include some form of biographical sketch and information of surviving family names and service time, day and place, if desired.

Be sure if you do allow the funeral home to prepare the obit/notice into its final copy that you ask the director to let you proof read it before delivery to its publication destination. This way if there are any mistakes or errors in the writing or editing it can be corrected before being put into print. There can be nothing more disappointing to a family than to have a wrong piece of information or misspelled name in the printed piece.

You may also want to inquire into the publication's policies concerning editing or reformatting the information once it is received by its editorial staff. Although usually not a huge issue but one worth mentioning, relates to sending the obit information one way and having it printed up in a different order. In other words, having the entire information printed but rearranged in

Some newspapers will run an obituary as a one time courtesy at no charge whereas others do not.

Check with the funeral director for guidance on how to publish an obit or death notice at no charge or as inexpensively as possible.

its order. It is well within the rights of any publication to print the information according to its standards.

Depending on the publication there also may or may not be a charge for running the obit or death notice also according to the publication's policies. Some papers are content to publish obituaries or notices free of charge as a public service. Others may charge just for a simple death notice, and then for obituaries add on a per-line charge and also charge if the decedent's picture is included. Other factors affecting the price is whether the decedent was a resident of the paper's trade or circulation area and whether or not the obit is to run more than one day, or in more than one edition. Check with the Funeral Director or with the publication(s) desired for price information when making arrangements, especially if money is an issue in relation to the total expense for the funeral.

Death Certificates
(Vital Statistics)

A death certificate is the official legal record of a person's death. It contains some variation of both the vital statistical information about a decedent's date of birth, date of death, places of birth and death, and the medical data relating to the death.

Death certificates are used to prove the death as needed to close and finalize the estate of the decedent and certified death certificate copies are normally needed for winding up bank accounts, insurance policies, investments, social security and veterans benefits.

The rules and requirements concerning death certificates are governed by the states, and most states require the certificate to be filed in the city, county or other jurisdiction where the death actually occurred.

Depending on whether the death was from natural causes or was accidental, crime related, or a physician was not in attendance usually determines how long it will take to file it with the municipal registrar, county clerk, or other designated authority. If the death was not natural, filing the certificate can cause a delay pending any investigation. In the case of an inquest that may await the results of toxicology or other tests performed from an autopsy, you will need to consult with your Funeral Director to find out if a provisional or temporary certificate can be issued for proving that death has occurred.

Since the various states have differing requirements for death certificates you will need to also find out from the Funeral Home what information you will need to bring to the arrangement conference to give to the funeral director for the certificate.

There are two important reasons for this. One is so if you have all the information as the informant/party responsible for making arrangements, it will allow the Funeral Home the leeway if it needs to get the certificate readied and hopefully filed as soon as possible, and two, if inaccurate or wrong information is recorded on the certificate and it has to be changed, an amendment to change it can be a lengthy and time consuming process.

The death certificate is an official legal document and certified copies that are issued usually consist of some type of bonded or unique fiber paper with a seal indicating that they are originals.

The cost of certified copies can range from $3-20 per copy and is added on the funeral purchase contract as a cash advance.

Permits

Another necessary item under certain circumstances, a permit is a written order issued by a governmental authority granting permission to do whatever the permit allows the Funeral Home to do on your behalf.

Also formulated at the state level, permits are usually needed to cremate, disinter or transport a deceased human body by common carrier or across state lines.

Any ethical, law abiding Funeral Home will want to do what is necessary to obtain the proper permit(s) any time it is working on a family's behalf to carry out arrangements made with that family. Sometimes a family may want to, for example have a deceased family member that they are making arrangements for cremated by a certain day in order to get the ashes to have a memorial service with the ashes present by "this weekend" when all the family will be together. If the permit-issuing authority does not issue a permit allowing the Funeral Home to cremate by "this weekend" then there will not be a cremation this week and there will not be ashes present at the memorial service. Any Funeral Director who is willing to do something for a family that requires a permit to be issued and is willing to do it without a permit is not an ethical, law abiding Funeral Director and as a result should not be trusted.

The governing authorities have good reasons for requiring a permit in cases like cremation, disinterment and certain transportation activities; reasons that are for the health, safety and general welfare of the society at large as determined by the state. As a result, in some cases it is well within reason for the Funeral Director to not act until he or she secures the proper permit(s) to move forward with the family's wishes.

So the bottom line here is that the Funeral Home does not issue or control the timing of when permits can be issued. The Funeral Home's job is to do their best to apply for and obtain the permit(s) needed as efficiently as possible on the family's behalf.

As with death certificates, permits are added to the family's bill on the Funeral Home's contract with the purchaser and depending on what the permit is for and what state you are in will determine the cost. Average costs are $2-25.

Cash Advance Items

These are charges that the Funeral Home places on its sales contract or statement of funeral goods and services selected that the funeral director incurs on behalf of the purchaser(s) in order to carry out the services requested by the purchaser(s).

Cash advance items usually include such things as flowers, motor escorts, obituary and death notices, musicians and officiating clergy honorariums, and also any charges from the use of an outside cemetery, crematory or the cost of using a common carrier such as an airline to transport a decedent.

What should be noted here is that the Funeral Home does not determine the actual cost of the item or service treated as a cash advance being provided to the purchaser but is simplifying things for the purchaser by doing the work of ordering and obtaining the cash advance item(s) needed to carry out the purchaser's wishes.

Some Funeral Homes charge you their cost for the goods or services they buy, others may add a service fee to their cost. The Federal Trade Commission rules dictate that those providers who charge on extra fee must disclose that fact expressly, however it does not require them to state the amount of their markup. The Funeral Rule does require funeral providers to tell you if there are refunds, discounts or rebates from the supplier on any cash advance item[7].

Miscellaneous Services

Because Funeral Homes and mortuaries are becoming more and more competitive with one another within a rapidly changing business and social environment where consumers want to have a wider range of choices, more and more funeral homes, in an attempt to capture and keep market share, are offering more and more nontraditional services to attract business. Some of the extra services offered by Funeral Homes to their clientele are as follows:

<u>Catering</u>: Going to make the funeral arrangements and deciding when and where to hold services can present the opportunity of providing families and their service guests with a

meal either before or after. Some Funeral Homes have made agreements with a local restaurant to provide prepared food either at the Funeral Home or at another place arranged by the Funeral Home on the family's behalf.

Usually this consists of the family telling the Funeral Director what type of catered meal they would like, when and where and for how many people. The Funeral Director will then take care of contacting and arranging the meal with the caterer. This service will usually be charged as a cash advance and added to the family's funeral bill.

Cooking/Food Preparation: Some Funeral Homes have a kitchen area or kitchenette that allows them to prepare food for families during the time they are at the Funeral Home. Depending on what type of facilitation is available such as oven, stove, refrigerator, etc. determines what can be done.

There are also some Funeral Homes that will send food to the family's house to lift the burden of them having to bother with cooking themselves. As with catering, any cost or expense is added to the contract.

Errand Running: At times when there is lots to do and not much time to do it, some Funeral Homes may offer to provide a courier to get out and pickup, drop off, and do some errands for a family when it is very inconvenient or troublesome for the family to do it themselves. The feelings and emotions associated with death can leave one feeling overwhelmed with simple chores and to dos. Such errands can include picking up/dropping off pictures to be developed, clothes at the cleaners, grocery items, mailing out letters, turning in library books, and a host of other things that the family may need to have done but because of the interruption caused by the death may not have time to do themselves.

Flower Placing: This is in connection with the arranging and setting floral pieces at the home or other place for a dinner, reception, or other event that the Funeral Home is not involved with in any other way.

One example of this would be after a funeral if the family

was to have a get together at a place intended for such and wanted the Funeral Home to take the flowers present at the service to the place of the gathering and arrange and set the flowers in an organized display. This service is commonly requested when the family is holding a memorial service without the Funeral Home's direction, but would like to have a Funeral Home staff associate to come solely to arrange and set all the flowers for the service.

House Cleaning: If you are in need of someone to come during or after the funeral to clean or tidy up the house that has been full of guests or the family has been too preoccupied to tend to this chore, the Funeral Home may offer this service.

When the Funeral Home does offer housecleaning or maid service it is usually only from the time of the arrangement conference through the day or a day or two after any services under the Funeral Home's direction are over.

Marker Setting: If you purchase a memorial table or headstone for your departed loved one's grave from the Funeral Director and then have it delivered to the Funeral Home when ready, usually the Funeral Director has someone on the home's staff that can take the marker out to the cemetery or memorial park and set it.

This is offered by some Funeral Homes for a set fee because of the handling and setting of the marker oftentimes can take special know how, especially if there are special cemetery rules about setting markers that the Funeral Home may already be familiar with.

Photography/Videographing: As with other special events in life such as anniversaries, birthdays, graduations, holidays, wedding, etc., some families do not want the special events of a visitation or funeral ceremony to pass without pictures or video footage. Some Funeral Homes have jumped on the bandwagon of having someone on their staff picture take or videotape some of the funeral/memorial service/visitation/committal at the family's request for such.

Expect the Funeral Home to charge a reasonable fee if using their own equipment for photographing, taping etc., developing film, processing videotape and the like.

Reception Hosting: Since some families chose to forego an actual standard funeral or memorial service and instead have a reception in its place, some Funeral Homes have or are planning to build on or renovate a part of its present facilities to accommodate receptions.

Also some families need a place to have a dinner or informal gathering before or after a service and the Funeral Home is usually a good place.

Because of the trend toward the more informal gather, visit, talk and mingle type of event in connection to a loved one's passing, the funeral industry today is creating an awareness for Funeral Homes to respond to this opportunity. Funeral Homes that facilitate reception hosting will usually provide the reception room and the chairs and tables. They may also provide drinks and refreshments and a few will even provide a piano for some soft background music while guests and family members visit.

Register Book Typing: A service that some Funeral Homes have been doing for years, this effort involves typing the names of those people who sent flowers to the family for the funeral into the register/memorial book.

Using the cards attached to the floral tributes sent, the Funeral Home staff will usually remove the cards before the service and have the Funeral Home's office staff to type the names onto the designated pages for such in the register book before presenting it to the family after the services are complete.

Most Funeral Homes include this service as part of their professional service fee while others may charge separately for it.

Security: Because the world we live in is not always safe, and there are places, circumstances and situations that may require that precautions be taken, providing a security guard or guards is a provision that a Funeral Home can usually assist with if requested or need be. Some Funeral Homes that are located in higher crime areas or when a ceremony or visitation is held after dark, or if there are problems within a family between a family member and someone else that may pose a threat to the safety or well-being of a family or family member, the Funeral Home usually has either a private security company it contracts with or can arrange to have a uniformed or non-uniformed off duty police officer come and be in attendance in case any problems should arise relating to family members, guests and attendees.

This charge will vary and may or may not be treated as a cash advance item.

Service Recording: While photographing or videotaping can capture the visual aspect of service events, recording the funeral or memorial service on cassette tape or CD can get the audio dimension.

Most Funeral Homes chapels have a cassette recorder and can record the service as another way to help the family later remember the event.

There may be a recording charge for doing this but some Funeral Homes do it complimentary for allowing them to handle the services.

Miscellaneous Products

As with services, there are various types of goods and merchandise that the Funeral Home may offer for sale to increase its revenues along with the traditional caskets, outer containers, burial clothing and guest-register books.

Usually the Funeral Home will have these items or information about such displayed in the area where arrangements are made and visible to consumers. However if these goods are not shown, you may ask about them if any of these would help you create a more meaningful service or way to remember your loved one afterwards.

Here are some of the items offered:

Bookmarks: These are not the ordinary type of bookmarks that you pick up at the library or a bookstore, but rather a durable laminated card with the decedent's obituary or death notice on one side and usually a poem, inspirational picture, painting, prayer or bible verse on the opposite side. If the Funeral Home possesses a laminating machine it can make personalized bookmarks using whatever type of picture, paragraph or other impression that can be placed onto the card or paper size.

Some Funeral Homes will charge to make the bookmarks, others will do them complementary so long as the family only requests several. If the family wants more than a certain amount, say 8 or 10, they may charge per bookmark after that set number.

Bookmarks make a great way to remember the deceased in a form that can be used for years to come and are ideal to give to friends or relatives after services that were important to the deceased or to those unable to attend the services.

Candles: Like bookmarks, candles can come with different inscriptions, symbols or emblems engraved onto the exterior surface of the candle holder.

The way that the candles are usually displayed for sale by the Funeral Home is by offering the candles that are placed in a glass or clear plastic outer candle holder that has the inspirational engraving or inscription on the outside. These candles can be bought either individually or in plural and are sometimes lit and burned during or as part of the Funeral or memorial service, or kept and burned later on.

Some religions such as catholic or Jewish faiths incorporate candle use during some part of their traditional rites or ceremonies. Others purchase and use them to simply add meaning or value to the period of mourning.

Cross/Crucifixes: Made of brass or some other hard metal material, these crucifixes usually are about 8 or 9 inches in length and are given to family members after the catholic funeral mass.

Many times a single crucifix will either be attached to the

inside head panel of the open casket or placed on top of the closed casket during mass.

The crucifix adds significant value to the catholic service and extras can be purchased at about $10-25 per unit for other family members that may want one as a keepsake.

Flag Cases: All honorably discharged United States veterans are entitled to receive an American Flag courtesy of the U.S. Government provided through the proof of honorable discharge.

Since Funeral Homes obtain the flag on the deceased veteran's family's behalf, many families want to display the folded flag that is given or presented to them at the service.

One way that some Funeral Homes help families in safekeeping and displaying the flag in their home is by offering flag cases that are triangle shaped made of wood and a glass front for viewing the folded flag.

Flag cases are made out of oak, cherry, mahogany, walnut or other type of wood and usually offer the option of engraving the deceased veteran's name and dates onto an attached metal plate on the front and also a circular medallion with the branch of service emblem on the front base of the case.

Flag cases are usually an item of enhanced value to those families who want to honor the pride of the veteran's service in the armed forces, and the flag case makes this patriotic display more meaningful.

Paintings: Using an individual photograph of the decedent, one way that a lasting tribute and remembrance can be created is through an oil painting.

Funeral Homes are a logical avenue of marketing portraits in oil for the artists who are skilled in painting because of the fact that the funeral directors usually ask for a photo of the deceased for obituaries, hairdressing, etc., and are also in the business of helping families create unique and lasting impressions of their deceased loved one.

The way that it usually works is that the Funeral Home will

often have an individualized oil painting on the wall of the arrangement room(s) or areas where families will see the sample painting and discover what can be done.

If you decide that using the decedent's photograph you would like to have a painting made, the Funeral Director will usually go over the size and color options and other details necessary to provide the artist or studio that the Funeral Home contracts with to do the painting.

Usually the larger the painting size, the pricier it will be. Also the more color and outline detail involved may also add to the

cost. Depending on distance, time, number of painting projects, etc. may influence how long it takes to have the painting finished and delivered.

Be sure to find out where the painting will be done, whether you will get the photograph used to paint the portrait back, whether the frame is included in the price quoted, as well as any shipping, delivery or receiving costs or any applicable sale tax.

<u>Picture Frames</u>: Separate from the paintings, picture frames are available for purchase at some Funeral Homes either individually or as part of some packaged funeral plans with other merchandise.

Since a portion of the funeral arranging process can revolve around imagery and the preservation of the deceased's likeness in life through photos, some people have an old cherished photograph that has not been framed out now with the decedent's passing; the importance of preserving it has now increased in value. And so some Funeral Homes will try to present the opportunity to fill this desire with custom picture frames usually in 8 x 10 but possibly also in other sizes.

Usually the frames offered are not much different from what you would find in a merchant retail store, but the Funeral Home may charge more for it based on the idea of buy it at the Funeral Home because you are at the Funeral Home now anyway, so save yourself another trip or another stop later.

Other Charges

Like other business enterprises, Funeral Homes must cover their costs in providing its clientele with services that are sometimes needed to properly carry out a family's wishes.

As a consumer, you need to have an awareness of certain miscellaneous items that may incur a charge that can be posted to your account.

Director Present: Different states have different rules concerning what situations require the presence and involvement of a funeral director/mortician, licensed by that particular state.

For example, your state may require that a Funeral Director be present for disinterring a decedent from one grave to be moved to another grave in that or another cemetery. Having a licensed person to come out for the disinterment may incur an expense on the part of the consumer arranging for the disinterment.

Also if the Funeral Home you are making arrangements with to transport your loved one to a cemetery a good distance away for an out of town burial may use an unlicensed staff member to drive him or her to the burial destination, however if the cemetery or the state requires a licensed director to be in attendance at the gravesite for the burial, the arranging Funeral Home may have a director from a local mortuary go out for the burial.

The underlying purpose in having a licensed director present for these and other situations involving the deceased is to be sure that proper supervision is provided for. In other words it is a form of consumer safeguard that gives assurance that the business of taking care of the dead is properly carried out and in compliance with all wishes and applicable rules and laws.

Flower Storage: Sometimes after a service is over and done and arrangements call for the Funeral Home to keep the flowers from the service for a specified time, there may be a storage fee or keeping them until delivery or pickup.

Most Funeral Homes will keep the flowers and plants from a service under their direction for a day or two after services have concluded but anything past that may incur a charge for keeping them.

If it will be more than a day after a service before the flowers and plants can be picked up or delivered, check with the Funeral Home about any charges.

Holidays/Evenings/Weekends: Doing business during regular business hours cost a lot of money in and of itself. Since Funeral Homes help families by serving them during nonbusiness hours for visitations, rosaries, prayer vigils, memorial services and weekend or holiday funerals, there is an extra cost incurred by the Funeral Home to provide service during these times.

As a result of additional costs, the Funeral Homes that provide after hours services must impose an additional charge to pay its staff and other expenses.

If you are interested in using the Funeral Home's staff and/or facilities for an evening or weekend funeral or memorial service, or on a holiday, be sure to get an understanding of what the total cost will be to have the service.

Overnight: This pertains to any charges in relation to the Funeral Home safekeeping, sheltering or holding a decedent at its facility overnight until disposition the next day.

Sometimes a Funeral Home that is in the local vicinity of the cemetery where the burial is to take place when an out of town

Funeral Home transports the decedent the day before the burial, the decedent will need to be held or sheltered until burial the next day.

If a local Funeral Home is approached to keep a decedent at its facility overnight for safekeeping it may have a charge for this that will be paid in some form by the arranging family.

In the case of having a deceased loved one transported somewhere distant for burial, find out if the decedent will be housed overnight at a local Funeral Home and if they have a charge.

Per Day: This can relate to such items as refrigeration of

decedent pending cremation or burial, holding of an embalmed decedent awaiting a family's decision about disposition or arrangements or holding the cremated ashes of a decedent after cremation.

Be sure to read the general price list given by the Funeral Home to see if there are any items charged on a per day basis.

Visitation or use of facilities for viewing is also charged on a per day basis by many Funeral Homes.

Recording Fees: If funeral or memorial services are to be held in the Funeral Home's chapel or facility equipped with sound and audio equipment, the Funeral Home may be able to make a cassette or CD recording of the service.

Some Funeral Homes will record the service complementary to the family; others may charge a nominal recording fee. Either way, if you would like to have the service audio recorded, ask your Funeral Director for details.

Sender Fees: In situations where you ask the Funeral Home to carry out a special request, such as notifying another party of the death by telegram, telegraph, overseas phone call(s), or mailing out letters or cards after the service, etc., the Funeral Home may charge you the cost to them of doing it. Phone, postage, overnight express mail, and other activities requested of the Funeral Director and his/her staff can add up fast, and again as with any business, covering the cost of doing business is the only way to stay in business.

Packaged Funeral Plans

Many Funeral Homes and mortuaries offer some type of funeral package plans that allow consumers to buy a package selection that includes both service and merchandise items that are usually associated with a traditional funeral service. Different packages contain different features that appeal to consumers such as receiving a discount for buying the funeral as a package rather than as itemized components. Other advantages may include certain products or services that may only be offered exclusively with the packaged plan such as long-distance calling cards, legal or financial service memberships, placements of obituary on the internet, gift certificates for food or other purchases. Another incentive for purchasing a packaged funeral plan can be uncomplicating and simplifying the arrangement process.

If, for instance, you know that you want to have a traditional funeral for your deceased loved one, the Funeral Director can show you the packages that are offered for a traditional service. It will usually allow you to select the casket you would like with all of the service charges included as well as other items that usually are part of a traditional service such as guest register book, service folders/programs and thank you cards, for example.

Instead of having to go over each and every item, piece by piece, the packaged funeral allows you to make one or a few decisions and then have the assurance that all the components

When Things Go Wrong

What happens if your relationship with your selected funeral home does not go as planned? If your wishes were not properly carried out, you are charged improperly or for something you did not need or request?

If you feel that you are or were not treated fairly, first talk to your funeral director and let him or her have a chance to address your grievance(s). If this is not addressed satisfactorily then go to the management of the funeral establishment and let them try to help you. If your concerns are not adequately dealt with here then you can normally go to an authority outside the funeral home or provider such as the Better Business Bureau, the governing authority over the funeral home, etc.

Chapters 12 and 13 in this book list those entities that can help you if this situation occurs.

that are part of a traditional service are provided, usually at a cost savings to you and allows you to be relieved of the more time consuming item-by-item burden at a stressful time.

The offering of packaged funeral plans is permissible under the Federal Trade Commission Funeral Rule so long as an itemized price list is provided. The offer of packages is optional to Funeral Homes under the FTC provisions and funeral providers are permitted to offer as many or as few packages as they wish.

The packages offered may also be presented on the basis of no deletions or substitutions of individual components that are part of a package. However in some cases where let's say for example an outer burial container that is a part of the packaged plan is not needed because the cemetery or memorial park does not require one, then the package offer may allow the outer container to come off and leave the rest of the package intact. If this is the case be sure to ask if an item or items can be deleted and if so which ones. Be aware of the fact that even though the FTC allows consumers to buy their casket from a party other than the Funeral Home providing the services, the Funeral Home can restrict discount package plans to those consumers who purchase the casket from the Funeral Home without violating the Funeral Rule.

This allows Funeral Homes to be more competitive with third party sellers by offering packages with discounted prices as a way to encourage consumers to buy their caskets from funeral homes. You should also know that since packaged funeral plan offers are optional, the funeral home or mortuary does not have to place the packages on their general price list under FTC regulations. So if you are shopping and obtain a funeral provider's GPL and it does not show any packaged plans for funerals or cremations, be sure to ask if you are interested in what packaged plans may be available.

Sample Funeral Contract as mandated by the Federal Trade Commission

FTC COMPLIANCE FUNERAL HOME

525 Vine Street, Suite 2200 • Cincinnati, Ohio 45202 • (513) 241-5540

STATEMENT OF FUNERAL GOODS AND SERVICES SELECTED

Charges are only for those items that you selected or that are required. If we are required by law or by a cemetery or crematory to use any items, we will explain the reasons in writing below. If you selected a funeral that may require embalming, such as a funeral with viewing, you may have to pay for embalming. You do not have to pay for embalming you did not approve if you selected arrangements such as a direct cremation or immediate burial. If we charged for embalming, we will explain why below.

____
Funeral Services for

______________ Date of Death

______________ Date of Funeral Service

A. PROFESSIONAL SERVICE SELECTED ______________ $ ______
Basic Services of Funeral Director and Staff ______________ $ ______
Embalming ______________ $ ______
Other Preparation of the Body:
______________ $ ______
______________ $ ______

B. ADDITIONAL SERVICES AND FACILITIES FEES
Visitation at the Funeral Home. . . . . $ ______
Visitation at Other Facility . . . . $ ______
Funeral Service at the Funeral Home. $ ______
Funeral Service at Other Facility . . . . $ ______
Memorial Service at the Funeral Home . . . . $ ______
Memorial Service at Other Facility. . . . . $ ______
Graveside Service . . . . $ ______

C. AUTOMOTIVE EQUIPMENT (local service 25 miles)
Transfer of Remains to Funeral Home . . . . $ ______
Funeral Coach. . . . . $ ______
Limousine(s) . . . . $ ______
Family Car. . . . . $ ______
Flower Car. . . . . $ ______
Other Automotive Equipment:
______________ $ ______

D. UNIT SERVICE CHARGES
Offering A . . . . $ ______
Services of funeral director and staff, transfer of remains to funeral home within 25 miles, embalming, other preparations of the body, use of facilities for viewing (1 day) and funeral ceremony or services in other facility, coach, committal or other disposition service, acknowledgement cards and register book.

Offering B. . . . . $ ________

Services of funeral director and staff, transfer of remains to funeral home within 25 miles, embalming, other preparations of the body, use of facilities for funeral ceremony or service in other facility, coach, committal or other disposition service, acknowledgement cards and register book.

Offering C. . . . . $ ________

Services of funeral director and staff, transfer of remains to funeral home within 25 miles, preparation of the body other than embalming, use of facilities for shelter of body and funeral ceremony or service in other facility, coach, committal or other disposition service, acknowledgement cards and register book.

Forwarding Remains . . . . $ ________
Receiving Remains . . . . $ ________
Direct Cremation. . . . . $ ________
Immediate Burial . . . . $ ________

TOTAL SERVICE SELECTED . . . . $ ________

E. MERCHANDISE SELECTED

Casket . . . . $ ________
Outer Burial Container. . . . . $ ________
Urn . . . . $ ________
Clothing. . . . . $ ________
Registration Book . . . . $ ________
Acknowledgment Cards. . . . . $ ________
Other: ____$ ________
Sales Tax . . . . $ ________

TOTAL MERCHANDISE SELECTED . . . . $ ________

F. CASH ADVANCES

Cemetery Charges . . . . $ ________
Flowers . . . . $ ________
Clergy . . . . $ ________
Death Certificates . . . . $ ________
Other: ____$ ________
____$ ________
We charge you for our services in obtaining: ______________$ ________
____$ ________

TOTAL CASH ADVANCES. . . . . $ ________

TOTAL SERVICES, MERCHANDISE and
CASH ADVANCES . . . . $ ________
Paid at or prior to arrangements, or other credits . . . . $ ________

BALANCE DUE . . . . $ ________

Contracts And Agreements
(Your Legal Rights)

At the end of the arrangements conference, the funeral home is required by federal law to give you, the purchaser, a statement of funeral goods and services selected, also termed the contract or purchase agreement. The Funeral Director is to fill in the contract from decisions made by the arranging family regarding services and merchandise offered by the Funeral Home, and present it to the responsible party. The agreement is to be signed by both parties and a copy given to the purchaser/consumer.

The funeral rule does not require that the purchase agreement/contract be in any specific format, however it must be itemized with each item printed on the contract and the corresponding charge written or printed correlating to the item chosen. This makes it easier for the consumer to receive non-deceptive pricing for goods and services selected and to only be charged for items selected or those items that are required by law or mandatory for the type of services desired.

The list must also disclose your legal, crematory or cemetery requirements in connection with certain goods or services purchased. If any charges are not known at the time of completing the arrangements, a good faith estimate may be given to you in writing. Also, be sure that the total cost is stated in writing on the contract as well. Usually the terms and conditions relating to the transaction between the Funeral Home and the consumer/purchaser will be part of the contract printed on the reverse side or another page. For full disclosure rules, see the Federal Trade Commission's Funeral Trade Rule in chapter 11.

In Summary
(Do I Have To Use A Funeral Home?)

The question is asked from time to time by callers who want

to know the answer to, do I have to use a funeral home? The answer depends on where you live and what the laws of that state or jurisdiction call for.

Usually a death certificate and the reporting of the death to the local or county registrar of vital records is required and there also usually are ordinances in place restricting where burials of human remains can take place.

There are certain situations that surface in life where we need assistance of others who are versed and qualified to guide *us* through. It is generally understood that when you need to buy or sale a house, you usually need the aid of a real estate agent or title company, that when you need a tooth pulled or cavity filled you go to a dentist. The same applies when a death occurs in the family. Not only are you in a state of deep emotional loss, but you and many others do not know what to do or how to do it. Because of the shock of a loved one's passing, the pyramid of details that must be analyzed and tended to along with meeting any and all applicable legal requirements, I strongly suggest that you let a funeral professional help you through the process, not because I am a licensed Funeral Director and want to create continued job security from now on, but because you and the ones you love are best helped by those of us who can and want to help you - the purpose of this book.

Chapter 2

Cemeteries & Memorial Parks

1. Introduction: what You Need To Know
2. Selecting A Final Resting Place: Price/Value/Beauty/Reputation/ Genealogical Access/Historical Significance
3. Types Of Cemeteries: Big vs. Small/Urban vs. Rural/For Profit vs. Nonprofit/Corporate vs. Independent/Public vs. Private/Religious vs. Nonsectarian/Difference Between Cemeteries And Memorial Parks
4. What Should It Cost? Type Of Disposition/Sections And Areas Within The Cemetery/Processing And Administrative Fees
5. Contacting The Cemetery: Down To Business
6. Buying Property And The Right Of Interment: What You Need To Know/Ground Space/Lawn Crypt/Mausoleum Crypt/ Columbaria/Specialty Statutory/Scattering Gardens/Churchyard Property/How To Save Money On Cemetery Property
7. Arranging A Burial
8. What Is Opening And Closing?
9. Vault Installation/Removal
10. Multiple Interments/Entombments
11. Witnessing Burial/Entombment
12. Temporary Burial/Entombment/Storage
13. Contracts And Agreements
14. Paperwork And More Paperwork
15. After Disposition: What Cemeteries And Memorial Parks Should And Should Not Allow. Rules/Regulations/Restrictions/Flowers And Decorations/Visiting The Cemetery/Holidays/Activities And Events
16. Endowment Funds
17. Perpetual Care
18. Non-Perpetual Care Cemeteries
19. Grave Do's And Don'ts
20. Markers/Monuments/Headstones/Vases: Sizes/Shapes/Finishes/ Borders/Designs/Lettering And Inscription/Emblems/Vases/Government And VA Memorials

21. Where And From: Purchasing A Memorial. Funeral Homes/ Cemeteries/Independent Dealers/Chain Dealers/Internet Sellers/The Process
22. Delivery And Transport Fees
23. Installation And Setting Fees
24. Engraving/Inscription/Lettering Fees/Scrolls
25. Marker Moving/Resetting/Reinstalling
26. Repair/Maintenance/Restoration
27. Continuity And The Cemetery As A Going Concern. Deeded vs. Undeeded Property
28. What Happens To Unused Property
29. Selling Unwanted/Unneeded Spaces
30. Exchanging Cemetery Property
31. Donating Unneeded/Unwanted Property
32. Transferring Burial Property
33. Statuary And Other Features
34. Prearranging Cemetery And Burial Services
35. Cemetery Associations
36. Disinterment/Exhumation And Reinterment
37. Exploring The Possibilities: Can A Cemetery Go Out Of Business?
38. Pondering The Possibilities: Do I Have To Use A Cemetery or Memorial Park?
39. Defending And Saving Old Cemeteries: Out with The Old, In With The New?

"There is a land of the Living and a Land of the dead and the bridge is love, the only survival, the only meaning."

- Thorton Wilder

Cemeteries And Memorial Parks

Many people have for a long time thought about funeral homes and cemeteries or places of final disposition as one. Although there are today more than ever before "combination" locations where the funeral home and cemetery or memorial park are on the same property, even in these cases of the one owner or under one roof idea, the cemetery or memorial park is usually a distinct separate entity and as a result should be looked at separately.

In this chapter I want to show you what cemeteries and memorial parks can offer you as a consumer and help you understand and know what to expect when time comes to purchase the services of a place of burial.

The same as buying funerals however is the luxury of thinking about and shopping for burial property before the time of need. One of the most difficult things to do in life is to have to go out and buy burial or final disposition property on the same day you are making at need funeral arrangements. If a service is already scheduled for day after tomorrow, you don't have time to research, call and look around for the best deal.

My purpose here therefore is to help guide you to make the best decision whether at need or looking ahead to the future.

Rose Hill Cemetery, Cleburne Texas

Judging A Book By Its Cover
(Selecting a Final Resting Place)

Location, Location, Location

Whether at the time of death or purchasing ahead of time, the location of the cemetery is a huge factor in deciding where to bury the family as they pass away.

Because of the mobility of our society and world today, it is harder to determine if the immediate or extended family will still be living in the same area 20 years from now. If a family should move it will probably be hard to sell a space or lot without taking a loss on the transaction.

Another consideration is the anticipated patronage. Will the surviving family members want to visit the gravesite frequently?

Driving 5 miles or 50 miles may enter in as a factor if someone who was close to the decedent wants to come to the cemetery once a week.

On the other hand, driving by the cemetery on the way to and/or from work everyday may be a constant reminder of the deceased and his/her death, and provide an obstacle to relegating his/her memory to the past and therefore being able to move forward with life.

Price

Cemetery space can be very expensive or very affordable depending on where the cemetery/burial park is located.

As a general rule, an urban and metropolitan cemetery located on major traffic thoroughfares will be pricier.

Cemeteries that are out "in the sticks" in rural areas tend to be less in price for spaces or lots.

Availability of spaces for sale can also effect the price of a burial lot or space. If a cemetery is fairly new (30 years or less) in existence, there may be a plentiful supply of spaces and the cemetery may be trying to sell the spaces by lowering the sales price.

If an older more established cemetery is nearly "sold out" and has few spaces/lots left to sell, the price may be rather hefty.

Whichever the case, be sure to get the prices for any property you would consider purchasing and evaluate it according to your wishes and needs.

Value

Very few if any people take the time to consider, evaluate and purchase something if it has no perceived value or significance. Cemetery property is no different. People want value for their money. They want a product that will meet their expectations.

What you will have to deal with is not just a piece of real estate or property to put a deceased family member in, but also the intangibles of familiar surroundings, upkeep of the grounds, expectations being met by the cemetery's administration, promises made being promises kept, etc.

Beauty

At the time of dealing with a loved one's death, how nice a cemetery looks may not be high on the list of priorities.

However in time it will.

How well the grounds are kept is a reflection upon a cemetery's ownership and management, and how important to them it is to have a place of beauty rather than just an area outlet for disposition of the dead.

Are the trees pruned or trimmed? Grass cut and manicured? Is there trash scattered along the yards and streetways? Is the lighting and fencing kept in a working condition? Making several visits to a cemetery on different days answers these questions.

Reputation

How esteemed is the cemetery among those who live in proximity to it? Is it an asset to its community, or a liability?

How responsive is the cemetery's contacts to requests from property owners? How committed is the cemetery to serving the public, its patrons its property owners?

Genealogical Access

Not as large a variable as some of the previous factors; how research friendly is the cemetery to future generations of family members who may want to come visit and obtain information about past ascendants?

Are grave markers and headstones easy to find and read? Is it easy to get information on where one is buried? Is the cemetery located so far off the beaten path that it would be too difficult to find and access?

Historical Significance

Also not necessarily a huge factor, but something to consider is a cemetery's significance from a historical standpoint. Are there any famous persons buried in the cemetery? Are there any historical markers or displayed information concerning some important past event or activity that adds too or lessens the merit or worth of its grounds?

How a cemetery deals with and handles its own history and the history of its ruminants speaks wisdom about how it will care for and honor its future stewardship.

Types Of Cemeteries

Cemeteries like most anything else, can vary greatly in size, shape, symbolism, surroundings, etc. The variances can be great but the basic objective the same: to provide the area or community with a place for the disposition of the human dead.

With this in mind I want to contrast cemeteries along the lines of black and white to help us understand the differences.

Big vs. Small

Besides the obvious variance of size, large cemeteries often employ full-time employees and staff for management, sales, administration, maintenance, grounds crew, etc. Small cemeteries often work as one or two person operations if that, depending on number of burials per month or year.

The thing to remember is that the larger the cemetery, the bigger the line of communication is likely to be concerning questions, inquiries, and the desire to obtain information.

Many (but not all) smaller cemeteries may not even have a phone number listed in the phone directory. For those located out in the country, unless there is a phone number or address posted on the cemetery's front gate, it may take some extra effort to find the point of contact.

Corporate vs. Independent

Ownership of a cemetery may be structured in different ways which I will discuss further in this chapter, but a cemetery may be owned by a corporation or chain conglomerate such as SCI, Stewart or Alderwoods (see Chapter 1) or by an individual or company that owns just the one cemetery property.

In many ways from the consumer's standpoint there may not be a big difference between the two except on paper. Many times corporate-owned cemetery chains may acquire a cemetery that was independent and continue to operate it under the name of the previous owner, not their own name.

Corporate cemeteries are covered or owned under the "corporate umbrella" of the cemetery being one of its many locations, whereas the independently owned and operated cemetery may be the owner/operator's sole livelihood and means of support.

Urban vs. Rural

Touched upon earlier in the Selecting A Final Resting Place section, rural cemeteries tend to be small in size (acreage) and urban ones large in size, however this is not always the case.

Because of its accessibility, cemeteries in metropolitan areas or cities tend to be more than just a place to bury the dead, but also a place for the community to esteem and value as a special place within its city.

It can be as simple as having a place to go for a walk away from the crowds or a place available for the community to source out civic activities such as hold special events or display artwork or statuary, for example.

Rural cemeteries on the other hand may go weeks or even months with no activity, no burials, no movement or visitors.

For Profit vs. Nonprofit

For-profit cemeteries, which originated around the time of the civil war, are structured to operate the same way any other for-profit business is, and can do just about anything that is legal.

Nonprofit cemeteries on the other hand are exempt from taxation under section 501 (c)(13) of the Internal Revenue Code[1]. The idea behind nonprofit status is that the needed service of aiding society in the disposition of its dead should be encouraged and therefore the creation of nonprofit status.

There are some nonprofit cemeteries of larger size that may also operate for profit subsidiaries such as mortuaries, flower shops, burial vault companies, etc. that do not affect the cemetery's nonprofit status.

Religious vs. Nonsectarian

Some churches operate cemeteries under the exemption of the church. These cemeteries are available for the use of the church's members and families.

Depending upon the church and its beliefs and policies, the cemetery may or may not be open to inquiry from non-church members.

Nonsectarian in contrast is usually open to those of all faiths or peoples regardless of beliefs. Most cemeteries today are nonsectarian in that they operate according to one's economic ability to buy or purchase property rather than one's religious affiliation.

Public vs. Private

Most states provide for district or municipal cemeteries with the idea of all cities, towns and regions have provided for, a place to bury its dead. This way, those places that are devoid of any private cemeteries will have grounds to dispose of its deceased.

Most public cemeteries today are in existence for the sole purpose of providing burial property to those citizens/residents in need of it. These activities are restricted due to the general concept of having government compete with private industry.

Privately held cemeteries are owned as a corporation, partnership, proprietorship or other private form of organization. They generally object to regulation by the governmental authorities that allow municipal or public cemeteries to operate without the same level or type of regulation.

This contention is just one part of the larger forum of debate over the issues of government vs. the private sector and regulation of business.

Cemeteries/Memorial Parks

Once called or known as graveyards, cemeteries are places designated for the use and to be used for the final disposition of human remains, where memorialization of the human remains may also be established.

A memorial park is a cemetery that does not allow or permit the use of upright memorials for the purpose of adopting a parklike setting. With the use of flat markers, memorial parks intend to create grounds that educate, inspire and uplift visitors by procuring a more inviting environment.

There are some cemeteries that coin themselves as memorial parks although they have upright markers, but have designated sections within the park that don't allow upright memorials.

What Should It Cost?

The most common and frequent question asked by people today regarding funeral and burial information is, not surprisingly, "How much does it cost to bury someone ?" The answer to this is, "It depends."

The same way that the cost of clothing will depend upon what type of outfit, what type of material it is made of and whether you go to Wal-Mart or Neiman-Marcus, the cost of burying someone falls along the lines of when, where and how. Since there are at least a minimum of several factors determining burial that will affect the cost, I will spend most of the remainder of this chapter discussing how cemeteries operate, what they do and don't require and how this determines your expense.

Types Of Disposition

If you want ground burial, the cost will vary depending on use of an outer container, single or double interment, and opening/closing fees. If you want entombment the cost will be different, as will the cost of purchasing a niche for cremated remains. If your cemetery space is a lawn crypt, your cost will differ from not having a crypt, and so on.

The first step is to decide what you prefer the most and the least, then do a cost comparison.

If your first preference is ground burial and least preferred is cremation with ashes going into a niche, you may chart it like this:

Most Favored:	1) Ground Burial
	2) Mausoleum Entombment
	3) Cremation- Ashes into Ground space
Least Favored:	4) Cremation- Ashes into a Niche

Then you will want to contact different cemeteries to find out what their charges are to do each of the alternatives listed. This will make it easier for you to make a decision.

Sections/Areas within The Cemetery

Some larger, well-established cemeteries have named sections within the grounds. The price of burial space property within each section may be different from the spaces in other sections. The reason for this depends primarily on where the section is located within the cemetery. The same way that property values in a city are determined by the part of town where the property is situated, the same principle applies to burial space.

Example: A space in the lakeside section of the cemetery is more desirable than one in a more remote part due to its pleasant scenery, features, accessibility, etc.

Processing And Administrative Fees

Some cemeteries may charge fees for processing the contract and paperwork related to providing the client/family with the services and merchandise requested.

This may be figured into the cost of the burial property or it may be placed on the contract as a separate item.

Nevertheless these charges basically represented the cost of the cemetery's staff, operational and/or administrative activities needed to procure the family's wishes.

Generally these charges may range from 1-10% of the cemetery's total charges. Be sure to ask for a price list and ask if all potential charges are on the list of prices and if not what else may be included. Charges may be worded in various ways but usually are known as one of the following:

Service Charge	Document Preparation Fee
Processing Fee	Overhead Charge
Recording Fee	Administrative Surcharge

Down To Business
Contacting The Cemetery

Whether your situation is at the time of death or you are wanting to purchase final disposition property in advance will depend on who contacts the cemetery.

It is the funeral director's job to contact the cemetery once death has occurred after gathering the pertinent information from the family to get the proper grave or burial space open. This includes information about the decedent and all facts needed from the next-of-kin concerning the exact space to be opened.

Advance planning for future burial should always be initiated by the one who wants to someday be interred in that cemetery and preferably along with a legal next-of-kin or other who is likely to survive him or her. This way when the person does pass away the one who accompanied the decedent to the cemetery earlier will be knowledgeable about the preneed discussions and therefore know what is expected from the cemetery.

The information one will need for contacting the cemetery will always be the name and date of birth of the one arrangements are to be made for, as well as the deed to the property (if already purchased).

Buying Property And The Right Of Interment
What You Need To Know

The first step is to determine what type of cemetery property you desire to purchase. Do you want a ground burial or a mausoleum entombment? And if the choice is cremation there is the choosing either ground inurnment (burial) or a columbarium (above ground) niche or space. A careful consideration and overview of each will be helpful.

Ground Space

By far the most traditional form of disposition is burial in a grave or space of ground.

What is for sale here is the right of interment or "burial" subject to the rules and regulations of the cemetery.

Although this is the most basic product offered by cemeteries, some providers sell spaces for either single (one burial per space) or double interment where two burials may be made in the same space- one at a lower level, (for example 8 feet) the other at a more shallow level (4 feet, for example).

As a rule of thumb the double interment or companion space will cost more than a space designated for a single burial.

Another thing to consider is the size of dimensions of the space. With a rapid increase in recent years of an overweight population, will someone fit in one space as defined by the cemetery? It may mean the difference in having to buy one space as opposed to two.

As far as pricing, cemetery ground spaces vary by a wide range depending on factors such as number of cemeteries in the area, available ground space, demand for spaces, beauty and maintenance of the grounds, etc. As a general rule, you can expect to pay more in the city or large metropolitan areas than in the more isolated rural areas.

Lawn Crypt Space

Also known as garden crypts, lawn crypts are regular ground burial spaces in appearance, but each grave space is constructed with a reinforced concrete chamber below the ground while the section of spaces is being developed. Lawn crypts may also be single or companion for two interments depending on how the cemetery has built them.

Since each crypt space has a built-in concrete structure, no vault or outer container for a casket is needed, therefore saving the consumer from having to purchase one. However due to the construction of the crypt within each space, expect lawn crypt spaces in a cemetery to cost more than a regular ground space.

Mausoleum Crypt

Opposite of lawn or garden crypts are mausoleum crypts which are above ground and can be either indoors or outside. They can also be community or family mausoleums.

The appeal of a community mausoleum is that it allows many more families to choose a burial form of disposition previously associated with wealth and power[2].

Family or private mausoleums are usually much smaller in size and may have the family's name inscribed on the structure.

Mausoleum crypts offer varied features such as embellishments that affect the price for a mausoleum space. Also the way that spaces are constructed with the crypts stacked from bottom to top, expect to pay more for a space at eye level and less for spaces higher up. The price of individual crypts may also vary on whether they are indoor or outdoor.

Large cemeteries are more likely to offer mausoleum crypts as an alternative to ground spaces, whereas few smaller cemeteries have community mausoleums.

Columbaria

Also called a columbarium, this is a building or other structure that is designed with individual spaces or niches used for the inurnment *of* ashes or cremated remains. A columbarium may be part of a mausoleum or a free standing structure on its on. Whereas crypts are designed for full size adult caskets and are made of concrete, a columbarium is much smaller in size and usually constructed to hold 1 or 2 cremation urns and are constructed of various materials with granite or marble being most popular.

Columbaria niche spaces will be less expensive if cremation is the choice of disposition, and with the growing trend toward cremation, more and more cemeteries are building and marketing columbaria.

Specialty Statuary

Some cemeteries that are looking for creative ways to offer options to consumers have developed product lines out of statuary features that can become part of fixtures within the cemetery. These would include benches, statutes, freestanding columns or other durable products, usually made out of marble or granite, that allow consumers even more choices in relation to disposition and or memorialization.

Granite benches for example, often can have the family name engraved on it, and may have preconstructed spaces for holding cremated remains.

Although specialty statuary can be pricey, a lot of cemeteries are working to make such features affordable to interested parties.

Scattering Gardens

These are areas or a section within the cemetery where cremated remains or ashes may be scattered or released from their container unto the earth.

The cemetery's charges for this may be for the space or area to release the ashes on and/or a service charge for accommodating or procuring the act of scattering.

There may also be a permit to obtain from the proper authority in the area and a charge for it.

The first step however will be to find out whether scattering of cremated remains is permissible at your cemetery of choice.

A Last Resort: Churchyard Property

Also known as charity spaces or Potters field, this is usually a section in the cemetery where indigent cases are interred.

These spaces for burial are either very inexpensive or at no charge if the family of the decedent is approved for assistance.

Unlike regular burial or disposition property however, there may be restrictions on the spaces. For one thing, there may not be an outer container permitted. Another may be that only simple wooden caskets be used. The reason being that the cemetery may reserve the right to reuse the space after so many years (usually around 20) for another burial in the future. In other words, the decedent is really only using the space long enough for decomposition to consummate and then it will be utilized again in the future for the next decedent in need.

How To Save Money On Cemetery Property

Burial or final disposition property can be the most expensive part of dieing but it does not have to be.

First decide what you want to happen after you die and take action now. Prices will, like most everything else over the long run, only go up on cemetery space.

If you want ground burial, check with other family members and find out if your family already has burial property with unused spaces that you and your spouse/dependents can use when the time comes. It is amazing how many people after talking with their extended family find out what's already out there.

If your family does not have space available, start shopping around, but not just in your area but possibly in other places that are further away but not necessarily too distant-prices on spaces can vary greatly within a 50-mile radius.

Next check with any associations or other entities that you or your spouse is a member of to see if they own cemetery property for the exclusive use of their members. (Some churches and fraternal organizations do this as a benefit or at a reduced price to comparable property in the same cemetery.

Another way is to look at the classified or obituary section of your local newspaper. Many times there are property bro-

> One variable you may want to consider before purchasing cemetery property is to talk with other relatives about whether your family already owns burial space(s) that are owned but not planning on being used.

kers who buy and sell cemetery spaces for less than market value. Also current owners of cemetery spaces may need to sell (moving, not needed, etc.) and are willing to do so at less than what the cemetery itself is selling spaces in that particular section for.

ARRANGING A BURIAL
(What You'll Deal With)

Once it is determined that burial or disposition is to take place within an established cemetery or memorial park, there is a fairly methodical procedure that is usually followed to arrange for such.

Depending on distance to the cemetery, the rigidity or laxity of the party in charge of it and the rules and regulations pertaining to arranging a disposition will all play a part in the process.

Since there are no federal laws controlling cemeteries, state law will be the authority on any issues of a legal nature. The first thing the cemetery will want to determine is the legitimate ownership of the property. When cemetery property is purchased, a deed is issued to the buyer upon proper consideration. If the original owner is the decedent, or is already passed away, the survivorship laws for the state in which the burial is to take place will take precedence.

Since it will be the funeral director's duty to contact the cemetery to arrange the burial, the family or party with the

As of this writing:

Cemeteries and memorial parks do not have to follow the same FTC guidelines that funeral homes do because a cemetery is not considered a funeral provider under the FTC rule.

Since the cemetery does not in and of itself provide care and preparation of the deceased services (such as embalming), it would not fall under the FTC jurisdiction.

right and duty to control disposition will need to provide the funeral director with the information that will be needed by the cemetery.

This will usually include (but not necessarily be limited to) the following:

* Full Name of Deceased
* Date of Death
* Next of Kin
* Next of Kin address/phone #
* Next of Kin Relationship to Deceased
* Deed number
* Property Description
* Deceased Social Security #
* Deceased Home of Record
* Type of Burial
* Casket/Outer Burial Case /Container names/types

The cemetery's sexton or superintendent will usually be the point of contact regarding burial arrangements and after collecting the information needed will then check their records to verify who the survivors are and the names of those entitled to make use of the space.

The sexton or superintendent will then indicate to the funeral director which family member must sign the cemetery's authorization form. Depending on the cemetery's policy will determine how this is done. Sometimes a cemetery will fax its paperwork to the funeral home to be signed in the funeral arrangement conference or the cemetery may require that the authorized person must physically come to the cemetery's office to handle any paperwork.

If the cemetery requires that the grave space to be used be physically marked with a marking flag (usually a foot in length with a bright color) then the family or one of its appointed representatives will need to visit the grave location with the superintendent to properly mark the correct location.

If the cemetery being used is a good distance away and it is not feasible for the family member to visit the cemetery before the day of the burial, the cemetery may ask that a form be signed releasing it from any liability if the wrong space is opened by accident. In the case that the family is arranging a funeral and has selected a cemetery in which to bury the decedent but has not previously purchased burial property there, then a trip to the cemetery to select a sight will need to be made before funeral arrangements can be finalized.

Since the cemetery (especially larger ones) have their own schedule and work format, the time that the family wants to arrive at the cemetery, the ceremony, rituals desired and the family's wishes concerning any other details must meet the cemetery's consent and approval.

The last item that must be weighted in arranging burial or disposition is payment for the cemetery's expenses. Depending on whether it is a situation of the property already having been purchased or not and whether or not there is any balances unpaid and owed for property, marker, etc. may determine how it is handled. Many times the funeral home will allow the cemetery's charges to be placed on the funeral contract and the funeral director collect the money for the cemetery as a cash advance or third party item.

What is Opening and Closing?

This refers to the process of digging the grave (niche, crypt, etc.), setting up for the service at the grave or place of disposition which usually consists of a tent or canopy, folding chairs, artificial grass (or carpet) under the covering and a stand or a lowering device to set the casket safely and securely unto the grave or crypt and then filling in the ground and placing the space back to the same condition as before the opening.

The opening and closing is usually arranged by the cemetery, or the funeral director may chose a grave service that it uses most of the time in that area, or if the cemetery does not have a contract or exclusive agreement with a particular grave service. The cost for opening and closing is usually a standard charge but may vary depending on certain factors such as:

*Whether the burial is a first or second interment in that particular space

*Whether an outer container is involved in the opening and closing process (more about this in a moment).

*If the grave already has an existing headstone or marker that will need to be moved in order to properly open and close the grave and then be reset.

*What the ground conditions at the cemetery are like, such as rock under the ground surface or having to pump water out after rain.

*Time of day or day such as holiday or weekend affecting overtime rates of pay for employees.

Each of these can determine the amount of time, effort and therefore the cost to the grave service of doing the work and therefore the cost to the consumer. The funeral director should be able to secure the amount or estimate when arranging the burial and contacting the grave service.

Vault Installation/Removal

In chapter one I discussed the purchase of an outer burial container and the reasoning behind it but here I want to talk about installation.

Some cemeteries that do their own opening and closing of graves will charge an outer container installation fee. This amount is for just as it states- placing the outer container, which usually is either steel or concrete, into the grave space and then securely sealing the container after the casket is placed inside.

This is separated from the opening and closing charge because some cemeteries- or possibly sections within a cemetery may not require an outer container.

In the case of removal or reinstallation of an outer container where double or triple interment takes place in a single grave it may be necessary to "remove" the original container if the second interment is to be placed on the bottom and then the original on top of the second. Because of the time and effort involved in this process, you may expect an outer container removal and reinstallation fee.

Multiple Interments/Entombments

Graves and mausoleum crypts can be either single or double spaces, or as in the case of some ground spaces, even triple in depth.

The purpose here is to save ground space or crypt space and therefore allow for more efficient use of the environment (land).

It is a good deal for the consumer family to try to buy a double depth grave space, for example, for a husband and wife, because it is less expensive in most cases to buy one space and have to reopen it later for the second spouse than to have to purchase a second space altogether.

As A Rule Of Thumb . . .

Generally speaking it will probably be cheaper to buy one double interment space rather than two single spaces that allow only one burial per space; however it will depend upon how the cemetery in question prices the property.

You must also consider not only the price of the spaces themselves, but also the total price of the burial(s), which will include:

- Space or spaces(s)
- Outer Burial Container if needed
- Vault (Re)Installation Fee(s)
- Cost to Open And Close the Space(s)

Be sure to get a written estimate of the total cost for each type of burial in each type of property.

Usually a cemetery will price its double interment spaces as more expensive than single interment spaces but less than two individual single spaces. The purchaser will still come out ahead in almost every scenario by buying the double or triple depth space.

Mausoleum crypts can be constructed the same way that is for a single or double entombment within a crypt space, however the placement of the casket usually will be horizontal (end-to-end) rather than vertical (stacked) as in a ground space. There may be instances where a mausoleum may have crypt spaces built for some other type of placement (such as side to side).

One other note concerning the second or third interment in a multi-burial space is the possibility of breakage of the outer container that is being removed and placed back into the grave on top of the second interment.

Although rare, be advised that there is a risk that should be explained by the funeral director or cemetery counselor that if in the event that the outer container breaks or is damaged in the installation/interment process, that a new outer container will need to be purchased. Be sure to get a clear understanding in writing if the cemetery grave service has insurance to cover this and whether it is covered in your charges for the opening and closing or vault installation, or if you the consumer are expected to pay for the new container. It is best to ask questions before waiting for the worst to happen and having an unexpected charge.

Witnessing Burial/Entombment

An option that many times is linked to tradition or customs is watching the cemetery grave staff close the grave, crypt or niche, and can be a part of the mitigation process for some families.

To see the process of lowering a casket into the ground or

other final resting place can help foster closure and the finality of death that may not be obtained through the funeral services and other activities marking the death.

Most all cemeteries will allow the witnessing of the burial or space closing process unless there is a safety concern or other rule prohibiting it.

There are also times that some families or other mourners in attendance want to participate in the closing process (such as helping to shovel dirt into the grave after the casket has been lowered down and the cemetery is ready to fill it in with dirt). This may or may not be allowed depending on various factors such as ground and weather conditions, cemetery policy, safety risk, availability of equipment at the disposition site (such as shovels), labor agreement between the crew's workers and the cemetery management and deal between the cemetery and grave service to name several.

If witnessing or desire for participation of the closing process is desired, the arrangement conference is the best time to ask the funeral director or cemetery counselor.

Temporary Burial, Entombment, Storage

There may be times in which circumstances warrant the temporary placement of human remains into a tomb, crypt or other designated place for storage until the desired circumstances or condition occurs that will permit disposition in the decedent's final resting place.

Such reasons that a decedent may need to be placed into temporary holding would include, but not be limited to the following:

* Space purchased in a cemetery or other designated final disposition place has not yet been developed and is awaiting completion before human remains can be placed within.

* Weather conditions such as snow and ice, flooding or other uncontrollable act of nature makes it temporarily impos-

sible for disposition to occur at the moment.

*Family members are scattered across the country and cannot come together for a service and desired presence for the final disposition of the deceased until a later time.

*The family or other financially responsible party does not at the moment have all the funds necessary to pay the funeral home and/or cemetery to carry out the final disposition.

* The mode of transportation or great distance to move the decedent to the final disposition place may be delayed or placed on hold for some reason.

Whatever the case may be, make sure that you understand what needs to happen to make the final disposition take place and what the charges may be to disentomb or remove the decedent from the temporary place, transport or move them to the final resting place and then make the burial, entombment, etc.

Some cemeteries may charge per day, per week or per month- be sure that you understand what the rental charge is and covers- get it in writing.

Also ask the funeral director or cemetery counselor that you be notified if it is your wish, when the decedent will be moved to the final resting place and if you can be present for any phase of the process- removal from temporary placement transport and placement into the final resting place.

Contracts And Agreements

Since the regulation of cemeteries is left to the individual states, and therefore the buying and selling of cemetery goods and services to each states appointed agency, there is a wide range of oversight regarding the sales agreements that cemeteries and memorial parks make.

Chapter 13 in this book provides a generalized summary of what the states allow or do not allow in relation to cemeteries.

Regardless of whether you are buying cemetery goods/services before or at need, there are several variables that you will

Sample Cemetery Sales Contract

Green Grass Memorial Park
100 Road End Ave., Seaside Florida

Deceased Name ______________________________

Funeral Home ______________________________

Time/day of service ______________________________

Place of service ______________________________

Burial/disposition date ______________________________

Type of disposition selected ______________________________

Property purchase description ______________________________

Purchaser/owner name/address/phone ______________________________

____

Certificate of ownership to purchaser: Y N

If no, certificate goes in whose name ______________________________

Arrangements:

Interment/entombment fee: $ __________

Property location: Space/tier __________ Crypt/niche __________

Section/sanctuary: __________

Property: _____ Spaces @ _____ per sp. Memorial: $ __________

$ __________ Description: __________

Outer container: $ __________

Description: __________ Installation fee: $ __________

Perpetual care: $ __________ Vase(s): $ __________

Total price of arrangements: $ __________ Sales tax: $ __________

Grand total: $ __________

Cemetery Representative's Signature: ______________________________

Purchasers Signature: ______________________________

want to make sure are included as part of any deal:

- Be sure that the agreement is in writing
- That it includes the name, address and phone number of the cemetery.
- That the charges for each item you are purchasing are itemized or listed separate from other items with dollar amount.
- That agreement is dated and signed by the cemetery representative/counselor and that you receive a copy.
- Also if agreement is preneed and financing is involved that the terms of payments, amounts, finance charges, interest rate, etc. is included on the/contract.

As with any major purchase, be sure to read the fine print on the agreement and get a clear understanding of the agreement's terms and conditions. Once you sign it, it becomes binding.

Paperwork And More Paperwork

Along with purchasing a final disposition place for yourself, a family member or other, be aware of the fact that cemeteries keep records and information of its activities and transactions and that due to changes that take place in the lives of property owners and heirs that changes to a cemetery's records and information may be needed.

These would include:

- Transfer of ownership by lot owner or heir to another party.
- Duplicate the property title or deed.
- Preparation of Affidavit of a lost deed or title of ownership.
- Name change or change in marital or family status.
- Request for records or information by interested party(ies).
- Change in address, phone number, other way of contact of the property owner(s).

As a general rule, most cemeteries will charge some type of processing, administrative or recording fee to change, update, procure or otherwise handle the request since they must incur time and expense to pay staff, make the changes, record, store and make access available to the cemetery's information.

AFTER DISPOSITION:
What Cemeteries And Memorial Parks Should And Should Not Allow

Each state will have various rules and regulations regarding designated burial lands. Chapter 13 of this book provides some basic guidelines into what the states allow on some specific issues.

<u>Rules/Regulations/Restrictions</u>

There are designed policies in place regardless of area or jurisdiction for the mutual protection of both the cemetery as an entity and the consumers or owners of interment rights within the cemetery. The enforcement of the stated policies will help protect the cemetery as a going concern and create and preserve its heritage.

Most cemeteries have general policies printed and available to property owners and visitors. The best way is to call, write, or if the cemetery has an office, to stop by and ask for a copy.

<u>Flowers And Decorations</u>

Although all cemeteries allow flowers and usually some type of grave decorations, there is a wide variance of what cemeteries do and don't allow. The following points can help you in regards to asking questions and gathering information on what can and can't be done:

* Fresh cut or live flowers are those that are purchased from a florist and will last a short time after obtained and are generally bought for the funeral of the deceased and then placed on the grave space and depending on watering, heat,

humidity, and other climate conditions will usually wilt shortly after placement.

* Artificial flowers are those usually purchased from a general retailer and will last longer than fresh cut flowers, but in time, they will fade and deteriorate through changing seasons and weather conditions.

* Decorations are usually defined by cemeteries as any non-flower items or objects left on or within the vicinity of one's disposition place as a symbol of commemoration or enhanced beauty of the place. These can include things such as pictures, toys, stuffed animals, birdhouses, brickbrack, jewelry, etc. that the lot owner(s) or other survivors feel helps honor the decedent's memory or adds value to the final resting place.

* There may be a rule about how flowers and/or decorations may be placed on a grave or final disposition space. Sometimes the cemetery may require that the item or items meet the cemetery's approval and be placed by the cemetery itself. Other times the cemetery may require that the item(s) be tagged or a description of the items be written in its logbook or otherwise authorized. Otherwise they may reserve the right to promptly remove it/them.

* There may be specified dates or times of the year that flowers can be placed or removed. Most cemeteries have clean up dates or times when certain items, flowers, etc. may be removed and discarded in compliance with the yearly scheduled policy. Be sure to check and find out when the clean up date or period is.

* Some cemeteries and memorial parks also specify and regulate the types of containers that flowers may be placed in. They may require that all floral pieces be placed into vases or other containers that meet the cemetery's approval. A lot of cemeteries do not allow glass, tin, plastic or any breakable objects to be placed. They may not even allow vases made for holding flowers be placed unless it is one that is permanent and part of the monument that is placed on the grave.

* Most burial parks will have rules concerning prohibited items that cannot be placed within its grounds. This can vary greatly from a flower piece that is not placed within a monument attached vase to anything that is a violation of public policy to have placed or displayed in view of the general public.

* It would also be worthwhile to find out what the policy of the cemetery is regarding responsibility for anything placed within the grounds that meets the cemetery's approval for placement. Most cemeteries expressly state that they are not liable for any flowers or decorations left, but it is in your best interest to get a clear understanding and statement of such up front.

Visiting The Cemetery

Whether as a lot owner or other guest or visitor to a cemetery or burial park, there usually will be rules of conduct for those visiting the grounds and although most cemeteries will post general rules of conduct at the entrance or roads leading into the property, some that do not will expect visitors to comply with the rules that will probably include:

- Speed limit while driving through the cemetery grounds.
- Where and how vehicles are parked while in the cemetery.
- Hunting, fishing and activity regarding wildlife while on the grounds.
- Planting, tilling, digging in the ground, landscaping or construction of any kind.
- Cutting, breaking, injuring or altering shrubs, grass, plantings or other fixtures without permission.
- Any sporting or recreational activity other than walking, jogging, cycling, skating or picnicking is usually forbidden.
- Leaving trash, littering or leaving other items not approved/authorized to be left in cemetery.
- Allowing animals or pets outside of vehicles or to run loose on the grounds.
- Using the cemetery as a meeting place for actions or activities of a loud, disruptive, threatening or partisan nature that may

defy the good of the general public.

Holidays

Some cemeteries (especially the larger ones) are likely to have special ceremonies or rules in connection to certain days of observance such as Christmas, Easter, Mothers Day, Fathers Day, Grandparents Day, Memorial Day, etc.

Whether planning a visit on or even close to one of these or any other day that you believe the cemetery may be making a special remembrance of or festivity in connection with, you should call ahead and find out in advance, especially if you want it to be a special visit.

One example that comes to mind is an annual Christmas service that was being held a week or so before the holiday at a large metropolitan cemetery. Although it was an annual event each year, well publicized and planned for, a group of visitors who were from out-at-state wanted to come by to see the grave of a long passed relative.

Since they were from out of town and knew nothing of the Christmas event at the cemetery, they were quite disturbed when they drove to within about 100 yards of the cemetery entrance only to find a line of cars with people coming for the featured event in front of them.

With the visitors only wish being to spend several minutes driving into the cemetery observing the grave and leaving the grounds quietly, their visit was a disappointment to say the least since the section they wanted to get to was closed off and cars were being routed to another area for parking. Although different cemeteries have emphasis concerning different holidays, Christmas and Memorial Day tend to be the times that will generate the most festivity.

Activities And Events

Holidays are not necessarily the only times that cemeteries do special things other than bury the dead.

Depending on the type of cemetery, the ownership or management, the level of involvement in the community or the cemetery's effort to generate interest or support from various groups, there may be other areas of influence that a local cemetery may try to have. Such events or activities may include but not be limited to the following:

- Holding the cemetery's association meeting for its lot owners on an annual basis.
- Facilitating the cemetery's board of directors meeting that may be open to interested parties.
- Allowing for the ceremonies of veterans or other organizations with a special purpose in connection to the cemetery.
- Dedication of a special monument or other statuary feature of a general historical interest.
- Host a special clean up day where a group of volunteers, community service participants or others come to clean up, to collect and discard trash, etc.
- Invite a field trip of school kids to come to the cemetery to learn about the significant place that the cemetery has been in the community's function.
- Have an annual picnic for the descendants and other relatives and guests of those buried on the cemetery's grounds.

The best way to know what is going on at the cemetery is to get on its mailing list and keep the cemetery's office up to date with your current address, phone number and email address.

Endowment Funds

These are monies that cemeteries use to, in essence, fund the future. Depending on the law in your state, when a cemetery sells a space in the cemetery for burial or disposition it collects an amount or percentage of the sale for deposit into the endowment care fund.

The fund's money is then invested, according to the laws of the particular jurisdiction, by a fund manager for the cemetery, into investments that are within the investment objective of the cemetery for the purpose of growing the money in the endowment fund so that there will be enough money throughout the future to maintain the cemetery as a going concern.

This becomes a big issue as a cemetery progresses toward selling out all of its available space. It is the continuing responsibility of the cemetery's management to provide for the future care and maintenance of the cemetery's property and grounds without additional charge or assessment to the owners of disposition rights.

Perpetual Care

Since one of the main purposes of cemeteries is to provide their communities with a sense of continuity, perpetual care provides for just this.

At some point in time, a cemetery will run out of spaces to sell and therefore end its main stream of income. However the upkeep of the grounds will continue.

Perpetual care makes it possible to maintain the cemetery for generations to come. By utilizing the income generated from the endowment fund, it is possible for the cemetery to be cared for in "perpetuity" on the assumption that the endowment fund is properly producing adequate returns on the monies invested in it.

It is important to know whether a cemetery is or is not perpetual care. If it is, you as a lot owner, patron or other interested party can rest assured that the grounds will be taken care of long after you are gone. Most perpetual care cemeteries will usually (but not always) post a sign stating such unless law requires it.

Non-Perpetual Care Cemeteries

If you have ever seen an old "graveyard" either in pictures, television, or perhaps driving down the road and seen the property in basic disarray- overgrown grass and weeds, crooked grave markers, rusted features, torn down fencing, then you have seen an example of a non-perpetual care cemetery.

What happens here is that once the last spaces have been sold and then the final burials made, the cemetery runs out of money to continue to care for the grounds and must cease maintenance and repair efforts.

There are some non-perpetual care cemeteries that-have continued the chore of groundskeeping as a result of donations from families of those buried within, from church or community organizations, or even volunteer groups who want to preserve the history and heritage of the cemetery. Sometimes even with these efforts, there have been cases where these cemeteries went out of existence. In these rare occurrences, usually the land will revert back to the state or county (Depending on the laws applicable). Several cemeteries in California in recent years went out of existence; one located in Whittier had the memorials removed and became a park. Another in Los Angeles was seized by the state and is an unresolved situation[3].

Grave Dos And Don'ts

Several brief remarks I want to make concerning grave or final disposition space at a cemetery that can seem rather common sense but also overlooked:

Do:

1. Find out what the rules and policies of the cemetery are.

2. Report damage or signs of vandalism to a grave space to the appropriate cemetery contact (if unknown, call closest local funeral home and ask who the cemetery contact person is).

3. Put in a request for repair to a space or property that you have an interest to in writing.

4. Once a request to the cemetery has been made, check after a reasonable period of time has passed to make sure its been done.

Don't:

1. Try to fix or alter something on a grave space you have interment rights on yourself if the contractual agreement calls for the cemetery to do it.

2. Gather names, dates or other information off of monuments in a cemetery without the cemetery or lot owner's permission if the information is going to be used for some public purpose.

3. Place or plant flowers, decorations, or other items or fixtures on a grave space without the lot owner's permission.

4. Rearrange a grave space's contents that is not yours or belong to you.

5. Do a rubbing (reproduction of the surface markings of a memorial/marker such as letters, numbers, etc.) without the cemetery or interment right/memorial owner's permission.

Markers/Monuments/Headstones/Vases
(Gone But Not Forgotten)

One of the most fundamental emotional needs we have is the need to adequately remember those who have gone before us.

Whether a very close relative or another who impacted our

21st Century Grave

According to an article in the May, 2003 issue of International Cemetery and Funeral Association Magazine, an Austrian architectural firm has designed a high tech monument/grave site utilizing solar cells to create a soft light.

Architects Simon Rummele and Gerhard Strohle have formed a company (also the website name) www.fuerrot.at that majors in state of the art cutting edge gravesites. Using the elements of earth and light, the architects also employ stainless steel to design and market individual graves, memorials, urns and other architecture.

life in an important way, memorialization is the manner we choose to mark and establish one's memory.

Whether you are making plans for your own memorialization or have an immediate need, choosing and selecting a cemetery memorial is a decision with lasting significance.

Once known or referred to as grave markers or tombstones, memorials seen today in cemeteries and memorial parks are more appropriately called monuments or markers, depending on several different variables.

Besides the obvious objective of acknowledging a life lived, a memorial should meet several other criteria as well:

* Is the memorial you are desiring going to stand up to and endure the weather conditions in this particular area?

* Is the memorial solid enough and able to withstand demarcation or the attempt of theft?

* Is the memorial durable to withstand the routine activity of the cemetery's operation of the grounds such as mowers, tractors, weed eaters, watering, etc. ?

* Will the memorial help serve the long-term goal of allowing future generations to seek the memorial out as an information piece for genealogy research or other historical significance ?

Cemetery markers and monuments today are generally made out of one of three basic materials:

Granite- durable and strong rock; needs no aftercare

Bronze- Metallic, copper and tin alloy

Marble- stone that will eventually need cleaning.

Most private sellers market mostly or all granite because of its traditional appeal, look, availability and suitability for the purpose at hand.

Bronze is also available and combination Bronze tablets on Granite bases are becoming more so; marble and bronze are primarily used by the United States Veterans Administration for V.A. markers. Bronze is used to make flat or flush headstones and marble for the upright monuments seen in national cemeteries.

One of the other advantages of granite is the different colors that it comes in, such as different shades of black, brown and gray. Also different bases for markers are usually either granite or cement.

The two basic types of grave markers are temporary and permanent. Temporary markers are those placed on a grave usually the day of the burial by the funeral home who is handling the disposition and is usually made of aluminum or plastic, has a smooth surface for etching the name of the decedent and dates of birth and death on with a pen or pencil, and usually has a spiked end or prong that can be easily pushed into the surface of the ground.

As the name expresses, temporary markers are placed on the grave until the permanent monument is ordered and shipped to the memorial park or cemetery and set in place.

Since the focus of this part of the chapter is on permanent memorials, we will not elaborate on temporary markers any further except to hit on the point that most funeral homes will take care of the temporary marker as part of its service to the family and will ready and place it after the burial without comment or mention (upon the fact that there is not a permanent

Memorialization

As the hearse (coach), limousine or casket is the symbol of the funeral home or mortuary, the marker or headstone/monument symbolizes the cemetery.

Whether it is a picture of an old graveyard perhaps centuries since its last burial or the modern looking green grass neatly cut and maintained to perfection, with flat markers and modern landscape, the monument purchased for a loved one will be the last, and the lasting material form of remembrance of that person from now on.

Regardless of simple or elaborate, the monument is the final act to keep the loved one's memory alive into future's end.

marker already on the grave). Other funeral homes may ask for consent or permission and may charge a small fee of $3-15 for the temporary marker, which if there is a charge, it should be on the sales agreement contract.

Of permanent memorials the two basic types can be either standard or customized. Standard memorials are those that are made in a 'process' making setting where the memorials are alike in size, shape, color, material, and a same-like format (such as name, date of birth, date of death). Customized memorials on the other hand are more one-of-a kind and usually begin from the buyer's imagination and evolves into a request for a special or custom made memorial. It may be square, heart shaped, have special designs or borders, and basically be a personalized tribute to the one it is made for.

Sizes

There are many different sizes for cemetery memorials as can be seen by visiting many different burial grounds. Although the imagination may not be limited as to the various potential sizes of memorials, usually the cemetery or memorial park will have restrictions. In essence, the sizes allowed will depend largely upon cemetery regulations. The keys to focus on will be whether the memorial is for one individual or for two people; a marker that covers two graves with one memorial is called a companion. This can also be the case for a double interment (two people buried in one space) in which the memorial would cover the one space but have the names and dates of both persons.

In the case of a triple interment, markers can be made to include the names and dates of all three persons listed vertically from top to bottom.

Ground space memorials can range in size from 6" x 6" for infants to 56" x 16" for companion markers covering two spaces. Obviously the sizes may be even larger when talking about upright markers that serve as the master memorial for a family lot of 10-12 spaces that usually inscribe the family's last name.

Shapes

Going along with sizes, memorial dimensions are also designed in various shapes depending on standard or custom made. The basic shapes include:

Upright- Consists of a base, die and a serpentine top (curvature).

Flush- flat or level with the ground.

Bevel- rises up at an incline from a flat base.

Slant- angled dimension that slopes from top down to the base.

Again, the cemetery may restrict what shape memorials it allows to be set. More and more cemeteries are going to sections that only allow the flush markers due to the ease of maintenance of the grounds.

Upright monuments

Flush/flat markers

Finishes

Modern memorials are made to look and stay attractive for the long term. Both granite and bronze can be ordered in different colors or finishes

There is a variety of colored finishes that both materials may come in including but not limited to brown, cherry, light or dark green, and gray. With the exception of the inscription, the color finish will be the most visibly distinguishing characteristic of any memorial.

Because of this, careful consideration needs to be given to the choice of finish taking into account such factors as landscape, shady or open to a lot of sunlight, the colors of other memorials in the section and visibility from common ways.

Borders

This will be the outer perimeter of the memorial, usually all the way around on all sides. Borders come in different etchings and may be straight, curved, indented, smooth or rough, simple or elaborate.

Borders add value and boundary to memorials allowing for a more valuable and meaningful tribute.

Designs

Designs are sketchings or artistic patterns that can be created as an added carving or decor to a memorial's finished product. Designs are added value items that can be used to transform a bland or otherwise unappealing memorial into something special. Designs can be part of the memorial's border or apart, and usually consist of flowers, tree leaves, specialized symbols, or even farm or garden produce images (such as cotton, wheat or corn).

Lettering And Inscription

The single most distinguishing characteristic of any memorial will be the words and numbers printed on the memorial surface.

Since this is the main feature, you will want to give very special consideration to different lettering styles, fonts, dates, words being abbreviated or spelled out, whether you want (or will have room for longer names) middle names spelled out or just an initial, etc.

Do you or can you have the family or person's last name inscribed in bold letters at the top (or on the backside if an upright monument)?

What letters show up well and will be easiest to read on the type of material being selected.

Will the lettering be in English or another language? Some memorial makers, such as Matthews, have an international segment that can do oriental/Asian expressions, for example.

Along with the name and dates of the person will be the choice of placing an epitaph on the memorial. An epitaph is a short inscription of a commemorative nature that is placed on many types of memorials. It is usually a few letters such as "together forever" on a husband and wife companion marker to a sentence or paragraph (space permitting) that may well summarize the honored person's life.

Emblems

These are the authorized castings that can be engraved into or onto the surface of the memorial that adds a personalized or descriptive value to the memorial.

There is a wide range of different emblems that can be selected from for memorials. Some are religious, some fraternal and some referring to interests in sports, college alma mater, hobbies, childhood, animals, etc. The best approach is to check with the memorial provider to see and explore available options.

Due to copyright restrictions, some emblems that are registered trademarks, trade names, service marks, etc., may not be used- always check and get permission before going forward.

Vases

Because some cemeteries started disallowing placements of flowers on the graves or ground areas because of maintenance and routine care, monument makers started making memorials with vase attachments as part of the memorial itself.

The vases are generally made of the same material as the memorial, and some are permanently affixed in an upright position to hold floral tributes while some are made to hold other articles such as candles.

Some of the bronze and bronze on granite markers have a feature where the empty vase can be turned upside down and placed down into a chamber for the vase when it is not in use. The vase is usually attached to the inside of the marker with a durable metal chain to deter theft of the vase. This way the vase is an affixed feature of the marker and today some memorials can be purchased with or without a vase.

Government/V.A. Memorials

Headstones or markers are available from the Veterans Administration upon application for an honorably discharged deceased veteran whose grave is unmarked, or memorial headstones/markers are available for remains not buried.

Provided at the government's expense are the marker itself, authorized inscriptions, and transportation from the maker to designated consignee.

The name, branch of service and years of birth and death are mandatory items on all V.A. markers. Other items such as month and day of birth and death, rank, religious emblem, war service and service awards are optional but may be inscribed at government expense.

All memorial markers (remains not buried) will mandatorily be inscribed with "In Memory of."

Government markers come in bronze, granite or marble in either upright or flush types. An illustration of the standard headstones/markers and authorized emblems are shown on the following pages. All V.A. government provided memorials remain the property of the United States Government after shipment and setting. For more information on eligibility and application, see V.A. benefits in chapter 6, Available Benefits.

Where And From
Purchasing A Memorial

Today there are different places that you can buy a memorial, including funeral homes, cemeteries, independent dealers, chain dealers and Internet sellers. Let's take a look at each.

Funeral Homes

Not all mortuaries are providers of cemetery memorials, but a number are. The way to tell is to look around the funeral home or the lawn outside the building for a memorial display (which usually will feature 3-15 different memorials). If you don't see a display, ask. It is also possible that the funeral home will sell memorials out of a picture book (like a picture album). This way the mortuary can free up space for other functions it performs such as staterooms, office, arrangement rooms, etc. Funeral homes usually will have firsthand knowledge of the regulations of most of the cemeteries in its area due to the fact that it usually has a working relationship with them. This allows the director or salesperson to know what can or cannot be set in the cemetery. However there may be drawbacks to the funeral home memorials such as the possibility that if the funeral home also owns, operates or is affiliated with a certain cemetery or cemeteries, and your purchase is for another burial ground for the memorial, they may not sell you one for that reason. Another possible disadvantage may be price.

Since funeral homes already handle the funeral service arrangements, the idea of buying the memorial at the same time saves you time and another trip somewhere else, but not necessarily money. The funeral home may profit by providing this extra convenience.

Cemeteries

Like funeral homes, not all cemeteries and memorial parks offer memorials, but some surely do. The ones that do sell will have firsthand knowledge of what types, sizes and shapes, etc. that memorials within its property requires. They also will know the details of handling the receipt and installation of the memorial.

If you find a cemetery that does sell memorials, be sure to ask if they sell just for their own grounds or for setting in other cemeteries as well. If you are shopping at a cemetery dealer for a memorial that is for aunt Mary's grave 20 miles away they may not handle your request.

Another potential drawback is price. Cemeteries may charge more for their memorials for the added convenience of buying on site; just another reason to shop and compare before taking the plunge.

Independent Dealers

Listed usually as monument companies, these sellers are retail establishments that deal primarily or exclusively with obtaining and marketing cemetery memorials of various kinds to the public.

Some are apart of the making and manufacture of memorials that simply serve as a retail outlet while others may purchase memorials from different makers and then offer to the public. They will usually always have a physical display or actual memorials on site.

> Since the purchase of a cemetery memorial is something that does not have to be bought at the time funeral arrangements are made, and in a fair number of cases it is purchased after services, there is usually plenty of time to shop around and get the best deal.

Independent dealers are usually owned by an individual or family who sets up as a "mom and pop" operation and the business is the owner or distributor's only place or location for selling memorials.

The key advantage of going to a sole or independent dealer is that the dealer will have first rate expertise about the product and the materials, designs, and other features of the memorials it sells and in general since the dealer or proprietor specializes in providing memorials as its only line of business.

A possible disadvantage to independent dealers is the time and energy-and as a result money- that it may take to drive around and look at what various dealers in your area have to offer. Comparing prices, terms, product availability, delivery and transportation, setting fees, timing, etc. may vary greatly from one independent to another.

Chain Dealers

Like independents, chain dealers are in the business of marketing memorials but they differ in that they have multiple locations to serve the public through. This may mean 3-4 outlets in a large metro city or have one location in a smaller town or rural trade area with other locations spread out in other towns or areas in the same county or metropolitan region.

Chain dealers, like independents, are very knowledgeable about their products and features with a solid understanding of memorials. They will also almost always have physical displays on hand and they also should have very reasonable prices due to better economies of scale and spreading out their cost of doing business to their number of locations.

Any drawbacks with chain dealers may come with not having on site access to some resources such as the owner or manager who may be at another location and possible flexibility limits if you are talking with a salesperson who is not authorized to make decisions on certain requests (such as special delivery, payments, setting by a certain time, etc.).

Internet Sellers

To date there are only a few companies that offer memorials over the internet but as time goes on there will probably be others who will join the opportunity to market memorial products via the web.

Monuments.com is a firm out of Seattle, Washington that has an extensive website. The crown jewel of Internet marketing is the providers abilities to make customized memorials.

The fact that information about the seller and its products is that it is as accessible as the computer, with Internet capacity, and therefore makes Internet sellers highly attractive.

Two possible drawbacks of Internet providers will be their potential lack of knowledge about cemetery rules and requirements concerning markers and also that depending on distance and carrier, transportation costs could be excessive.

However if an Internet seller can make a customized memorial that others cannot provide at a price that you can pay, any transportation costs may not be a big factor.

The Process

Regardless of where and from whom you decide to purchase a memorial from, the process that you should go through in order to guarantee that you get what you desire is as follows:

A) Find out the cemetery's requirements. Each cemetery has its own rules and regulations about what type of memorial is allowed on a specific grave or lot. You don't want to have a monument delivered to the cemetery that will be rejected due to nonconformity.

B) Analyze And Decide. Once you know the constraints and boundaries that have been set by the cemetery you may choose a memorial that will be accepted by the cemetery for setting. Remember that you are making a choice on something that will last from now on. Ask yourself: Will the material I chose the marker to be stand-up to weather conditions over the long term? Will it be easy to read with this color? If I choose to have a word or phrase engraved on it at a later date will it be permissible? If so, at what cost? Be sure to take your time. Purchasing a memorial should take as much thought as any other major purchase you'll make

C) Place The Order. This will consist of transacting your wishes with the seller of the memorial and should always include a written contract. The agreement should include type, size, color, inscription(s), cost (including sales tax, if applicable), payment method and terms, as well as any wording that will express what both parties are obligated for, when, where and how, in order to prevent any problems or misunderstandings later. When in doubt, ask questions, you are the customer.

D) Pay in Full or Payout. Virtually all memorial dealers allow payout or payment plans when purchasing preneed (before burial or setting). Usually, an installment plan can be set up to allow monthly payments that include a finance charge that consists of a portion of the monthly installments. Depending on the price of the memorial, the payout period can go 60 months or longer. Once the payments are made and the memorial is paid in full, it will be shipped to the designated cemetery for setting. Paying for the memorial in full at the time of purchase will have the obvious advantages of saving on finance charges, being able to get the memorial ordered and shipped right away and getting the transaction consummated as soon as possible.

E) Make/Manufacture. Once payment is secured and collected by the seller, the order will be sent to the plant/facility that makes the memorials for your dealer of choice. The timetable from the point of sending the order till the manufacturer shipping the memorial will vary depending on such factors as workable material available for making the memorial, whether there is already a stock of unengraved memorials ready for carving and engraving, how many orders the maker already has to process and distance and the mode of transportation. Because of the variables involved, ask your dealer for an approximate time for receiving and setting the memorial; the dealer can usually give

Potential Memorial Dealers

	Advantages	Disadvantages
Funeral Homes	1. Knowledge or rules/ requirements of local cemeteries, or will have ability to obtain rules/ regulations swiftly 2. Can purchase at same time as making funeral arrangements; part of the one stop shopping theory	1. May only sell memorials for cemeteries it is affiliated with or operates. 2. May be pricey
Cemeteries	1. Will know and communicate all Its rules/regulations concerning memorials at its interment grounds. 2. Will also know details about getting and installing.	1. Generally will not sell memorials for placement in other cemeteries. 2. May also be pricey
Independent Sellers	1. Will have first rate expertise concerning the materials, designs, and other features of memorials it sells, and in general.	1. Will need to shop around and spend time and energy researching and comparing with others to find the right dealer.
Chain Dealers	1.Also very knowledgeable about memorials and cemetery features 2.Should have very reasonable prices due to better economies of scale	1.Have to do separate from funeral and burial arrangements. Make another trip; deal with another entity separate from the mortuary or cemetery.
Internet Sellers	1. Ability to make customized memorials at a premium. 2. Information highly accessible by consumer with Internet without having to call, write or visit.	1. No Knowledge of rules/regulations of area cemeteries. 2. Transportation costs may be high.

rough estimated time of arrival after conversing with the maker.

F) Ship or Store. If the memorial is paid for in full and ordered and made before need, the option may exist if you already own cemetery property to have the memorial stored by the manufacturer or dealer if it is not your desire to have it shipped and set. The point of having the memorial stored until needed can vary, but in the case of not purchasing cemetery spaces yet or buying spaces that have not been designated yet (such as an undeveloped section of a cemetery that will be developed in the future), there would be a need to have the memorial(s) stored somewhere since there is not a place to set it. Another reason may be the wise economic choice of buying it at today's price to hedge against future price increases, or not wanting to have a visible fixture to remind one of his/her own mortality. If a memorial is purchased ahead of time for cemetery space in a cemetery whose requirements and rules for memorials is known, it is possible to purchase and store it until burial or the purchaser is ready for it to be sent.

What is important for you to know and do is upon payment in full, have the seller send you a certificate of title for the memorial and place the certificate in a secure place; it conveys all the rights and title for the memorial to you as the legal purchaser. Ask the exact physical location where the memorial is stored also. The memorial will remain stored until you or an authorized representative request that it be shipped for installation.

Delivery And Transport Fees

Once the desired memorial has been selected, purchased, paid for and ordered, the next step is getting the product from point A to point B.

The size and weight of the memorial as well as the distance it is transported will determine the cost. Sometimes the delivery and transport fees are figured into the sales price of the memorial but sometimes not. The sales invoice should itemize clearly any shipping charges if separate from the price of the memorial.

If you would like a memorial shipped as priority, as with anything else, expect to pay more for a rush order. As a general rule, memorials can be transported anywhere in the U.S. or world that a shipping company will deliver to. If not, check with the cemetery or place of final disposition if it is located in a remote area to see if they will pickup at a drop-off point for the shipping company. If so, expect to pay some type of fee or charge for this depending on distance and size/weight of the memorial. Remember to make sure that the delivery company has the name, physical address and phone number of the cemetery to be transported to, as well as a contact person at the cemetery if confirmation is needed. They will also need to know the hours of operation at the cemetery so that there will be personnel available to receive and accept proper delivery of the memorial.

Installation And Setting Fees

The cost of placing the memorial at the location of final disposition is usually separate from the price of the memorial itself.

However if you are buying the memorial from a dealer who is going to install it for you, the dealer should itemize the charge on the same contract, as the memorial sale.

Since some cemeteries do not allow outside parties to set memorials in its park, there will be a setting fee for installing the memorial that as a general rule, will be a percentage of the sales price of the memorial.

If the cemetery does allow outside parties to set memorials within its grounds, expect to pay to have it done, unless stated otherwise. Most cemeteries will not install the memorial until payment in full for the setting is made. Whether or not they will accept the memorial for setting without the fee(s) paid in full is also a point to find out about.

If they do receive the marker/monument delivery without

the installation being paid in full, they may only hold it for a certain period of time before assessing a storage fee.

Engraving/Inscription/Lettering Fees

Whenever a memorial is bought as it is displayed with the predetermined design(s), border(s), names and dates, etc. that are a part of the standard memorial for that particular type, the lettering, inscribing and engraving are usually part of the sales price of the memorial.

If you desire to have any allowable engraving, inscriptions or extra lettering over and beyond the basic standardized memorial, you are probably looking at some type of surcharge to have it done. Again this will depend on the size, amount, time, effort, font, etc. involved in the request. Special requests for any permissible "extras" to be placed on a memorial that is granted by the dealer and/or cemetery will probably lead to a delay in the shipment and setting of the memorial.

If you have ever looked around at memorials in a cemetery that are complete except for a final date, you are seeing memorials that have been purchased, delivered and installed ahead of time- or before death-so that the buyer can get the memorial they want and freeze the cost at the time of purchase. The only thing left will be a final/date inscribed, engraved or added to the memorial after the burial.

Adding on final dates is a service the cemetery or memorial dealer provides at a very minimal cost. It usually is handled by an independent contractor that specializes in placing final dates on cemetery memorials.

On granite and stone markers a special engraving instrument is used to inscribe final dates, whereas on bronze, it may be a scroll, which is a small plate with the date that is screwed on or permanently attached to the memorial. Most companies will visit larger cemeteries once a month and do all the final dates for that month at one visit, whereas smaller cemeteries it may be longer depending on how often the contracting engraving specialist comes to the area. In the event that after a memorial has been set and regardless of final date or not, what if you as the purchaser would like to add an inscription or engraving to the memorial? This will depend on whether the cemetery will allow it according to its rules and regulations, and if it can be done once the memorial has been set, whether it would require the contracting engraver coming to the site to do something simple and basic (like a cross emblem) or the memorial being taken up, transported back to the factory or shop and then brought back and reset, unless otherwise stated, expect to pay for all facets of what you're requesting.

Marker Moving/Resetting/Reinstalling

Although a rare occurrence, moving a memorial from its space and then placing it again can happen in the following instances:

1. In the course of opening a grave for burial, the grave service/must move the marker in order to adequately do the burial as contracted.

2. A cenotaph (a memorial in honor of a decedent not buried there) is transported to another location and set in a new designated place.

3. A decedent is disinterred and reinterred in another location in which the memorial would need to be moved also.

Whatever the case may be, find out what the charges are and who is responsible in the event of damage to the memorial. It would be a good idea to inspect it before and after transport if possible.

As far as resetting/reinstallation is concerned, does the party that transports the memorial also reset it or does the receiving cemetery, and if so at what cost? If the receiving cemetery does, ask when the memorial will be set. If you can't get a straight answer, ask for an estimated or projected time and if it can't be reset/reinstalled upon arrival, ask to be contacted and notified when it can.

Repair/Maintenance/Restoration

There are various events that can take place that can cause cemetery memorials to need attention in the way of repair, maintenance or restoration. Such possibilities include but are not limited to:

*Natural disaster such as flood, earthquake, tornado, mud slide, or other act of God.

*Human initiated events, such as vandalism, attempted theft, act of war or other civil violence.

*Human error such as chipping with lawn mower or weed whacker, accident or other mishap.

*Normal decay through the course of time such as fading, cracking, weathering, etc.

Whatever the case may be, in the event that a memorial is in need of fixing, the first step will be to get the copy of the contract/bill of sale and see if the memorial is covered under any type of warranty and if so for how long. Depending on from whom and when it was purchased and set may depend on whether the seller will handle any repairs for a certain period of time.

Sometimes the purchase agreement will state whether or not there is a warranty and if so, what types of damages it covers. Some purchase agreements may include an insurance option where you may pay an amount added to the purchase price that will cover all or at least some of the occurrences mentioned above. Just because a cemetery or memorial park is a perpetual care property does not always mean that the markers/ memorials on its grounds are covered under the perpetual care umbrella. If the memorial was bought and installed by an outside dealer, is the damaged memorial the responsibility of the buyer, the seller or the cemetery? It is better to know ahead of time than to wait until some type of work or repair is needed.

In the case of repair or restoration that is needed and is the buyer's or buyer's heirs responsibility, there are companies that

Cemetery memorials come in various shapes and sizes; some can be made with personalization.

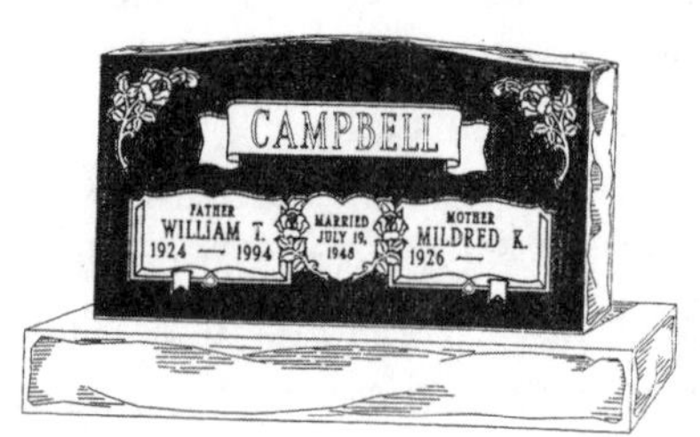

Upright companion marker made of granite on a granite base.

Single upright granite marker on a granite base.

Flat bronze companion markers on a granite base with vase for two separate ground spaces.

Flat companion marker with vase for a double burial in same space.

Single flat bronze on granite marker with vase.

Single bronze marker on granite base without a vase

do monument and memorial restoration work and usually can be contacted direct.

The best way to find a memorial restoration entity is to call a dealer or the (any) cemetery and ask who does that type of work in your area. If they cannot provide a referral, call a funeral home in the area where the cemetery/memorial park is located that contains the memorial that needs attention.

Continuity And The Cemetery As A Going Concern
(Carved in Stone)

Up until this point in this chapter I have discussed the basic ideas of cemeteries, memorial parks and the related activities of evaluating, choosing, purchasing, establishing and maintaining your cemetery and memorialization property. What I want to spend the remainder of this chapter discussing is the cemetery or memorial park as an ongoing entity far into the future with the various matters that may occur needing a solution.

Deeded vs. Undeeded Property

When cemetery property is purchased but not completely paid for at the time of its purchase, the space(s), lot(s), crypt(s), or other real property of the transaction is "undeeded" meaning that since the buyer has not paid for the property being bought in full, that the seller of the property will keep the deed as collateral – so to speak- until the purchase price has been completely paid for.

The same way that when a house is purchased by a buyer who makes a down payment and then makes monthly installments over a fixed period of time, the deed or title to the house is held by the party receiving the payments until all the payments are made. When a real property transaction takes place regarding cemetery property, once the property (space, lot, crypt, niche, etc.) has been paid in full, the property or interment right to the said property then becomes deeded or the buyer will receive the actual title to the property.

What Happens To Unused Property

An issue that comes to mind for most people at some point in time is the matter of cemetery spaces that are not ever used.

Chapter 13, Cemetery Laws By State, lists state-by-state how each individual state deals with the issue of unused, abandoned or unclaimed lots or spaces.

These spaces or property is defined as interment or disposition property that was purchased for the purpose of interring or making disposition of deceased human remains but through the course of time the property goes unused through at least several generations removed from the original purchaser(s) and the probability of the property ever being used is minimal or extremely remote to the point of the property reverting back to the cemetery, the state, the original owners, etc. whoever the authorities have determined the property should "go back" to.

How does the state know when burial/disposition property should be reclaimed? It could be after a certain number of years have passed since the last burial on a lot, or after three or more generations have passed away since the property was purchased and no burials on the site have occurred despite the fact that the purchaser's descendants have also passed away (being buried somewhere else). For others it may be some other criteria. Find out what your state does with unused/abandoned property. For states that do not reclaim disposition property the spaces will simply go unused.

Selling Unwanted/Unneeded Spaces

If your family possesses rightful title to a space or spaces within a cemetery or memorial park that after consideration you have determined will not be needed by any potential family members for future use, one option would be to sell the unused spaces.

This could happen for many reasons (moving, other property you'll use somewhere else, decision to be cremated, etc.) but the first step after deciding to sell the space(s) will be to determine the best way for you to sell.

A lot of times people try to approach the cemetery where the property is located about buying the space(s) back. However since most cemeteries are in the business of selling burial and disposition property themselves, the chance of them repurchasing the property is remote unless it is at a drastically reduced price with their intention of reselling it at market price.

Your best chance usually is to go to your local newspaper and place an ad for the property at less than market (or what the cemetery is selling comparable spaces for). Someone that wants the spaces for their own future needs will usually be interested if it is priced less than what the cemetery is asking for the same type of property.

Another possibility would be a cemetery broker. This is a third party who makes a living working to buy cemetery spaces at less than market price and then turns around and tries to sell it to another purchaser for a profit. Most metropolitan areas have at least one broker who deals with buying and selling cemetery property for a profit.

If you list the space(s) you want to sell in the paper, usually you will get a call from a broker due to the fact that checking the newspaper(s) for spaces placed for sale is part of their routine.

Also don't forget other relatives or friends that have established "roots" in the area where the cemetery is located. Sometimes these may be the best candidates depending on the situation. Being able to sell cemetery property to other relatives can be an assuring way of keeping the property "in the family" so to speak, or even a sale to friends or acquaintances can produce a reassuring peace of mind.

Exchanging Cemetery Property

Because our society today is on the move and constantly changing, statistics indicate that the average American family will move about every 6-8 years. Because of this fact, the chance of needing to obtain cemetery property in your new area is a real possibility.

The American Cemetery Association has created the Lot Exchange Dollar Credit Plan that allows a person who lawfully possesses a deed or certificate of ownership or right of interment to property and non-personalized merchandise in a participating member cemetery to receive a dollar for dollar credit toward the purchase of a selected property and merchandise in an ACA participating member cemetery in the person's new town or area once a permanent change of residence takes place that is more than 75 miles from the original cemetery[5].

The lot exchange program is subject to the conditions and restrictions set by the ACA and not all members of the American Cemetery Association are participants in the plan. If you have moved recently, plan to move or are considering a permanent change of residence to a new area, and know with all foreseeable assurance that you will not want burial/disposition in the cemetery in the area you will be moving from, once you find a cemetery in your new area that you are interested in, contact that cemetery about the possibility of their participation in the ACA exchange plan. If they

Swap Meet

Most cemeteries and memorial parks today want to accomodate consumers as much as possible. For this reason, if you are or have moved and want to try to exchange cemetery property in your old area for burial/disposition property in your new place, contact both cemeteries and see what they are willing to do.

If one or both cemeteries are not members of ACA or any other lot exchange network, the two entities more than likely will converse by phone, E-Mail, fax machine, etc. to try to work something out for the benefit of each party involved.

Building goodwill and helping future potential customers is what good service is all about.

are not participants in the plan, check with other cemeteries in your area till you find one that is and talk with them about obtaining property on their grounds through a lot exchange with the cemetery in your old area.

Donating Unneeded/Unwanted Property

One alternative for disposing of burial or final disposition property that some people do not think of is donating it to a person, family or organization that can make use of it.

There are some churches, missions and human relief agencies that will accept burial property as a gift of charity that can be used for the benefit of indigent families without means to financially acquire their own burial place.

You may also wish to consider donating burial property to relatives who may use it, or to friends or other groups or organizations that may use it as part of their benevolent outreach to others.

Such donations of final disposition property may be tax deductible as a charitable contribution of property under certain circumstances. Because of the nature and complexity of the federal tax laws it would be best to consult with a tax accountant or to ask the organization you're contemplating donating to about any tax deduction benefits or implications from a gifting transfer.

If you do decide to donate unneeded disposition property, be sure to properly transfer the deed and get the transaction documented in writing for your records.

The advantages of donating property that you have clear title to include spending less time than it would usually take to sell the property, the possibly favorable tax implications, and the goodwill that is created by doing something to help someone else.

Transferring Burial Property

Moving the title and right of interment from one party to another is an event that may become necessary anytime that someone who holds the deed to final disposition property wants to tender it to another either for or without compensation or benefit.

Transfers of property can take place for many reasons, some of which may be for example, sale, gift, donation, inheritance or estate reasons, bankruptcy, divorce, etc.

If you desire the transfer of cemetery property to or from another party, contact the cemetery and ask what the procedure is for doing a transfer of property (varies from state to state). The party that wishes to transfer the property will need to have a clear deed (uncontested title to the property being transferred) to it. In most cases the cemetery can handle the actual transfer transaction but there is also usually a nominal charge for handling and processing the paperwork involved. The paperwork involved can include:

- Each transfer of ownership by lot owner(s)
- Each transfer of ownership by heir(s)
- Duplicate Certificate of Ownership
- Name change only
- Preparation of Affidavit of Lost Certificate of Ownership

Depending on the number of individuals involved (for example: six children who inherited a lot in the cemetery to one of the six) will determine the amount of paperwork, time, effort and resources expended to consummate the transfer. This will increase the cost and may also involve an administrative or filing fee by the cemetery and/or county if the transaction needs to be filed in the deed records at the courthouse.

Statuary And Other Features

Cemeteries come in different shapes and sizes and oftentimes distinguish themselves apart from each other by establishing landmarks and other types of fixtures that add to the value, quality, and eye appeal of their property.

Commonly known in cemetery jargon as features or specialized statuary, cemeteries attract potential customers by building or placing such fixtures as statutes, gazebos, water fountains, pavilions, walls, benches, etc. in their respective parks to enhance the scenery and environment. This in turn will provide visitors and others with a place where they would want their loved one's and/or themselves placed when their time comes.

As a general rule, the larger and more modern the cemetery, the more likely it is to have features that attract notice and awe from visitors and passersby. Since the cemetery usually bears the expense of statuary and features, this in turn would increase its cost which in turn pass the costs on to the consumer with higher prices on lots, crypts, memorials, etc.

As with anything else in this world, the fancier, the more elaborate the product, the higher the price to be paid by the consumer, and cemeteries are no exception.

Pre-Arranging Cemetery And Burial Services

The concept of selling cemetery property and services before death actually occurred has been around since at least the beginning of the 20th century, and is probably around to stay. Prearranging for disposition consists of two components: preplanning, which is determining and specifying expressly what property to be buried in and the kind of memorialization wanted. Prepaying is funding or financing the preplanned items either through a lump sum or installment payments. This includes a price guarantee that freezes the products/services selected at the price stated when the prearrangement contract is executed.

Also involved in the mix is whether the items and services which are now sold in advance being available in the short-term or present/very near future, if needed as opposed to the purchase of something that is not ready for consumption.

Those items that can be tendered to the purchaser immediately are called deliverables. This would be developed cemetery property, for example, that can be utilized immediately if paid for in full up front.

Goods that can't be consumed until a future time are non-deliverables. This would include a mausoleum crypt (space) that is predeveloped and purchased as such but cannot be utilized until it is built and construction is completed.

In cases like this it is important to find out from the cemetery seller what will happen if death occurs before a non-deliverable is ready for use, and at whose expense? If a temporary entombment, etc. needs to be done for an undetermined amount of time, who will bear the expenses of temporary disposition, disentombment, transport, etc.? As stated in other parts of this book, get in writing what the seller's intentions and obligations will be. The written contract can be your best friend.

The practice of selling property and services is well established throughout North America, and by contrast, it is very hard to discuss disposition prearrangement on anything but a general basis due to the fact that state laws are often complex and vary considerably.

For this reason I want to spend the remainder of this section telling you why it is in your and/or your family's best interest not to ignore prearrangement of final disposition property and services.

REASON #1: I can't bring myself to think about it.

Nobody likes to think about dieing and one day no longer being apart of this world. Nobody likes to go to the dentist either. But have you ever bought accident insurance for your car? Fire or flood insurance on your home or possessions? How about health insurance or major medical for hospitalization? You don't want these things to happen either yet you've thought about the consequences and prepared accordingly.

Buying final disposition goods and services is one more provision that you can make because in contrast to the events described above, death will happen- it is only a matter of when. If you die and have not prearranged, you are leaving a tremendous burden upon your survivors. Decisions made at the time of death can be skewed by emotion and not made by reason. What would you have wanted- a cemetery or a memorial park? How much of your estate would you want to go toward your burial and memorialization? These are simply some questions that only you can answer, and only you can take the guesswork out of the situation.

REASON #2: I Have Insurance.

Life insurance policies are named such for a reason. They are for life, or the living of the beneficiary(ies). No insurance policy tells your family where to buy cemetery property or how much to pay for it. Your insurance benefits may not go toward the purposes you intended, since you won't be around to direct your heirs and survivors and their choices. Most insurance policy proceeds that the beneficiary receives that is used for nothing but living expenses of the spouse and/or dependents is usually completely used up in 3-5 years if not before then.

REASON #3: I cannot afford it now.

Burial property and services purchased at the time of need must be paid for up front before disposition will take place. When you buy it preneed, you can choose from a variety of installment plans that oftentimes can be worked to fit almost any circumstance. If you show a responsible willingness to act and prepay, you are exercising free will and the ability to choose and be in charge. When you buy today, you buy at today's price. This way you are transferring as much risk as possible from you the buyer to the cemetery the seller who will then be obligated to provide you with the agreed to items at the price at the time of purchase, despite increases in price inflation.

If you do not choose prearrangement, your survivors will pay more later and they'll pay it all at once.

REASON #4: I want to be cremated.

No matter what form of disposition you choose, you are in

charge when you prearrange. As the decision maker in the preplanning role what will happen after the cremation? Although cremation is a form of disposition, it is not a final act preparing for memorialization. In other words, what happens to your ashes? Are your cremated remains to be scattered? If so where? And by whom? Are there lawful restrictions pertaining to scattering at this place? What if you want the ashes put in an urn- what kind? And then what is supposed to happen to it? With prearrangement you guarantee that your wishes will be carried out if you purchase a ground space, columbarium niche or urn space to place your remains in. This way you are communicating to your survivors what you want done when the time comes.

REASON #5: My family already owns property.

The first question to ask yourself is do you really want to be buried in the cemetery your family owns property in? Your parents may have acquired a family lot when you were younger and perhaps your father even told you there was a space for you in this family lot. Chances/are that you do not even have the deed, meaning that you need the deed holder's written authorization before a space can be opened for you or your spouse. It is also possible that other family members will use it before your part of the family needs it. Are there currently six spaces on the lot for example, but seven family members who will potentially expect to use it? Somebody is going to be left out.

The time is now for you to communicate with the rest of the family to determine who's going to do what and when.

REASON #6: I'm not from this area and move frequently, and don't know where I will end up.

It is true that some people because of job or other reasons move a lot and know that where they are today may not be where they'll stay. The place where you grew up is no longer your home and it may be years at a time between your visits back to your hometown. Not growing roots in one area does not mean that you do not have a need for prearrangement; you and your spouse will still someday need final disposition property.

Purchasing property today and freezing it at today's price works in this sense like an insurance policy- hopefully you will not need the benefit, but if you do, you'll have it. Then later on in life if you do settle down in a particular area, you may do a lot exchange and request a property transfer.

REASON #7: My kids, brother-in-law, nephew, best friend, cousin, etc., will take care of my final arrangements.

If you are fortunate enough to have a close tight-knit family who are willing to make major decisions for you without your consent then that's your business. Since there will be many decisions to make at a stressful time concerning where and how to handle your final disposition: why place this trusted person into such a pressured situation? If the purpose of a friend or loving family member is to help them and make their life more enjoyable why subject them to deciding things for you that you can make for yourself? It is not wise to depend on other people if you can help yourself or do something for yourself.

Cemetery Associations

A cemetery association is a group of people who own property or interment rights in a cemetery or memorial park who organize to represent their interest in the cemetery/memorial park as one voice.

Cemetery associations can have varying functions depending on the size, volume, activity, location and other factors in relation to the cemetery. If the cemetery is not perpetual care, the association's main function may be to raise money for the upkeep and maintenance of the grounds.

The association may have a board of directors that work on behalf of the property owners with the cemetery's management in relation to issues and strategic plans for the purpose of protecting the association members' interests.

Most cemetery associations at a minimum have at least an annual meeting which usually includes a day of open house at the cemetery grounds, the yearly business meeting, a luncheon or dinner fellowship meal and printed material with news and updates pertaining to the cemetery for the past year as well as any plans or upcoming changes or activities relating to the cemetery.

The best way to find out if a particular cemetery has an association is to visit it and look for any signage with a contact name and/or phone number or call the closest area funeral home and ask if they can provide any contact information.

Disinterment/Exhumation And Reinterment

Disinterment, also called exhumation, is the removal of a dead body or remains from its place of disposition after such has been completed.

There is a very strong sentiment against disinterment in virtually every jurisdiction in western civilization. Most authorities have legislated policy stating that disinterment is not a matter of right and that there must exist a valid reason and good cause to permit the exhumation of a decedent in repose.

Disinterment may be authorized by law on public or private grounds. From a public standpoint, exhumation may be granted by a court or legal authority with reinterment in the same place for the purpose of collecting evidence to be used in the course of a criminal investigation or for a civil case.

The state may exert its power to exhume a body if there is reasonable cause for believing that foul play may have been involved in the death, and that the decedent's remains may answer questions or provide facts in relation thereto.

In civil suits, a party may allege that a cause of death be affirmed or disaffirmed in connection to an insurance policy or the settlement of an estate. Disinterment may be permitted by a judge if human remains can verify or deny the existence of fraud or intent to deceive relating to the original cause of death determination.

In such civil cases, a much stronger burden of proof is usually required than in criminal cases. Eminent Domain defined as a government's power to take private land for public use for a fair compensation may occur if a grave needs to be moved to another location that is in the public interest, such as providing access for transportation, for example. Another possibility would be if bodies buried in a certain place have come to pose a threat to public health, for instance the contamination or threat thereof to an underground water supply that serves the surrounding area. The governing authorities would have an overriding interest to act for the common good against any objections from any private individual or party.

Private reasons also exist for wanting to disinter a deceased human's remains and generally speaking exist for the following reasons:

1) Reinterment in same cemetery
2) Reinterment in another cemetery
3) To replace the casket or outer container
4) Procure another form of disposition

1) Sometimes a decedent may be disinterred and moved to another space in the same cemetery or memorial park. A good example would be if the decedent's family purchased a single space to bury the person's remains years ago and then later decided to buy more spaces for other family members only to learn that all other available spaces around the decedent's grave were already sold.

In this instance the family may buy a lot of spaces in another part of the same cemetery and want to have all the family's members buried together and so disinterring the lone family member and reinterring in a space in the new family lot would be permissible. Some states do not require a permit if reinterment is to be made in the same cemetery.

2) The same as in number 1, if a family moves or buys a lot or group of spaces in a cemetery and would like the whole clan

buried together in the same lot then disinterment and transporting to another cemetery for reinterment can be an option.

Another example of this would be a veteran who is buried in a single space in a private cemetery whose surviving spouse would like to be buried next to her husband by minimizing her own future cost of burial.

By having her husband moved to a V.A. cemetery and reinterred, she can someday qualify (as his spouse) for free burial next to him in the V.A. cemetery, saving her and her survivors the expense it would take to bury her in the private cemetery that he was previously buried in.

3) Taking a decedent out of a closed grave to place into another casket, alternative container or vault is a rare occurrence but has happened. Perhaps at the time of original burial the decedent's casket was placed into a simple concrete box that was non-protective and the family decided that they made an unwise choice at the time of the decedent's arrangements. Now they realize it would be better and give them more peace of mind to know that grandpa was in a protective vault.

In this case, a disinterment could occur with the casket or alternative container being removed from the box or original outer container and placed into a new container and then reinterred into the same space. Having these second thoughts after the fact is rare but not nonexistent whether the motive is better protection or some other reason.

4) Choosing to cremate, entomb, carry out some other form of disposition after a burial is an option that some have decided to do also. One good example of this was a family here in Texas that was moving to Iowa and decided three years after the death of one of its family members that they wanted to disinter, cremate the remains and take the ashes with them to their new area. After paying the cost and obtaining the necessary permits, this request was granted. In another instance, a surviving spouse purchased several mausoleum crypts and had his wife who was ground buried, disinterred and placed into one of the purchased crypts.

These are just several reasons why a private disinterment/ exhumation may occur and there may be others as circumstances change. It is an indictable offense under common law and statute to disinter a dead body without proper authority regardless of the purpose or motive[7].

Any time you are considering disinterment for whatever reason, consult an attorney, funeral home or cemetery, or the local or county authority in the jurisdiction where the decedent considered for disinterment is located to get advise and council for following proper procedures.

One of the biggest factors to consider in any exhumation/ reinterment will be the cost of doing such. There normally will be a disinterment fee that can run 2-3 times the normal interment fee at the cemetery.

Other things to consider are permit(s) that may need to be secured, transportation to the new disposition location, outer container reinstallation, opening and closing the new space, crypt, etc. where the new interment will take place, any funeral director or cemeterian fees that the law may require as well as the removal, transport and reinstallation of any monument or memorial from the old site assuming it meets the requirements for memorials at the new cemetery or memorial park.

Anytime that you do decide to do a private disinterment/ reinterment, be sure to read the contract closely and ascertain who bears the cost of any mishaps or unforeseen events such as breakage or cracking of a container or marker, accidental or unintentional damage of another sort that may happen during the process.

Exploring The Possibilities

Can A Cemetery Go Out Of Business?

The question has been asked about whether or not a cemetery of all things can actually go out of business, be shut down, close, fail or go out of existence. The answer unfortunately is yes; the good news is that it is a very infrequent occurrence. Anytime that a cemetery or memorial park does cease to exist it has failed. Business failure is not totally foreign to the cemetery as to any other commercial enterprise. Bad management as well as other uncontrollable economic factors have led a few cemeteries to not be able to continue as viable entities. Inadequate sales volume to pay current expenses, lack of endowment care money and poor financial maneuvering have preempted closure, bankruptcy or insolvency.

Some cemeteries have ceased to be such in the sense that they have been forgotten or abandoned. Burials eventually ceased and if a non-perpetual care property, nobody cares for the area. Since burials are in existence and memorials are placed at the graves, the property is still a cemetery.

What becomes of these cemeteries varies greatly. An article that appeared in the *Los Angeles Times* in 1998 told the story of an incident near Tehachapi, California where a developer found six graves during the course of building a project. Some old timers from the area guessed that the property had previously served as a family cemetery for some early settlers in that region. In one other instance a/failed cemetery became a public park where the memorials that had marked the individual lives of those buried there were gone.

Another old cemetery in Whittier, California was transformed into what the state calls a "pioneer cemetery." The memorials were all removed and it became a park. No cemetery of any age, size, or type has a monopoly on the potential for failure.

Pondering The Possibilities

Do I Have To Use A Cemetery?

America has been called the Land of opportunity. Add to this the current trends to be creative, save money and explore options, and the idea comes to mind of disposition somewhere other than a designated cemetery.

The best answer to be given is that it will depend on what your state and/or city allows. It is possible to establish an area of ground as a cemetery if the laws applicable to such are followed.

The potential factors involved in the establishment of a burial ground may include location (in or out of city limits), health ordinances, dedication of land, depth of graves, access and records of disposition/interments.

There are some people that just like to do things different and have inquired to bury on the family farm, ranch or other acreage. Even the question of "can we bury dad in the backyard under his favorite shade tree" has been asked.

There are some organizations that have even investigated the whole issue. A July 2002 article in the *Wall Street Journal* stated that some colleges and universities eager to find new sources of revenue in a shrinking economy are beginning to offer on-campus burial plots and columbaria (for cremated ashes) for alumni. The University of Virginia, universities of Richmond (Va), Centre College, Danville, Ky., St. John's N.W. Military Academy (Delafield, Wis.), St. Mary's College (Emmitsburg, Md) and Bucknell (Lewisburg, Pa.) are among those that have jumped on board the on-campus disposition train, according to the article.

As society progresses and becomes more complex, the sky is literally (see end of chapter 3) the limit on the forms of disposition under consideration.

Out With The Old, In With The New?
Defending And Saving Old Cemeteries

Although modern times are bringing us rapid industrialization, global mobility, changing trends toward cremation and less and less time to deal with practices that are likely to take or keep us out of our daily routines for too long, there is a spirit and attitude of interest in things of historic and sentimental value such as cemeteries.

Even though technology, the super information highway and the continuing development of once barren or unused land is changing every facet of our lives, society, I believe, still yearns to be connected with and show reverence for the past.

There is an interest in cemeteries for many different reasons. For some it is satisfying a need to visit relatives' gravesites on a regular basis to remember and reflect. For others it is an interest in history and the connection to the past by skimming the memorials. For others it may be the outdoors and a chance to get outside to walk, relax or enjoy the fresh air. Sometimes an old cemetery is the only piece of property left in an area or neighborhood with development and modernization all around it.

Some people have even seen or heard about cases where a real estate developer has developed over or tried to 'remove' a cemetery in the name of commercial expansion. Cemeteries that are inactive or overgrown are sometimes threatened by those who believe in "progress" or "moving forward" without consideration for the sacred grounds at question. Protecting old historic cemeteries can be a real challenge. States have a variance of laws governing these treasures and enforcement in some of the stricter jurisdictions can be lax.

However there are several ways to help preserve the past that cemeteries aid us with in remembering the roots of our communities. One way is by joining and supporting our local cemetery associations. This way it will show that there are people that are still interested in a particular burial ground.

Historical societies in your town or county also offer a way to get involved in preservation efforts regarding cemeteries as well as other objects of nostalgic value.

Genealogical clubs or groups can aid and abed a cemetery's worth to a town, city or area because of the information contribution that is often made from the memorials within its boundaries. Even a neighborhood or community group or a group of you and your friends or family can merge together to keep an old graveyard or cemetery from fading into only a memory.

There are several websites that I have listed in the Resources Available in Chapter 10 that can help you to find and save graves online. Fortunately there are people who recognize the intrinsic importance of these sites and have cared enough to record and assist in preserving their and our heritage.

Cremation bench with compartment for set or sets of cremated ashes.

A mature cemetery with lots of history; notice the statuary and marble-covered graves.

Small chapel used to hold services at the cemetery.

Chapter 3

Cremation & Alternative Forms of Disposition

1. Introduction
2. What Is Cremation?
3. Should I Consider Cremation?
4. What Should Cremation Cost
5. Government Regulation/Legal Requirements
6. Funeral Home Requirements
7. Direct Cremation
8. Crematory Requirements
9. Expectations From A Crematory
10. Arranging A Cremation
11. Transportation Involved
12. Permits Needed
13. Alternative Containers
14. Cremating Items with The Decedent
15. Witnessing Cremation
16. Ceremony Or Rites At A Crematory
17. How Long Should It Take
18. What To Do With The Cremated Remains: Scatter/Keep/Inter/Entomb/Inniche/Inbench/Ossuary/Monumentalize/Divide/Comingle/Transform/Propel Into Space/Shipment, Transport, Handling Charges/Unclaimed Ashes
19. Urns And Cremains Containers: Porcelain/Metal/Marble/Wood/Bronze/Plastic/Biodegradable/Cloisonne/Jewelery Keepsake (Memento)/Temporary/Outer Containers
20. How To Save Money On Cremation
21. Preplanning/Prefunding Cremation
22. Memorial (Cremation) Societies
23. Do I Have To Go Through A Funeral Home To Do A Cremation?
24. Other Forms Of Disposition (What's The Alternative)
25. Immediate Burial: Viewing Without A Service/Witnessing Burial

26. Donation To Medical Science And Research
27. Organ/Tissue Donation
28. DNA Storage
29. Mummification
30. Burial At Sea: Bodies/Cremated Remains
31. Body Dissolution
32. What Is Cryonics?
33. Is Cryonics Something I Should Consider?
34. What The Future May Hold: Outer Space Suspension?
35. Explaining Cremation And Alternative Disposition To Children

Introduction

The single biggest area of change in the funeral industry over the past 20 years is cremation. Whereas in the era of our parents and grandparents, cremation was a rare type of disposition we may of heard of for someone we may have known through media coverage or other person we may have had knowledge of, today cremation is a mainstream way of dealing with death in our society.

What I want to discuss here is what cremation is, what happens in cremation and describing the process of arranging for it and giving you some facts to determine if it is for you or someone in your family. Grouped along with cremation are the other alternate methods of disposition including immediate burial, donation to science, burial at sea, and last but not least, the controversial subject of Cryonics.

What Is Cremation?

Cremation is the irreversible process of incinerating a deceased human remains using extreme heat. A deceased body is placed in an appropriate casket or alternative container that/is then inserted into a chamber known as a retort (furnace). The heat or fire then reduces the body and the enclosing container to ashes.

Should I Consider Cremation?
(Thinking The Unthinkable)

Statistics show that cremation is on the rise. Depending on what part of the country you live in probably determines how much cremation takes place as a form of disposition.

Canada's British Columbia had a 75 percent cremation rate in 2000, the highest in North America, whereas the state of Alabama had the lowest rate at 4.82 percent, according to the Cremation Association of North America.

What was one time taboo (cremating a body) is now almost commonplace, with the expected cremation rate in the U.S. tittering close to 50% after the year 2025 (see table).

Like other major decisions in life, deciding on whether or not you want to be cremated will depend on different factors. Some of the variables that weight into the cremation decision include money and expense, religious beliefs, desire to save land, preference over burial, other family members being cremated, or the idea of more simplicity and convenience over other forms of disposition.

Cremation Rates

Year	Deaths	Cremations	%
1980	1,989,841	179,086	9%
1990	2,162,000	367,975	17.02%
2000	2,400,122	597,630	24.9%
* 2010	2,634,000	1,033,582	39.24%
* 2025	3,235,000	1,552,153	47.98%

* - Projected

Source: Cremation Association Of North America

If any of these reasons are of interest to you then cremation may be your best option. Several studies that have been conducted to try to define the cremation consumer have determined that the people who have selected cremation have done so because it fits into their ideas of what is important. They feel that it is simpler and causes less hassle for survivors, that it allows for more opportunity for individual expression and has more choices as far as disposition of the remains (ashes). It also allows one to be in control of what happens after they pass away (families rarely choose cremation for other family members).

Some things to think about in arriving at a decision on cremation include:

-Are you one who places a lot of emphasis on tradition? Since cremation is a relatively new alternative as far as social acceptance, interment may be a better option if you are not opposed to the idea of burial.

- Do you want to keep things very simple and to the point? If you are not into pomp and ceremony, planning and going to a lot of trouble and many decisions, direct cremation may be for you.

- Is the body no longer sacred after the soul has left it? If your world view of the afterlife sees the human body as no longer a vessel to be preserved after the occurrence of death, cremation may be your best choice.

Whatever you choose, deciding about cremation as disposition, remember that it is an irreversible process. That once someone is cremated there is no going back unlike burial where once laid to rest can (and in some instances have) be later disinterred and then cremated.

What Should Cremation Cost?

This is a hard question to answer because "cremation" will usually include removal from the place of death, transportation to the crematory, fees for any required permits and a container to place the ashes in after the cremation. This is over and above the crematory's charge to cremate and a container to place the body in before putting the deceased into the cremation chamber to start the process. Because these are all separate charges and there are a wide range of variables that go into each item, cremation costs will vary considerably from place to place across the country.

In researching the writing of this book I have found that cremation without any ceremonies, urns, flowers, or other accompanying items or services that can potentially supplement a cremation purchase, that the general range is anywhere from $600-$3,800 for the basic act of cremating a human remains. The best way to find out cremation costs in your area is to call around to area funeral homes and get quotes over the phone.

Government Regulation/Legal Requirements
(Abiding By The Law)

Cremation is currently regulated at the state and local level. Due to the horrifying events in February, 2002 in connection with the Tri-State Crematory in Noble, Georgia, where it was found that the Crematory's operator, Ray Brent Marsh, had taken money to perform over 300+ cremations that did not take place, but instead dumped the bodies in the surrounding area, most states have or are in the process of revamping their cremation statutes as a result of this tragedy.

The good part is that the large majority of both funeral homes and independent crematories in North America are honest, ethical and law-abiding. It is however in your best interest to check and find out what the cremation laws are in your state if you are seriously considering cremation.

The rules and regulations vary widely but most jurisdictions require a waiting period before a decedent can be cremated. The local coroner, justice of the peace or other authority must issue a letter or permit before a cremation can proceed. Unlike burial or entombment, since cremation is irreversible, the authorities have an overriding say as to whether an investigation into the death must take place before disposition can proceed.

Along with a letter or release from the coroner, the city or area where the crematory is located or jurisdiction where the death occurred may also require the funeral home or crematory to obtain a permit from them also. The issuing governmental entities must receive a signed certificate or statement from a licensed physician who treated the decedent prior to death and is familiar with his or her medical history before issuance of any permit.

All of this red tape can take at least several days if not longer and because of this, cremation is usually not a "rush into event."

Funeral Home Requirements

Most funeral homes will have certain rules in place regarding cremations and do so in order to protect themselves from liability.

If a decedent is not to be embalmed due to the fact that cremation is desired, the funeral home will require the decedent to be refrigerated until the time of the cremation. Since refrigeration retards the decomposition process, this will allow the funeral director time to secure the necessary paperwork to schedule the cremation without the decedent's remains to posing a health threat to the funeral home's employees.

An identification tag or bracelet is also becoming more and more commonplace as a requirement. Most funeral directors now will not allow a deceased's remains brought onto the premises without an ID bracelet attached because of the liability exposure involved. Especially in larger cities in high volume funeral homes that handle many calls each year.

Funeral homes will also require some type of signed authorization form before proceeding with the scheduling of a cremation. What the form contains and whom they will require to sign the authorization may vary, but again cremation is a large area of potential lawsuits. Mortuaries like any other business must shield themselves by obtaining the needed authorizations in order to cremate.

Crematory Requirements

Along with funeral homes and mortuaries, crematories will have their own regulations in order to make sure it operates efficiently.

Verification of the decedent's identification is usually a must before a crematory will proceed. This comes in the form of a signed ID form by the next-of-kin or other party or a form that states refusal to identify. At this point the funeral director will usually supply the crematory with a statement that he or she performed proper identification using information derived from interviewing the family when making the arrangements. This will usually be a scar, tattoo, birthmark, photograph or other means that will allow the crematory to satisfy itself that it is cremating the right body.

Placement of the decedent into an approved container is also a requirement of any reputable crematory. The idea of placing a body uncovered and unencased into the cremation chamber is unethical and immoral if not illegal. An approved container must meet the crematory's requirements as far as size, weight, material and composition. Usually any wood casket or container made of wood or wood products will be okay.

Any other materials of alternative containers will need to be approved by the particular crematory and some containers, such as ones made of metal will be forbidden due to potential harm to the cremation chamber and/or inability to burn.

A reputable crematory will also always require the proper permits be obtained by the funeral home and submitted to it before scheduling a cremation. Depending on what the particular laws in the said state or jurisdiction are needed to meet legal requirements will effect what the crematory will want to meet its requirements.

Expectations From A Crematory

The main point to know about any crematory is that it has its own schedule to keep and as a result usually works on a first come first served basis. Once the paperwork and other requirements are satisfied, the crematory will usually have other cremations also and it may be a day or longer before they can do yours.

It must be remembered that crematories have fixed capacity (only so many retorts) and that regardless of demand- and demand as pointed out earlier is on the increase- that the crematory cannot just automatically enlarge its working ability in a snap.

Usually the funeral director can help explain to you what and what not to expect from the crematory that his or her firm uses and can answer any questions you may have concerning the cremation.

Direct Cremation
(The Process)

As defined at the beginning of the chapter, cremation is the act or process of transforming by heat, human remains to small particles of bone fragments through reduction and evaporation.

Before the process begins, any items, objects or mechanical devices such as pacemakers that may cause harm to the cremation chamber must be removed. Other types of implanted devices may be removed also if they are metallic or contain batteries or other contents that may explode during the cremation.

The cremation begins when the human remains encased in the approved container are placed into the retort (chamber).

Identification Concern

Today because of the disaster at Tri-State Crematory in 2002, there is a legitimate concern relating to knowing whether the loved one was cremated and whether the ashes that are returned to the family are actually your loved one's ashes.

Some funeral homes are utilizing an undetachable stainless steel bracelet with an engraved identification number onto the wrist of each decedent to be cremated.

This bracelet is designed to withstand the cremation process itself and is contained within the container of ashes returned to or shown to the family. It is just one extra measure employed by some funeral directors to give peace of mind to the families they serve.

Open flamed fire raises the temperature up to as much as 2000 degrees Fahrenheit, for an appropriate period of 1½-3½ hours, depending on variant factors with each human remains.

Depending on whether or not the cremation is performed at a crematory with a secondary chamber the partially cremated remains are moved to this secondary chamber for completion of the process. For crematories without the secondary chamber, the partially cremated may be repositioned by the crematory operator to secure completion of the cremation.

After the process is complete, the cremated remains are removed from the retort and put into a cooling tray and then processed to their final state of bone fragments or cremated remains. Although often called ashes, from a technical standpoint they are not ashes in reality.

Any metal or other objects that need to be removed after the cremation that may have broken into smaller pieces during the operation such as screws, hinges, prostheses, jewelry, dental metallic, etc. may be taken out of the cremated remains using a metal detecting wand magnet or other means that is scanned over the cremains and removed and disposed of according to crematory rules and/or local laws.

The cremated remains are then placed into a container according to the family's wishes. Most remains weight between 5-8 pounds depending on the size, weight and bone structure of the decedent and type of casket or container the human remains went into the retort encased in.

Arranging A Cremation
(Great Expectations)

Once that determination is established that cremation is the desired objective in the disposition process, the funeral home will require some type of conference be set to arrange for the cremation.

One of the first priorities that the funeral director will need to establish is who has the right to authorize the cremation. The general rule in force in most states is that the legal next of kin will have the authority to arrange the cremation in whatever definition is given to next of kin in that particular place.

Next count on the director explaining and defining cremation, going over the funeral home and crematory rules and requirements and having the legal next of kin sign an authorization form. There will be decisions to be made on the type of alternative container to be used for the cremation, whether or not an urn for the cremated remains are desired and if not what type of receptacle the cremains will be placed in; whether or not you want to be told when all the requirements have been satisfied to schedule the cremation, be notified when it is scheduled and whether or not you wish to be present to witness the cremation.

You may also expect to be asked whether or not you or other family members would like to see the decedent before cremating. A lot of funeral homes require a visual identification or a signed refusal to identify where the funeral director will try to ascertain information about the decedent's physical characteristics that will positively identify him or her.

Along with arrangements preparing for and carrying out the cremation will be discussion about what to do with the cremains after the cremation. The next of kin authorizes the funeral home to be given to him or her, the authority to mail to a designated recipient such as a cemetery who will bury or entomb the cremains for example, or authorize another person such as a family member or executor to pick them up from the funeral home or crematory.

Also the issues of whether the decedent's cremains are desired to be present at any memorial services as well as memorialization options should also be points to be touched upon and decided about. The arrangement conference is the opportunity to ask questions and obtain answers about any concerns you may have.

Several things that might come to mind are how long does it generally take between arranging for and doing the cremation; it is it possible to visit or see the crematory and is it normal to be present for or know the time of the cremation. These are questions that your funeral director can answer for you.

Transportation Involved

Unless the crematory that your funeral director uses is located at the funeral home, expect there to be a charge to transport the deceased from the mortuary to the cremation site. Sometimes this charge is contained in the charge for basic or direct cremation, but be sure to ask. The fewer surprises the better when it comes time to pay up.

If you or the funeral home you are using to handle the cremation is located in a rural or more isolated area, there may be an additional mileage charge for the transport for each additional mile outside the funeral home's normal trade area. If for no other reason, it makes sense to ask the funeral director where the crematory is located that will be used. If it is outside the funeral home's trade area, be sure to find out what the charges are and what portion is additional mileage.

Permits Needed
(The Thicket Thickens)

Earlier in this chapter we touched upon some of the requirements states and local authorities impose in connection with cremation.Now I want to elaborate further in order to come full circle on the issue of obtaining proper permission to cremate.

Although your funeral director should be well versed in what is needed regarding cremation and the subsequent cremated human remains, it is important for you as the consumer to have a basic awareness of what permits may be compulsory in relation to the entire process.

First, make sure to ask if any type of permit(s) will be needed to take the decedent to the place of the cremation and if so how long it should take to get it.

The law may also require your funeral home and/or crematory that will do the cremation to have a permit to hold custody of the body until cremation. This area is usually covered under the licensing of the funeral or crematory establishment, but it never hurts to ask.

After the cremation is complete and the decedent's body is transformed to ashes or cremated remains, there may be a permit or document needed to possess to transport the cremated remains. Be sure to ask about this also. The last thing you would want would be for someone to get in trouble for not having the proper paperwork while possessing or transporting your loved one's cremated remains.

Possibly the most important consideration is any permit needed to procure disposition of the cremated remains. Any time you are taking cremains with you by common carrier and/or wanting to dispose of the ashes in a public area you will need to be sure you are within the bounds of the law. Your funeral director can advise you as to any paperwork such as a burial transit permit or certificate of cremation you may need to carry cremains with you on an airplane, bus or other public mode when traveling.

If your objective is to dispose of said cremated remains, check with the proper authority in that area to see if you will need any type of permission to do so.

Alternative Containers

A cremation casket or alternative container will need to be chosen for the cremation itself. This outer encasement or container is needed, usually as a crematory requirement to help protect the interior of the cremation retort.

Any type of container for the cremation can be used so long

as it meets the crematory's requirement. Usually any wood casket that is part of a funeral home's selection is acceptable for cremation due to the combustibility of the wood.

Cremation caskets are made with less ornamentation and from different materials that may allow the cremation to go faster. Some funeral homes offer "rental caskets" that consist of an outer frame and exterior and a removable interior in which the decedent can be placed for viewing or open casket funeral, and then afterwards, the insertable cremation container with the deceased enclosed is removed from the ceremonial or permanent part of the unit and the frame part of the casket used again.

The interior alternative container is what the decedent is cremated in. Alternative containers are named so because they are made for the purpose of an alternative form of disposition such as cremation. They are usually made of cardboard, fiberboard, chip wood or other material that is conducive to the cremation concept of easy combustibility and rapid burning.

Alternative container manufacturers are also focusing on making containers that are environmentally sound also.

Cremating Items with The Decedent

Placing certain items with the one to be cremated is becoming a more popular and commonplace idea along with the rise in cremation as a form of disposition.

The symbolic gesturing of putting things with a decedent at the time of disposition is nothing new but interest in the concept of having keepsakes, personal belongings or other treasures go with the decedent adds to the beauty of the sentimentality of saying good-bye.

The only thing that most crematories forbid as a rule from being cremated with the deceased are metal materials, batteries or battery operated devices and anything of an explosive nature such as firecrackers.

The crematory operator will usually use a hand held metal

detection wand and scan over the body to ensure that there are no items or objects encased that may be cremation unsafe.

Some of the things that I have been given as a director to place with a decedent to be cremated have included a deck of cards, photographs, blanket or quilting, a piece of clothing, and nonmetallic jewelry pieces. Other things I have seen or heard about include candy bars, peanut butter crackers, a yo-yo and handwritten letters and cards.

Anything that cannot be cremated with the decedent should be documented and returned to the person making the arrangements by the funeral home. It would probably be a good idea to make a list or an inventory of the items given to the funeral home to be cremated with the deceased and keep it for your records.

Witnessing Cremation

One area that is growing within the growing trend toward cremation is being present at the start of or witnessing the cremation. This very simply consists of being present at the crematory as the decedent is rolled up to the cremation chamber and loaded into the retort, usually by an automated loading devise that resembles a forklift or escalator pad and watching as the cremation gets underway.

More and more crematories are being built with or adding on a witness room that allows anywhere from a handful of family members up to a small amphitheater/stadium like setting for larger accommodations of people to be present at the cremation start. Some crematories allow families who desire to do so to press a remote or panel control button to begin the cremation process. This is usually in part of some religious customs.

Witness rooms usually are constructed next to the cremation control room that houses the crematory's retorts and is separated from the witness room by a large glass wall. This way families can watch the start of the cremation either seated or standing up.

Since the cremation usually lasts several hours, most families that wish to witness do so only for the start and leave after the first 5-10 minutes. Witnessing cremation usually must be scheduled with the crematory by the funeral home and sometimes includes a witnessing fee due to arrangements and special coordination of scheduling that must take place to accommodate the requesting family's wishes. Also you can expect each person who chooses to be present to sign some type of waiver or release holding the funeral home and crematory harmless for any emotional distress that one may develop as a result of witnessing the cremation.

Ceremony Or Rites At A Crematory

Along with witnessing cremation, there are some, because of religious or philosophical reasons, or a desire to have some form of closure at the time of the cremation, who request to have a service at the crematory.

Most crematories and the sponsoring funeral homes are very accommodating to these requests and there are several factors that must be considered before making plans to try to have a ceremony at the crematory.

First, you must determine what type of service you want to have and what you want to include. Is it as simple as having a short prayer? Do you want a reading, music or speaker? How long do you wish it to last? These will all be important considerations.

Second, is the crematory conducive to this service/ceremony plan? Is there a place to play music? How many people can be comfortably accommodated? As a general rule most crematories are not yet "visitor friendly" so far as facility lay out. This will probably change in the future as the demand for ceremonies and rituals at crematories increase in demand.

There will probably be some type of charge for holding a ceremony at the crematory possibly by both the crematory and the funeral home if a licensed funeral director is required to be in attendance. There may also be a time constraint placed on how long your party may occupy the designated ceremony room or space at the crematory.

If the crematory has other cremations and other families to accommodate on the same day, there may be a restriction on how long the ceremony will have to be completed. Be sure to let your funeral director know what you have in mind so that he or she can advise you and get you the information you'll need to make it a success.

How Long Should It Take?
(Hurry up and Wait)

Although many people link cremation to a form of practical or immediate disposition without a lot of fuss, the timeliness of the period between death and when the cremation will be performed may vary considerably.

Getting signed death certificates, cremation letters, permits and other required paperwork can take time. Also considering the schedules of the funeral home staff, crematory personnel along with the waiting for the proper governing authorities to submit paperwork needed to schedule a cremation, it is a wonder that it happens as fast as it does sometimes.

Texas has a 48-hour waiting period between when a person dies and when they can be legally cremated. Different states have varying laws and rules and any legitimate funeral home or crematory will want to abide by those laws. To answer the question how long should it take is going to depend on how quickly all of the legal, funeral home and crematory regulations are met. It may take 2 days or it may take 10 (usually not likely to take 10).

When you take into account weekends and holidays when most public, legal and medical offices are closed and the period to schedule and carry out the cremation may be extended. As a very general rule of thumb, you can expect 3-5 business days on average for the funeral director to secure the paperwork and procure the cremation. Try to remember however that there are lots of different factors involved outside the funeral home's direct control in getting required paperwork and it may take longer. Because of this I would strongly advise against, for example, scheduling a ceremony with the cremated remains present before the cremation is scheduled.

There have been too many instances where one of the permit-issuing entity's held up and did not submit a required document in as timely a fashion as they "usually" do, and therefore delayed the cremation being scheduled.

It is best to never schedule anything with the cremated remains being present until after the cremation has taken place or is at least scheduled to occur on a certain day.

What To Do with The Cremains
(Adding Meaning to Memory)

What many consumers don't understand is that cremation is only a process; it is not a form of disposition in and of itself.

It is not a form of disposition of the remains. Having a body cremated doesn't dispose of it; it merely alters its form. Because of this, there is the issue of what to do with the cremains. Since a lot of people choose cremation because of its simplicity and its perceived "elimination of having to make big decisions," I want to present the possibilities of what can be done with the cremains once received.

Scatter

The idea of scattering the cremated remains of a loved one seems very sentimental and somewhat romantic as portrayed in the movie *The Bridges of Madison County* with Clint Eastwood and Meryl Streep. However there are some serious considerations to take into account when thinking about scattering.

The first is the location at which you would like to scatter the cremains. The local laws and ordinances should be checked to make sure that releasing cremated human remains is legal in the place in which you are considering.

Second is the fact that scattering cremains is, like creation, an irreversible act. Once it is done there really is no practical way to retrieve the ashes and go somewhere else.

If scattering is the choice, some cemeteries have a scattering garden that allows families who wish to scatter but have no place to do so to scatter a loved one's ashes. Oftentimes the family prefers the scattering to be private and informal and may include the family members or those present to participate by each person using a scoop to take and scatter a portion of the cremains in a way that creates a special significance.

Wherever the place is that you select as a scattering site be sure you are within the bounds of the law in that area and that if it is a place you want to visit in the future, that you will have a "reasonable assurance" of access to the place in the years to come, such as the ocean, a protected land reserve or other nonrestricted place.

<u>Keep</u>

One of the favorite reasons that some people choose cremation is so that they may retain their loved one's cremated remains. This becomes important if one moves a lot or anticipates moving in the future and being able to carry their loved one's cremains with them wherever and whenever they go.

There is an entire line of urns and keepsake urns (holds a smaller portion of the cremated remains) available that serves this very purpose. There are some who desire to place their loved one's ashes in their home close by and display on a table or mantle as a daily reminder of the decedent's memory. Others prefer to store or place the cremated remains in a more out of sight or out-of-the way place.

Another key advantage of keeping the ashes is that retaining them alleviates the financial burden of having to purchase a place for them at a cemetery or memorial park. Keeping the cremains also allows plenty of time to think about and plan any possible options of disposing of the cremains without any time pressure, deadlines or being in a position of having to make a decision now.

Inter

Placing cremated remains into the ground is another popular option that some people choose because it is less expensive than traditional casket ground burial but still allows for a permanent placement of disposition as well as traditional memorialization opportunities such as a flat headstone or upright monument.

Interring the cremated remains, also called inurnment, is a desirable alternative if for example both a husband and wife want to be cremated as opposed to buried. In this case the couple can buy one cemetery space and both sets of cremains can be buried in the same space, subject to cemetery rules.

If the case arises that one spouse wants to be buried and the other cremated, many cemeteries allow urns to be buried in the same space as a previously interred casket. It may be possible for as many as 4-6 inurnments (burying cremains) in a single space in some cemeteries.

Some cemeteries and memorial parks require urn or cremated remains container vaults the same as vaults for casket interments as discussed in chapter one. As with casket burial, urn vaults protect the urn and the ground from sinking after the inurnment. Expect to incur a charge for the urn vault (if required or desired) to open and close the space, and possibly a vault installation fee.

Entomb

An alternative to interring cremains in the earth is to entomb or place the cremated remains into a mausoleum crypt. This also is usually cheaper than casket entombment but as with burial, allows the cremains a permanent final place of disposition.

Again if in the case of a couple, if one partner desires cremation and the other traditional casket entombment, both partners can be placed in a crypt (as allowed according to cemetery rules) one casketed according to his or her wishes and the other who wants to be cremated, the ashes also placed, according to his or her wishes.

If both want to be cremated, a regular adult size mausoleum crypt would be more than large enough to accommodate both sets of cremains whereas in contrast to ground inurnment, with a mausoleum crypt there would be no need for an urn vault(s) as may be the case with inurnment (ground burial) of the cremated remains.

Inniche

Putting cremated remains into a columbarium (defined as a structure, room or space in a building or other designated place specifically built for the placement of cremated remains) niche as final disposition is called innichement. Columbariums are constructed for the sole purpose of placement of cremated ashes.

Innichement will be cheaper as a general rule than either entombment or interment/inurnment due to the plain fact that we are talking about a smaller space than a regular size ground space for burial or mausoleum crypt for entombment, because there will also be no need for a vault and the cost to open and close the niche should be relatively inexpensive.

Niche spaces are tailor made for cremains and most all niche spaces are large enough for most any type of urn or container but the key thing to remember is to find out from the cemetery, memorial park or other niche provider the dimensions of the niche space.

The last thing you would want to happen would be to purchase an urn or cremains container and after the fact find out that the niche space is too small for the urn or container to fit in. If innichement in a columbarium is your desired choice, get the niche space measurements before purchasing an urn/container to place the ashes in.

There are also specialty niche properties available from some cemeteries that allow either companion niches (side-by-side for two), a group of niche spaces to be purchased together as a group similar to a lot of spaces for ground burial for an entire family. This will vary from place to place so check with your cemetery of choice.

Inbench

Along with innichement is the concept of placing or "inbenching" the cremated remains into a specially made bench for the disposition of cremains.

More and more modern cemeteries and memorial parks are establishing some types of marble or granite benches within their grounds that are built for cremated remains to be placed within.

These benches usually have spaces for at least 2 sets of cremains or possibly more. Some benches allow for the family's name to be engraved on the bench the same way that names are engraved onto cemetery memorial markers at grave spaces. The benches are permanently set at predetermined places in the cemetery. Inbenchment is a great option if one desires distinction, status, and a more prominent disposition of cremated remains, however expect to pay more for this form of cremains disposition than the others.

Ossuary

Once defined as a property for holding the bones of the dead, today an ossuary is a shared or commonplace receptacle for cremated remains, or memorial place for holding cremains that are buried in the ground below a sculpture column that encases a locked cover.

Ossuaries are not offered by some cemeteries or memorial parks, but the ones that do sometimes also offer a place near the ossuary structure to memorialize the decedent through cenotaph or placement of a name plaque or other memorialization. Check with the cemetery or memorial park that you may be interested in to find out if they have an ossuary and the applicable terms, rules and price information.

Monument Structures

Today some funeral homes and memorialization providers are offering cremains monuments that can be placed in an outdoor setting such as a cemetery or in the backyard or lawn as part of the landscape.

These combination urn/monuments are usually offered in some form of granite, rock, marble or bronze and feature such desirable qualities such as security, closeness, relocatability, and cost effectiveness. They may be eligible for placement in a cemetery or memorial park that allows above-ground markers or statuary, or if placed in a lawn, can be moved to a new residence property if you move.

The urn monument structures contain a built in shaft or chamber within that houses the cremated remains. They also come with a feature on the exterior to affix a plate or plaque with the decedent's name and dates and other information if desired.

Cremains monuments are an ideal way to place cremated ashes if your goal is to keep your loved one's memory (literally) close to home. They are durable structures that usually weight between 50-100 pounds and yet are small enough to be relocated elsewhere. They can also serve as symbolic monuments for cremated loved ones whose ashes have been scattered elsewhere or buried in a far away cemetery that is inconvenient to visit routinely.

Divide

Dividing up the ashes of a decedent after a cremation is an option that is growing in occurrence among families who want to keep the cremated remains but with more than one survivor with an interest, such as a family with four or five grown adult children for instance, who all want to keep mom's ashes. The way to solve such a dilemma is division of the cremated remains.

There are smaller type cremains containers for dividing ashes into smaller portions, which I will discuss in the next section on urns and containers.

If your family's choice is for cremation of a deceased loved one and there are at least two surviving family members who express a desire to possess the ashes, serious consideration should be given to dividing the ashes. Most funeral homes can give advice and direction to the particulars of this when making arrangements, and will also handle dividing the cremains and placing into the various chosen containers.

While I do not personally know of any funeral homes that charge a handling fee for this service, it may be wise to ask your funeral director.

Co-Mingle

A not-so-common request that still occurs on occasion deals with the issue of co-mingling or mixing the ashes of two or more persons who have been cremated, together in one receptacle. This occurs mostly with married couples who are cremated and then "joined together" again for eternity.

Regardless of the final disposition of the cremated remains, co-mingling is usually a service that is done by the funeral home (however a family may chose to do it themselves) by simply taking the two sets of cremains and pouring them into one of the two existing containers or together into a new one that is large enough to house the newly mixed set of ashes. Many times after the first spouse dies, the funeral home will either hold the cremains in a container selected until the second spouse dies or return the first spouse's ashes to the family for safekeeping. Later after the second spouse dies, the funeral home will retrieve the first spouse's ashes or obtain from the family and comingle together as requested.

Several things to look at here are does the funeral home have a charge for holding the first set of ashes until the second cremation, and if so is it based on time? If so you will be off taking the first set and keeping them yourself until the second passing and subsequent cremation occurs.

Also the issue of a container for the first set of ashes- if there is a charge for the temporary or utility container to house the first set of ashes until the second set becomes available (an unknown factor) you will be better off purchasing the permanent container up front and then later simply adding the second set of ashes. This way you will have the decision made on the permanent container and eliminate any charge for the temporary container or storage/holding fees for the first set.

Transform

Knowing all the options that exist helps you to make a good decision by being well informed. A relatively new and still evolving option is to have your loved one's cremated remains transformed into diamonds. This is now possible through a new high-technology process that extracts the carbon from cremated human remains and is turned into a synthetically produced diamond. The idea of making synthetic diamonds is not in itself new as the General Electric Company pioneered the achievement in the early 1950s. Since the process has now been refined and improved upon through the years, we are now able to create higher than the quality of natural stones synthetic diamonds using the carbon from human cremains.

On average there is enough carbon in the human body to produce 50 or more diamonds of different sizes up to a carat. The carat diamond can then be set into a ring or other piece of jewelry.

Costs, as with anything new, are usually pretty exorbitant depending on exactly what you want to have done. However if you think of transformation in terms of getting a product that will last forever and can be passed down as an heirloom from generation to generation, it can be worth the price.

The real benefit is in being able to keep apart of the decedent with you from now on. Transforming cremains allows this to happen. A bizarre idea for some people indeed, but if it provides comfort and connection for the bereaved, it can be a good idea.

Propel Into Space

If you ever wondered whether or not the sky was really the limit, guess again; with services now available to consumers, there is actually a way to launch cremated remains into space!

Ever since the earliest days of mankind, humans have looked to the skies with wonder, awe and fascination. For those who want to travel in space, now there is a way to do so.

Celestis Services, Inc. of Houston, Texas provides several different options of how cremains may be propelled into outer space for earth orbit and return, then vaporizing, for lunar surface destination, or for permanent launch into deep outer space for eternal drifting. The company also offers a service to transmit a digital memorial message to the stars in honor of an individual who's passed away and disposition of the remains is to occur in some other way.

As can be expected, the cost for these services starts at around $1,000 and goes upwards (no pun intended) to as much as $15,000. This is just for these mentioned services, not including the cremation itself or the goods and services discussed throughout this chapter rendered by a funeral home and crematory.

If your ultimate idea is to "reach for the stars," you may want to seriously consider space propulsion if your desire is to someday be cremated.

Shipment/Transport/Handling Charges

If cremated human remains are to be sent, transported, shipped, couriered or otherwise moved from point A to point B via a third-party such as the U.S. Postal Service, Federal Express or other shipping entity, you can expect to pay the cost of shipping and handling and any other related costs that may be incurred to procure the transport. A good example of this is if the family asks the funeral home to mail the cremated remains to a cemetery some distance away, where the ashes are to be interred in or otherwise disposed of, the funeral home may have a fixed charge for shipping within the continental U.S. or if they are sent even further it may be at the postal prevailing rate.

Cremated human remains may be sent as such by registered mail, return receipt, provided they are packaged as required. Other carriers may have different requirements for transporting. One of the advantages of letting the funeral director handle this task is because he or she is generally familiar with the rules and requirements of shipping cremated remains. If you want to do it yourself, call and make sure you get all the information needed to ready and properly send the cremains according to your wishes.

Unclaimed Cremains

So what happens in the case that a legal next-of-kin authorizes and the providing funeral home does a cremation but arrangements are not made or followed through on as such and the cremated remains go unclaimed?

It usually will depend upon the funeral home's policy for unclaimed ashes and/or if there are any laws or ordinances dealing with how these ashes are to be handled. Some funeral homes that also have affiliated cemeteries may take all the unclaimed ashes every so often (6 months, year, etc.) and bury in a designated lot in some remote part of the cemetery. Others that have a mausoleum or crypt space available may place the unclaimed in there. Others may simply have a storage shelf or cabinet in the funeral home that they retain unclaimed ashes indefinitely and will deal with the issue at some future time when space runs out and they must act.

Most funeral homes however will not keep unclaimed ashes for extended periods of time. If you find out through researching the family tree that your long lost aunt Mary was cremated by XYZ Funeral Home in 1948 and you can't find that anyone ever went to pick up her cremains, don't get your hopes up that XYZ funeral home has them in a locker by the receptionist desk.

Urns And Cremains Containers
(To Have And To Hold)

Once the cremation has been completed the cremains are removed from the chamber and, need to be placed into some type of holding receptacle.

An urn is simply a container or vase with or without ornamentation that is specially made to house cremated remains. An urn can be made out of various materials or hybrid. In this section I will describe the different types of urns that are available to consumers today and discuss the possible features of each.

Urns come in lots of different shapes, sizes, colors, finishes and designs. Some are manufactured in a basic form and made in such a way that symbols, emblems or other types of personalization such as engraved name and/or dates, decorative emblems, symbols, attachments, or ornamentation can be added at the consumer's request upon purchase.

Some are made for a particular use in mind such as scattering the ashes, where the urn may include a retractable carrying handle, latch door to open and release the cremains, or display or placement urns where once the cremains are placed within, the intention is for them to permanently remain within. These containers will usually have a screw on base or permanent fit lid. Other types are made to express the individualism of the decedent whose cremains are within such as artistic designs, chimes, birdbath, sundial or other unconventional forms to display the decedent's uniqueness.

Since urns and containers are usually classified by sellers according to the material the object consists of, I will discuss urns on that basis. However when looking at urns to choose one to purchase, the single most important factor to keep in mind is, "what am I going to do with the urn that contains my loved one's cremains?" The reason for this question is that, for example, you want to place the urn into a niche that you've bought at a local cemetery. The niche space measures one foot wide by one foot high. The urn you are considering is one and a half feet high. Your urn will not fit into this niche space and if your heart is set on this particular urn, you will have to either find another niche or other space large enough for the urn or get another one that will fit.

So first ask yourself what if you want to do with the cremated remains that will go into the chosen vessel and then start looking at your options.

Porcelain

Porcelain is a strong glazed ware consisting of translucent ceramic that can be useful in making pottery. This also makes it a good material for urn construction. Porcelain urns are usually good display urns since they are manufactured with some type of decorative painting or exterior. Due to their fragile texture, if a porcelain urn is to be kept for display purposes, it should be placed where it cannot be easily touched or knocked off a table or other fixture.

Metal

Metal urns come in steel, sterling silver, carbon steel and pewter or some other type of alloy of metals. Steel urns are usually made of iron and lesser amounts of carbon. Stainless steel like the caskets will not ever rust or corrode, and pewter urns are metal alloy compositions mostly made from tin.

Metal urns are among the most durable and are the logical choice of container if the cremains are to by buried or placed in a niche or other space. These urns can come in various sizes, shapes and colors with painted finishes. Metal urns also can usually be engraved depending on other variables.

Marble

Marble is a hard, solid limestone capable of taking a smooth polish after being fashioned from solid blocks of stone. As a durable composite material, marble urns are well-suited for either burial or display purposes. Because of its hardness and strength, marble urns may not be required to be encased by an outer container for ground inurnment. Like metal, marble can usually be engraved for personalization and come in various types of marble colors.

Wood

Wood urns are among the most popular in existence today among cremation consumers. Wood urns provide warmth, beauty and value and come in a variety of different types including oak, cherry, mahogany, walnut, poplar, maple and basswood.

A wide range of personalization choices go with the wood urns that can be handsomely hand-crafted and stained including applique attachments, engraved designs, medallion attachments, embroidered tapestry and name and date engraving.

Cherry and mahogany usually run more expensively and oak and poplar tend to be more modestly priced by most urn retailers. Regardless of final disposition, hardwood urns are among the best cremains containers on the market today.

Bronze

Bronze is a brownish colored alloy consisting of cooper and tin. There are basically two types of bronze urns, cast and sheet.

Cast bronze is bronze formed by pouring into a mold to form the desired object's shape and dimensions. This casting process is used to make special design type urns such as keepsakes and statuary that have unique designs.

Sheet bronze uses a thin layer or layering process to shape and produce more standardized urn types such as square or rectangular shaped objects like chests, boxes, cubes, and compartments.

Bronze urns can usually be engraved if space provided is big enough to allow lettering and like marble, bronze urns can come in various colors and finishes. Bronze is also very durable and cast bronze products tend to be among the highest priced, however some sheet bronze keepsakes are very affordable.

Plastic

Plastic of course is either natural organic or synthetic material that can be shaped when soft then hardened into the desired object.

Plastic urns usually are designated as such by the user of such (the consumer) since urns made of plastic are not readily made and marketed as containers for cremated human remains by most urn sellers.

Because of its composition and the related economics, most urn providers prefer to offer the types of urns made of other materials that usually allow more profitability and higher revenue. Plastics also are at a competitive disadvantage from the personalization standpoint in that it cannot be readily engraved and imprinted upon as the urns made of harder, more durable substance.

Plastic containers can work very well as urns however if the cremains within the plastic urns are to be entombed, interred with an outer container, or otherwise placed within a durable final resting place. Plastic is also among the most inexpensive receptacles and can be purchased at various types of retail stores.

As a general rule, the urns for sale at the funeral home may tend to be more expensive than a container that could be bought at a retail store for the same general purpose.

Compare the prices of some of the funeral home's urns with comparable containers that you may be able to get somewhere else.

Biodegradable

Made with environmental issues taken into consideration, the biodegradable urn is a product capable of decaying and being absorbed by the environment.

Created by the Options Division of Batesville Casket Company, the Reflections Series Biodegradable Scattering Urns are made of pressed cotton and when placed gently into water will float for one to five minutes at the water's surface before descending. This allows a time for any ritual or ceremony to take place at the water's edge by those gathered as a way to complete their good-byes.

The biodegradable urns measure about 23" in diameter and 4 1/2" deep and comes with a choice of designs most fitting the decedent including floral, soaring eagle, Signature (allows loved ones to write a short message) and Sailboat Reflections. They are competitively priced along with other types of urns.

Cloisonne

Among the elite of hand-crafted beauty, cloisonné is an ancient art form where different colors of molten enamel are poured and separated by metal wire or bands into compartments.

Cloisonne urns come in various colors and designs of artwork and are very fragile. They are made much like a vase in that they have a base container in which to place the cremains in, and a removable lid top that is simply placed down over the opening as any other decorative vase or table/mantle display piece.

Cloisonne urns are available from most urn retailers and tend to be on the pricey side due to the material, hand-crafting and eye appeal. These urns are also usually good if your objective is to keep the cremains and set on a table, cabinet, shelf or mantle.

Keepsake

Keepsake products primarily consist of jewelry and smaller

sized capsules of cylinders for the purpose of holding small portions of the cremated decedent's remains.

A relatively new concept in marketing to the cremation consumer, keepsake products are made of many types of materials such as aluminum, glass, crystal, granite, brass, and even gold along with those mentioned (metal, bronze, marble, etc.).

The range of items available includes rings, pendants, necklaces, miniature urns, engraved commemorative display plaques and memento boxes.

Some products such as some of the keepsake pendants allow for a small photo of the deceased, engraved name and dates of birth and death, or even photo laser engraving if you wish.

Since not everyone is okay with the ideas of carrying around mom's or dad's cremains with them, these other memorial keepsakes have been developed.

The memento chests are available for those who wish to have a special receptacle for storing items of the cremated decedent as a safekeeping heirloom. Memento chests are ideal for the placement of photos, jewelry, papers, medals, and other individual items and some chests are made with a separate compartment for all or some of the decedent's cremains as well.

Keepsakes are ideal for those who wish to memorialize their loved ones in a tangible way that can serve as a constant reminder of their memory.

Temporary

Just as the word says, temporary urns are those used to hold the cremated remains for a time until the permanent urn or container is ready to place the cremains into.

Temporary urns are also called utility urns and usually consist of cardboard, plastic, hardbound paper or rugged wood composite material.

Many times the crematory will always place the cremains into a temporary urn to give back to the funeral home who will then place into the urn or container selected or provided by the family.

If no urn or "permanent" container is selected then the temporary urn is the permanent container and will serve as such. Because these temporary units are usually made of durable material, the "temp urn" can work fine and often times a funeral home or cremation provider will keep the cremains that go unclaimed in the temporary urn.

Outer Containers

As stated earlier in this chapter, whenever cremated remains are to be interred in the ground at a cemetery or memorial park either through requirement or the desire to protect both the urn and/or the grave, an outer burial container may need to be considered.

Like the outer burial containers used for caskets, urn vaults are made of copper, steel, stainless steel, galvanized steel or reinforced concrete. If you are going to bury the cremains and the cemetery requires an outer container, it will keep the grave from sinking in after closing; if not required what you need to think about is the urn itself, of whatever material it's made of buried beneath the ground by itself. The choice will be up to you.

Urn outer containers or vaults usually measure about 2 feet wide both ways as a square box and one to two feet high or deep in order to accommodate most any standard size urn. In the unfortunate event that two family members pass away at the same time (an accident, for example) and are both cremated, it may be possible to place two sets of cremains into a standard size urn vault (again, depending on the urn sizes). Urn vaults usually are priced about the same as urns themselves, without any extra fees for shipping, handling, transportation, etc.

How To Save Money On Cremation

Simply by making the choice to be cremated, you can save a lot of money over traditional burial. "Depending upon the cost of the various factors relevant to cremation that have been discussed so far in this chapter will determine how much can actually be saved.

If you employ the same services leading up to the cremation that equals exactly the same as would take place before burial the amount of savings will obviously be less. Generally speaking, a nonprofit memorial society can arrange a cremation for less than a traditional funeral home. Purchasing a container on your own from a retail store that the cremains will fit in is less expensive than what some funeral homes will sell their urns for. Holding a memorial service or a visitation/reception saves money if it is held at a private home or other place without the direction or involvement of the funeral home. This makes sense if you are expecting a small gathering as opposed to a large crowd for a memorial service, in which case you will need someone with experience in charge to run things.

For the cremation itself, since most crematories accept any type of rigid combustible container for the deceased to be placed in for the cremation, you may be able to provide this yourself for much less than a funeral home or crematory would sell its minimum cremation container for. Find out what the crematory requires and go from there.

Preplanning/Prefunding Cremation

Making arrangements for a cremation before need can be one of the soundest decisions one can make because it takes the guesswork out of your survivors wondering what your wishes were after you are gone. Since cremation usually has more legal requirements and red tape involved in preparing for the cremation than for traditional burial or entombment, the effort to make your wishes known ahead of time can save others a lot of pain, hurt and heartache in cases where surviving family members are in disagreement about whether to cremate or bury.

Some steps that you may want to take in prearranging for cremation are: - Sign an Authorization for Cremation form and have witnessed and/or notarized according to legal requirements in your state or jurisdiction.

- Prepurchase for cremation arrangements with a funeral home or mortuary and file the contract with the provider, with your attorney and with a trusted family member or next of kin.

-State your directive for cremation and file it with or as a part of your will.

Prefunding a cremation just adds more icing to the cake in that cremation prices will continue to rise as will funeral expense costs. By creating, signing and funding (paying for) cremation prearrangements you give yourself simplicity, control and the satisfaction that what you want will be carried out unaffected by future price increases.

Prepaying your arrangement plans may also qualify for SSI/ Medicare asset exemption and allow you, as with funeral pre-arrangements, to payout the plans on the contract over time.

Memorial/Cremation Societies

With the many rapid changes taking place in the funeral/ cemetery/cremation/disposition industries today, with more and more information available, third party casket, monument and other sellers coming on the scene, the inquiry has been made about what is a memorial society, what is a cremation society, and are they the same thing?

Memorial societies and cremation societies are not one in the same and actually have some key fundamental distinctions from one another, which can best be discussed consecutively.

Memorial Societies

Memorial societies are nonprofit membership organizations that collect and distribute information about funerals and possibly assist people in making prearrangements. They may also monitor state and local laws pertaining to the funeral industry, do price surveys, educate the public about choices available and can also operate as a cooperative for its members by negotiating discounts with participating mortuaries.

Technically speaking, memorial societies are hard to classify; they are neither funeral homes nor cemeteries and do not actually render any goods or services other than disseminating information and assisting consumers. Generally they are not regulated and the relationship they have with local mortuaries could place them in the category of a brokering service.

Cremation Societies

Cremation societies are for-profit organizations that provide low-cost disposition of a body through cremation. They are also usually membership entities that charge their members a fee in being for-profit, but due to the way they are structured, have much lower prices.

Cremation societies do not have the investment in facilities, staff and overhead the way that most funeral homes and cemeteries do and they also work very hard at producing operating efficiencies in order to lower their costs as much as possible. They are regulated at various levels as discussed earlier in this chapter. Since a lot of states are in the process of initiating and implementing regulation systems over cremation, these rules will affect these societies for the years to come.

Do I Have To Go Through A Funeral Home To Do A Cremation?

As stated in the previous section, you may go to a cremation society instead of through a funeral home in some places if all you want is a basic cremation. Since the various states have different rules and laws you will need to check and see what the laws are in your state. You will also want to look around and contact various providers to see what they offer, at what price, and whether they are willing to be up-front and provide information you are asking for.

Since unfortunately there are unethical and unscrupulous operators out there, I would recommend contacting someone you can trust. Even if I was not a funeral director, I would still advise you to call a funeral home that has a good reputation and long- standing tradition of service in your community to handle cremation arrangements. The funeral director is there to help, give guidance, support and information on choices during a rather difficult time, as well as provide resources and assistance through necessary paperwork and procedures.

What you may save in monetary terms by going to a low cost provider without a proven track record may be sacrificed in other areas such as dignified and respectful/treatment, good rapport with other providers and with previously served consumers. Check out potential providers with an area memorial society, the better business bureau and any other entities that may provide referrals or advice.

Other Forms Of Disposition
(What's The Alternative)

So far in this book we have dealt with the traditional types of disposition, namely ground burial, entombment, and the growing choice of cremation.

Now I want to talk about forms of disposition that are either new, previously not practiced, virtually unheard of in mainstream society or in the process of evolving into methods of disposition for the future.

We live in a rapidly changing world. Technology, economics, the individual desire to be different, the development of new resources and the accessibility of the super information highway are just several of the factors that are making not only the way we live and our lives different, but also changing our deaths and our manner in dealing with such.

Immediate Burial
(What's The Hurry?)

Also known as immediate disposition or direct burial, immediate burial is the disposition of a decedent through ground burial usually within 24 hours of death. It is usually also characterized by no rites or ceremonies with the body present. Embalming is also usually not performed since there is no health reason to preserve the body from decomposition since burial is to take place so quickly.

Most of the time immediate burial is done for religious reasons where the belief system dictates that disposition must take place within a day of death, for health reasons where there is a highly contagious communicable disease involved and disposition must happen swiftly, or simply because it was the wish of the decedent as stated before death. There are also instances where a family may have no money and cannot afford to have a service or the charges of a funeral provider and must go a cheaper route.

Whatever the case may be, there are several things that you need to know about concerning immediate burial.

First is that immediate burial means immediate burial in that the funeral director will schedule a time and day with the cemetery to go out and do the burial and that time needs to be honored in that both the funeral director and the cemetery usually have a schedule to keep regarding their work for the day and when a direct burial is requested that means to go out to the cemetery, place the decedent into the grave and close it without fanfare. Sometimes the family will ask if they can be present at the burial, which is usually alright so long as those present stay a reasonable enough distance out so the cemetery staff who will have the job of closing the grave may work.

There are other times when a family may want to say a prayer share a few words or have some other short rite at the gravesite at the time of the burial. This is usually also okay so long as it is very, very brief. Anything that last a minute or less is usually okay with most funeral directors but anything more and you will probably need to have a graveside service. The difference between an immediate burial and a graveside service is almost the difference between night and day from a funeral director's and a cemetery's standpoints. There are many details to attend to any time there is a death and planning a direct burial to a funeral director means go to the cemetery at 10:00 am Monday, transfer custody of the deceased over to the cemetery and stay at the gravesite until the cemetery staff has lowered the casket down into the grave. The cemetery also sees immediate burial as the deceased will arrive at 10:00 am and be ready to bury upon arrival. And so everyone plans their schedule for the rest of the day accordingly. The cemetery staff will be at the site ready to take the deceased and bury upon arrival and having to wait upon unplanned rites or ceremony acts as an inconvenient disrespect of their time and work schedule, and rightly so if these were not the arrangements made.

With immediate burial you are still looking at incurring charges for the funeral director's basic surcharge, removal from place of death, refrigeration (in lieu of embalming), transportation to the place of burial, casket or burial container, an outer burial vault if desired or required, opening and closing of the grave. This does not include other optional items such as newspaper notices, death certificates, flowers to place on the grave afterwards, or a marker for the grave space. Depending on the funeral home and cemetery at issue, there may be a charge for placing the decedent into the burial casket or container, a vault installation fee and a witnessing the burial charge. As with anything else, check or ask if unsure.

Many times unless there are health hazards involving airborne pathogens, a family may want to view the decedent before leaving the funeral home to go to burial. This can usually be arranged but again there may be a charge for viewing (use of state or viewing room) and/may require signing an authorization form for minimal preparation of the decedent which may include bathing and closing eyes and mouth if needed. In this case there may be a charge as well as an authorization to sign. No matter how direct or immediate you may wish disposition to be, there will still be decisions to make and issues to encounter.

Donations To Medical Science
(It Is More Blessed To Give)

Medical and dental educational institutions throughout the continent need bodies for teaching and research purposes. Since it is possible to store bodies for a specified time period, most medical science entities are willing to consider applications for body donations.

If you wish to donate your body to medial science after death, it is important to contact the institution for which your bequeathal is intended to ascertain what the terms and conditions for accepting a body are. Since not all body donations are accepted- and acceptance or rejection of a donated body is usually decided by the medical school at the time of death- an alternative plan such as burial or cremation should be in place.

Some entities may refuse bodies that have major organs or limbs missing, that have been autopsied or mutilated or that do not fit within a predetermined age and/or weight and height range.

If body donation is your choice of disposition, you may still have a funeral service with a viewing and visitation in most cases. You will need your funeral director to contact the school you are choosing to donate to for any special instructions regarding embalming and preparation procedures.

In the case of no funeral or viewing with the body present, the deceased may be transported immediately to the medical school. Some institutions will pay this cost and some will not. Most pay for the transport within a certain distance.

Many funeral homes are willing to work with medical and dental schools and are able to assist families with body donations. Both the funeral home and medical facility are aware of the psychological benefits of a funeral or a memorial service to the family and will make every effort to accommodate and help the survivors.

Since there can be various factors involved in a death such as time, place, and cause, etc., a funeral director's services will usually be needed in connection to death certificate filing, meeting legal or other requirements, transportation, and death or obituary notices.

As for planning purposes, it is important to make your wishes known, preferably in writing to your family, to the designated donee school and to your attorney, executor or other trustee so at the time of death there will be no question of your intent.

Donations are beneficial in the continuing progress of medical science and donors can take a great deal of comfort in the idea that they are contributing to the future of that progress after their earthly life has ended.

Organ/Tissue Donation

If the idea of donating your entire body to medical science and research doesn't interest you, another contribution you can make to humankind after death is the bequeathal of organs, tissues, bones or other useful parts.

We have experienced great advancements in transplant operations in the past quarter century and many people donate

predesignated parts or any organs that would benefit any potential donee. Some parts that are in great demand include but are not limited to the following:

Heart	Pancreas	Blood Vessels
Lungs	Eyes	Livers
Kidneys	Skin	Bones

The procedures and details of harvesting these parts can vary. If a person is to donate an organ for example, his or her body is put on a respirator so that oxygen can be pumped into the organs until an operation is performed to remove the organ(s) sought so it can be rushed to the recipient's hospital for transplant. As a general rule, the younger the donor the better the chances are of acceptance of parts. Medical personnel desire organs that have the best chance of functioning for at least several decades, if not longer. If you are 85 for example, the organ(s) you wish to donate may not be useful in say a 40 year old. The option of donation is provided to families as they begin to make end-of-life decisions for their loved one[3].

Once the decision is made to donate, normally the recovery of parts is a surgical procedure that normally takes place in a hospital operating room. The process may take 10-30 hours and consists of the agency that handles the donation procurement determining what organs and parts can be transplanted, finding recipients and carrying out the harvesting, carefully handling encasement of and transport of the parts/organs to the recipient destination, and coordinating all the resources involved in making the donation a success.

Here are some things you should know about organ donation, as provided by the United Network for Organ Sharing:

* Organ Donation is consistent with most religious beliefs.

* There is usually no cost to the family nor is there any payment made for the donation.

* Organ Donation does not affect or delay customary funeral arrangements and usually should not disqualify the desire for an open casket funeral or viewing.

* Medical expenses prior to the donation and funeral expenses afterwards remain the responsibility of the donor's family.

* Most organs and tissues can be stored for a limited period of time and can be transported to any location where needed.

* Patients awaiting a transplant are registered on a national computerized system. Organs and tissues are shared by centers across the world and when donated, this system helps distribute them where they are most needed.

* One donor can help many recipients through the gift of different organs and tissues.

* It is not necessary to mention organ donation in your will.

* Individuals under the age of 18 may sign a donor card with the consent of a parent or legal guardian.

* There is most likely a hospital or community or area doing transplants. Any questions you may have can usually be answered by contacting the hospital and asking for your local donor program.

It is very important to discuss your desire to be a donor after your death with members of your family and although every state has laws making the unselfish act of organ and tissue donation a simple legal matter, consent from your legal next-of-kin will still need to be obtained at the time of death despite the fact that you have given permission to and have signed a donor card and/or designated yourself on your drivers license as a donor.

Regardless of age or medical history, everyone should consider themselves a potential candidate for some type of donation.

Although not everyone will be able to donate all parts upon death the fact that each year the list of those waiting for transplants increases provides amble incentive to consider donation (less than half of those waiting will ever be transplanted).

Even if you chose to not be a donor, the issue that goes along with deciding to not be a donor yourself and your family's future decision to ratify that choice to not donate organs/tissues/parts, comes the possibility of you being asked to decide for someone in your family who has died. This can be a difficult decision, but donating organs provides great consolation and comfort for those who say yes. The future of transplantation depends upon the freewill support of people like you.

DNA Storage
(The New Frontier)

DNA is short for deoxyribonucleic acid, which is the genetic material that determines a person's features such as blood type, sex, and eye color. Each person's DNA has a unique order that contains 40,000 genes.

As scientific researchers learn more information about genetics and how they work, documenting one's genetic makeup is becoming more and more important. By retrieving one's DNA, various types of objectives may be met including documenting genetic ancestry, helping predict risks of specific diseases, assisting genealogy and providing insight in deciding lifestyle and medical issues, among others. Since many of us are proud of our heritage and ancestry, learning more about each family member's unique personal story written in the DNA code may only make sense.

Some funeral homes and mortuaries now offer a DNA retrieval and storage program. Once a body is buried it is very difficult to retrieve DNA, and impossible once cremation takes place. If cremation is being considered as an option, it is critical to make a decision about DNA before scheduling the cremation since there will be no second chance.

DNA is collected by retrieving cells from the body that contain DNA. They are then treated with proteins and fragments are produced at varying lengths. These fragments can produce a visible pattern called the DNA fingerprint. These fingerprints or profiles are processed and stored at a DNA laboratory and can be kept for about 25 years.

Confidentiality is often a key factor regarding DNA banking, with profiles kept strictly confidential with accessibility authorized only by legal next-of-kin or other appointed family members. Genetic and tissue information can be set up where data about stored DNA only being able to be released to other parties with the express written consent of the donor or donor's designated legal appointee.

Whether DNA retrieval and storage is something that you should consider for you or a family member will depend on different variables. Some of the questions that you will want to answer will include where DNA will be retrieved, the time factor of retrieval taking funeral ceremonies/rites and form of disposition into account where it will be stored (what lab or DNA bank) and what the cost will be and who will be responsible for the payment. Contact your local funeral home, memorial society or DNA Connections on the Internet at www.dnaconnections.com[4].

MUMMIFICATION
(Reinventing The Wheel)

The arrival of the new millennium has now brought us a union between ancient history and modern technology through the process of mummification.

What we all spent time in world history class in school learning about the Egyptians of centuries ago, preserving their dead through very elaborate and detailed preparations of corpses is now available to us again today as a viable form of disposition.

Available as of this writing through Summum Mummifications and Mummiforms in Salt Lake City, Utah, a deceased body may be mummified through a process that will allow for the indefinite preservation of the body that will also allow a longer term preserving of the DNA within the mummified remains. It also offers an alternative to the more traditional forms of disposition that gives distinction, class and an increased cultural standard regarding disposition.

This ancient practice has been updated and modernized to

mummify those among us today who chose long-term preservation as the ruling classes did in the days of King Tut. Already used on the deceased animals of former pet owners who wanted to preserve their remains, Summum has organized a way for arranging the mummification of human remains as well.

The mummification process basically works as follows:

After the body of the deceased is transported to a funeral home in traditional fashion, it is prepared for any viewing and/or services. Following these services, the body will be transported to the chosen mummification facility (currently only Summum in Salt Lake City).

The body will go through the mummification process by licensed Thanatogeneticists which will consist of the removal, cleansing and replacement of internal organs, immersion into a preservative liquid solution, removal after enough time allows for maximum penetration, cleansing again, covered with a lotion, wrapped in cotton gauze and a permanent seal of polyurethane membrane applied.

Then the body is to be wrapped in a layer of fiberglass and resin, and then encased in a standard casket or mummiform (or art form casket), filled with amber resin to completely surround the deceased (mummy), and the openings in the mummiform are welded shut.

The mummy is then to be transported to the designated cemetery or memorial park for mausoleum placement or ground interment.

A minimum of 30 days or more will be required for the entire process due to the thorough nature of the transformation that will last permanently. Because mummification can be started after a funeral or visitation rite and/or ceremony, mummifying a decedent does not represent a break from current tradition but can rather complement it.

Along with the service of procuring mummification, the "mummiform" is a specialized container provided by Summum made of metals ranging from bronze to gold and also contain the option of inlaid precious gem or jeweled crests. They are also made to represent various belief systems such as Christian, Jewish, Buddhist, Moslem, or others according to your own choosing.

In order to carry out mummification for yourself or in helping another who chooses to be mummified, these services will need to be recorded in you last will and Testament, and a signed Power of Attorney. A body release form will also need to be signed by your legal next-of-kin and copies distributed among the mummification company, your family and your attorney who you will want to consult with regarding any other legal requirements that may need to be met concerning the procurement of the mummification after you pass away, according to your wishes.

You may contact your local funeral home concerning all of the costs in connection to mummification. Most persons arranging for mummification purchase a life insurance policy naming the mummification company as owner and beneficiary of the policy. You may be able to deduct the premiums you pay on the policy from your taxable income since the IRS has issued a revenue ruling currently declaring mummification tax-deductible so long as the payments are treated as a charitable donation. This can be accomplished through preplanning your mummification through a nonprofit organization as designated by the IRS. Making your donation through the life insurance policy makes paying for these arrangements more affordable.

Whether your desire is to do something completely untraditional or to be preserved in as natural a state as possible after death, mummification may be the answer to being held in the highest esteem possible by society after dieing, and achieving eternal memorialization for centuries to come.

Burial At Sea
(At The Waters Edge)

Humankind, it seems, has always had an awe and fascination for the oceans. Whether it is the desire to sail and travel the world by ship or simply sit on the sandy beaches to watch the waves roll in, there is a certain attraction we have and endure to the seas.

Although nothing new as a form of disposition, burial at sea is an idea worth considering for those who have a lifelong love for the ocean. Various funeral homes and mortuaries offer this service in association with charter boat companies for families who wish to bury their loved one at sea whether it be the Atlantic or Pacific oceans, the Gulf of Mexico or other ocean.

A funeral or other ceremony or ritual may be held traditionally at a funeral home chapel or church and then arrangements made for transportation to the boat launch site, or the ceremony held on the chartered boat itself with the burial launch as one of the final act{s) of the ceremony.

Embalming is usually required by the boat company for burial at sea, and the decedent's body placed in a standard casket or wooden box which will be properly weighted so it will sink. Coast Guard regulations dictate that burial at sea be done at a distance of at least 60 miles out at sea and in water at least 600 feet deep.

Cremated remains may also be placed for sea burial or scattering with the rules somewhat different depending on the governing jurisdiction of the waters in which the cremains are to be dropped.

Costs for body burial at sea only, excluding other charges not related to the sea burial range from $2500-5000. Whether you want burial at sea or cremains buried or scattered at sea, consult with a local funeral home, the port or maritime authority or Coast Guard concerning all requirements.

Body Dissolution
(Now You See It, Now You Don't)

A new process developed by scientists with the help of professor Gordon Kaye of the Albany Medical College, has devised a method to dispose of the human body- by dissolving it!

According to professor Kaye, dissolving a deceased human body is the most environmentally friendly way of final disposition of human remains.

The process utilizes chemicals in an alkaline hydrolysis to break down the remains through high temperature, pressure, sodium or potassium hydroxide to chemically change the remains into a liquid. This process can also sterilize any bacteria or disease that may have been present in the body, according to Minnesota law that, along with Florida and Michigan are the first states to permit this process.

The first initial drawback of this method of disposition is the cost. The machine that can perform dissolution is well over $185,000, which presently makes it too difficult for most funeral homes to consider offering to the public[5].

What Is Cryonics?
(For Crying Out Loud)

Brought into the national spotlight by the death and subsequent cryopreservation of baseball legend Ted Williams in the summer if 2002, cryonics is a growing industry in which a deceased human body can be indefinitely preserved by a company that offers such service.

The idea is to freeze corpses that one day can be thawed out and with the assistance of technology yet unknown be awakened from death. With many deaths attributed to causes that today have no known cure, the theme underlying cryonics is that someday when a cure is found, that cure can be applied to those bodies that are cryopreserved awaiting a remedy that caused the death.

Although there is nothing in science presently to suggest this to be possible, cryonics is a on an upswing. Currently there are several thousand people who have signed up for the process with various companies that offer cryonics.

The way it works is that shortly after death, the decedent's body is packed in ice and immediately transported to a facility that is equipped for the procedure. Blood is then removed from the body and replaced with a glyceria contained liquid. The body is simultaneously cooled with ice, cold air or dry ice.

The body is then placed into a container and floated in incredibly cold liquid nitrogen for as many years as necessary until medical science finds a cure to apply to the decedent's cause of death.

Most of those who have signed up for cryonic storage do so by taking out a life insurance policy naming the cryonics provider as beneficiary and designated the policy amount enough to cover the expenses of cryopreservation. It is unclear what the fees are of cryonic disposition. Some reports say that one can sign up for as little as $1,200 while others say $25,000-150,000 as the price range, depending on what company you sign up with.

Is Cryonics Something I Should Consider?

For those who would give cryonics serious consideration, the factors you will need to think about and resolve include finding a cryonics provider to designate as your body's recipient after death, executing a written agreement with the provider, funding the agreement through life insurance or other means, and consulting with an attorney so that there is a clearly expressed legal understanding that cryonics is what you want done with your body after death, avoiding the terribly unpleasant situation that resulted from the Ted Williams case.

Since you will in most cases need the services of a funeral home when you pass away to remove your body from the place of death to the funeral home where arrangements will be coordinated to have your remains prepared for transport to the cryonics provider's facility, it will be wise to notify the funeral home you want to handle the removal so that they will know your wishes and plan accordingly (few funeral homes or mortuaries to date have ever handled a cryonics case).

WHAT THE FUTURE MAY HOLD:
Outer Space Suspension?

Earlier in this chapter I briefly discussed the future is now idea of cremated remains being propelled into space for eternal orbit.

Well with the advent of DNA storage, cryonics and modernized mummification, can suspension of a deceased human remains be far behind? Technology and research are changing every facet of our society almost daily. It only takes staying up-to-date on current events to realize that what was unthinkable yesterday is reality today.

The idea of placing the remains of a loved one upon a special mission spaceship for the purpose of flying outside the earth's gravitational belt to place a casketed decedent into orbit for eternity does seem farfetched (no pun intended), but only time can tell! Twenty years ago who would have thought cremated remains could be sent into space; can full body disposition really be that far behind?

IN CONCLUSION
Explaining Cremation And Alternative Disposition To Children

Cremation and the other forms of disposition we have discussed can be difficult when taking the absence of traditional forms of disposition into account. This is true of everyone, but especially children.

Children are a unique and important group of family members in that they are very impressionable. It is imperative that their experience with the loss of someone they knew be as positive and as healing as possible.

Several points to take into consideration with youngsters when a deceased loved one is cremated or otherwise not buried or entombed:

1. Children can cope with what they know. They cannot cope with what is kept from them.

2. Children are literal and concrete, not abstract. Use simple visual type language with them.

3. Be brief and follow the child's lead in answering his or her questions.

4. Whatever information you need and your adult family members choose to share with the child, be sure to use words they will understand.

Helping your children through a difficult loss will be important as they develop into adults. More about helping kids in chapter 7 about grief and mourning.

Chapter 4

Personalization & Practical Ideas For Memorialization

1. Introduction
2. What Is Personalization/Memorialization
3. How To Personalize A Funeral Or Memorial Service
4. Using Technology
5. Using Symbols And Articles
6. Eulogies And Readings
7. Funeral Celebrants
8. Funeral Facilitators
9. Including Friends And Relatives
10. Including Children
11. To Ritualize Or Deritualize
12. Memorializing One Whose Remains Are Not Present
13. Memorializing One Whose Remains Have Not Been Recovered
14. Memorializing One Declared/Presumed Dead
15. What If I Don't Want A Funeral Or Memorial Service
16. How To Personalize A Visitation Or Wake
17. Other Types Of Ceremonies And Rituals
18. Receptions And Reunions
19. Holding Anniversary Rituals
20. Commemoration Rituals
21. Chapter 4 Summary
22. 100 Practical Ideas

One of the many ways our society at large has battled and overcome the monotony and predictability of certain ritualistic practices (including the perception of funerals) is to personalize certain events. Whereas in previous days you could attend a wedding, funeral, church worship service or other event or ceremony and know ahead of time what the event would and would not include. That day is passing.

Today our culture cries out for personalization, unpredictability (within parameters) and something different. People want their rituals to be special in a deeply personal way and funerals are no exception.

Contained in the paragraphs and pages ahead is a look at personalizing funerals and the passing of a loved one in unique fashion. Memorializing someone now gone will also be put under the microscope and discussed within the text of finding ways to remember someone that fits that someone only.

What Is Personalization/Memorialization ?
(Honoring A Loved One's Memory)

When we talk about personalization we are really defining the individual. Who was this person who has passed from amongst us? What were their likes, their dislikes, their hobbies and interests, their career(s) and activities?

Was the decedent a people person or more of a loner? Did they spend a lot of time talking about their family and growing up years? What was their favorite color, favorite song, favorite place to go or visit? Asking and answering basic questions such as these starts the personalization process. It is thinking about, deciding on and putting together a tangible history of sorts on a person's life.

Memorialization has been discussed in chapter 2 in the context of cemeteries and places of disposition from the standpoint of monuments and markers as permanent fixtures to serve as a continuing memorial to that person's life.

The memorialization that we are talking about here refers to the action (verb) of providing a program or ritual of tribute to the decedent which can be quite broad in definition depending on how you want to go about memorializing the person in the funeral, memorial service, visitation, etc.

In essence, personalization is the act (how) of gearing an event, place or thing in such a way as to fit the specific individual, and memorialization is the objective (what) or goal of what is to be attained.

How To Personalize A Funeral Or Memorial Service
(Cookie Cutter Or Outside The Box)

Funeral service today is going through a radical change-a change from the traditions and rituals of the past into innovation, uniqueness and creativity. Although personalization is the current buzzword within the funeral industry, different funeral homes and directors are at varying levels in connection to fostering and facilitating the changes that consumers want regarding personalized funerals or other services. Regardless of what firm or funeral director you select when your time of need comes, my goal in this chapter is to help you to understand the concept and the possibilities that exist to plan a service that will be meaningful and create a lasting memory.

In talking about the "how to " of personalizing the rituals of a loved one's passing, the process starts by asking and answering some simple questions:

Who was this person?
What did they do?
How did they relax?
What did they like?
What was the person's favorite:
- Animal
- Book
- Color/Charity/Cause

Event
Flower/Memento
Food
Hobby
Holiday
Job
Movie
Picture
Scripture
Song
Souvenir
Sport
Story
TV Show

What was the person's:

Best Moment?
Highest Achievement?
Greatest Accomplishment?
Most Memorable Experience?

Once you get started thinking a little deeper on these questions and their answers, you will begin to develop and determine how you want the person remembered at the service you want to personalize.

No matter how simple or elaborate you plan to go with it, here is a basic outline I've devised that you may want to follow:

#1 Decide what type of service you want

#2 Identify what you want to include as a part of the service

#3 Gather the things/resources you want as part of the service

#4 Organize these resources in a way that will make the ritual a success.

#5 Implement the ideas/resources into the service.

#1 The Type Of Service

This can be created by deciding where and when you want to gather to hold the service.

Chapter 8 of this book will deal with the role that tradition plays if you want to hold the service at a church that is structured in what is or isn't allowed as part of its doctrinal beliefs surrounding funeral rituals.

You will need to therefore consult with the church or a funeral director to determine what's permissible with the church you are considering holding services at.

Do you want a funeral (deceased in casket present) or a memorial service (deceased casketed remains not present)?

Do you prefer an open or closed casket? Is the service going to celebrate the life of one who went the full trajectory or one tragically cut short?

Do you expect a large (150 or more) or small attendance (50 or less)?

How much time will you have for the service? If the ceremony is at a funeral home or church do they have other services or activities planned later the same day?

There are a lot of factors to consider and think about. The end of this chapter will provide a summary of how to best decide what you want the service to be.

#2 What To Include In The Service

A good way to think about what the service should consist of is to ask: How would this person want to be memorialized, or, what would he/she want to happen as the social event marking the end of his/her life? If you are preplanning of course it would be how do I want to be memorialized/remembered at my funeral/memorial service?

Is a eulogy or obituary reading by a minister appropriate? Should there be one song or three or four? If so what type religious or secular? Should there be a slot of time made available for those in attendance to share stories or memories? Do

I want to display pictures or belongings of the person at the service to make it more special?

#3 Gather What's To Be Part Of The Service

Whether it is old photographs, handwritten letters, mementos, CDs or other items that are to be used in some way in the ceremony, getting things together can take longer than expected- especially if it requires a trip across town or even out of town and back. Gathering items of significance can also open the door to adding more things to be a part of the service.

An example of this was one time when a lady's elderly father had died and she found an article that had been written about her father years before about his military service- she then remembered that there were two other writings about his service experience and wanted to display them as a set however she wasn't sure the location of the other written pieces in all the boxes that were in storage. To say the least, it took her several previously unplanned hours to locate the writings in time to carry the idea through for the service.

Order of Service

Traditional Example:

1. Song- *Rock of Ages*
2. Opening Remarks/Prayer
3. Obituary
4. Song- *Amazing Grace*
5. Message- Church Pastor
6. End with Prayer & Song- Beyond The Sunset

Contemporary/Personalized Example:

1. Play Deceased Favorite Song
2. Lighting of Candle(s)
3. Obituary/ Moment of Silent Reflection
4. Video Presentation with Song
5. Eulogy
6. Closing Song

#4 Organize The Resources For Success

Success meaning that the service will accomplish what you wish for it to. That the things, items, and other contributing factor will produce a service that will be memorable for attendees and memorialize the decedent as the unique individual that he or she was.

Considerations to think about here would be the order of service that serves as an outline for what's to happen when.

Should the service open with the family being formally seated by the funeral director? What is best to start, with introductory remarks by the minister or officiant, or with a special song played?

Does the eulogy have to go before a prayer or after? Would it make a big difference in reference to what else will happen during the ceremony?

Try to think through the ceremony and piece together the various parts and inclusions. If I have a painting or picture of the deceased, should I display it at the front of the sanctuary for the service or in the foyer when people first arrive?

Your funeral director can be a valuable resource in providing guidance in these areas.

#5 Implement Into The Service

Your minister or service officiant can take care of conducting the ceremony from beginning to end following the Order of Service.

The funeral director's job will be to set up the facility according to your desires, arrange flowers, pass out programs, seat guests, answer questions by attendees and be sure that musicians, readers, other speakers, etc., know what's to happen when by getting the Order of Service to all those who will be taking part. In other words, the carry through and carry out of what you've decided on, identified, gathered and organized will hinge on communicating with the service officiant and funeral director what's to take place, when how and where. It is their job, what they have been trained to do to implement for the desired personalized, memorial tribute you wish. The end of this chapter will list 100 practical ideas of ways to personalize services.

Using Technology
(Its Showtime)

Virtually every area of our world today is affected by the continuing upgrades in technology- the funeral service is no exception.

In the past two decades, use of various forms of electronic media to print, capture, record, play and produce have propelled the possibilities of personalizing funeral and memorial goods and services to new heights.

Here I want to talk about what is available through the existing technological avenues by placing the differing modes into three general categories: audio, computerization, visual

Audio

Cassette Tapes (Is it Live or Is It Recorded?)

Cassette tapes are one way to make services more personal whether to play special songs or meaningful background music. Audio dialogues or monologues also add a touch of personalization that can be very helpful.

Recording the funeral onto a cassette tape is a service that more and more funeral homes are offering either at a nominal fee or on a complimentary basis. If the funeral home does not have a cassette player or recording equipment ask if you may bring one in for either purpose.

Compact Discs

Compact Discs or CDs serve the same purpose as cassettes. Some people like to bring a decedent's favorite songs or music to play at the service, which can be played at the funeral homes that have CD players. Some funeral homes have a collection of CDs that they have purchased or leased for the purpose of having songs available to families that may want particular music that the family itself does not have a copy of.

It may also be possible to download a particular song off the internet onto a blank CD through the computer's disk drive if the computer has the capacity. With CD-ROM, computers can play compact discs on the hard drive and also can read CDs that are recorded on from other sources.

Cassette tape recordings that are converted over to CDs provides a way to produce an avenue for playing recordings on CD if that is the only means that one has for listening.

Computerization

Getting Connected

Nothing has brought people together without physical presence quite like the computer. The amazing revolution that has taken place the last 10-15 years continues to evolve with new and/or improved attachments, accessories, innovations, etc., whether hardware or software. Funeral service has been impacted in a very positive way by computerization from the customer service standpoint of retrieving and transforming information into data that can produce more personalized meaningful services.

Electronic Mail

Electronic messaging, or email, is one of the most common forms of communication today both for businesses, households, and individuals. Email can be used to send and retrieve all types of data, anything that can be captured imprinted and sent.

Email can readily be used in obtaining factual information used for obituaries and death notices, printed media such as songs, poems, charitable donation addresses and relevant data that can be used to move information very quickly for inclusion in personalization efforts.

The Internet

The Internet is now being used by some funeral providers as a way of making available to consumers an avenue for publishing obituaries, memorial tributes and even electronic guest register books for those unable to attend services. There is a variety of new companies that have partnered with mortuaries for the purpose of collecting, posting, sharing and maintaining life stories on the Internet.

Different packages offer varying levels of service from simple one-paragraph death notices to conglomerations of content that can include thousands of words, pictures and documents.

Printers

Printers are of course the computer compliments that make getting what's on the terminal screen onto paper. The computer would not be nearly as effective without the attached printer.

Since personalized cards, folders, obituaries and other information can be processed through computers, it is the printer that can output the poem, tribute, write up or other printable image for sundry purposes.

Scanners

Scanners are the hardware attachments to computers that can digitally convert a photograph placed on the scanner's glass into images that are then electronically transformed and then printed in the same form as what's on the picture.

These devices are commonly used to send photographs from the funeral home to a newspaper that has Email capacity for publication with the written text of an obituary. Scanners can also be used to imprint photos onto program or service bulletin handouts for the funeral or memorial service.

Visual

A Picture Is Worth A Thousand Words

Being able to see what is discussed, described or talked about aids any type of process and memorialization is no exception.

Camcorders

Camcorders are normally thought of in relation to special happy events such as birthdays, anniversaries, weddings and reunions, but now the funeral is also included.

Since there are usually those who cannot attend the funeral and/or visitation, camcorders can capture the event and allow those not present to later experience the ceremony second hand.

Cameras

Cameras have long been a useful tool in visually recording the event(s) on film for later viewing and reflection. Although cameras have long been a phenomenon on the societal frontier, there have been a good number of regretful families who later said they wished they had brought a camera (forgetfulness or overlooked details are a common symptom of grief).

The idea worth mentioning here along with film developing, instant production and disposable cameras is the digital camera that saves a picture taken as an electronic image rather than on film. This electronic image can then be transferred to a computer and viewed on screen.

Closed Circuit Television

If the service is being held at the funeral home or at a church and there is an overflow crowd expected, the facility may possess closed circuit TV capacity. Some larger churches and funeral homes may have an adjacent room with chairs and a large screen or TV monitor that can be used to view the service if there is not enough room to seat everyone in the chapel or sanctuary.

You may ask if the place where the funeral is held has closed circuit TV if it will help you feel better about those attending the service that may not be able to get seated in the auditorium or chapel.

DVD

DVD, which stands for Digital Video Disk, is a way to place pictures and music together on a special DVD player. Some funeral homes are requesting their client families to bring in photos, which the funeral director can then use to produce a special DVD tribute to the decedent that can be played as part of services.

Since this is still a relatively new area, there is as of this writing, a number of funeral homes that have not delved into this area. If you have services at a mortuary that does not yet produce DVD memorial tributes, you may be able to do your own with the proper equipment needed. A video or audio/visual company in your area may be able to provide some guidance in this area and can usually be found in the yellow pages of the phone book under video/visual.

Fax Machines

Facsimile or fax machines are, like cameras, no stranger to today's mainstream public. However use of facsimile technology in the transference of ideas and information concerning personalized funerals is still lagging among much of the public.

Faxing information for use in funerals and memorial services is the best option for those without Internet access.

Montages

Montages are photo images produced by combining parts of different pictures through superimposition. Photomontages add a definite flair of personalization to any type of service or ceremony and have not been widely used to date as part of funerals.

Photomontages can be done best by someone who has the

technical know how. Usually a video production service company will be able to do this for you. Whether or not it can be done in a timely and economical fashion will vary.

Photographs

Photographs are widely used in funeral service for some aspect of the funeralization process. What generally is not known are the many options that are available in using photos. One way that we encourage families at our firm to make the service more personalized is through the use of a magnetic board that sits on an easel stand. The board can hold as many as fifty 3 X 5 snapshots. The response to displaying the picture board at services has been overwhelmingly favorable.

Slides

The showing of slides as part of the funeral/memorial service is another way to personalize. Nothing better tells the story of a life lived than through use of the slide show. Most funeral

Paying Tribute to a Life Lived

People today want value for dollars spent. Funeral service is no exception to this, and more and more funeral providers today are responding by offering various types of options that provide some type of electronic presentation or tribute.

Using old photographs, video footage, and other visual items, a customized production can be made, usually with the accompaniment of music, narration and taped eulogies or interviews. Usually the electronic tribute lasts from 3-10 minutes and is implemented along with the other parts of a traditional funeral or memorial service.

Talk to your funeral professional about any packages offered by the funeral home, or if your family wants to put together their own, ask if the funeral home (place of service) has the capacity and/or resources to facilitate an electronic presentation.

chapels are conducive to the required projector screen and electrical cords and lighting needed.

Video Collages

The video collage is much like the use of slides. A collage is a work of art made by pasting various materials onto a single (video) surface. Instead of showing slides during a service, a video collage is a way to do a picture tribute using photographs.

Video Tape

Another option for the wide screen at a service would be the videotape. If there are any videos that have been taken in the past that includes the decedent being featured, transposing the VCR tape is a great way to pay homage to the one whose memory is being honored.

Since this idea is using something that already exists (the video tape), the challenge here is to arrange the set up and play of the tape at the service.

Video Conferencing

Video Conferencing is the process of using a camera and microphone to capture (videotape) a subject and use it to interact live with another party through a computer terminal. Through use of video conferencing, it is possible to transmit the funeral ceremony live in progress to a viewer(s) through a computer. This concept is like watching TV on the computer and is already in use primarily for news and information broadcasts, and by large businesses to transmit business meetings to colleagues at other physical locations.

Using Symbols And Articles
(Hearts And Flowers)

One of the most tangible and colorful ways to make services more individualized and meaningful is through the use of symbols and articles.

Symbols allow us to express ideas and emotions for which words are inadequate. They can help convey the message of respect, honor and love.

Articles are items that belonged to the decedent that he or she may have identified with through work, school, hobby, leisure time, home life, or whatever, that distinctly tells a story or characteristic about one's life.

If the decedent at one time in his or her life was part of a basketball team, for example, and that was an important and fulfilling event in his or her life, the family may want to bring a basketball or a jersey worn to display at the service.

For another, if sewing was a lifelong pastime with many joys and good times, bringing some of the garments made to layout at the service may be a good way to personalize the service.

To give you a general idea of how to think about the value of symbolism and articles as part of a service, I've listed some common basics of both types to consider as a starting point:

<u>Symbols</u>

Christian:

- The Cross- Crucifixion of Christ
- Lamb of God- Jesus's innocence
- Triangle- The Holy Trinity

Event, Career, Family:

- Muscled Worker with Hammer- Organized Labor
- Multi-Colored Wreath- Eastern star
- Letter G with Drafting Tools- Masonic Lodge

Flowers, Fruits, Plants:

- Lily- Resurrection
- Daisy- Innocence
- Rose- Eternal Love
- Tulip- Charity

Jewish:
- Menorah- Seven Days of Creation
- Star of David- Divine Protection

Miscellaneous:
- Anchor- Maritime
- Harp- Music
- Rainbow- Promise
- Scroll- Literature

<u>Articles</u>

Bible	Books
Candles	Certificates
Clothing	Degrees/Diplomas
Eating/Drinking Items	Letters
Medals	Newspaper
Sporting Equipment	Wall Hangings

Many times the funeral director can help make suggestions about obtaining and displaying symbols whether it is setting a metal crucifix up or placing a Masonic easel next to the casket.

Articles can be gathered from the decedent's personal belongings and many times can be placed around or in an open casket. This often creates more meaning and helps tell the story of the decedent's tastes, likes, faith, beliefs and history.

For those times when words alone cannot communicate the entirety of a life lived, using symbols and articles go a long way in helping.

Eulogies And Readings
(It's Story time)

As the funeral or memorial service usually consists of at least several parts, the eulogy is an opportunity to add a material touch of personalization to the ceremony.

In essence, a eulogy is a period of simply remembering and talking about the unique life that the decedent had lived and thereby paying tribute to that person's life. It is an opportunity to say good things about the person being eulogized.

The eulogy may be delivered by a friend, family member or clergy person, who is called the eulogist. There can also be a participant oriented eulogy where the service officiant may ask anyone who wishes, to come and share memories and stories about the decedent's life.

In other words, the eulogy may be very structured with a single eulogist who may spend much time planning, rehearsing and outlining the eulogy or very impromptu. Either way the key goal to remember is that the eulogy is a chance to tell about the uniqueness and individuality of the one whose memory is being honored.

Readings are also apart of the speaking portion of the service that typically includes at least one of the following:

The Obituary
Scripture or Poem
A letter or Script
Favorite Quote

Appropriate readings add a spark of personalization to the event in that they can help capture the personality and character of the person who has died.

Readings may be given by the officiant or main speaker at a funeral or memorial service or by different individuals with each reading a different one.

It is also possible to chose a reading such as the 23rd Psalm out of the Bible for example and make copies of the Psalm to pass out to attendees and then as a congregation recite it together. The reading may also be printed in the bulletin for those who may not want to read to help them feel included.

Funeral Celebrants
(One, Two, Three)

In recent decades our society has become more secularized and pluralistic. In any given community today, less than half of the families are active in any church. We are less religious and hold fewer ties to structured religion or religious entities.

A celebrant is someone who is trained and equipped to meet the needs of people during their time of loss by providing a funeral service or tribute that reflects the deceased.

Some funeral homes are responding to sociological changes by having someone on staff or available to help serve families who do not wish to use a clergy member.

A celebrant can help and work with you to personalize a funeral or memorial service that is directly tailored toward the personality and unique life of the individual who has passed.

Celebrants can help grieving families in their time of need regardless of religious or nonreligious ties since some religious families may opt for a service at the funeral home, graveside or other place that is less structured than what a service at their church may allow.

Celebrants can also be trusted to hear and discuss any ideas you may have for a service that may seem eccentric and that you may feel uncomfortable talking about to a funeral director or clergy person.

Funeral Facilitators
(Order Out Of Chaos)

Since the mortuary and memorialization industry is going through a revolution so to speak from old to new, traditional to less traditional, religious based to more secularized and structured to less formal, the term funeral facilitator is still not completely and officially defined.

There are some in this profession who are replacing the

word officiant with facilitator because the former is usually a clergy person.

In this book I would like to refer to a funeral facilitator as one who provides the avenue in which a personalized ceremony can take place. There are several parties that would fit this bill including but not limited to the funeral director, funeral home, church, cemetery, clergy, officiant, etc.

Facilitating the service can also include one who provides an alternative place to have the ceremony such as a private residence, a commercial business establishment, or other place that may aid and abed the personalization of the service.

One example that comes to mind of a funeral facilitator is a gentleman who was a manager of a private club in the community whose longtime friend- a member at his club, died. The deceased friend had been a loyal patron for many years and spent lots of time at the club with other club members.

The club manager offered use of the club for a memorial service and the decedent's family thought it was a great idea. In this instance the club manager is the facilitator. In other circumstances it may be a neighbor, friend, relative, former teacher, student, employee, employer, whoever.

Although the funeral facilitator does not have to play a huge role in the memorialization process, their contribution can be a vital link in their supporting capacity.

Including Friends And Relatives
(The Big Tent Theory)

There are many ways to be inclusive in connection to funerals and memorial services. Whether it's acting as an active or honorary pallbearer, sharing a song or poem or giving a eulogy, it is important to include others that may not be part of the immediate family for several reasons.

One is that friends and relatives can be affected by the loss as much as an immediate family member and have the same need to grieve and be given a channel to work through their grief.

Another reason is that there are many things that need and can be done to be a part of the funeralization process.

We all have certain traits and special talents and ways that we can make a contribution in this world and the loss of a life is no exception.

Look around at your family's friends, extended family, associations, etc.; who is good at speaking, at singing, at playing a musical instrument or at cooking, organizing, consoling others or whatever? Whether it is part of the actual ceremony or not, be sure to look around your sphere of influence and see who needs to be included in the services- it will make a big difference for you and for them.

Including Children
(Something For Everyone)

Traditionally children have been left not only out of participating in the funeral in any way, but left completely out of the ritual itself.

This is because oftentimes parents want to protect kids from pain and the funeral can be a painful event. It is so because funerals are our way of beginning the process of healing our grief. Children (defined here as ages 3 –12) need to go to and be present at the funeral and even participate in some way that will help them to heal also.

We are not talking here about minors necessarily eulogizing or officiating at funerals, I'm referring to something more like lighting a candle, being able to place a memento or drawing into the casket, write a letter to the decedent. In chapter 7 I will spend some time talking about children and death more from a psychological and emotional standpoint.

Here I simply want to advise how to help children by helping them be a part of what is happening within age and circumstance appropriate parameters.

From this vantage point think about the child and their relationship to the decedent. Try to evaluate how the child's presence at the funeral will be perceived by the child and go from there. If he or she expresses an interest in actually taking part in the funeral, do not discourage it; they need to feel important enough to be allowed to express themselves.

To Ritualize or Deritualize
(For Better or For Worse?)

Because of rapid sociological changes that have and are continuing to take place in our culture, the ritualization (or act of ceremonial rite or solemn observance) of death has been on the decline.

There are many factors that have influenced these changes such as longer life spans, a fast-paced mobile society, self-reliance, and a lack of proper understanding of what facing a loved-one's death head on is supposed to heal.

The rise in direct cremation, I believe, is a result of our population not wanting to face the reality of death when it does come to our family or inner circle, and thereby foregoing the funeral or ritual. The rise in the cost of funerals is another variable that some use as a reason to skip the "dog and pony show" in favor of the "simplicity" and "relative convenience" of cremation or immediate burial.

Although deritualization is somewhat trendy, less time consuming, more efficient and less expensive monetarily speaking, there will be a much larger price to pay in the years ahead emotionally speaking for not stopping, grieving and in some shape, form or fashion, ritualizing the loss. (I talk more about this in chapter 7).

The rest of this chapter is earmarked for the purpose of presenting ritualization as a piece that can fit into any kind of puzzle.

Let's face it, circumstances and conditions surrounding death can come in many different forms, and death is no respect or of persons regardless of age, status, color, creed, etc. There are times and situations where ritualizaton may be completely dismissed, but what I want to propose is that there is a solution to the problem of needing to ritualize one's passing.

Memorializing One Whose Remains Are Not Present

Having a service or ceremony for one whose casketed remains are not present at the ritual is known as a memorial service.

Since the deceased is not present in body, it is a time of remembering or memorializing the one who has passed.

Memorial services are becoming more common because of direct cremation but also due to immediate burial or burial before a memorial service. Also alternative forms of disposition such as cryonics or donation (discussed in chapter 3) are also occasions for a memorial service.

Most memorial services have a centerpiece or focal point in place of a casket, which is not present. Many times this is a framed photograph of the decedent but it can also be a painting, a cut arrangement of flowers or a candle, as examples.

Memorial services can also be held at anytime after the death and many times families that live far apart or cannot leave at a moment's notice for whatever reason may opt for a memorial service at a day and time that allows for inclusiveness of all those related and connected to the decedent.

In the rare instances where one has died and is not to be embalmed because of personal choice, religious beliefs, economics or other reasons, and is to be buried directly without a funeral, a memorial service may be needed to allow those who wish to gather and have a formal ceremony.

As a general rule, memorial services can be as much like a funeral as a funeral with the one exception of the deceased's casketed remains not present at the service.

Memorializing One Whose Remains Have Not Been Recovered Or Found
(Getting Prospective/Getting Closure)

Accidental or untimely death has seen a reality for millions of families at one time or another, whether the death has been the result of war, fire, explosion, natural disaster or other unexpected or sudden event where the decedent's remains have not or can not be recovered.

Regardless of the tragic loss of life involved, there needs to be an event held to recognize the life lived and to embrace the pain of the decedent's passing from this earth.

A memorial service is the only real option here since the remains are not recoverable. Because of the circumstance of suddenness involved, time should be taken to plan a memorial service that can be made as personalized as possible. It should include as many of the decedent's friends, family and acquaintances as possible and center around getting everyone in attendance to participate in some way- even if it is as simple as placing a flower beneath a picture of the deceased.

Since the goal is to get closure on the life of the one being honored, make it as personable as possible, make it participant friendly and include as many as possible who knew the deceased.

Memorializing One Declared/Presumed Dead
(Is There Anything To Celebrate?)

Many of us at one time or another have seen news stories and/or heard of instances where someone has disappeared, or been taken or otherwise been missing for a long period of time without resolve.

Many times these events are linked to kidnapping, abduction or other presumed or established crimes where a long period of time has passed with no developments or activity. Different states and jurisdictions have a varying number of years that must pass before one is declared dead.

Once the legal time has passed and there is no realistic hope that the person in question will resurface from an objective point of view, it will be time for the family to consider a legal declaration of death and to hold some type of ceremony or ritual to formally mark the person's death.

Although many times there are family members who will "never give up hope" of their loved one's return, it is at some point in the best psychological and emotional interest of the survivors to have some point of closure so that they may move on with their own lives.

This does not in anyway imply that they are having a memorial ceremony to forget the presumed decedent or to "give up" their memory, it simply means that once the authorities, family, friends and other parties involved in finding the person have exhausted all variables, have spent years of mental, emotional and financial resources dedicated to recovery and return that an approach is taken and adopted to understand that it is time for the survivors to come to terms with the very high probabilities that the missing loved one is dead and therefore obtain closure so that those still here may go forward without forgetting the loved one.

This type of memorial service tends to be very healing for survivors because those involved may have been in the place of being left for too long to wander in the emotional limbo of not knowing one way or another if the person is dead or alive.

Much like other memorial services, the ceremony should focus on the person's life as much as possible and include personal belongings of the presumed decedent, pictures and a way that everyone who wishes, to be involved. It should (although against human nature) refer to the decedent in the past tense, and serious consideration should be given to establishing some type of cenotaph (memorial marker placed when the decedent's remains are not buried there) in a local cemetery or other properly designated place to give survivors a permanent tangible place of remembrance since there are no remains to bury. Having a place to go and remember the decedent is a psychologically important thing also.

What If I Don't Want A Funeral Or Memorial Service

Many people at one time or another upon contemplating the death of a family member or perhaps thinking about what should happen when they pass away, have asked the question, "Do I want a funeral or memorial service?" Because of so many changes in our world regarding death and rituals, some have answered, what if I don't want a service for myself, for my spouse, mother, father, whomever? What then?

If you are the legal next-of-kin to one who has died, you can decide if you want a service for them or not. But how do we define service?

Many people have been turned off by the traditional funeral because it is too expensive, too sad, too rote, too uncomfortable. These misconceptions are one reason I have written this book.

You do not have to have a funeral or memorial service and it will be OK. What you do need to have is some type of event or ritual that will start you and others connected to the decedent on a process of resolution and closure concerning the deceased.

It can be the affirmation of life through a reunion of family and/or friends. It can be exchanging memorabilia, old stories, eating a meal together, meeting for refreshments or informally chatting and reminiscing; as long as the underlying theme and central point is the decedent and the impact that his or her life has had on those involved and in common.

Service - No, Ritual- Yes
How To Personalize A Visitation/Wake
(Lasting Treasure)

Generally speaking, the funeral or memorial service is the formal time for paying tribute to a departed loved one. The visitation or wake however is the opportunity to personalize on a different level. At the end of this chapter I'll give specific ideas about personalized visitations and wakes.

The concept however deals with the issue that visitations and wakes tend to be informal, more flexible, less structured, and relaxed. Since this is a time for talking and chatting among friends and family, being able to show and tell what the decedent was all about has its moment.

One of the things that my mother and aunt did at my grandmother's visitation was to create a picture board using various family photos from throughout her life to tell a story about who she was.

One family I recently served brought in numerous boxes filled with hats, medals, newspaper clippings and other memorabilia in which we set up folding tables so that these items could be well displayed for visitors who attended the visitation.

For an avid sports man or woman it may be bringing a set of golf clubs or his or her bicycle to place in the stateroom or visitation area.

The more creative one is the more ideas that can be brainstormed. Since personalization is gaining popularity in the funeral industry, most funeral directors can be consulted to help come up with ideas and the best overall way to create a memorable personalized wake or visitation time.

Other Types Of Ceremonies And Rituals

Although formal funeral or memorial services are the way that most people today continue to choose in ritualizing the dead, alternative services are also available to meet the needs of those who want something simple. Here are several kinds of ceremonies that can help get closure for survivors and uniquely personalize the deceased.

The Stateroom Gathering

This is basically utilizing one of the staterooms at the funeral home for the purpose of having a small ceremony of less than 20 people.

It resembles a formal funeral in that chairs can be set up facing the same direction and using a register stand or portable podium so that an officiant or speaker may talk to attendees.

Music and other audio and visual stimuli can be used as part of the service also.

Usually the stateroom service will last from 10-30 minutes and is anchored in the traditional ceremony of speaking, music, prayer(s) and fostering- divine meaning and contemplation.

The Celebration Of Life

This ritual focuses on the life of the deceased and tends to be an event of praise and festivity rather than sadness and sorrow.

Oftentimes held at a private residence or alternate facility, the life celebration does just that- it celebrates a life! It is an upbeat time of sharing the life lived by the decedent and the activities focus on him or her the person.

The celebration of life tends to take a historical look at the decedent and what he or she did during their lifetime. Eulogy will be a very important part if not the entire agenda at the life celebration.

The use of readings, pictures, life accomplishments, activities, etc. will grab center stage.

The Rites Of Passage

A more structured ceremony than the celebration of life, the Rites of Passage revolves around an initiation or "send-off" into the afterlife.

Depending on one's religious beliefs and philosophy about life after death will dictate whether this ritual would be relevant or not. The stronger one's views on eternity and the afterlife are the more likely that some form of Rites of Passage will take place.

In the Judeo-Christian tradition, the committal service at the gravesite or place of disposition serves as a type of rite of passage into eternal life.

Other faiths and belief systems may have their own rites and ideas concerning the decedent's status once he or she is dead.

Placing clothing, food, money or other tangible items with the deceased before disposition is practicing the idea that he or she may need these things in the afterlife.

Rites of Passage can manifests in many different ways whether an event or a process, tangible or intangible, now or later. It is the concept of the decedent's state in eternity and how survivors chose to ritualize the crossing from life on earth to life afterwards.

The Community Affirmation

Unlike the previous three, the Community Affirmation focuses more on the family, friends and others connected to the decedent.

Focuses on survivors not in the aspect that the decedent is ignored or not acknowledged but on affirming and consoling those left behind to carry on.

The ceremony is usually held at a place important to the survivors and centers on how the decedent's life impacted each person touched by the decedent. Memories are shared, remembrances imparted, gifts or tokens may be exchanged and each person is enriched from the act of coming together and having "community" in the honor of the decedent.

Now lets summarize all four through this grid chart:

	Stateroom	Celebration of Life	Rites of Passage	Community Affirmation
Place:	Funeral home	Place Import-ant to Deceased	Any Appro-priate Setting	Place Impor-tant to the Living
Focus:	Traditional but in smaller setting	The Deceased Before Death	The Deceased After Death	Survivors
Activity:	Speaker(s), Mu-sic, Prayer, etc.	Upbeat/Joyful	"Send Off"	How The De-cedent Impac-ted Survivors
Goal:	Describe, Eulo-gize Decedent	Celebrates the Decedent's Life	Appropriate Initiation	Affirm The Living

Receptions And Reunions

A majority of the time, most formal ceremonies or rituals end with a meal or informal time of gathering to casually chat and share memories, eat and try to relax and support each other.

This informal time to release and transition back to life again from the events surrounding death oftentimes takes place at the home of a friend or family member, a restaurant or a church meeting room.

I have titled this section Receptions and Reunions with Receptions used in the ordinary sense of the word, but Reunions not so in that when we think about reunion, we are thinking family, high school, college, etc. But when a family member dies and relatives come together it is a reunion in that a gathering is to take place, in this instance due to a death in the family.

Receptions and reunions in place of formal funeral or memorial service is becoming more common due to cremation and alternative forms of disposition. Some families are opting out of the formal ceremony altogether and choosing to hold a gathering or reception instead.

There are various ways to make the gathering/reception meaningful and personable.

One key factor is ambience. Having food, background music, flowers, drinks, photo albums or a picture board and memorabilia all are ways to add value to the informal gathering or reception.

Also allowing for comfortable chairs, tables and the creation of a relaxed, laid-back atmosphere will also help transform a somber time into a time that refreshes the body, spirit and soul, and will help those in attendance to feel that they have participated in an alternative event that allows them to deal with their grief in a more casual, nonthreatening way.

It's a Family Affair . . .

Families are different. And as there are no two people that are exactly similar, the same goes for family units.

One of the cornerstone strengths of our society is that most families get along well together and enjoy being together. Unfortunately, some do not.

Receptions and Reunions, because they are less structured and more interactive socially speaking, a family's true character is more likely to surface in this type of setting. Add in the emotionally charged variable that a death has taken place within the family, and you have a setting of true feelings and emotions coming out.

If your family is one with "issues" among or related to the death of the one now passed, carefully consider the reunion/reception carefully before making the decision to do it.

Holding Anniversary Rituals
(Honoring A Loved One's Memory)

Once a loved one is gone and life goes back to its normal routine so to speak, oftentimes the first year that passes since the death tends to bring reflective emotions to surface.

For some, holding a ceremony or remembrance on the date of the decedent's passing is a way to deal with lingering or resurfacing emotions.

This can be formal or as informal as you wish and can be held in a home with just a few or in one case I know about, the family chose to come back to the funeral home and reserve the Chapel a year later and hold a structured one hour service of remembrance.

For some it may be a one-time event a year after the death, for others an annual observance for several years or every 5 years, 10 years, etc. The main theme for several of the anniversary services I've had knowledge of have focused on how the decedent's legacy continues to impact the lives of those still living; of how the person's life has shaped who the survivors are and how they live their own lives today. It shares in essence how the decedent's memory is continuing to be lived out today.

Commemoration
(I Will Remember You)

Whereas the anniversary ceremony or ritual is the "event" of honoring a loved one's memory at key points in time, commemoration is the process of memorializing the decedent's memory in the day to day motion of life..

It may be as simple as putting the decedent's picture on your night stand to see each evening when going to sleep or waking each morning. It may mean printing and framing a quote or statement made by the decedent during his or her life and hanging on the wall as a pleasant reminder of his or her wit and insight.

Depending on the circumstances surrounding the death it may include the development of some form of shrine.

How, when and where you decide to commemorate and remember someone can be as simple or as complex as it needs to be. The idea to remember is that it is something that will allow you to effectively create the memory you want and need to hold.

Chapter 4 Summary

Personalization And Practical Ideas For Memorialization

Questions To Ask:

Who was this person?
What did they do?
How did they live?
What did they like?
What was the person's favorite:
Thing, Activity, Job, Possession, Event

Planning A Service:

#1 What type of service do you want?
#2 What do you want to include as part of the service?
#3 Gather together what you want to be part of the service
#4 Organize resources to make it a success
#5 Implement the ideas/resources into the service

Using Technology:

Audio Helps- Hearing & Sound
Computerization- Efficient Output
Visual- Seeing & Sight

Articles And Symbols

*Help convey the message that words alone cannot
*Express Ideas and Emotions
*Identify a part of who the decedent was.

Including people to participate as either leaders or followers help all to feel included and worthy of the occasion. Nontraditional ways of memorializing the deceased exists and offers an alternative method of personalizing and presenting rituals to honor his or her passing.

Other Types Of Ceremonies Include:

The Stateroom Gathering
The Celebration of Life
The Rites of Passage
The Community Affirmation

Each one has a different setting, focus, mode and goal involved.

100 Practical Ideas For Personalizing Memorialization
(Let Us Count The Ways)

1. Make a memorial donation in memory of a loved one, friend or associate.

2. Place the decedent's favorite possession with them for visitation.

3. Bring the decedent's favorite book, magazine, reading, etc. to visitation for placement or display.

4. Consider bringing a favorite pillow, blanket, chair or other comfort to place with the decedent.

5. Order flowers for the service that are made with the decedent's favorite color.

6. Have the florist attach a ribbon to the flower piece with a meaningful inscription, word, phrase, etc.

7. Find photographs of the decedent to display on a table or board for the visitation and/or service.

8. If allowed, bring a candle(s) to the visitation to help foster a calmer more personable atmosphere.

9. Bring the decedent's old scrapbook to the visitation/reception/gathering for visitors to look at and discuss.

10. Have an item or items representing a hobby or favorite past time brought in such as sewing machine, golf clubs, bicycle, chess set, paint brushes, etc.

11. Bring the decedent's favorite outfit or clothing piece to the funeral director to have him or her dressed in for burial.

12. Have the decedent's favorite piece of jewelry placed on him or her for the visitation and/or funeral.

13. If a collector of stuffed animals, bring some of them to the funeral home to be placed in casket with deceased.

14. When choosing a casket, ask if there is one available to match the decedent's life (certain color, fabric type, head panel, engraving or inscription).

15. If having a meal before or after the funeral, fix and eat his or her favorite dish in his or her honor.

16. If art was an interest, having some favorite paintings brought and displayed for visitation or gathering.

17. Play the decedent's favorite type of music as background for the visitation, reception, gathering.

18. For the funeral, play at least one of the decedent's favorite songs.

19. At the funeral, display a banner as a backdrop that shows some trait of the decedent (career, military service, club membership, church affiliation, etc.).

20. Allow attendees at the ceremony/ritual to write a short letter to the decedent (as part of the service) and then place it in the casket during the final viewing/pass by.

21. Make the service special with a video tribute using photos and special music to create a personalized portion of the funeral.

22. In place of traditional funeral flowers, request that people send a vase with the person who died's favorite flower.

23. Display a large poster-sized photo of the decedent as a memory portrait.

24. Consider dressing (or helping the funeral director to dress) the decedent.

25. Put out a memory book next to or close to the register

book where guests can write down a special memory.

26. Hold the visitation or reception someplace special to the family like a garden, the beach, a park, lounge (there may be permits and other issues for public places).

27. Create a personalized obituary for the newspaper that focuses on how the person impacted his/her world.

28. Look at holding the funeral itself at a place special to the decedent rather than the traditional chapel, church or graveside.

29. Allow children in the family to draw pictures and write letters to place in the casket with the deceased.

30. At the end of visitation gather everyone together in a circle holding hands and have a special prayer together.

31. Create a bulletin/service handout for the funeral that gives a summary of the person who died's life.

32. Ask the funeral home if a personalized set of thank you cards with the decedent's name can be inscribed on them.

33. Have the minister or service officiant read any quotes, sayings or poems that were special to the decedent at the service.

34. Consider showing slides at the funeral with photos of the deceased and using a microphone to talk briefly about each slide during the presentation.

35. Using various articles from the decedent's life, create an article board or display to set up for the visitation and/or service.

36. Instead of (or along with) flowers, consider obtaining some helium balloons for the services that can add color and variety.

37. Bring the decedent's favorite blanket or bedspread to lay across the foot end of the casket instead of a traditional flower piece.

38. Consider asking other members of a club or group that the decedent was apart of to serve as pallbearers.

39. Bring souvenirs that the person who died collected on trips if he or she was a traveler.

40. Ask the funeral director if there is a selection of register books to chose from in order to find one that will fit the decedent's life.

41. If possible, see if the decedent's photograph can be computer scanned and placed on the front of the service folders

42. Make laminated bookmarks out of the newspaper obituary as keepsakes for friends and family.

43. See if preprinted laminated bookmarks are available; there are various themes possibly available such as golf, public servant, fishing, Armed forces, cooking, animals, etc.

44. Have a portrait in oil painted of the decedent using a snapshot.

45. If the person who died was a musician, have the instrument that he or she played brought to and played or displayed at the service.

46. Choose a commemorative head panel for the casket to share a certain aspect of the decedent's life with others.

47. If decedent was a longtime member of a club or organization, have a special part of the seating for the service reserved for its members and to have them ushered in and seated together in unison.

48. If funeral and burial are being held in close proximity, ask if a horse-drawn carriage could be arranged for taking decedent's casket from funeral to gravesite.

49. Place a large blank sheet of cutting paper on a table at the service and visitation with pens where guests may write a special message to the person who died to be rolled up and placed in the casket with deceased before burial.

50. Place candles at the front of the chapel and have family members come up and light them as part of the service.

51. Plant a tree in honor of the decedent's memory in an appropriate place that will always remind you of them.

52. Have the decedent's name and dates engraved on the exterior of the casket (if possible).

53. Have some other type of insignia, design, or symbol

engraved on the casket (as available by casket manufacturer).

54. Customize the casket with decorative symbols that are built into the four exterior corners of the casket (also as available).

55. Personalize the burial vault with the name and dates and a symbol engraved on the exterior (as available).

56. At the graveside, have a balloon release at a specified moment that will provide a special memory for attendees.

57. At the end of a chapel funeral, as mourners pass by the casket, give each person a long-stem rose to place in a large vase next to the casket.

58. If the decedent had any pets, take a snapshot of (each) the animal and place it in the casket to be buried with the deceased.

59. At the gravesite, after the service have each attendee sprinkle some of the dirt from the grave on top of the casket.

60. Have an "open mic" time slot at the funeral where attendees may get up and take several minutes to share a special memory connected to the deceased.

61. Ask the funeral director if a lock of hair can be obtained from the person who died as a keepsake.

62. At the end of the graveside service, have a pigeon release where the birds are let out of their box at a specified time.

63. For cremation, ask about options available for name and dates inscription on the urn.

64. Purchase a special piece of statuary to have set in the yard or other appropriate outdoor place in honor of the decedent's memory.

65. Select a display/keepsake urn for cremated ashes that reflects the decedent's life.

66. Hold an Inurnment Service if the cremated ashes are to be buried or inurned at a cemetery or memorial park.

67. If decedent was a veteran, request Taps be played at the graveside service and the flag folded and formally presented to the next of kin.

68. Purchase a keepsake pendant with a small portion of the cremated ashes and their name engraved on it.

69. A keepsake pendant with the decedent's picture can also be obtained as a personalized keepsake.

70. Place a picture of each of the decedent's children, grandchildren, great-grandchildren, etc., into the casket to be buried with decedent.

71. Pass out roses to guests at the graveside service and have each person go by and place rose on top of casket at the end of the service.

72. When burying cremated ashes in the ground, an urn vault may be able to be inscribed with the name and dates of the deceased.

73. When the funeral chapel and burial site are in close proximity, have the pallbearers walk behind the coach to the gravesite.

74. Place a commemorative obituary in the local paper to honor the one passed away on first birthday after the death or a first anniversary of death.

75. Play a medley of photos of the decedent on DVD at the visitation.

76. See if a special exterior casket can be purchased to allow mourners to write special messages onto the casket itself.

77. Have a special symbol or inscription indicative of the decedent engraved on his or her cemetery monument.

78. Hold a special memorial gathering or service for the decedent on the anniversary of his or her death.

79. Put together a memorial scrapbook of the person's life with photos, clippings and other memorabilia as a keepsake.

80. If purchasing a cemetery memorial with a vase, have a laser etching of the person's name and dates placed on the vase

81. Purchase a memorial tablet cemetery marker that has a brief biographical description of the person's life.

82. If allowed, help the cemetery crew fill in the grave with shovels after the graveside service.

83. Buy a cemetery memorial that will allow the decedent's picture to be placed on as part of the marker.

84. Create a special shrine in your home as a tribute to the decedent using belongings, memorabilia, pictures, etc., set up in a corner, a bookcase, table, etc.

85. If the person was a member of a club or other organization, have one of the entity's members say some special words at the funeral.

86. If holding a diner or reception as part of the services, propose a toast to the decedent's memory.

87. If cremation is the method of disposition, see if a cenotaph with name and dates can be placed in a cemetery as a permanent, durable memorial.

88. If decedent was a veteran, look into purchasing a wooden flag case with name and dates inscribed on and attached to the case.

89. Each year on special dates- birthday, anniversary, etc., order and have special flowers placed on decedent's grave, tomb, final resting place.

90. Plant the decedent's favorite type flowers in a special area of flower bed, garden or yard each spring as a commemorative tribute to him or her.

91. If decedent was member of a church or other special organization, see if memorial donations can be made in his/her memory.

92. Record a special video or audio tribute of the decedent as a biographical summary of his/her life and give copies of it to various family members, as a lasting tribute.

93. Using computer technology and the Internet, create a special electronic tribute to the decedent that can be viewed by other friends and family members by computer.

94. Have everyone attending the service for the decedent sing together as a congregation a song paying tribute to him or her.

95. Purchase keepsake cremation jewelry that can hold a small portion of the cremated ashes and divide up ashes into small portions and give one to each family member to wear / have.

96. At the funeral, if the person liked a particular type of candy, buy a bulk of samples and pass out one per guest at the service.

97. Play an audio or video recording of the decedent at the service talking or shown doing something as a legacy tribute.

98. On the way to the place of final disposition, have the immediate family members walk behind the casket holding hands in quiet procession.

99. During the funeral, have a moment of silence (one minute) to allow attendees to meditate and think about the decedent.

100. As the casket is being closed for the final time, ask if family members can help by lowering the lid to close it.

Chapter 5

Financing & Payment

1. Introduction
2. What Your Options Are
3. The Contractual Agreement
4. Cash/Check/Money Order
5. Debit Cards/Credit Cards
6. Life Insurance Assignment
7. Prearrangement Policies
8. Pre Need vs. At Need
9. Bank/Savings Loans
10. Credit Union/Insurance Policy Loans
11. Retirement Plan/401K Loans
12. Factoring Structured Settlements
13. Selling Other Receivables
14. Liquidating Assets
15. Organizational Membership Benefits
16. Employee/Company Benefits
17. Accidental Death Benefits
18. Credit Card, Other Account Benefits
19. Benevolence Assistance From Membership/Association With Certain Groups, Entities or Charitable Organizations
20. Assistance From Social Organizations
21. Installment Payments
22. Finance Agreements
23. Service For Service
24. Barter
25. Local, County, State Government Benefits
26. Like-Kind Exchanges
27. Totten Trusts

One of the stickiest issues surrounding death for all parties involved in the matter of what to do and how to do it is in the area of financing and paying for the final arrangements made for a departed loved one. Since funeral and burial costs have unfortunately- for a number of reasons- risen faster than the rate of inflation, the problem of paying the funeral home and/or cemetery for services rendered, has become a serious concern among many.

The focus of this chapter is to give you various options of how to prepare financially for the inevitable whether thinking in advance or faced with a death today. Since some funeral homes can be flexible to some extent in making financial arrangements for services planned, most of the following methods will be possible alternatives that the funeral home or cemetery may accept as payment; since most establishments have defined policies of what types of payment arrangements they will or will not accept, it is a good idea to discuss these with your funeral director.

Facing The Inevitable
What Your Options Are

Paying for the services and/or merchandise of a funeral and/or cemetery business is a very unique experience from the customer/consumer standpoint. What is happening is that the customer (family) of the decedent is in a position of having to make a purchase that 1) must take place regardless of whether the customer wants to be in the position of consumer or not and 2) must expend money to take care of the task of memorializing and/or procuring proper, lawful disposition of the deceased.

Since some people are unprepared for, underprepared for, or unsure of what expectations need to be met, or even how to measure them, paying for these services and merchandise is usually difficult at best in handling and dealing with the problem of death.

Because funeral homes and cemeteries are in the business of

handling death and its related burdens, oftentimes the public views funeral directors and cemeterians as holding most of the marbles in so far as making the arrangements for payment. To a degree this is true because as business entities if funeral homes and cemeteries don't charge for and collect their monies, they will cease to do business and no longer be able to serve anyone.

The remainder of this chapter is a presentation and discussion of different ways and methods available that may suffice in creating ways of paying for the final expenses of a family member or loved one. Having and knowing what potential options there are can be priceless and save more grief and heartache than what one may already be feeling just from the death itself.

Getting What You Pay For

The Contractual Agreement

In Chapter 1 I talked about contracts and agreements from a legal and ethics standpoint, but here I want to briefly discuss it from a financial aspect.

Since the Federal Trade Commission requires that all funeral provider contracts be itemized—or simply show the specific amounts for the goods and services selected—it is convenient for customer families to evaluate each charge for each item, and therefore know how much they're spending for what. This way the customer family has an itemized bill of sale and may make better spending decisions on items they may or may not want as part of the services being purchased.

It also answers the important question of exactly what are we paying for, and therefore the best way to pay for it.

Cash/Check/Money Order

Almost too fundamental to mention, there are relatively few businesses that do not take currency, personal or cashiers check or money orders.

In reference to the above importance of the itemized contract with the total to know how much to write a check for or how much cash to get, always be sure in the memo portion of the check to write what you are paying for. For example if you are buying goods and services at a funeral home that includes both funeral and burial expenses, write: Payment for funeral and burial expenses of decedent's name, not just funeral expenses. This way it is clear that you are paying for both with one check.

The same on money orders and printed cashiers checks. Be sure you have the bank print on the memo portion of the paper exactly what you are paying for with it.

Also be sure to have the provider of goods and/or services write and give you a receipt at the time of payment—especially when paying cash. This way you have a provider generated document to show that you've paid.

Debit/Credit Cards

Most funeral homes and mortuaries take either debit or major credit cards such as Visa, Master Card, Discover and American Express. If you are considering paying this way, be sure to ask when talking with the funeral director to set up the conference to make arrangements.

If transacting business over the telephone, ask the director to call you back with the approval number given by the bank or credit card company in processing the card, or ask to have the card machine receipt along with a funeral home payment received receipt to give you a documented record of the amount charged.

Life Insurance Assignment

A very traditional way of paying for some or all the costs of funeral and burial expenses is use of a life insurance policy or policies.

Some people buy these policies for the intended purpose of their family or survivors to use the insurance policy to pay for their final expenses, whereas others may buy the policy for a surviving spouse and/or dependent children to use to help cover their living costs after the death, but use a portion of the insurance policy's proceeds to pay the funeral and/or burial expenses.

Whatever the case, most funeral providers will accept assignment of an insurance policy upon verification of its in force status. This means the funeral home will ask for the policy and file it for you and have the policy's beneficiary sign an assignment form. The funeral home will then do the legwork of filing the policy or policies for you.

When calling the insurance company, the funeral home will give the total amount of the contract or expenses to verify that the policy will cover the funeral home's charges. Most insurance companies will not give any third parties the amount of the policy or policies due to privacy. The funeral provider will then proceed to take an assignment only on the amount due for its expenses.

For example, if the Smith family incurs $10,000 of funeral expenses on its contract with Jones Funeral Home and gives the funeral home a $25,000 life policy, the funeral home will take assignment for $10,000 meaning the insurance company will mail the funeral home a check for $10,000, and a separate check for $15,000 directly to the beneficiary on the policy.

Research And Planning

Prearrangement Policies

Started in the 1930s to combat the problem encountered during the Great Depression by people unable to pay the funeral expenses of a deceased loved one, the funeral industry came up with the concept of selling insurance policies to prefund one's final expenses.

In a nutshell, prearranged funeral plans are policies that can be bought by consumers through funeral establishments to preplan (decide and document what types of items and services one wants at the time of death) and pre-fund (pay for the preplanned arrangements through a single payment or installments) their final arrangements.

Driven by the desire to buy funeral services for the future at today's prices, and to save family members from having to make big decisions at the time of death, many consumers are prearranging now, responding to the aggressive marketing initiated by funeral homes in their desire to lock in future business for their firms.

There are two basic types of prearranged funeral plans: trust and insurance. A trust prearrangement works in such a way that if the prearrangement is being paid for in an installment payout plan over, say 5 years, if death takes place before all the 5 year installments are paid, the unpaid balance would become due and payable before the seller would be obligated to provide the goods and services in the prearrangement policy.

Example: Ms. Smith's son buys a $9,000 prearrangement for her in which he will payout in monthly installments of $150 over 5 years. ($150 month x 12 months/year x 5 years= $9,000). In year 2, Ms. Smith passes away after the son pays in 18 months of premiums (150 x 18= $2,700). Ms. Smith's son will now need to pay the remaining $6,300 (9,000-2,700) balance for services to be rendered.

An insurance prearranged plan however works like a life insurance policy. This way, regardless, of whether the death takes place before all the payments are made in an installment plan or not, any unpaid balance will be paid off at the time of death. In other words, the insured prearrangement is a type of life policy that will pay for the funeral/final arrangements in full regardless of when death occurs.

Regardless of which type of plan one buys, trust or insured, prearranged funerals are designed to provide great advantages to consumers in that by making choices, benefactors are able to have the arrangements they want, they spare their survivors the anguish of having to make the decisions for them, often under

Consumer Preneed Bill of Rights

(National Funeral Directors Association)

Prior to purchasing any funeral goods or services or signing a pre-need funeral contract, we urge you to ask us any and all questions you may have regarding your pre-need purchases.

To ensure that you as our client family, have a full understanding of the pre-need funeral transaction, we guarantee the following rights and protections:

We will:

1. Provide you with detailed price lists of services and merchandise before you select services and merchandise.
2. Provide to you, at the conclusion of the funeral arrangement conference, a written statement listing all of the services and merchandise you have purchased and the price.
3. Give you a written pre-need funeral contract explaining, in plain language, your rights and obligations.
4. Guarantee in the written pre-need contract that if any of the merchandise and services you have selected are not available at the time of need, merchandise or services of equal or greater value will be substituted by us at no extra cost to you.
5. Explain in the written pre-need contract the geographical boundaries of our service area and under what circumstances you can transfer the pre-need contract to another funeral home if you were to relocate or if the death were to occur outside of our service area.
6. State in the written pre-need contract where and how much of the funds you pay to us will be deposited until the funeral is provided.
7. Explain in the written pre-need contract who will be responsible for paying taxes on any income or interest generated by the pre-need funds that are invested.
8. Inform you in the written contract whether and to what extent we are guaranteeing prices of the merchandise and services you are purchasing. If the prices are not guaranteed, we will explain to you in writing who will be responsible for paying any additional amounts that may be due at the time of the funeral.
9. Explain in writing who will receive any excess funds that may result if the income or interest generated by the invested pre-need funds exceed future price increases in the funeral merchandise and services you have selected.
10. Explain in the written pre-need contract whether and under what circumstances you may cancel your pre-need contract *and how much of the funds you paid to us will be refunded to you.*

emotionally charged circumstances, and are able to freeze the cost at today's prices, thereby hedging against future increases.

Rules and regulations over prearranged funeral/burial/cremation plans differ widely from state to state so it is important to know what the applicable laws are in your area.

The following are some tips to keep in mind when shopping, buying or considering prearranged funeral plans:

1) Have two (2) other people who in all probability will outlive you be present and have knowledge of the prearrangement agreement to prevent any misunderstandings at the time of death.

2) At a minimum, preplan your final wishes in writing, stating what kind of services you would like with instructions.

3) Do not put funeral wishes in a will (it's usually found and read after the funeral or disposition); put it where it can be found quickly.

Simply Stated . . . It Can Be Complex

Although prearranged funeral and cemetery plans have grown in popularity in the past 20-25 years, there is still a segment of the population that is skeptical about buying prearranged services.

If you are on the fence so to speak about whether to prearrange or not, shop around. Providers can sell practically anything before need that can be sold at need (with exceptions).

Research prearrangements the same way you would before purchasing a home, a car or any other major purchase. Learn about trust funded pre-need plans; price guarantee vs. non-price guarantee plans, revocable or irrevocable plans, etc.

Check with your state's attorney general's office, insurance and/or banking commission, funeral/cemetery oversight board, etc. to learn the rules by how to measure what potential pre-need sellers present against what they are required to disclose.

4) File your wishes in three (3) separate places- friend, relative, funeral home, attorney, etc.

5) Get an annual statement of the preneed fund that your money is deposited into to pay for your services. You may call the funeral home or the prearrangement company that has underwritten your policy to get information about the fund.

6) Be certain that it is set up in a fund that is insured.

7) Get your agreement from the preneed seller in writing. Ask questions about anything and everything you don't understand. Get explanations in writing also.

8) Have the salesperson write on the prearrangement contract any items or services that will be needed at the time of death that are not part of the contract to avoid any surprise such as cash advance items.

9) What happens if the funeral home sells to another owner? What happens if they go out of business? Be sure that any relevant what ifs are addressed now rather than later.

10) What if some of the merchandise in the prearrangement is no longer available when death occurs? The terms on the contract will govern the agreement.

Saving Money: Preneed vs. At Need

Since not everyone is ready or comfortable making and paying for their final arrangements ahead of time, there is an alternative to prepaying through a preneed policy and that is done through establishing an individual bank account for this purpose. The account can be set up at a bank under the terms of the money being made payable to your funeral provider of choice as payee. This solves the problem of having funds available at the time arrangements are made. Be sure the account is set up "in trust" for your final expenses. This way no one can get to the money before you pass away and proof of death will need to be supplied to the bank before funds can be disbursed to the funeral provider.

Opening the fund as a savings account will allow it to draw interest, although it is usually a low rate; it will still be earning some increased value.

Putting the money into a bank CD can accomplish the same principle so long as it can be liquidated quickly and hassle-free to pay the funeral provider at a moment's notice (also see Totten Trust at the end of this chapter).

Bank/Savings Loans

Banks and Savings and Loan institutions are in business to loan money. Many banks can approve potential borrowers over the telephone, sometimes in a matter of minutes. Others may require a visit to their branch office to fill out a credit application

Supplemental Security Income/ Medicaid Eligibility News

The government allows an applicant for social security administration and state Medicaid benefits to, in some cases, not count certain items in determining total asset values which may include pre-need funeral/final disposition funds as excludible assets.

Medicaid/SSI Exclusions:

- The value of a pre-need trust to fund an irrevocable prearrangement contract which is set aside to cover future burial expenses. There is generally no dollar limit on this type of contract.
- The provision of a burial or final disposition space is excluded if the value of the actual space, crypt, urn, casket, vault or other repository for human remains is also exempt from being counted as part of the applicant's resources. The applicant himself or herself must actually own the site, space, crypt, etc.
- A burial fund amount up to $1,500 can also be excluded if it is clearly designated to cover the cost of expenses not covered under the burial/space exclusion.

in person. Nevertheless, funeral and burial expenses are expenditures that may require the taking out of a loan to pay for.

Most adults today have at least a bank checking account in their town or city of residence that they bank with. This would be the logical place to start in asking for a loan. Sometimes however the person making funeral arrangements may not be able to get approved for the full amount to fund the arrangements made. At this point it may be necessary for two or more family members to work together as a family to create a line of credit sufficient to receive a loan(s) to pay for the funeral/burial expenses.

I have met with several families in the past where this was the situation that the next-of-kin did not have amble credit for a loan but several other family members stepped up and used their credit to get the funds needed to pay for the funeral.

Credit Union/Insurance Policy Loans

Like banks or Savings and Loans, Credit Unions may be a source of getting a needed loan for funeral expenses.

Home Equity as a Borrowing Source

Now permissible in all fifty states, taking out a loan using the equity in one's homestead as collateral is an option to those who need or want to obtain money for any number of expenses.

A home equity loan may be a viable option if there is enough equity in your house to take out a note to cover the funeral/burial expenses incurred.

The key to remember in considering a home equity loan is the repayment of the amount borrowed plus interest. If for some reason you cannot meet your obligations to repay, you may have your home as another loss over and above your loved one's passing to cope with.

Credit Unions will loan money for certain expenses of employees who are a member of the credit union. Whether or not funeral expenses is something that a particular credit union will loan money to one of its members is subject to the union's agreement with its employees.

One of the main advantages of getting a loan for some or all the funding for one's funeral expenses is the relatively low rate of interest of paying back the borrowed money compared to commercial banks and savings and loans.

Another way of borrowing money at a usually lower-than-market interest rate is against the face value of one's life insurance policy. If the next-of-kin or other family member has a life policy through an insurance company that is willing to loan money against any equity in the policy, the policyholder may find this to be a helpful way to obtain needed funds.

The insurance company will issue a check to the owner of the policy for said amount and will reduce the amount of any proceeds that will be paid out on the policy until the loan is paid back.

The Time Is Now: Retirement Plans

401K and other retirement savings plans are another source of obtaining loans to help pay a decedent's final expenses.

Subject to the terms and conditions of the plan, there are circumstances in which one may apply for a loan or hardship withdrawal from a retirement account.

Usually the maximum amount available for withdrawal is the balance in the retirement account or less. The plan will make a loan to the plan participant secured by the amount of the balance in the account. Contact the plan's administrator for information on loans and hardship withdrawals.

THE FUTURE IS NOW:
Factoring Structured Settlements

A structured settlement is an order handed down by a judicial or other governmental entity, or through a business agreement between parties where one party obligates to pay the other party through time payments. Settlements can take many forms but an example would be an award from a lawsuit where XYZ Company must pay John Individual $1,000 a month over 25 years.

Let's say that John Individual's mother passes away and he makes funeral and burial arrangements totaling $15,000. If John I. has no other way to pay for these arrangements he may sell or factor the remaining payments he's entitled to from XYZ to a third party buyer for a discount. A factor is someone who will buy the settlement from the receiver for a discount of the payments to be made, usually for a percentage anywhere between 30-80 % of the amount.

To illustrate let's say John I. is at the end of year 5 of the 25-year payout. John contacts a third party factoring agent who agrees to buy the remaining payout from XYZ for 60% of the value.

Amount of Settlement (25 years X 12 months/year X $1,000/mo.)	$300,000
Amount of Settlement paid by XYZ Company to date, 5 years X $12,000 per year	<60,000>
Amount of Settlement Remaining	$240,000
Amount of money that Third Party Factor agrees to buy settlement for from John I. (40% of $240,000)	<96,000>
Amount that John receives in sale of the settlement	$144,000

John I. now pays the funeral provider the $15,000 due and goes home with $129,000. Although this situation is not very common, for those people who receive monthly payments from a mandated settlement, it is a possible option worth mentioning.

Selling Other Receivables

Along with structured settlements, it may be possible to sell at a discount any other amounts due over time that one's entitled to receive. This may include but not be limited to notes, bonds, securities, contracts, annuities or other paper that serves as proof of future payments to be paid but not yet received.

Again these may be sold to another party at a discount in order to get cash money today.

The Axe Is Laid At The Root Of The Tree
Liquidating Assets

Next is the alternative that most cashless people think of the most but want to do the least and that is asset liquidation. This is the selling off of any assets, tangible or intangible to pay the funeral expenses. Most of the time the decedent may have some assets as part of their estate that can be sold or liquidated for cash. This list may include but not be limited to furniture and fixtures, clothing, jewelry, appliances, household accessories, automotive vehicles, collectibles, antiques, souvenirs, etc. This may include assets of the deceased or next-of-kin and/or/other family members.

Since liquidating assets usually takes time and the funeral home will usually want its money before rendering services, this option may only be feasible if it can be done quickly (1-3 days), or if the funeral home is willing to wait until after services (in good faith) to receive the proceeds from the liquidation. This will depend on the funeral home's payment policy.

Organizational Member Benefits

If the decedent was a member of a particular group or organization such as the Masons, Eastern star, Knights of the Pythias, Elks Lodge, Daughters of the American Revolution or one of the many other member only groups, these organizations may (and also may not) offer some type of financial assistance to help pay funeral costs up to a certain amount.

This can vary greatly from group to group and depends on the organization's policies or bylaws. If the decedent was a member (or previous longtime member) it may be worth asking if the organization has any financial assistance for final arrangements available.

Employee/Company Benefits

Most employers offer or provide life insurance as an employee benefit and some may be willing to pay the funeral expenses of a deceased employee or former employee depending on the circumstances.

If the decedent died while working or in the course of performing work-related activities (like traveling), then the company may have a policy to pay the funeral expenses (up to a certain amount) in some cases.

For those who are retired or no longer working after a long tenure of service, a decedent's former employer may help cover or pay some of the final expenses as defined by the company's policy or discretion.

If the decedent died in the course of work, work-related activities, had a long tenure or left/retired after a long period of employment, it may be worth checking into.

Accidental Death Benefits

In the unfortunate event that one dies in an accident, which is an unforeseen sudden loss of life due to traumatic incident, the decedent may have accidental death benefits due to his/her estate or next-of-kin.

This may come as a result of connection or affiliation with different associations such as travel clubs, auto clubs, professional groups, etc.

Accidental death insurance would also fall under this category, which means that accidental death must be defined as "accidental" by the certifier of the death certificate for any benefits to be paid.

Any application for accidental death benefits by an applicant usually must be by the next-of-kin or designated beneficiary of one's estate.

<u>Credit Card/Other Account Benefits</u>

Along with accidental death are benefits that one may receive as the holder of a credit card. Some of the major credit companies, like Master Card, Visa, Discover, American Express and others include accidental death benefits subject to the cardholder agreement. The coverage for death benefits may be very restrictive and may come simply as a result of being a cardholder or may have to be purchased at a fee that is usually billed through the card's account.

Brother Can You Lend A Hand?

Benevolence Assistance From Charity/Human Relief Organizations

Some cities and towns may have nonprofit organizations that in the case of more dire circumstances may assist financially in helping less fortunate families.

Since death is a reality that will affect every family at some point in time regardless of financial or socioeconomic status, your community may have a charity, mission or relief organization in town that may help in this unavoidable and irreversible event of death.

If a benevolence organization is willing to monetarily assist the family with funeral expenses it is usually very limited and will probably only cover one or some of the funeral home's non-declinable fees such as embalming or refrigeration or transportation to place of burial, etc. The benevolence entity also may send the check directly to the mortuary to be applied to the decedent's account rather than entrusting the money with the family to take to the funeral home.

Assistance From Churches Or Religious Organizations

The involvement of churches and church organizations in the funeral process is nothing new. There is a very wide range however, of how involved a church or religious entity will get in helping a family who has lost one of its own.

As a funeral director I have come across several churches that have had pastors come with the family to the funeral home for making arrangements and along with offering to officiate the funeral or memorial service, also offer to get pallbearers, musicians, and payout of the church's funds for some portion of the funeral home's charges.

There are many factors involved in determining assistance from a church or religious organization such as budget and resources available, programs established to deal with death and funerals, size and influence of the congregation, autonomy and ability to make decisions on assistance matters and possibly also the decedent's or decedent's family's association and/or involvement in the church.

If you or your family is affiliated with a church it may be worth your time to find out if and what the congregation offers to families and members families who have experienced a death.

Take The Slow Road

Installment Payments

Fewer and fewer funeral homes today are accepting installment payments from families as compensation after the fact.

The reason very simply is because the mobility, urbanization, and quite frankly, the sometimes less than honest intentions of the buyer(s) to perform their end of any payout agreement.

Installment payments are basically the concept of purchasing merchandise and services and then paying it out over a future period of time. Due to the promises or verbal commitments to payoff funeral services, the funeral home is acting as creditor and is reliant upon the buyer's honesty and integrity to make the payments as agreed upon at the time the deal is made. This is because unlike other types of buy now pay later arrangements that are common place for banks, automobile dealers, and other lender/creditors, the funeral home does not have collateral or anything a part of the deal that it can foreclose on or repossess if the buyer decides not to pay. For this reason, a lot of funeral homes, especially in large urban areas are not likely to accept payments after the death has occurred and services and merchandise have been rendered or agree to any installment payout plan.

Counting The Costs
Finance Agreements

Like installment payments, finance agreements are also defined as the monthly or other periodic paying out over time for goods and/or services rendered but include the addition of interest.

Similar to taking out a car loan or mortgage on a home purchase, finance agreements would allow for the pay back over a future period with a portion of each payment going to principal (the contracted amount of money for items purchased from the funeral home) and a portion going to pay the interest or the cost of the purchase after the rendering of services.

This way the funeral home can keep up with inflation and the rise in the cost and prices it pays for resources in producing the services it provides. It also allows the funeral home to make a minimal increase for the risk involved for entering into the agreement, which, like an installment plan, relies on the good faith intentions of the buyer(s). This method may include the filling out of a credit application and the funeral home may want a co-applicant as well.

Since most funeral homes generally do not act as lenders or finance companies for its clientele, this may likely not be an option for situations where death has already occurred, but may be worth asking your funeral director about if other options are ruled out.

SERVICE FOR SERVICE

Back in the "good old days" when a pack of gum costs a nickel and a gallon of gas was 29 cents, exchanging one proprietor's services for the services of another was not extremely unusual.

Today in the modern world of superhighways, computers, space flight and wireless telephones, the idea of paying an established business with an exchange of services for services is mostly remote, but not altogether extinct.

If you are a service provider yourself who performs or produces a service that the funeral home/funeral director may need routinely throughout future years, this may be worth mentioning. Regardless of whether your service is carpentry, repair, furniture-making/sales, hairstyling, computer programming, accounting, medicine, or whatever your service, if you are short on cash, mentioning a service for service swap may be an answer to a portion to if not all your funeral bill.

This option is probably less likely to work with a corporately owned or chain owned funeral establishment as opposed to a small town independently owned and operated mortuary, however there are no givens.

Funeral directors have to deal with suppliers, employees, vendors and other parties who expect payment in money, so it is not at all unreasonable for them to ask for monetary payment also.

Barter

Barter is the exchanging of goods or more tangible personal property for the merchandise or goods of the other party.

Bartering today is like service for service, not extremely common in the economic marketplace, but again, could be a viable alternative under the right conditions. If you or your family is "cash poor" but "asset sufficient," the funeral director may be open to listening to what you have available to barter for his or her goods and services.

Possible barter items may include but not be limited to financial instruments such as bonds, stocks, receivables to more tangible items such as vehicles, furniture, machinery or equipment.

Barter exchanges are few and far between in the funeral business but if you possess goods or assets that could be of interest to a funeral director and would be difficult to liquidate or turn into cash in a short period of time, this may be the way to go.

Taking From Peter To Give To Paul

Local, County, State Government Benefits

For families who have no funds, no credit lines, no assets, no means of payout and no extended family with any means to pay for a deceased family member's burial, application for assistance can sometimes be made to the location's governing entity whether it be city, county or an agency of state government.

When all other payment possibilities have been exhausted from family and private sources, the funeral director, on the family's behalf may be able to apply to the government agency in the appropriate jurisdiction for reimbursement to the funeral home for basic burial costs. This is subject of course, to the laws concerning public assistance in the said area. Most states and counties within have an established public policy on how to handle indigent cases.

After application is made to the appropriate authority, the

governing agency will more than likely proceed with a verification process to determine that the decedent's family/next-of-kin is indeed qualified for public assistance before approving the release of funds to the funeral home.

This usually means that the funeral home will only provide its minimum casket or burial container (or alternative container if cremation), transportation to funeral home from place of death and then transport to place of disposition (cemetery or crematory). The allowance may also include cost of a minimal outer container if the cemetery requires one or crematory fee.

If the family wants to have a ceremony or any rites, this is usually only a short graveside service if at a cemetery with no viewing or an open casket. Some funeral homes do indigent cases like immediate burials with no service. If cremation is the case, the family will be expected to hold its own memorial ceremony.

The key variable to remember about public assistance is that eligibility for help must be established and the criteria for carrying out disposition is very, very minimal, meaning family options and desires are considered secondary to the service provider's.

Like-Kind Exchanges
(Is it Likely?)

Where bartering to pay for final expenses deals with personal property, a like-kind exchange deals with either personal or real property. These are exchanges that are business for business or investment property for business property that refers to the character or nature of the property rather than the property's grade or quality.

Since there are at least several variables involved in like-kind exchanges such as paying for a portion of the transaction with one type of property and the other portion with a different type, there may be tax or other economic consequences triggered. For example, property that is exchanged that is not defined as like-kind is labeled "boot" which is not included in the definition of a nontaxable exchange.

If you are dealing with a funeral home that is flexible enough to consider such a transaction, consult with an accountant, attorney or tax advisor before consummating the transaction. The last thing that you will want to have happen is to do a like-kind exchange for funeral and/or burial expenses and then find out later on down the road that you have incurred a tax liability on the exchange as defined by any applicable tax laws.

Totten Trusts

Simply stated, a Totten Trust is a special bank account that is set up for the sole purpose of paying funeral expenses upon death. Instead of buying a prearranged funeral, you may go to the bank and open a Totten Trust that is a "pay upon death" or "in trust for" account payable directly to the funeral home or whomever you designate upon death.

The money is used only to pay the funeral costs of the designated person.

You may consider going to your bank or financial institution and discuss with them the details and whether or not they offer Totten Trusts.

Chapter 6

Available Benefits

1. Introduction
2. Pre Need vs. At Need
3. Preplanning vs. Prepaying
4. Social Security
5. Veterans Administration
6. Other Government Benefits: Employee/Public Servant/Crime Vic tim/Etc.
7. Employer Sponsored Benefits
8. Affinity Relationships
9. Spouse/Significant Other Protection
10. Child/Grandchild Protection
11. Travel Protection Plans
12. Bereavement Travel Fares
13. Personal Planning Guides
14. Aftercare Helps: "Estate Settlement Aids/Legal Clubs Financial Kits

Introduction

One of the silver linings behind any difficult situation we face in life is knowing that there is help available to assist in conquering the challenge.

The fact that there are resources out there that can help ease the pain in some aspect of saying good-bye to a loved one can be worthy of consideration.

In this chapter I want to show you some resources that are available that you may qualify to receive either due to your or the decedent's status in connection to or affiliation with certain entities.

Although not everyone may qualify for some, there are others that may be acquired in advance to hedge or insure against the sudden or unanticipated.

Why Today

Pre Need vs. At Need

In chapter five we talked about the value of having a prearranged funeral from the aspect of not only saving money but retaining value. Now I want to discuss the nuts and bolts of why prearrangement is so beneficial. In one sentence: To save you and/or your survivors headaches.

The beauty of preneed is being able to make decisions when one is thinking clearly and able to choose wisely under normal mental capacity- that is, before a death takes place and decisions are not so emotional, and therefore, more practical and reasonable. Having final arrangements made before needed is one of the best benefits available today to those who are willing to face the inevitable and take the first step to do it.

You Better Shop Around

Although prearranging is a sound idea as a general rule, where and how you prearrange can make a big difference. There are several ways that you may prearrange. One you can go directly to the funeral home or mortuary that you want to provide the services when death does occur, or you may go to a funeral planning or memorial society that provides information but does not offer services. In other words they do not later carry out the arrangements made but to take the agreement to whatever provider you chose, who will honor the plan to carry out the arrangements at the time of death.

Whichever establishment or preneed planning company you choose, be sure that your wishes are recorded in writing and that you are given a copy of the prearrangements made so that later on when the preneed becomes at-need you will have in writing what services and products the entity has agreed to provide.

Timing Is Everything

Preplanning vs. Prepaying

Where preplanning is the process of deciding what services and merchandise one would like to consume to carry out the final arrangements made, the act of prepaying is where a contract is actually executed between the seller and the buyer of the prearrangements to fund the services and merchandise when needed.

Since the costs of funeral, burial and other final arrangement expenses continue to climb, one of the crown jewels of preneed arrangements is prepaying or prefunding the arrangements in order to hedge against future price increases. In other words, you will only pay the costs of the arrangements made when you make the arrangements regardless of the rise in the costs on down the road.

As with preplanning, be sure to get a written agreement and to get a copy (Federal Trade Commission Rules are in Chapter 11) of the prepaying agreement to take with you. Different states have various rules about the regulation of prepaid funeral/final disposition policies so it would be wise to contact the governing authority in your state. (Chapter 12 includes a state-by-state listing of regulating entities, which would be a good place to start).

IT NEVER STOPS WORKING
Social Security

The Social Security Act of 1935 was enacted for the purpose of helping Americans receive protection benefits that include payments to survivors. This is to help ease some of the financial burden that may follow a death. Anyone who has worked and paid FICA taxes has been earning Social Security benefits for his or her family.

Qualified family members who usually can get benefits include:

* Widows and widowers over age 59.

* Widows and widowers at any age if caring for the deceased's child(ren) under age 16 or disabled.

* Divorced wives/husbands over age 59 if married 10 years or more.

* Widows/widowers, divorcees/wives/husbands age 50 or older if disabled.

* Minor Children (17 or younger).

* Children 18 or 19 if they attend school full-time.

* Children over age 18 who become disabled before age 22.

* A deceased worker's parents age 62 or older if they were being supported by the worker.

Also a one-time payment of $255 can be paid to a domestic spouse who was cohabitating with the worker at the time of death. In the event that there was not an eligible spouse, the one time payment may be made to a child(ren) eligible for benefits.

Applying for social security benefits may take place by calling, writing or visiting any social security office. Check your local phone book or information for listing. The toll free number is 1-800-772-1213. Representatives will answer 7 am - 7 p.m. on weekdays. The representative will be able to tell you what information you will need to apply for benefits.

A final note concerning social security benefits is that if one is planning on applying for the lump sum death payment of $255, application must be made within 2 years from the death of the insured worker unless good cause for failure to apply can be shown.

It should also be noted that the $255 benefit is not assignable to a funeral home or the person paying the funeral bill for the deceased worker's expenses as was the case before September 1,1981.

The funeral home must complete a Social Security Administration form 721, Statement of Death By Funeral Director.

When the Social Security office receives SSA-721, they will generally mail form SSA-8 directly to the person making the claim.

SALUTING A HERO
Veterans Administration

The United States government provides those who served in the armed forces who have died with at least several benefits to those who are eligible and were honorably discharged. V.A. benefits may vary based upon such factors as the veteran's length of service, wartime or peacetime duty and whether the veteran died due to causes initiated during his/her time in the service and whether death occurred while in a VA hospital or facility.

The very first step is to have a readable copy of the veteran's discharge papers, which is usually either a certificate or a DD-214 form that shows details of the veteran's service and discharge. Neither the funeral provider or the VA will move on providing any benefits until the proof of honorable discharge is submitted. If no discharge documentation can be found, the nearest Veterans Administration office should be contacted. The funeral home or cemetery can usually provide this phone number, or, one may call your local congressional office to get the number/point of contact. If not already on file in the VA's records, the following information will be needed:

1) Full name used at time when in the service.

2) Date of birth/place of birth

3) Social Security number

Once the proof of honorable discharge is established, the application for benefits can begin. Covered here is a brief summary of what may be provided for deceased veterans.

American Flag

All honorably discharged veterans are entitled to a United States flag that may either drape the casket, be folded into a triangle shape and displayed or simply given to the next-of-kin after services. The application for the flag known as VA90-2008 is usually filled out by the funeral director and signed by a relative or funeral director. Flags will not be issued after burial unless circumstances making it impossible to obtain one can be shown. This would be documented on the form VA90-2008.

Presidential Memorial Certificate

An embossed paper certificate inscribed with the veteran's name and bearing the President's signature can be obtained to honor the memory of deceased vets who were honorably discharged. These certificates may be framed or displayed as an ongoing commemoration of the deceased veteran's service to our country. Requests for and information about PMCs may be made to any V.A. regional office or by writing to:

Memorial Programs Service
National Cemetery Administration
U.S. Department of Veterans Affairs
810 Vermont Avenue, NW
Washington, D.C. 20420

National Cemeteries

All honorably discharged veterans and their spouses and

dependent children are permitted burial in a VA cemetery. This privilege may also be extended to some military related service civilians and some public health service personnel.

There is no charge for the burial space, grave marker, opening and closing of the grave or for the vault or outer container. Any other expenses are generally the responsibility of the veteran's family (such as transportation to the cemetery, for example).

Contact your nearest regional V.A. office or log on to the VA's website listed in chapter 10 under websites.

Marker/Headstone

A standard headstone or marker made of marble, granite, slate or bronze may be place upon the unmarked grave of any honorably discharged deceased veteran. Service completed by a vet after September 7, 1980 must meet special requirements however.

The Memorial Programs Services branch of the Department of Veterans Affairs administrates this service, which tries to ensure that no veteran's grave goes unmarked. This can be one of the most significant benefits a veteran can receive.

To be placed on an unmarked grave, anyone having knowledge of the deceased can make application. V.A. form 40-1330 is used to apply for a marker/headstone and can be obtained from any V.A. office, funeral home or cemetery.

Application for a memorial headstone/marker to be placed in a cemetery or memorial park to commemorate a veteran whose remains are not buried there may be made only by the veteran's next of kin. There is no time limit for filing application for a headstone/marker and a cemetery counselor or superintendent may be helpful in filling out or helping to fill out the VA40-1330 application form. The form itself may also be obtained from the cemetery or from the Memorial Programs Service address stated under the Presidential Memorial Certificate address given previously in this chapter.

Basic Burial Allowance

An amount not to exceed $300 may be paid for the expenses of burial and funeral of an eligible deceased veteran. The allowance includes not only burial but the other recognized methods of disposition such as cremation, burial at sea, etc.

Eligibility for the Basic Burial Allowance is limited and application must be made on VA Form 21-530, which can be obtained from your funeral director. The claim can be filed by the person whose funds were used to pay the vet's final expenses; the/funeral director if he/she is still owed money or the veteran's estate executor/administrator. The time limit for filing the claim is 2 years from the date of the veteran's final disposition.

Burial Plot Allowance

An allowance not exceeding $150.00 for expenses incurred for the burial space of a veteran when death occurred on or after August 1, 1973 in a private or other non-national cemetery may also be made on VA Form 21-530. The term plot is defined as the final disposition site of the deceased remains. Eligibility is limited as to the same requirements/conditions as the Basic Burial Allowance. The time limit for filing is also 2 years from date of the vet's final disposition. Contact your funeral home/director or the V.A. for more details.

Transportation

The costs incurred to move the deceased veteran from the place of death to the funeral home/place of burial may be made by the VA if death occurred in a V.A. facility. This allowance will be within the limits set by the Veterans Administration and details may be obtained from the V.A. or your funeral director.

Service Connected Disability

An amount not to exceed $1,500 may be paid in lieu of other burial benefits for veterans who die of a service-connected disability. Eligibility criteria are established by the V.A. and there is no time limit for filing a claim for this benefit.

Military Honors

In January 2000, the National Defense Authorization Act went into effect mandating the Department of Defense to be responsible for procuring its Honoring Those Who Served Program, which calls for at least two military representatives to attend the burial ceremony of any honorably discharged vet whose family requests military honors, to play taps and present the U.S Flag to the designated next-of-kin (as defined by the V.A.). Due to the realities of limited resources, the government may not provide a volley firing party or play taps with live music. The Department of Defense has authorized recorder Taps be played in C.D. in recent years due to manpower shortages.

With proper proof of honorable discharge, your funeral director may arrange military honors from the Defense Department (pending war or peacetime) at the family's request (this is also affected by the availability of personnel).

Private Benefits

Some funeral homes, cemeteries, casket manufacturers, burial vault makers and other providers have jumped on the bandwagon of providing special incentives to veterans and their families by promoting numerous types of offers such as flag cases (usually made of wood), discount certificates for providing funerals, engraved burial vaults, casket head panels with the flag or other military emblem, etc. to try to capture the veteran business. Contact your funeral home, cemetery of choice, memorial society, or cremation society to find out what they may offer.

V.A. BENEFITS SUMMARY

Benefit	Form	Applicant	Time Limitation
Flag	VA90-2008	Funeral Director	Before Burial*
Presidential Memorial Certificate	Contact Nearest VA Office	Anyone with Knowledge of Veteran	None
Marker/ Headstone	VA40-1330	Anyone With Knowledge of Veteran	None
Burial Allowance	VA21-530	Varies	2 Years From Date of Disposition
Plot Allowance	VA21-530	Funeral Director or Responsible Party	2 Years From Date of Disposition
Transportation	VA21-530	Funeral Director or Responsible Party	2 Years From Date of Disposition
Service Connected Death	VA21-530	Varies	None
Military Honors	Proof of An Honorable Discharge	Funeral Director	By day of Service (Ceremony)

*Unless dire circumstances can be shown

Government
A Servant Of The People

Some municipal, county or state governments offer death benefits to employees and their dependents as part of the packages that are offered along with health insurance and other perks for choosing to be an employee of that entity. There may be other programs also that benefit citizens within a governmental jurisdiction as a way to compensate families of a decedent for their loss.

Employee

Some governmental entities may cover some or all of the funeral and/or burial expenses of a decedent who is employed with them. This benefit may be contingent of the death being on the job or employment related or simply from working for that particular entity. Other death expense(s) benefits may be extended to retirees (usually those who served a certain number of years) and possibly to dependents. Check your employee benefits packet or with the human resources contact to see if there are any type of benefits available to cover funeral and/or burial expenses.

Public/Servants

Many police, fire, emergency or other departments that have personnel who die or are killed in the line of duty may also provide special benefits. Frequently the department of a fallen public servant will pay all of a large portion of the final expenses of one whose life was lost on the job. Again, check with the department's human resource contact to determine these benefits.

Crime Victims

Innocent victims of violent crime may be eligible for compensation under the laws of some states or other jurisdictions. The next-of-kin or dependent(s) of a deceased victim or other(s) who lived with a victimized decedent may receive monetary or other payment under compensation funds set up for that purpose. Funeral and burial expenses usually qualify as a cost that can be compensated to the crime victim's family.

Eligibility may vary from state to state but most compensation funds are established to help ease the financial burden and pay expenses to assist those dealing with deep trauma.

Contact the attorney general's office in your state, qualified legal council or call your state's public information phone number for help.

GETTING DOWN TO THE BRASS TACKS:
Employer Sponsored Benefits

Along with life insurance policies that are available today from most employers for their full-time or other eligible employees, some companies are offering funeral benefits as part of their benefits packages. The benefit may be set up like an insurance policy where the employee's designated beneficiary is given a check or voucher for a certain amount to be redeemed at any funeral provider the beneficiary may chose, or like a prearranged funeral plan where the benefit is set up with a particular funeral home or funeral company affiliate. This benefit may also offer the opportunity to preplan (make merchandise and/or service selections before need) or simply enroll in the program and receive payroll deductions to fund the employee's benefit for making the decisions on merchandise and services when needed.

Whichever is the case, this benefit can be worth a lot not only in monetary terms but also provide peace of mind.

THE PROOF IS IN THE PUDDING
Affinity Relationships

An Affinity program is a structured agreement between a funeral provider and another company or organization through which funeral benefits are provided by the funeral home/company to the employees of the contracting company or organization.

In recent years due to increased competition from other funeral providers, many funeral homes have developed a new way to capture future business through affinity networks. This allows the funeral provider the guarantee of future business and provides the company in the affinity relationship a way of offering a new voluntary benefit for its employees and their qualified family members. When signing up for the funeral benefits program the employee is usually given a membership card identifying him/her as a participant in the plan. The funeral benefits program offers the funeral and cremation benefits at a discount as a result of entering into the affinity program. The discount usually is anywhere between 5-25%.

Affinity programs are a great employee benefit from the standpoint that the money the employee pays into or is payroll deducted from the employee will be realized at a future date (the time of death) whereas some employee benefits paid for by the employee may never be used (such as disability insurance, cancer insurance, other health policies, etc.).

To Have And To Hold

Spouse/Significant Other Protection

Like a life or health insurance policy, when applying for enrollment in a funeral benefits program, it may be possible to add coverage for a spouse or domestic partner for a higher premium. This would allow the other to receive up to the same level of benefits as the primary enrollee. With the exception of children/grandchildren, the terms and conditions of the program/plan will determine whether other extended family members could be covered.

Finding Value
Child/Grandchild Protection

Nobody wants to think about the tragedy of losing a child or grandchild. But in the event that the unfortunate does happen, a child/grandchild protection policy may be available to cover the funeral expenses up to a certain limit. Some funeral homes and insurance companies that sell prearranged funeral plans will give the buyer an opportunity to add this protection (usually at no additional cost). The protection covers all children and grandchildren up to 18 or 21 years of age.

Some plans that are attachments to prearranged funeral policies that will provide funeral or cremation services free of charge up to the level of service, originally selected by the purchaser. Others will provide goods and services free of charge up to a certain dollar amount ($3,000 for example). Such protection for minors is extremely valuable but is often subject to conditions and restrictions of the seller (such as non-transferability for instance).

Fly Like An Eagle
Travel Protection Plans

Today more than ever before people are traveling; whether for work, vacation, or a quick weekend get away, our society is mobile and on-the-move. As a result, the chances of dieing away from home are also much greater.

Travel protection plans, or Away from Home protection, are insurance-like plans designed to handle all the details in the event of the death of the plan participant if more than a certain distance away from his or her residence (usually 50-100 miles).

The plan is designed to ease the burden, stress and possible high expense that is normally associated with trying to bring a loved one home. For a minimal one-time fee, a travel protection plan will issue a wallet size card to the participant that provides brief step-by-step information of what to do if death does occur away from home.

This type of protection is ideal for anyone who travels for either business or pleasure and is even better for people who travel to and from foreign countries. The travel plan will - with one phone call- handle and navigate through the red tape that often accompany the language and cultural barriers of death in a foreign country, alleviating at least some of the emotional stress that normally comes with the death of a loved one. These plans normally cover either all or most of the costs of getting the decedent back home from the place of death, all for an affordable investment that will be well worth the money spent.

The Road Less Traveled

Bereavement Travel Fares

Unlike travel protection plans that take care of getting the decedent back home, bereavement travel fares deal with getting one to where the funeral or memorial services are going to take place. These are discounted airfares that are offered by the airlines and possibly other common carriers such as bus companies, train and other travel providers.

Some funeral providers may also offer discounted travel fares as a result of choosing their particular firm to provide services for the decedent. These travel discounts may be offered over and beyond what the travel provider offers. Before making any travel arrangements or reservations, check with the family member/person who is making the funeral arrangements, and with the airline or travel provider to find out what is available. There are some providers that may also offer discounts on hotel accommodations, rental cars and restaurants also.

Getting Organized
Personal Planning Guides

These are folder type booklets that can be used to document vital statistics, funeral wishes, personal information and other valuable data about one's life that is used as an important reference for one's family and heirs.

Most funeral homes provide some type of personal planning guides free of charge to anyone who calls or requests one. There is no one standard format for a personal planning guide but most will have pages with spaces to fill in needed information about one's life and desires to be carried out after death such as estate and obituary information, family members to be notified and location of valuable documents (such as social security, military, life insurance, etc.). There is also space to detail one's wishes regarding his/her own funeral including but not limited to songs to be played, who to serve as pallbearers, who will speak, type of flowers to order, etc.

Personal planning guides are powerful tools for giving one's heirs and family a solid foundation for arranging one's final wishes and also for taking care of estate matters afterwards. I have included for your or a loved one's use a personal planning guide at the end of this book.

Staying Organized
Aftercare Helps

More and more funeral homes today are offering services and products to assist families with handling practical affairs after the service and/or disposition of the decedent. I want to mention just a few here that merit brief description because of their potential value to you.

Estate Settlement Aids

Some funeral providers sell or provide packets that deal

with managing business affairs and closing out the estate of a decedent. There can be many details, some of which may require immediate attention.

In order to help families get through this process estate settlement aids can help organize and streamline the activities in a non-confusing manner.

These aids may be in book, notebook or box form and usually include a way to document, track and take care of business in an organized and timely manner. Some estate packets are more elaborate than others containing prewritten letters, tips on how to deal with lawyers, accountants and others you may contact as well as prepaid postage for mailing and phone cards.

Simply basic estate aids may be furnished at no charge, whereas the more complete, comprehensive aids may run $100-350. Even if the estate of the decedent is not large, complex, unorganized or won't necessarily require a lot of time and attention, the top-of-the-line settlement aids are still a very good buy for the money and can save you confusion, unnecessary service charges and other hassles.

<u>Legal Clubs</u>

Along with estate settlement organizers comes legal plan memberships. These legal clubs can provide members with free and/or discounted legal advise and legal services concerning wills, probate, estates, trusts, and many other legal matters.

Usually included is a packet with a membership card, registration form and documents to get you in touch with obtaining the guidance you will need concerning any outstanding legal issues of the estate.

Legal plans can be valuable tools in helping you know where to start and where to go on handling these often-complex matters.

<u>Financial Kits</u>

No Aftercare/Helps list would be complete without mentioning financial assistance services.

Tracking and documenting the money from an estate is as important as anything else, and since most states require some form of inventory or appraisement of an estate, financial kits can be invaluable.

These kits can also come in book or box form and often contain record-keeping forms, bank account reconciliation guides, advise on how, where and when to pay estate expenses, taxes, and investing the monies from the estate, just to name a few. Even for the analytically minded and super-methodical, financial kits tailored for estates are priceless.

Chapter 7

Dealing With Grief & Mourning

1. Introduction
2. After The Funeral - What To Expect
3. What Is Grief And Mourning
4. Myth vs. Reality
5. Family Reorganization And Transition
6. Death And The Culture
7. Soul Searching
8. Becoming Disenfranchised
9. Cause And Manner Of Death
10. Sudden vs. Anticipated Death
11. Untimely Death
12. Children And Death
13. Teenagers And Death
14. Anticipatory Grief
15. Loss In Early Life
16. Loss in Mid Life
17. Loss In Later Life
18 Special Situations: No Services Held/Delayed Disposition/Delayed Services/No Viewing
19. Grief That Does Not Seem To Go Away
20. What Is Aftercare
21. Getting Help From The Helpers
22. Family And Friends
23. Funeral Directors as a Source of Help
24. Clergy, Ministers And Churches
25. Social Service Organizations
26. Counselors And Psychologists
27. Physicians And Psychiatrists
28. Social Workers
29. Support Groups
30. Attorneys

31. Certified Public Accountants
32. Financial Planners And Consultants
33. Estate Planners
34. Insurance Agents
35. Literature And Available Helps
36. Pets And Animals Can Help
37. Making Sense Of It All
38. How To Resolve Grief And Recover
39. Helping Other Friends And/Or Family; Supporting Others
40. Troubleshooting 101- Getting On with Life Again
41. Dealing With Business Issues
42. Conclusion
43. 25 Ways To Overcome And Get Through Grief

If the subject of death were as easy as making funeral/burial arrangements and then "moving on" to a normal life after the passing of a loved one, then dieing would not sting the way it can in the days following the services and disposition of one now gone.

What is now left to deal with is your life- your day-to-day living and the lives of those most impacted by the death.

Aftercare, what it is and how to cope with bereavement and the grief that is sure to follow is the feature here. Part of handling these issues of sorrow and mourning, we will first of all look at how the loss is manifesting itself and then apply the help that's available. What you will find is that different people- even those of the same household or upbringing- can react dramatically different to death. We will also take a look at the various tasks that often must be handled concerning business issues and what to expect regarding an estate.

After The Funeral - What To Expect
(The Morning After)

There can be a myriad of things to deal with once the services are over and this can seem overwhelming. Certain emotions not felt previously may now surface; the feeling of a void may be felt once friends and family who were with you since or shortly after the death occurred have departed to continue with their own lives. Although there is usually a sense of relief that you made it through the services and initial stage of the loved one's death, a difficult task may lay ahead with the readjustment into your day-to-day life.

For some people, a deep level of grief can take hold within their own soul, making living difficult and hard to endure. For others, bouncing back can be easier and getting back to a routine is more elementary. Most mourners however fit somewhere into the middle of the two extremes of deep mourning and sorrow and the reemergence into contentedness and well-being.

Since the death of a loved one can affect survivors in so many different ways and on so many different levels, the discussion of grief and mourning is rather complex and the scope rather large.

What Is Grief And Mourning

Anytime during the course of our lives that we experience a loss or disappointment of something important or meaningful to us, the foundation is laid for us to experience grief and mourning.

Whether it is the losing of a job or important position, not achieving the grade or desired outcome in a class at school, a favorite sports team losing an important game or the loss of a relationship through abandonment, separation or death, the fact that we attached ourselves to something or someone gives us the opportunity to deal with the departure or disappointment when we no longer have, achieve or experience the desired outcome or relationship.

In its most basic form, grief is the experience of thoughts, feelings and attitudes that one has toward a perceived loss and can be manifested physically, psychologically or socially. Grief can be acute (short-term) or chronic (long-term). Since grief is internal or "felt on the inside," a person can feel it and choose to try to ignore and not deal with these feelings. Many times we refer to someone in grief as bereaved.

Mourning on the other hand is the expression outwardly of what a person feels as a result of a loss or undesired outcome or event. Whenever someone is crying, talking about the one passed away, attending or participating in a ritual or ceremony for the departed, this is the act of mourning.

Grief is the inner reaction to a death or other loss; mourning is the outer expressing of the grief felt. One may put off or chose not to mourn, but grievous feelings will remain inside the one grieved until they are felt or "dealt with" by the griever.

Myth Vs. Reality
(Honesty Is The Best Policy)

Separating myth from reality (your reality) is one of the first most important steps to be taken when confronting grief.

Realize that grief does not move in an orderly or predictable process. One minute you may feel fine, the next you are sad about your departed loved one. You may go days, weeks or even months and feel no sadness or bereaved feelings and then all of a sudden you are shaken with the loss again. Sometimes these feelings can be triggered by a stimulant such as seeing the deceased's picture or driving by the house where he or she lived, etc.

Another myth is that you should try to " get over" the loss, try not to cry or express any emotion, or avoid anything that would provoke you to face your true emotions about the loss. Avoiding, ignoring or turning away from grief does not make it go away but oftentimes only prolongs it over time. Remember that you and everyone else on this earth are unique, so are your feelings, perceptions, emotions and reactions. How you deal with and how long it takes you to resolve your grief is a process that is as unique as you are.

Family Reorganization And Transition
(If The Shoe Fits Wear It)

Just as you the individual must experience and reshape your life as a result of losing a significant person in your life, so must your family. When a family member dies there is a process that the family as a unit must go through to readjust to life without mom, dad, grandma, grandpa, or whoever.

Since most families depend upon each individual family member in some way to contribute to the family unit, the new absence of the deceased family member creates a new void that will need to be filled by someone else in order to keep equilibrium or balance for the family. If the decedent was the one who cooked all the family's meals, for example, someone else will need to step into that role. Because of the huge range of jobs or roles that family members can have, the role to be filled may be very simple or enormously difficult depending on whether it was taking out the trash or the sole breadwinner who made the family's living with a six figure income.

Whatever your family's situation is, be aware of the serious repercussions of reassigning roles or duties to family members who may not be suited for the task. It is unfair to ask a little boy to now be the "man" of the house if he is the only male. Likewise if little Suzy is given the job of now being the cook and homemaker for the house, you are only asking for more problems.

Furthermore, it is imperative to realize that reorganizing a family is a large challenge in and of itself, but add in the grief factor- the idea that you have x number of family members dealing with the death in his or her own way—and at best you have an intense situation.

Several things to keep in mind are that it is important to weigh the family unit as a whole to the needs of each particular family member- a balancing act may need to take center stage. Families need to compromise in order to survive in the 21st century. Along with the myths discussed earlier, families cannot expect each individual within its clan to have the same needs- personal differences must be taken into account. Be gentle and be patient.

Death And The Culture
(Do You See what I See)

Along with many other social changes that have taken place in western society the past 3-4 decades is the fact that death is not taboo as it once was. What is experienced today is a more open attitude toward funerals, more inquisitiveness about what happens at funeral homes, and a curiosity about death itself that may not be new, but has evolved into an open-ended expressiveness.

We are not afraid to talk about or hear about death, funerals and mortuaries as we once were, but there is among some a preservation of denial that we ourselves, or someone we know, is grieving over a loss that they cannot (or will not) face. Our culture's rugged individualism says real men don't cry. Stuff it. Suck it up. Be an adult. You've probably heard others. Death is not taboo but dealing with the grief inside of us is.

What is happening to some extent in our country today is a result, I believe, of people who have suffered the loss of someone close but have not properly dealt with it. What happens instead is a manifestation of unresolved grief: drug abuse, alcoholism, addiction, co-dependency, marital problems, divorce, gambling, compulsiveness, eating disorders, anger, rage., etc. Not all these problems are necessarily caused by unfelt grief from a death, but some are. Recognizing how you or someone you know and care about feels and behaves is a step in the direction of positively resolving problems at hand.

Soul Searching
(Up Close And Personal)

If you want to have an impact in your family, your community and even our country at large, your heart is in the right place. But the place to start is with you. How are you?

Since the death of your loved one have you analyzed your own thoughts and feelings? Have you mourned?

Several questions to ask yourself and look at are:

* Do I feel overly emotional to the point of being out of control? Do I feel completely numb?

* Am I as sociable now as I was before _ died? If not, do I want to be again?

* Do I feel angry or irritable? If so how do I deal with it, and am I lashing out at those I love the most, risking their withdrawal or absence?

* Have I lost or gained a lot of weight? How have my eating habits changed, and if so should I be concerned?

* What do I do to relax and get my mind off my worries? Of course there are many others you can ask and answer but the main idea is to define how the death has and is affecting you. Before you can really help someone else you must be in a stable place yourself. The problems don't go away by themselves, there is action to take and work to do.

Becoming Disenfranchised
(Heartbreak Hotel)

One of the toughest parts in the unspoken language of post death etiquette is learning to handle "your world." Many times friends stop calling or corning by because they may think you want to be left alone. You may think, "I wish someone would call or stop by." When a spouse dies for example, you become single again. Maybe for years all your social activities were with other couples. Now what. You are not a couple anymore; you are just you. Maybe you and your spouse did things with other couples as a group. The group has plans to get together and go do something, however now they feel too awkward calling you to join them. They feel like you will decline an invitation and assume you will feel too awkward as the only single in the group without a partner. You on the other hand feel rejected by them for not contacting you. And so now you're in a place of dealing with "two losses" instead of one. Loss of a spouse among other deaths- of a child, parent or sibling-can and often does change your social status, but later in this chapter I will present some ideas and considerations that may serve as solutions. For now let's look at how a loved one's passing effects you and other family members in relation to different stages in the lives of survivors.

Cause And Manner Of Death

When, where and how a person died is perhaps the single biggest factor in determining how a survivor will cope with, and how long he or she will cope with the death.

If the decedent was quite elderly and died at home while asleep in familiar surroundings after a long full and enjoyable life, this will be quite different for survivors to deal with and heal from than one who may have died quite young while going through deep troubles, many problems and the questioning of "why."

It's true that death is death and departing this world on either "good" or "bad" terms is still hard at best. But psychologists have told us that the shock, horror and senselessness that's perceived and experienced in cases of accident, disaster, homicide, suicide and outcome unknown (such as a missing in action solider in war after many years), can be devastating.

Did the loved one die at peace or while suffering? Is there evidence of other crimes or actions committed that complicate the death such as torture, assault, mutilation, decapitation, dismemberment, burglary, threats announced against others, etc.? Violence and pain to a loved one taken invokes extreme anger, rage, helplessness, fear and vulnerability. There is often a very harsh sense of insecurity for a long time afterwards. There can be a lot of guilt also in the survivors asking themselves "why wasn't I there?" "I could have prevented this if only I was there." Such questioning is very normal. There is nothing rational or logical about some types of deaths, there will be nothing rational or logical about coping with it. There may even be other family members or friends that may blame you for the death (and manner it happened) of the loved one. They are also feeling very guilty and so guilty that they project blame onto someone else (you), in order to try to deal with their own feelings of hysteria.

You may feel accused, but realize that the feelings of others are their feelings whether right, wrong or indifferent. Be realistic about any blame you accept and be careful not to internalize the attitudes of others.

Sudden Vs. Anticipated Death
(A Closer Look)

A family in our community that we'll call the Anderson's recently lost Mr. Anderson, age 52, at the prime of his career, to a surprising out-of-the blue heart attack. A complete and total shock to his wife, kids, neighbors, relatives and community. No warning, no signs, no sickness or recent illnesses, just here one moment, gone the next.

Several doors down, another family we'll call the Jacksons, are caring for, as they have been now for four years, Mr. Jackson's elderly mother, who has Alzheimer's, a prolonged form of cancer, and at age 89 is slowly wasting away, little by little until one day she quietly passes away in her bed, surrounded by family who are almost surprised she lived this long.

Both families are now dealing with a death in their midst, but circumstances very different. The Anderson's still have many financial obligations, kids to get through school, commitments to fulfill and now the shock of the family's leader and breadwinner gone in an instant. The Jackson's have other issues that although less stressing in a sense of financial security and leadership, can still be difficult in that a fixture who has always been with them is now gone. Maybe the family member(s) who waited on and cared for her have lost a part of their identity in that caring for the family matriarch for so long and "needing to be needed" by someone has now displaced their sense of usefulness.

Both families will go through some changes and it is important to know that it does not really help to compare losses in order to decide which one is the worst. All losses are painful, just in different ways.

In examining sudden death, we have to understand that although a person is taken like a thief in the night that there will be two basic separate but also intertwined issues: one is the suddenness and surprise of the death, the other is the mode of the death. With the sudden death there is shock, disruption, overwhelming unpreparedness (in most cases). The loss does not make sense and there is an onslaught of emotion and anxiety.

The fact that you have been robbed of the expectation you had to continue your life with the decedent as part of your future is now gone. You had no chance to say good-bye, no opportunity to control your own plans. Now you have bewilderment, anger, maybe depression.

How about mode of passing; lets take a look at several to identify impact and response.

<u>Accident</u>

There are two types of accidents- natural disasters such as flood, earthquake, hurricane, avalanche, etc., and accidents due to human error such as a house fire, plane crash, car wreck, etc. The survivors of those who've died in unpreventable circumstances tend to fare better after the fact than those who've perished in some perceived preventable incident.

If your loved one dies in an earthquake there is no one to blame. If he or she is killed in an automobile by a drunk driver there is. Someone is responsible and action should be taken. It could have been avoided and so you must deal with anger usually directed at the one responsible.

When a natural disaster or unavoidable, uncontrollable event comes and takes a loved one who happened to be at the wrong place at the wrong time, you will more or less feel powerless and possibly try to blame yourself although subconsciously you know it would not and could not have altered the outcome.

If death comes from a natural event, expect to feel helpless, powerless, unfocused and confused. If the death is caused by an error or mistake in human judgment, there is an opportunity for blame, anger, and a desire to find and place responsibility and a fixation on wanting to punish that responsible party(ies).

Homicide

Because of the violent and traumatic nature of this type of death, the grief and mourning that accompanies it are rather dramatic. The shock and repulsion that someone made a choice to take your loved one's life and robbed you of that person send shock waves of enormity over the lives of those affected. If the assailant was someone your loved one knew, you may have extreme anger that he or she was involved with that person. You may even have guilt about whether or not you could have done something to prevent your loved one from being at the crime scene.

Grief resulting from homicide tends to last an extremely long time and can be accompanied by paranoia, unfairness, feeling out of control, and a sense of injustice. Some even feel victimized by the criminal justice system depending on how the case is handled and the timeliness of the action. Many survivors of homicide victims state that they cannot begin their own healing until the legal system administers proper justice to the wrongdoer and resolution of the legal issue at hand.

Suicide

This is maybe the hardest type of death for survivors to accept because of the fact that the decedent chose to die. Like homicide, it did not have to happen but it did anyway.

Oftentimes family members of a suicide victim feel confused, embarrassed, betrayed, rejected and shamed. There is an intense pain and stigma attached to suicide and sometimes the survivors feel guilty enough about the death that they may want to punish themselves, sometimes in conscious ways such as threatening suicide themselves, inflicting pain or pushing themselves beyond reasonable limits, or in more subtle ways such as workaholism, not eating (anorexia), not getting treated for a sickness, etc.

There is much confusion and unanswered questions that some survivors do not know how to cope with even though they may want to. Do not be afraid to ask for professional help. If you are a suicide victim's survivor and are wondering if you do need help you probably do. I'll talk more about this later in this chapter in getting help from the helpers.

Natural-Acute

What we are talking about here is apart of the discussion on sudden death. The difference is that there is a quick occurrence in some physiological malfunction that causes death, such a as heart attack, stroke or dieing in one's sleep. In these situations you are spared from having to deal with a personal agent's responsibility for the death as opposed to the previous forms of suicide, homicide, and accident. However it can be easy to identify and blame any possible contributing factors such as long-term smoking, alcohol abuse, overeating, etc.

Some survivors will still try to blame themselves for not doing more to guide the decedent to possibly make better choices during life. "If only I had pressed him/her harder to give up smoking years ago; If only I had insisted he/she go on that diet." Although there is always prodding that could have made a difference, it also could have not. The decedent was the one who had ultimate choice and responsibility concerning issues that may have led to the timing of his or her death.

Natural-Chronic

There are various illnesses and life-lingering situations that may cause a loved one to approach death more as a process rather than as an event. Although people who have lost someone very suddenly may think the families of chronic illness patients are blessed, these families often see it very differently.

A multitude of factors and variables enter into the long-term care equation and many special problems and dilemmas are created that demand attention and action:

Is our family equipped to handle this process?

When will it end? How exactly will it end?

Lengthy periods of anticipating the death
Remissions, relapses, uncertainty
Emotional, financial, physical and social pressure
Treatment options, facilities, doctors, methods

When death does finally come, you and/or other family members may be so exhausted that you may be too depleted emotionally, physically, and financially that you cannot grieve.

Your life may have become so altered in caring for the deceased that you gave up hobbies, interests and a social life to tend to them. Recognizing that a huge amount of resources in your life may have been spent to the point that you are now "out of gas." Consider the reasoning that it's imperative that you give yourself and other survivors a much-deserved break to replenish yourselves following such a stressful and demanding time.

Untimely Death

One of the saddest and most tragic things we see in the funeral profession is the one who has died "before his or her time." Regardless of the other factors and circumstances involved, when a person dies before age 65-70 in most cases or when the decedent still has a full slate of unaccomplished goals, mountains to conquer, tasks to do, there is still an added degree of grief on what could have been.

Whether a lingering condition or a sudden event, survivors of untimely deaths usually go through an extended time of reflection and looking for answers. "How could this happen?" He/she still had so much to live for. Usually there is some form of guilt or blame. "If I had only been a better ... (husband/wife/friend/brother) maybe this would not have happened," you state. Maybe in the large overall scheme of the universe, perhaps it was their time to die for reasons unknown. Because of the untimeliness of the passing there are usually many business related matters, estate issues and loose ends to tie up. This may delay the grieving process because the immediate need may be to deal with these pressing matters first.

Untimely death, sudden or not, will involve some long-term grieving and a trying to understand why? If there are dependents of the decedent they will need the most attention because they have lost someone they were depending on for support, parenting, care giving, etc. Don't expect a quick passing of issues, feelings or anything else; it may take quite some time to get things and survivors back to a settled, balanced life routine again.

Children And Death

Grief in children is very real and very personal. Kids are much more in tune with what is going on than we think many times. Whether it is the death of a sibling, parent, grandparent or other significant person in the child's life, it is important to understand that children grief similarly to adults, but are dissimilar in how they show it.

You must learn that children are in a unique situation regarding the death in that they will live longer with the memory than anyone else, in that they have had death illustrated to them that they too can die, and that they may feel anger at their parents for not preventing the death from happening. Children also in a sense feel the grief of their parents and may either presently or in the future try to "act out" in such a way as to create a distraction so that other family members will not have to think about the death.

The bottom line is that children grieve. They need the help of their parents and other adults especially in coping with major loss. Most psychologists believe children become aware of a death, that someone is missing or gone, from about age 2 ½ to 3 years. Your focus should be on several areas. One is to include your child or children in the funeral, memorial service or other ceremony for the decedent and two is to support normal grief responses from children rather than allow unhealthy ones.

You will need to pay close attention to how you communicate about death to your child. Use words and ways that he or she will understand given his or her age and capabilities. Be clear and honest about what happened. Be straightforward, realistic. It is not wrong to try to protect the child from too much information if the death was traumatic, violent or very dramatic. Using deceit or deception, however, will backfire. Someday even if it is years later, the child will be able to learn the truth. If you are dishonest and tell something to the child that is untrue, they will then also feel resentful toward you for not being honest.

And so, several words of advice in dealing with children when a death occurs close at hand:

1. Be honest and truthful without getting graphic or too overwhelming with details.

2. Tell the child about the death as soon as possible to prevent him or her from hearing it from someone else.

3. A parent or someone very close to the child should tell him or her in surroundings the child is familiar with.

4. Let the child know that a very sad thing has happened and that the adults are upset.

5. Tell the child what to expect at the funeral home and/or the place where the service/ritual will take place.

6. Reassure the child that you are there for him or her, that he or she is loved and will continue to be taken care of.

7. Allow the child to ask questions, be held or participate in ways that will be helpful to them.

When A Child Dies

In her book *Marilyn*, about the life of the late Marilyn Monroe, Gloria Steinem talks about the actresses death at such an early age in comparison to others and writes: "When the past dies, there is mourning, but when the future dies, our imaginations are compelled to carry it on."

The most profound form of bereavement comes from the

death of a child. Profound in that it is the most intense, unpredictable and longest-lasting grief. Regardless of age—stillborn, infant, toddler, preadolescent, a part of the future-your future-has died. All of the hopes, dreams, expectations, plans and wishes have now gone upside down.

A child's death is multi-faced in various respects. When a minor passes away from whatever cause or manner, along with the ideas and intentions that child's life represented, the parents and other family members lives change also. If you are the parent, all of a sudden the role you saw for yourself in relation to the child for the years to come has ended. You now will have an altered role for your life. Even if you have other children or may have in the future, a unique individual is gone and you're impacted by it.

Different family members will react differently to the child's death but still have deep grief issues. Parents, siblings, grandparents, extended family, will all have some repercussions in dealing with the shock and disappointment. No matter how you calculate it, a child's death upsets the natural balance of things. Children are supposed to someday bury their parents, not the other way around. As a result there is a tremendous opportunity opened to respond in such a way that can create more problems in the future because of the confusion, distress, disbelief and hopelessness that can surface.

What you do or don't do in connection to this loss, whether you are the parent of the deceased child, a family member/relative, or a friend of someone who has lost a child, may be the most important thing you ever do in your lifetime.

Usually the immediate family of a child who has died is so shattered and shaken that how they are helped, supported, affirmed and dealt with may make a difference toward their own future. Unfortunately there is a higher rate of divorce among couples that have lost a child. There is more addiction, alcohol and drug abuse, more dysfunctional behavior and long-term social problems from families where a child has died. Concern in these situations is critical. Here are some things that need to be done:

1. Realize the Truth- This Is Out of Order. Everything may now seem illogical and unstructured. Allow yourself to feel your emotions; Allow yourself to feel numb.

2. Talk About Your Loss. When you share, you heal. When you don't share, you don't heal. This may not be easy; you may even feel like you're going crazy or losing control. Speak from your heart not just your head.

3. Support Others Also Affected By The Loss. Be there for your spouse, surviving children, whoever else needs support. You may need to prioritize your life to do this but it will have definite long-term benefits.

4. Find Out what Your Limits Are And Respect Them. Yes, be there for the other survivors. Develop a support system, but realize that you are human, not machine. Impaired judgment, marginal decision making, low energy level, fatigue, depression, sadness can wear you thin. Care for yourself. Sleep, eat, watch a show, call a friend, go for a walk or other activity.

So much hoped for so much gone. Many who've lost a child have had to go for professional help in order to survive. Don't be afraid. There is a reason for everything. If you feel like you or someone you love needs extra help there are those ready to help. Later in this chapter I'll discuss what's available along with resources in chapter 10.

Teenagers And Death

Each year thousands of teenagers experience the death of someone they know and love. Whether it is a parent, grandparent, sibling, friend or other significant person, there is a legitimate feeling of sorrow for a person who helped shape their own fragile identity.

Since teenage years are normally difficult anyway from the developmental stage of adolescence, many young people are at various levels of both physical and emotional maturity. Since physical development does not always equal emotional maturity, some adults are apt to tell teens to "be strong" or to "suck it up," "welcome to the real world", or even worse, in the case of a parent or other contributing family member, you're now going to have to help "carry the load" (whatever that may mean). Since no period in life is as filled with change, volatility and self-doubt as the teenage years, many teens tend to not share their feelings and thoughts about what has happened, and this can lead to long-term problems for the teen.

The death that comes is often sudden for teenagers and as a result there is a heightened sense of unreality added to an environment where support is usually lacking. Most teens cannot talk to their friends about the death because most teens peers may not have gone through the same experience yet themselves of losing someone close.

Because of the normal process of developing and forming an identity and life apart from their family, teens are less likely to approach them for help. As a result, the teenager may feel lonely, betrayed and form a low self-esteem as he or she progresses toward adulthood.

Some teens in grief may begin to behave in ways that are inappropriate or out of the norm such as the following:

1. An aloofness or separation from family, friends, others.
2. Living in denial about pain while acting strong or mature.
3. Change in habits, academic performance, or interests in activities previously excited about.
4. Restlessness, rebellious, depressed, sleeping difficulties or change in social temperament.

Along with sitting down with the teen one-on-one to talk about the death and its impact on both of you and the rest of the family, it is important to convey that it's OK to mourn and be expressive about the loss. Teens need a caring adult to tell them it is alright to feel a range of emotions when someone dies.

Another consideration is peer support groups that are becoming more available for teens. Many are realizing that when teenagers can connect with other teens that have had a similar loss it can be very beneficial and appreciated.

When A Teen Dies

Adolescence begins the period of separation from parents. When a teenager dies it can be disheartening for parents especially from the standpoint that the parent is deprived of ever seeing the "finished product" or getting to enjoy the fruit of their labor in the adult child.

Each year also, thousands of teens die prematurely with auto accidents and suicide among the leading causes. Many times there is anger and deep resentment toward society at large because the death in many ways seems unfair. All the years of teaching, nurturing, sacrificing and preparing the teen for the future all seem a waste.

Usually there is some level of community support immediately after a teen dies but unfortunately it can dissipate quickly when people get on to their normal lives again. There is usually a huge void left because the house is now without him or her.

The point here is to realize that you'll feel as if you have lost a major investment of your time, energy and other resources in giving someone else (the teen) a future that is now destroyed. Your biggest challenge will be to deal with the void that is left. This will come from sharing your disappointed expectation with someone who can empathize with you.

Support groups or networks are usually a vital link as well as talking to family, friends and others who are available.

Loss In Early Life

Young adulthood is usually a time of change, establishing oneself and making and implementing the plans that one intends to unfold in making one's mark in this world.

Most people between 18 an 35 have developed their ideas about the world at large including death, funerals and disposition. They will probably see the death of an older adult in a very conventional way but a sudden or untimely death in a more dramatic manner.

For example, a 25 year old who is finished with school, out on their own and working in their first big career position and all of the sudden their 50 year old parent falls dead of a heart attack. Since he or she is now on their own and no longer dependent on dad, there may be a deep ground swell of emotion based upon the evolved relationship coming to an abrupt end.

In functional family situations once the adult child leaves home finishes school and sets up shop for their own life, a normal course for the adult child-adult parent relationship would be to move from one of dependence and support to one of friendship and mutuality. A chance for parent and offspring to enjoy each other's company rather than fulfill duty-obligation, dependence-submission.

A sudden death that robs the young adult of being able to have this type of relationship can be unbalancing and disappointing to say the least. Young adults are in a position usually to be less impacted from a financial, dependent standpoint but perhaps more from not being able to relate adult to adult for the desired length of time.

Young adults who lose a significant person in their lives may develop maturity issues. The passing of someone close can either speed up or slow down the young adult's maturation process depending on some of the other factors involved in the relationship.

Being available to listen and encouraging the young adult to talk or share their feelings will be both helpful and appreciated. Everyone needs a friend and a shoulder to lean on when a loss occurs.

Death Of A Young Adult

Much like the death of a teenager, the death of an 18-35 year old leaves survivors focused upon what could have been, what should have been. Many variables again enter the equation here, -marriage, children, education, goals anticipated, goals met, a legacy left.

For parents of a young adult now gone there is still the deep anguish that will be felt by parents at any age of death of a son or daughter. Even accomplishments and things done leave little gladness for the parent of a departed child of any age.

Regardless of the facts, there is usually a great outpouring of support for the spouse (if married) and kids (if applicable) of the young adult decedent. There is also a questioning about why this young man or woman was not allowed to reap the rewards of life usually sown while growing up.

One of the most overlooked issues regarding the death of a young adult is in acknowledgment. Acknowledgment of the death itself. The person that he or she was-apart from a spouse, apart from children, apart from work, status or anything else.

The death of anyone in the energy and vigor of their youth leaves everyone feeling vulnerable and insecure. Being able to focus on the decedent as an individual- a unique person will help survivors deal with the loss at hand.

Mid-Life Crisis

The segment of our population in the 36-64 age bracket represents the engine and drive of our society. This is the age group that predominately provides the resources, raises the kids, build the homes, create the jobs and businesses, pay the taxes, care for the elderly and manage society.

This group tends to be more settled than the 18-35 segment, more financially stable, independent rather than dependent, want to be in control, appear strong, and do things their way. A good number of those we see to come to make funeral arrangements are in this age group whether it be an at-need or preneed situation.

Death of a loved one appears to affect mid-lifers the least. They tend to get "busy" after a loss with work or other activities to numb themselves of the pain they feel over the loss. They are weaker on the inside than they appear to onlookers, but with lots of responsibilities to take care of, often allow their little inner voice to tell them that mourning is for weaklings, that grief can be put off until retirement or a more convenient time because there are many commitments to keep, projects to finish and tasks to complete.

However important the business of getting on with life seems, grief doesn't go away until it is fully felt. It is no respecter of persons or ages of persons. No matter how many clubs you've joined, organizations you support, boards you serve on, employees you manage or chores you do, you still need to grieve. What happens when you don't grieve a loss? It goes underground. It organizes a coup in your inner spirit. It demands to be recognized and felt. Mid-lifers are expert at stuffing emotions and getting away with it. However, stuffing is for turkeys on the holidays.

So what do you do? Whether it is you or someone you care about, there needs to be a call to come out of denial (if this is the case) and come to terms with the loss. There will probably be some work to do to pry open the container of emotions and start to feel the unwanted feelings. The memories of the past about the person needs to be shared good or bad. Experiences need to be relived with a friend or other trusted person. Recognizing these needs are vital in an effort to help yourself or other who wears the face of strength and/or control when that may not be the case.

Death Of The Mid-Life Adult

Because of the characteristics of carrying the rest of society stated previously about adults in the 36-64 range when someone in this stage of life dies it often comes suddenly and without warning. Even when death may come after an illness such as cancer for example, there can still be a cry of questioning and confusion because of the idea that he or she "overcame every other obstacle or challenge in life", so why die now?

The passing of a mid-life adult will shake survivors considerably. There is usually a great creation of insecurity that will surface and for dependents of a mid-life adult who dies, a feeling of alienation, desertion or even betrayal. Because of their active status and abilities, leaving the world in mid-passage can lead to very significant needs in jeopardy of not being met. The stories of wives being left with 2-3 kids to continue raising and only enough life insurance to continue the family's current standard of living for about 3 years is common. Mid-life deaths also lead to large family changes in other ways- emotionally, socially, etc. New unexpected problems to deal with added to the work of grief and mourning can complicate things exponentially.

It is very important for the surviving family members of one who was making big contributions to the family's welfare to unite and help support one another, to communicate their thoughts and feelings but to also give each person their space.

Loss In Later Life

When someone who is retirement age or elderly dies, survivors usually have some feeling that the decedent lived a full life by respect of making it to or having a chance to retire kick back and relax. When an elder adult passes away there is a sense of the grief not being as complex as a death in other stages of the human cycle. Senior adults have, for the most part, had a chance to live life to the fullest, to make choices and take risks and see the results of those choices.

Regardless of the status of the elder adult at death, there are some very real grief issues that must be faced. Many adult children who lose a parent still feel vulnerable despite the fact that the death of parents is the single most common form of bereavement for adults[1]. The death may or may not be expected due to the fact that people today live well past retirement age by as much as 20+ years. An older adult may be very active, have always lived in good health and glided into the winter of life with little slow down. The death of an age 65+ adult is not insignificant. Depending upon your relationship to the one who died, it can potentially be as devastating as any death at any age. The longer a person lives as a significant role model, matriarch, patriarch, leader, teacher, advisor, counselor, whatever to someone else, the more that person's life becomes a part of you. If it's a parent, aunt, uncle, godparent, older sibling or lifelong friend, realizing all of a sudden that he/she is not here anymore can be threatening.

Older adults have so much to give, so much wisdom and insight as a result of running the race, of going the distance and learning lessons each of us can learn from. When death comes it is like a link to history, to the past, has died, and, in a sense it has.

If your relationship to an elder adult who's died was less than perfect or problematic, there may be guilt feelings to recognize and confront. When you've experienced the death of a person whose life has gone the full trajectory, expect a lot of pondering, reminiscing and reliving the relationship. Take some time to do this and heal.

Senior Survivor

What about the 65+ adult who loses someone. This is usually a spouse; however it can be a sibling, close longtime friend, etc. It can also be the death of an adult child, grandchild, or other. Since older people have weathered many storms through life, grief in older people is often overlooked. Most people assume that senior citizens will "get past it." This may or may not be the case. Grieving can be the greatest among older people. They must face and deal with the death head-on.

Oftentimes there is not a full schedule of activities and engagements that afford the older population the opportunity to deny the loss by "getting busy and involved again." It may not be as simple as moving forward and "putting this behind us." A senior adult's entire life is "behind" them in the sense of living each day within a historical context or framework. The present and future is oftentimes viewed through the eyes of past experiences.

And so, with age comes an eventual decline of facilities and stamina. Some older people who have lost a spouse after 50+ years of marriage oftentimes may want to give up. It is not unusual for a surviving spouse to pass away within 1-2 years of their husband or wife if they had been together for so long.

A senior adult survivor will need a lot of support. Not just emotional but in other ways also. It isn't easy losing someone you have known and loved for so long. Time spent with others means emotional bonding, common experiences, and shared memories. The senior survivor will need to be listened to, embraced, thought about, helped and most of all, shown that you care for them and understand their loss and its significance to him or her.

Anticipatory Grief

Anticipatory Grief is the situation that occurs when a person is dying as a process or has reached the age in life when death is imminent. Whenever a loved one dies suddenly, there is nothing that can be done to change the experience of death since the person is already dead. In other words you are at a place of dealing with death past tense. You must pick up the pieces.

With anticipatory grief, whether the situation is a slow-moving cancer, Alzheimer's or a natural withering away of someone at the end of a long life, there is a valued opportunity to say and do things that may help both you and your dying loved one.

There are basically three different time frames that grief and mourning center around in anticipatory grief. These consist of:

Losses that have occurred in the past
Losses that are taking place at the present
Losses that are yet to happen

When someone is going through a dying process although still living, in anticipation of death, the dying individual and his or her family start the grieving process by mourning the person's past life; the life of a healthy person who, though alive, has "passed." Present grieving deals with the situation as it now is which is usually a secluded, bedridden, or confined life style that also alters the life of caregivers and family members who are tending to the loved one. The future of course centers around dreams, plans or wishes that will never be realized.

This is what makes anticipatory grief so difficult—that there are various types of mourning taking place simultaneously. Although it is true that survivors will mourn past, present and future after someone is gone in the present and future sense that the decedent is not here now nor will be a part of the future, anticipatory grief allows you the golden chance to create and share experiences during the dying loved one's last days that will have a profound effect on your grief after death occurs.

And so the goal of going through anticipatory grief is to grieve the loss of your loved one without detaching emotionally now. This is and can be a real challenge from the standpoint that you can be pulled in the three opposite directions: toward him or her as a person you love during the illness, as ongoing involvement continues, your distance with him or her stays the same, and a moving away from emotionally because of the fact that he or she will not be present with you in the future.

While you are caring for your dying loved one there are several things that you can do to make the situation a little easier for everyone involved, including yourself.

1) Resolve your relationship with your dying loved one. This means allowing yourself to express any unfinished business you have with them in a delicate and caregiving fashion. Share your thoughts and feelings about your relationship in an affirming manner.

2) Encourage other family members and loved ones to resolve their emotional issues and relational variables with the dying loved one. Each person probably has a different type of relationship with the ailing individual. Prod but do not push each one affected to have a chance to spend time with him or her.

3) Give the dying individual a chance to resolve his or her relationship with each family member. If the loved one is totally immobile and asks to see someone, make every effort to invite that person to come and visit with the dying loved one.

Anticipating a loved one's death is not easy or simple, but taking some basic steps to accommodate the desires and wishes of each person connected to the situation will help everyone to feel a little more relieved and balanced. Giving everybody a chance to share, participate and be involved can go a long way in helping one's ability to cope with and handle the grieving process and change lives for the better.

Special Situations

Sometimes there are circumstances that for various reasons do not allow for conventional avenues for mourning the loss of someone you know and care about. Although the situation can be because of variables beyond anyone's control or due to the choices of the person or persons in charge of making arrangements, there is still grieving to do because our emotions don't always wait for a more convenient time or dissipate due to circumstances.

No Services Held

There have been times in the past where a death occurred

but there were no services scheduled for honoring the decedent's memory.

There can be different reasons for this, from the deceased's own wishes to no legal next-of-kin or anyone willing to hold a service. There can be other reasons also such as not wanting to acknowledge the death and opting for immediate disposition only or not recognizing the value of the life lived. Sometimes there may be confusion or distrust of others involved.

Different people have different ideas about things and death is no exception. If you experience the death of someone you care about, if no ceremony or organized ritual is held, that does not eliminate your need to acknowledge and honor the decedent's life. For you and others who knew the decedent, it may be gathering for a brief moment of silence together or simply getting together to share memories or stories about the person. Chapter four on personalization and memorialization may give you some ideas about practical ways to honor someone's memory.

Delayed Services

This tends to happen mostly because a key family member or members are unable to come immediately for planning or attending a service. It can also occur due to a lack of financial resources to pay for a funeral home's services or because of a dispute or disagreement about what should happen among family members.

Any time that services are delayed because of a conflict of interest, it can lead to anxiety, stress, or chronic fatigue because of the uncertainty involved. The delay can also lead to problems because of the lack of closure needed for good mental health.

One of the most important things you can do at the time of the death is to make an acknowledgment of the fact in a way that is meaningful to you. This may be in making phone calls to notify others, taking time off work, writing a letter, etc.

Another important goal will be to communicate with the

person or persons who will be responsible for making and planning the services. Although the party or parties that will set the ceremony may take a "don't call us we'll call you" approach, let them know that you have a need to talk and converse about it as one of your ways of dealing with the loss.

Most family members will be understanding of this fact and realize the importance of at least setting a future date or approximate time (Labor Day weekend, for example) if there is enough certainty involved (such as knowing when cousin Ted will be back from an overseas trip).

Delayed Disposition

Since services for a decedent and disposition do not have to take place on the same day, or at the same time, delayed disposition can occur also because of extenuating circumstances. Many times this is a weather related delay such as snow, ice, flood, etc. where disposition is impossible or infeasible at the present time.

This can also lead to a lack of closure and the experience of various emotions such as panic, fear, anxiousness, and fatigue. As with delayed services, the greatest need may be to stay in close contact with the party or parties responsible for procuring disposition. If there are circumstances involved that are beyond your immediate control, patience is the name of the game. Do what is necessary to take your mind off the delay. Relaxation, meditation, or healthy diversion through reading, movies, and entertainment can work wonders in relieving stress and worry.

No Viewing

Having a closed casket or no viewing of the decedent between the time death occurs and disposition can leave a bitter memory in the minds of mourners. They will always retain a mental image of ugliness and shock[2]. It is or can be very difficult to view. However in most cases it; can be even more harmful not to view.

Regardless of whether it is because of the personal preference of the party responsible for making the final arrangements or because the manner of death will not allow it, if viewing of the deceased is not to take place, it can take longer to recover from the death. From a psychological standpoint, you may not fully realize the person is gone without seeing yourself. That is the reason that we in the funeral industry spend a great deal of time and effort to make viewing a possibility and encourage it if at all possible.

However there may be a situation where it is not possible and the death must be dealt with as best as possible. As a general rule, there will need to be more ritual and ceremony involved when viewing will not take, place. Since the visual aspect of the grieving process is removed, compensation in respect of the other senses will need to happen if possible. This can be more speaking, more music, more opportunities to express one's grief. The use of pictures or photographs may need to be incorporated by placing the decedent's picture on top of the closed casket, placed by the register book at the visitation and funeral or printed on the front of the service folder or bulletin.

Talk to your funeral director about any other ideas concerning what ideas can be implemented to otherwise replace the lack of viewing.

Grief That Does Not Seem To Go Away
(Blessed Are Those Who Mourn)

We all know to some extent that life goes through seasons; that there is a time to mourn and work through our grief over a loved one lost and then move on with our lives. However, experience shows that not everyone heals in the same way or within the same time frame. It is also true that time alone does not heal all wounds and it cannot if we do not even acknowledge it.

It can be really difficult to determine how long it should take someone to mourn and move on. Factors such as our own personality, history with and attachment to the one now gone, cause and manner of death, the number of our losses and other issues to deal with, are just several variables, along with the level of support from others, that can affect the grieving process.

It is possible to think you are over a loss until you go to a certain place, hear a certain sound, see a particular sight or other stimuli that can trigger feelings of grief again. When grief does not lift after a certain period of time and feelings of sadness, depression, anger, sorrow, pain or hopelessness persist, there is a general indication that we have not properly and/or completely expressed our feelings and emotions to the level needed to get it out of our system. This does not mean that you forget the decedent and put them and all reminders of him or her away by eradication, but simply that the memory of his/her life does not strap you to the point of not being able to live and conduct your own life in normal fashion. Pain may still surface when thinking about the person, but it will not be so intense that you must handicap your own functions and activities from now on.

When grief and mourning linger, we call this complicated grief or a condition where your emotional state becomes chronic, excessive, or prolonged. This is a place where you may want to consider help and care over and beyond what you have done so far.

What Is Aftercare
(Taking Care Of You)

In his handbook on Grief Counseling and Grief Therapy, J. William Worden states and describes what he calls the four tasks of mourning: 1) To accept the reality of the loss; 2) To experience the pain of grief; 3) To adjust to an environment without the lost person; and 4) To reinvest emotional energy in life[3].

Experiencing the pain of grief felt can be the challenge and the focus in the state we call Aftercare. Aftercare is what takes place following the death and funeral that a survivor may need to go through to adjust to life after a loss. It is a way of providing survivors with helpful services including but not limited to education, counseling and structured support systems.

Some people will just plain need more assistance than others in overcoming the death of a loved one and aftercare is the way that funeral homes and mortuaries are reaching out to their clients and the community at large with information and help to deal with complicated grief.

Some aftercare programs are very elaborate and well established and others very simple and informal. As a rule of thumb, if you inquire into what a particular program has to offer and it does not fit your particular needs, usually getting a referral to another program can be very useful. If you or someone in your family is having a particularly difficult time with a death, some form of aftercare will be needed to help restore you or them back to a normal life again.

The best place to start your aftercare regimen is with what you do for yourself. Although it may seem elementary and common sense, realize that grief can manifest itself in unclear thinking and in not always remembering to do things for yourself. Look at how you are dealing with life right now; ask yourself these questions:

- Am I feeling stressed out constantly or in spurts? If so how am I coping?

- What am I doing to relax? When I try to unwind can I get my mind off pressing issues?

- Am I getting enough exercise? If not, what can I do to start being more physically active?

- What about diet; Am I gaining or losing too much weight?

- What's my attitude like? Are people a burden or a delight to see and communicate with? If not, why not?

- What are the finances looking like? Is the checkbook out of balance, spending money under control?

You can probably add some more but properly evaluating your life initially can help you determine what type of help and what level of help you may need.

Getting Help From The Helpers
(Now That You Mention It)

Once you tell yourself honestly "I can't handle this anymore", and decide to get some input from another party, you can do your own needs assessment to determine what you can do. A needs assessment is a basic process of answering questions about your situation. Sometimes talking and getting feedback from a close friend or relative can be very enlightening. Also going to an objective third party such as a counselor for example, can help you gain insight into whether you need more or less assistance than you realize.

After recognizing that you or a family member could benefit from organized assistance in grieving, simply knowing this and choosing to take a first step is a sign of great strength. What you will need next is a proper perspective because the experience of grief and mourning can greatly cloud one's thinking and impair good judgment. Making decisions on some of the simplest things can seem monumental. You don't want to add to your grieved state by going wrong.

Ask yourself the question of "who do I trust," and start there.

Family And Friends
(Asking For Advice)

Most everyone has a least one or two family members and/or friends they can confide in about what they're going through. Being able to express your feelings is liberating and for a good number of people this may be all that is needed for them to heal.

For others it can be more difficult to turn the corner and get over a loved one's death. Perhaps gathering with a few other family members or friends after a period of time has past since the death to see how everyone is doing may be an idea to explore. If you and some of the others involved live a distance away, a conference call by telephone may be one way to interact with one another without travel. If your family is close at hand you may ask them to evaluate your handling of life since the death and seek their opinion.

Getting some feedback from friends and family can definitely help you decide if you are doing well enough with the support system you already have in place or should look further.

Funeral Directors As A Source Of Help
(Turning On The Light)

Funeral Directors are in the business of helping people in a time of great need. The profession has evolved from that of taking care of and burying the deceased to one of also adding the duties involved in aftercare for the bereaved.

Most funeral home professionals are involved in aftercare to some degree whether it is providing elaborate well-planned support programs for survivors or dispersing information that can give guidance.

Funeral directors act as counselors, advisors or consultants in different areas that survivors will deal with after a death. Funeral homes can be an excellent source for information referrals to counselors, community support groups, psychiatrists, or other professionals in the helping professions. If you are new to your community and have not had time to establish ties in some social areas, contacting the funeral director who helped you at the time of your loved one's passing for guidance is not farfetched or out of line.

Assisting families after the funeral is the thesis of aftercare and virtually every funeral home today expects to continue helping families for as long as necessary to deal with and overcome the burden of bereavement.

Clergy, Ministers, And Churches
(Seeing The Light)

Perhaps this is the first place you turned when death in the family occurred. Ministers, pastors and clergy members are among the most trusted and respected people in society. They also tend to be able to help us in our darkest hours.

Some pastors and ministers do counseling themselves, others in usually larger churches tend to delegate this work out to associate pastors or other qualified church staff. More and more churches are offering either counseling or support groups or programs for those in mourning after a loved one's passing. Many clergy today have had some professional training in counseling from several classes up to postgraduate degrees in psychology. If you do contact a minister, whether it was the officiant at your loved one's funeral or memorial service, or the pastor or other clergy at your church, you may want to ask if he or she has much training or knowledge in this specific area, and if so how much. Just because someone can do well at officiating at the service does not necessarily mean they are the best person to council with you about grief, mourning and bereavement.

Social Service Organizations
(Rock Of Ages)

Social Service organizations are also known as human service or human relief organizations that are usually either government supported or nonprofit entities that help people in a variety of circumstances.

Social service groups can be small or large, local or multinational and tend to focus on alleviating social problems that are not properly approached by others. Some of the larger well-known organizations like the United Way, Goodwill, The Salvation Army and Red Cross reach out to those in distress or difficult circumstances and attempt to help people in ways their resources will allow.

Some of the more localized groups may also do charity work, fund-raising for a specific cause, provide temporary housing or other community investment services. Some social services may help those in bereavement by giving referrals, providing counseling or guidance and establishing possible solutions to dilemmas concerning donating items to charity, assistance with mentoring young people, providing meals, and helping senior citizens.

When a death in the family leaves a void that cannot be replaced by resources currently existing with the surviving family group or support system, social services organizations are a valuable resource available in most communities to help either temporarily or long-term to meet the needs of people.

Some other social service organizations widely known include:

Big Brothers/Big Sisters
Catholic Charities
Meals On Wheels
Boys And Girls Clubs
Y.M.C.A.
Senior-Citizens Services

Finding out what your local area or city offers can usually be found in the yellow pages of the phone book or the local chamber of commerce.

Counselors And Psychologists
(Heart To Heart)

Seeking and finding professional help from the mental health field is more and more common today because going for assistance from a counselor or psychologist has lost the stigma it has had in the past.

There are several factors to consider when wondering whether or not you or a family member you are responsible for or care about should go for professional help. Several general indicators to evaluate include:

* A sufficient amount of time has elapsed and you feel stuck and unable to move (back) into the mainstream of life.

* You find your thoughts and mindset completely focused on the decedent and act as if he or she was still alive.

* You are increasingly involved in addictive behaviors or forming bad habits such as drug-use, alcohol consumption, gambling, overeating, constant craving or smoking or inappropriate sexual behavior.

* You think you might need professional help.

* Others tell you they think you might need professional help.

Once you decide and explore the options and alternatives of getting help from a counselor or psychologist, the next step is to look for a qualified professional who can best help you.

One of the best ways to find the right person is through a referral from someone who has been down the same path and received proper help from them in obtaining successful treatment. Getting in contact with professional associations of counselors or psychologists/psychiatrists can also be a valuable source of referral (check your telephone directory).

When you do obtain a professional contact there will be some valid questions that you will need answered before you do commit to going to the counselor or psychologist:

- What are his or her credentials?

- What type of education and training does he or she have?

- What and how much experience does he or she have with bereavement (specialist or nonspecialist)?

- Can I come at times that are conducive to my own schedule?

- What type of payment terms does he or she accept? Is insurance accepted?

There are different levels of expertise for counselors and psychologists with several different listings for both. Most professional counselors will have at least a masters degree in psychology while psychologists will hold a Ph.D. or doctorate. Be sure the individual is qualified to be doing what they advertise. The main factor of course will be whether once you meet the professional that the two of you are compatible as clinician and client. Progress can take time, work outside the sessions and have realistic expectations about getting better, Ask questions, don't be afraid to speak your mind and express your feelings. Try to set an objective timetable for going to the counselor or psychologist. If you are not making progress after a while, you may need to try another professional. Be encouraged, for those that have chosen this path of dealing with bereavement, there are stories of success.

Social Workers
(Grief Support)

Social workers are trained persons who help and guide individuals, families and groups. They may be connected with either public or private agencies. The professional social worker is trained to help others through skilled knowledge of human behavior on various levels of interaction.

Social work is carried out through many different channels including day care and children's homes, clinics, clubs, churches, community centers, hospitals, schools, courts and other entities.

Since there are different categories that social workers may work under, a social worker that does casework or is a caseworker, is the type that most commonly deals with individuals and families. Dealing with relational problems within the family unit or between individuals or families and others such as neighbors or friends is a common area for a caseworker.

Social workers may help those in bereavement by helping them find solutions to the problems of everyday life. For those in grief, it can be a major challenge to maintain one's own life or family. Household management, budgeting, properly raising children, keeping favorable standards of health, education, security and general well-being are things that social workers help people with along with relational issues that must be faced.

Most social work is performed whenever people reach out and ask for help from an organization that employs social caseworkers. The entity will usually assign a caseworker to help the individual or family who asks for it.

Physicians And Psychiatrists
(An Apple A Day)

Physicians or doctors need no real introduction on the premises that they are in the business of treating people for physical ailments. Some people who have struggled with grief without relief have gone to see their doctor for help. A medical doctor may take various approaches in helping patients in bereavement, which may include a change in lifestyle habits such as diet, exercise, sleep, or the issuance of prescription or nonprescription medications.

People are very different from a physiological standpoint and there are numerous factors and variables about a person that the doctor must take into consideration when treating a bereaved patient. If making some lifestyle or social changes has not helped, you may want to go see your primary care physician.

Psychiatrists are medical doctors who take on more extensive training into the field and treatment of mental disorders.

Since a very upsetting experience such as the death of a loved one can shock the system, psychiatrists are the professionals that can help those who need the deepest level of treatment using a wide range of techniques. Oftentimes after going to see a family practice doctor for depression, sadness or other grief symptoms without favorable results, the general practitioner may refer or send the bereaved individual to a psychiatrist who is more specialized in helping more severe cases of grief and mourning.

Most psychiatrists use discussion of one's problems, drugs or a combination of the two as therapy. A good number of cases are treated at the psychiatrist office or clinic. More severe cases may require outpatient service or hospitalization. When a survivor gets to the point of not being able to function at all in day-to-day living, psychiatric treatment is usually required.

Support Groups
(What's Good For The Goose May Not Be Good For The Gander)

Recent decades have brought our society many radical changes in the family unit and social conditions altogether. Many people do not always have a tight knit group of friends, family or social support available and able to give them the help they may need. Families tend to be smaller and more fragmented, people often may live great distances away and others may have jobs or busy schedules in general that prevent getting together and being there for one another. Each person connected to a loss may also be affected by the death at a different level or in a different way.

What support groups do is to bring people together who have experienced similar losses. They serve the purpose of providing a network of support to help people adjust to their loss

Originally conceived as an idea to provide help to widows and widowers, support groups have gained more and more popularity among people after a death and the initial phase of funeral or memorial service. Many funeral homes today are offering some type of support group either sponsored by the funeral home as a complimentary aftercare service to families after the funeral or referring families to a support group in the area. Larger churches, nonprofit human service organizations and other entities dealing with helping people deal with issues also provide support groups to mourners.

There are also support groups that deal with more specific types of losses such as widowed persons, sudden infant death, families of homicide victims and survivors of suicide. These and other groups have helped countless individuals deal with the lingering pain related with the grief that can continue after the funeral and that initial stage of realizing the loved one is gone.

Talk to the funeral home that served you, your church or a local social service organization for information about any groups that meet in your area.

Attorneys
(Laying Down The Law)

Choosing a lawyer or sound legal council can be as important a decision you will make after the death of a spouse, child, parent or other family member with whom you have an interest in their estate.

An attorney can guide you through the legal maze of business that needs to be taken care of in the days following a death. This can be especially true if the decedent did not have a valid will (about half of all Americans do not) or any post-death instructions in place on what is to happen when he or she dies. If someone passes away without a properly written will, the court will step in and distribute property according to the laws in the applicable state. Few people outside the legal system and law-practice industry have the knowledge or skills to deal with these problems on their own.

Finding the right attorney for you can be a challenge in and of itself. Even if the decedent had a valid will and well-thought-out documented instructions, an attorney who is knowledgeable in the area of estate law who can properly lead you through any red tape is worth a bundle.

If you do not have an attorney or anyone you liked who handled any legal matters for you in the past, the American Bar Association or your state bar association may give you some leads. A law firm that served you well in the past concerning unrelated issues might be able to give you a referral to an attorney or law firm that specializes in or is well-versed in wills/estates/trusts, etc.

Certified Public Accountants
(It's A Numbers Game)

Whereas attorneys are a good source of help in the realm of law and legal issues, accountants or CPAs are invaluable in assisting with financial and business issues.

CPAs go through 4 years of college to earn a bachelor's degree in accounting and must pass a rigorous four-part exam to get certified. Accountants like other professionals can specialize in different areas but CPAs in public practice can give you needed guidance after a death.

Along with preparing tax returns for the decedent's estate, CPAs can be consulted about various issues including audits, inventorying an estate, disposing of assets or the sell off of a business and valuations of holdings. Accounting fees are very reasonable for the work done and you may well need the accountant's help to get estate tax returns filed properly and within the law's framework. The CPA can also be consulted before making decisions that will have a financial impact upon a decedent's estate and upon your own financial status in relation to an estate.

Financial Planners And Consultants
(More Bang For The Buck)

Financial planning is the concept of evaluating your financial situation at the present, setting goals for the future and developing a plan to reach the goals. It is a basic step-by-step process to help take you from where you are now to where you want to be in the future.

For many, the journey into planning for the future financially can be a voyage into unfamiliar territory. Because the death of a loved one can create a genuine crisis point in one's life, the period of time following the death is one where certain big decisions must be made that will have a large impact financially for years to come, but one's mindset of grief and heartache can make good decision making difficult even for the most financially astute.

This is where a financial planner can be greatly beneficial to you. A financial planner is someone who assists you by using the process of gathering and examining financial information, originating and planning a strategy to help you meet you and your family's future financial goals. The financial planner uses a model that inputs your needs that include meeting expenses, budgeting, saving, insurance, taxes, investments and retirement planning.

Although there are resources available that can help you do your own financial planning, I recommend that during the first 6 months to a year following a major loss such as the death of a close family member that you utilize the services of a certified financial planner.

In choosing a financial planner to work with, be sure that he or she has the proper training and credentials, that the planner has the necessary experience in helping others in the same situation you are in (after a death), that the planner is focused on your needs first and has gathered enough information about your financial status to be able to recommend a course of action tailored properly to meet your needs.

Estate Planners
(Your Family, Your Life)

Planning your estate is basically the end extension of financial planning. An estate planner is someone who provides you with advise, council and guidance regarding an estate and can put together a strategy to maximize the results of financial planning and set up orderly management and transition of your assets at the time of your death.

A qualified estate planner will help you identify and create the documents that you will need such as a will, living trust, declaration of guardian, powers of attorney and the details of planning your estate including all property owned, type of will needed and transferring assets.

While various types of professionals such as lawyers, accountants, financial consultants, bankers and others can give advice and provide input into an estate, estate-planning professionals generally are practitioners of only estate planning and many hold the AEP or Accredited Estate Planner designation.

Insurance Agents
(In Good Hands)

An insurance agent is one who is authorized by an insurance company to offer, sell and service various types of insurance policies including life insurance which is often used to either pay for funeral expenses or help pay future expenses of surviving family members after the death of the insured.

Insurance agents are licensed by the state in which they practice to sell the various insurance products that their particular company offers. An agent can be the point of contact at the time of death to collect the proceeds from the insuring company to the policy beneficiary. Agents can give service to clients and potential clients by advising them of their insurance needs, help them understand various policies that are available and even work out a plan to pay for the policy desired.

Many insurance agents carry the Chartered Life Underwriter (CLU) designation and are able to help you purchase life insurance that's customized to your particular needs. Independent agents can write policies for more than one insurance carrier and assist those wanting to but a policy to find the best deal for them.

Literature And Available Helps
(A Rule Of Thumb)

Where do you go in your time of need? Knowing what is out there and what is accessible to you can be a big relief in and of itself. We live in an information-driven world today and no matter where you are or what you are seeking, knowing that vast resources exist and are there for people like yourself who want to know and learn and grow through the grief experience is valuable.

Since everyone is different, the journey through grief will be a different road for each who travels it. Some will find wellness through interacting with others. Some will predominately receive the healing hand through reading, studying and learning from the printed word.

Chapter 10 of this book entitled Resources Available contains a listing of books, literature and other helps that are accessible and obtainable to those who seek them. My desire is that you will look at and consider some of these and the references to other listings that exist so that you may discover the literature and resources that will help you best complete your journey back to wholeness and healing.

Pets And Animals Can Help
(Man's Best Friends)

When Abraham Lincoln was 9 years old living with his parents and 12-year-old sister in the Indiana frontier, his mother suddenly died. It was a time of great sadness and loneliness for Abe, his father and his sister. One day shortly after Mrs. Lincoln's passing, he saw his sister sitting on the steps of the house crying. Young Abe knew that she was sobbing because of their mother's untimely death. Abe decided to try to do something to cheer his sister up so when he found a baby raccoon near the cabin, he brought it to his sister. Although the animal could not, as no other creature could either, replace their mother, the little coon seemed to cheer Abe and his sister up. Abe felt good trying to do something to help, and his sister seemed to accept that he cared for her in bringing the little critter to her as a pet.

Although I am not advocating giving wild animals as pets,

the morale of this story is that animals have been successfully used to help the bereaved recover. Whether it is offering to give a puppy or a kitten to someone who's had a recent loss, animals help people to refocus and reinvest themselves in something stimulating.

Pets have been especially beneficial to both older persons and to young children who have lost someone very close to them. There is something therapeutic about adopting and caring for, or just simply receiving a visit from someone with a pet dog, cat, bird, ferret, whatever.

Every person is different and circumstances vary; there may be cases where giving someone a pet to take care of is not feasible, but for those who like animals and enjoy pets, it can be a very healing gesture that can pay dividends for both the person recovering from grief and the pet.

Making Sense Of It All
(Creativity Out Of Chaos)

Information overload. Do this. Don't do that. Be cordial. Fake it till ya make it. You'll be OK. It was God's will.

Most of us have heard these phrases and many more from others who care but oftentimes don't understand—people who haven't walked in our shoes. It is OK to have well-wishers in life, but it is rare to have someone who really knows what's going on within. It is called life turned upside down. Today will end and tomorrow will begin, but what will I feel when it starts? There are no easy answers. Maybe it is time to try to make a little lemonade from this lemon.

Realize that accepting your feelings and thoughts for what they are is OK. Grief is an animal like no other. Changes are a part of the process. You may feel sad. You may feel bad, but they are your feelings. Make choices- sure, that's easy to say, but much harder to do. Start with "do I want fries or onion rings with my burger?" Somewhere under the emotions of craziness and facing the unknown there is a dilemma. As a human being you can choose to be bitter or to get better, to understand that making the right choice can still involve pain, suffering, heartache, heaviness and second-guessing. But you are what you are at this instant- a survivor.

How To Resolve Grief And Recover
(The Light At The End Of The Tunnel)

The questioned asked is, "How do you resolve and recover from grief? " Someone who asks this is also stating How do I get well. It is really like asking "How do you get from Atlanta to Chicago." The answer, of course, depends on a lot of things. If you go by jet airplane nonstop it will be the fastest. If you fly indirectly through another city and then take a connecting flight it'll take longer. How about passenger train or bus? Or by automobile- there are various intersecting highways between the two cities to choose from but many combinations can end at the same location.

And so it is with the experience of grief and mourning. Your journey may take longer or shorter than someone else's. There is no formula, no exact timetable because the different factors involved concerning your relationship with the decedent, your history, your emotional makeup, your dependence on or independence from the decedent, and many more. Being attached to someone in some way will require a grief experience of some sort.

So what can you do when there are variables that are not completely within your control? Here are some things to consider:
<u>Realize</u> that you are going through a period of grief. That this is not abnormal after the loss of a loved one. Realize that you have a legitimate need to grieve and to take the initiative in doing so.
<u>Recognize</u> that us humans are emotional, feeling creatures. If you feel sad, you feel sad for a reason- someone you knew, cared about, loved- is missing and will not return. See it for

what it is, nothing more, but also nothing less.
Analyze your situation for what it is at face value. Don't be afraid to look at your feelings from different angles. Look at, not away from your loss. Turning away and refusing to see it can lead to bigger problems.
Communicate to appropriate others in your life what you are feeling, going through and thinking. Let others know what you need and expect to happen. Other people are not mind readers. If you tell someone legitimately that you are grieving and they don't accept it, they have a big problem themselves.
Express your thoughts and feelings as appropriately as possible when possible. Hiding and repressing your emotions will not help you heal in the long run. There may be certain times and settings that are not ideal for expression but let yourself feel the loss.
Accept yourself for where you are. You will not hurt or feel sad forever. Whether it is you or another family member, realize that bereavement is for a season; it is not a lifetime sentence.

Helping And Supporting Others
(A Friend In Deed)

Perhaps you are not the one going through grief, or you are further along in your journey to recovery and seek a friend, family member or other person who has been affected by a death and is struggling with either the initial stages of grief or who is involved in some type of complex or complicated grief and you want to encourage them.

There are many ways to help others (some people may experience anger and not want help) and it is important to grasp the basic principles of the stages of grief and then lend a helping hand. These stages normally include shock (the first reaction to the death), denial (telling oneself it is not true), reality (realizing that the death has happened), anger (feeling guilty or bad that it has happened, is irreversible and that no one prevented it), and acceptance (receiving the event for what it is and choosing to have peace about it). Understanding these five stages help you to see the other for where they are.

Here are some ways to reach out and help support others:

Be A Friend

Make yourself available as a friend who will be there. Be a listener. It is much easier to talk than to listen but we each have two ears, one mouth. Act accordingly.

Offer To Help

Doing chores, running errands, cleaning, answering the phone are a few ways you can show someone that you are supporting them while they are not 100%.

Share Some Food

Eating and friendship go together and offering something to eat is an important way of showing you care for them.

Be Objective

It is also easy to be moved to act emotionally rather than logically. Think with your head rather than your heart in relating to someone who's grieving.

Don't Use Cliches

Saying, "you'll get over it," "don't worry, be happy," or " you still have ____," etc., are not helping a person who is bereaved. They can do more harm than good so avoid using words and phrases that will not help.

Define Your Boundaries

No one person can help everyone every time. Understand that some problems and pains are beyond anyone's control to solve. Your heart is in the right place when you want to help someone recover, but don't do more than is necessary or try to take over someone's life for them.

The most important thing to remember is that your friend, family member, etc., must walk their own walk. By offering your support and walking "with" them, not "for" them, you are giving them the ultimate gift of friendship.

Troubleshooting 101
Getting On With Life Again

In this chapter I have covered a number of issues that grief can present as problems socially, psychologically, and physically. These have been presented to some degree on a theoretical or analytical basis. Now I want to talk on a little more practical level and discuss some possible difficulties and suggestions for solving them.

<u>Birthdays And Anniversaries</u>

After a painful loss, you may feel that you are progressing until a date that has previously been important comes up on the calendar. If it was your spouse it can be your wedding anniversary, his or her birthday, your first birthday without him or her in x number of years. There are many people who fell into a depression or took a step back when an important date from their relationship came up after the loss.

What you feel is real and legitimate. You miss him or her, and the date, whether it's a birthday or anniversary date, is a reminder of what you did have that is no more.

First, don't repress or deny what you feel. It is OK to express your feelings of sadness and unhappiness. Stuffing your emotions does not help you.

Second, consider doing something symbolic or commemorative to honor the loved one on the special day. This could be visit the person's gravesite, placing their picture on the fireplace mantle for the day or anything else that will help you to cope and remember.

Third, ask for what you need from appropriate others. You may need to talk to someone or be with other people. Think about how you can do this for where you are.

<u>The Holidays</u>

Holidays can also be very tough to handle because they are

unavoidable and have the added stress of being advertised and magnified by society at large. When everyone is working for and gearing up for the holidays, it just makes it that much harder. There are ways to take control of the situation however by realizing that the holiday will happen anyway. By anticipating and planning ahead for what you do or do not want to do that day is something you can exercise some control over. If you adjust your expectations to a more realistic level ahead of time it will be easier to deal with.

Since holidays are usually spent with other family or friends, communicate how you feel about the holiday and any gatherings or events that you will (or can) be apart of. Oftentimes others are feeling some of the same emotions, and letting someone you will be with on the holidays know where you are at can be helpful for them also.

It is also important to deal with this holiday for now; meaning do not worry about future holidays. Deal with today and don't fret about setting a precedent for all future holidays. Live one holiday at a time.

Living Alone

This situation is most common when an older adult whose children are grown and out on their own losses a spouse. Living alone can be hard at any age because as humans we are made for fellowship and community. It is not natural for us to be alone. However a death can leave us that way.

There can be several issues here but the most important one will be to try to reach out to other people. Getting involved in others lives can be very healing. It can be calling others on the telephone to chat, joining a social group, doing volunteer work or visiting others who also live alone.

Several people I have talked to said that just having the radio or TV on helped alleviate some of the sting of living by themselves. Whatever your circumstance is, there are connections that can be made, tasks that can be done and places that can be frequented in meeting people.

Being Single

Your spouse has passed away and you are single again, perhaps after a long time of being married. Now you may feel very uncomfortable and awkward especially if most of your social connections are other marrieds.

One of your primary needs will be to resume social relations with the opposite sex again at some juncture. Society has stamped its own predetermined "period of mourning" on widows and widowers and assumes that after 6 months - 2 years, the widowed single should be ready to date again. I think it is interesting that the folks who usually announce this time frame for grieving are people generally who have not been widowed themselves, so take it for whatever you think it's worth.

What you will need to do is to know within yourself that you are at a point in your own life when you can pursue a social life without any guilt about it or be able to deal with any feelings in a constructive way. Finding a replacement or someone to simply help you try to forget or not think about the past will not work.

There is also the issue of children and the status of their lives. If you have young children who are still at home and dependent upon you this will be very different than if your children are adults with their own families somewhere else. Think carefully about starting any relationship that may impact your present relationships. Seek advice and council, look at every angle and be careful to take it slow.

Remember, if you are single again and trying to hurry up and rush into not being single again, you probably have deeper issues than just being single.

Talking About Death

A point of deep concern and apprehension to some survivors is communicating the death to others after the fact when those you come in contact with are unaware of the passing. This can be quite awkward when you run into an old friend you haven't seen in years, someone who moved away and now has moved back, etc.

There will be several factors to consider including the nature of the passing, how it occurred, what stage of life the decedent was in and where you are presently in your own bereavement. The important thing to remember is that you were not able to control the loved one's death, but you can choose how you communicate it to others. You are not on trial and can choose how you want to disclose the quantity and detail of information that you wish to and no more.

You are entitled to your grief and there is nothing wrong if you cry and become upset in some other way that is not harmful to others. There will be some people that you may want to confide in about the loss and others that you care not to discuss it with. Disclosure is something very much within your power to do or not do.

Going Back To Work

This can mean one of two things. One is reporting back to your job after so many days or weeks off to arrange for services, tend to business, do any traveling and other necessary tasks when a death occurs. The other is reentry into the work force after the death of the primary breadwinner or one who contributed financially to the household and now is faced with going to work to help make a living.

In the first scenario, resuming one's job is the official act of going back to life's daily routine. It may take several days or weeks to get back in rhythm again. Most workplaces are very supportive to those who've had a loss and will allow workers "space" to get back into the groove of labor. The same basic principle applies here as with talking about the death to others. You are entitled to your grief and the old idea of leaving your personal life completely at the door into the work place each day does not always happen. We are mental, emotional and social creatures. We can't just drop these parts of us off at the door each day. If the burden of grief does seem to continue to affect your work performance as time goes on, it would be wise to incorporate a new dimension of support into your life to help whether it be a support group, reading grief literature or seeing a counselor or physician.

In the scenario of going to work again to make ends meet financially, the best policy is honesty. Some potential employers may ask about time out of the work force and refer to your reasons for wanting to work. Letting someone know the truth about the change in your family status is being up-front about your situation and motives. Since it is beyond the scope of this book to provide complete information about what should or should not be disclosed, consulting with one of the contacts or organizations mentioned earlier may be of assistance.

Accepting New Responsibilities

Whether it is a young widowed spouse who now must try to be both parents to minor children or taking on the duties of managing an estate, or other chores, the main theme that underlies any new burden is "can I handle this or not."

Stress is often the added ingredient to one's life when you are still grieving and now have more responsibilities in order to fill any voids left by the decedent's absence. It can be challenging and demanding but also anxiety provoking depending upon the input needed to meet the new demands.

Here are a few things that may help you cope and adjust:

- Take time out each day to meditate. Get alone and take the phone off the hook, close the door and silence the pager. Turn off the cell phone and think.

- Take out several hours each week to go do something you enjoy. Read, go to a movie, eat dinner at a favorite restaurant, play with the pets, something to relax and de-stress yourself.

- Get some exercise. Walk, bike, lift weights. Swim, throw

a bail or Frisbee, or just simply stand up and do some stretches and bending. It is incredible how a little movement and physical activity can change one's mood, clear one's mind and help you feel better.

Dealing with Business Issues
(Details, Details, And Even More Details)

On top of the myriad of emotional issues to deal with after a death, there are usually a number of business concerns that need to be taken into account such as settling an estate, paying outstanding bills, notifying interested parties, returning borrowed items and redirecting mail, just as examples. There may be things you'll need help with and other things not. To know which from which ask yourself these three questions:

1) Am I qualified to handle this matter on my own?
2) Do I have sufficient knowledge about what should be done regarding this issue?
3) Is there anyone within my social network of friends and family that may be able to assist me with this problem?

What you cannot do, the help of those listed earlier in this chapter can be of great assistance to you and your household. The very practical considerations such as chores, childcare, housing, shopping and transportation, will also need attention as to the who, when, where and how in getting the things done to maintain your life and the lives of others affected by you. Here are some tips and pointers on some matters of high regard:

<u>Canceling Unneeded Services</u>

Make a list of those who render some type of service or who filled some need when the decedent was still alive that is no longer required. The list should consist of the name, address and phone number and hopefully a contact person. Send each service provider a notice that the customer (the decedent) has passed away and that the service is no longer needed. Be sure to document when you contacted the service provider about canceling service in case they try to continue to send bills or invoices to be paid. Examples of services that may need to be cancelled include newspaper or magazine subscriptions, cable TV, health club or spa memberships or other club memberships.

Changing Records And Accounts

This can be simple or difficult depending on whom the account is with. As with canceling services, make a list of entities or parties that the decedent had dealings with or may have held jointly with you and contact the party about the change. You may be required to submit a death certificate or other proof of death to make some changes so it may not be as easy as a phone call or sending a notice in the mail. Most businesses have procedures in place on how customers can close accounts with them. It may be a good idea for you to find out what the procedure is in case you run into any problems in trying to close out the decedent's account with them.

Disposing Of Personal Property

There are many ways to unload articles and property that belonged to the decedent that are unwanted, however some ways are better than others. Placing items in a publication for sale can open the door for potential thieves or others who may want to scope your house to have a chance. If you want to sell items the safer approach may be to go to those who buy and resale used goods, a consignment store, an estate liquidation company or at an auction. For items that don't sell and you want to get rid of, you may be able to donate to the Salvation Army, Goodwill or other nonprofit entity and receive a tax write-off for the estimated value if you itemize on your tax return.

Filing And Collecting Insurance

Different companies will have various procedures for filing insurance policies. Some will require surrender of the policy itself and a certified death certificate; others may want additional forms and documents such as their own company's claim forms, a copy of the funeral contract, statement of beneficiary, or other requirements. Filing insurance can be tedious and time consuming if you don't know how to "work the system" that is getting through the red tape that some insurance companies have in paying claims. Some funeral homes will help you file policies as part of their service even if they don't take an assignment on the policy. Since funeral homes deal with filing and collecting on insurance as a routine, you may ask your funeral director if he or she can help you with this.

Getting Organized

This can be something different to everybody. It is working out a way for you to get the business that you have to deal with, put into a methodical order that works for you. It is getting together all the paper, forms, documents, receipts, bills, checks, policies, and whatever else you have that needs attention into a place where it will get the attention that it needs when it needs it. The idea is to place everything together into groups or stacks with similar papers and file together for the purpose of easy reference. The most common way is to get manila file folders and label each one with what the contents are such as utility bills, legal papers, credit card statements, bank checks, etc. You may be able to put everything into 2 or 3 files or you may need metal filing cabinet space to hold all your relevant data. You can put the files in alphabetical order with the first file labeled "Priority" or "Current Attention" file. You may also want to make use of a carry size calendar to remind yourself of tasks and appointments, other obligations and when they need to be done.

Protecting Yourself

Unfortunately we live in a world where there are shysters and villains among the general population who would try to take advantage of the bereaved and those who have experienced the death of a spouse or close family member.

Usually these low-lifes will target older widows or widowers who now live by themselves or women whose husbands have died. Most scams that are devised usually revolve around someone showing up at your front door step or sending you something in the mail where you must pay to receive something that the decedent ordered before he or she died or must pay for something the decedent supposedly used or bought before death. If there is no proof or documentation provided, the approach is probably bogus. Everything from purse snatching to car theft to home burglary has been reported by survivors in incidents the days following a death. Some would think that no one would stoop so low as to assault or stalk a family in grief, but think again. Some of the things for you to remember are:

* Do not leave spare keys anywhere outside your home.

* Do not leave your car unlocked or unattended with keys, purses or other possessions inside.

* Keep lighting on inside and outside your house at night.

* Have someone stay at your house during funeral, visitation or other services, especially if it is announced in the newspaper.

* Be careful about disclosing information to close family or friends on a cell or mobile telephone. The conversations can be intercepted and listened to by someone with electronic equipment within a certain radius of the transmission.

* With identity theft on the rise, do not give out social security, drivers license or other numbers to strangers over the telephone or to anyone without knowing why they need the information.

Writing And Mailing Correspondence

You may want to keep a record or a log sheet of anything you send out through the mail with the date sent, what the correspondence refers to, what response (if any) is needed, and if response is needed the date it is received. This can be used for thank yous and acknowledgments, business, legal and estate matters. If you have access to a copy machine you may also want to make and keep a photocopy for your records.

Talk To Your Bank

This means the bank where the decedent had an account or accounts. They can advise you concerning the money that the decedent had and the bank's rules and procedures as well as applicable laws in your area in connection to the monies. They may also be able to guide and direct you in connection to investments, trusts, multiple accounts, transferring money, converting assets, and lines or letters of credit.

Transferring/Distributing Assets

In conjunction with disposing of personal property, transferring and/or distributing assets, generally means the changing of hands of those assets that are real property (houses, buildings, land) or of greater monetary value. In these cases it may be necessary to find out if there is a deed or title to the asset, and if so, the proper way of transferring or distributing it to another party (buyer, donee, recipient, heir, etc.) It may be a transaction that will require an oath, affidavit, notarization or other requirement or documentation. When in doubt/always consult an attorney or other qualified council. You may need or be required to do an inventory or listing of the asset(s), so find out what the rules are and follow them.

Conclusion

In review, this chapter has been about the grief and mourning period that comes after the funeral or other services and disposition. Bereavement which is the intense feelings and emotions experienced after a death of a loved one can be very complicated and take a period of time to get through. There are various helps available from other family members and friends to benevolent organizations to highly trained professionals who are skilled in dealing with a grief-related issue or issues.

Since the goal of this book is to give practical guidance and direction, I've decided to end this chapter with some suggestions or ideas that can help you or someone you care about who is going through the hard transition time that can follow a loss through death.

25 Ideas To Overcome And Get Through Grief

1. Live one day at a time. Try not to focus too much on either yesterday or tomorrow.

2. Eliminate the negative by realizing there are certain things you cannot change and choosing to look at the "upside if life"

3. Review your thought processes and analyze whether your thinking patterns are irrational or controlled too much by emotion.

4. Go for a walk, every day if possible. A morning or late afternoon trek can help you feel more refreshed.

5. Read the comic section of the newspaper. Sometimes reading something humorous can change your mood to a more cheerful outlook.

6. Listen to music. Turn on a radio, tape or other recording of music that will relax you or help you loosen up.

7. Give a little time to a worthy cause. It can be making a phone call, writing a letter or volunteering to help a good work. Reaching out to aid someone edifies you more.

8. Go outside. Whether it is to a nearby park or out in the back yard, look around at the sky, nature, the world.

9. Give yourself mercy. Instead of accepting a heavier burden because you are trying to live yours and the decedent's life, realize your own limits and set boundaries.

10. Visit a library or bookstore. Look at the various publications in print and find something that interests you to read about.

11. Eat a snack. I did not say snacks. Since we are becoming an overweight society, do not use food as a way to make yourself feel better. However an occasional cracker, cookie, or handful of nuts can ease the moment.

12. Encourage yourself. Go look in the mirror and tell yourself that since you are choosing to handle your grief in a positive way, you deserve to be content and have a good life.

13. Do some chores. Sweep the porch, mop the kitchen floor, dust off furniture, etc. Tidying up the house will help you feel and be productive and accomplished.

14. Keep a journal. Have a notebook or diary where you can write your feelings and express your thoughts.

15, Hold a mini-ritual. Either by yourself or with a friend or a family member, have a brief time of honoring the decedent through pictures, talking or meditating in a ceremonial conducive setting.

16. Take deep breaths. Unless you have a special medical condition and can't, sit down be still and take 3-4 long breaths. This can instantly help you feel better and calmer.

17. Watch a favorite show on TV whether it's an old comedy or new episode of a current airing, refocus your mind through entertainment.

18. Eat good food. Junk food, binging, skipping meals, loading up, etc., all can be harmful and cause or contribute to mood swings, and depression. Get on a steady nutritious diet that includes the 4 basic food groups and proper intake of calories.

19. Get some exercise. Physical activity stimulates the mind and body. Find an exercise you enjoy, can do routinely and is okayed by your physician.

20. Get some extra rest. Take frequent intervals during the day and stop what you are doing and relax. Try to get some place where you can be alone for 5 minutes at a time and rest

21. Be sociable. It may be difficult, especially at first, but try to step out and involve yourself with others whether it is a support group, volunteering your time, visiting others, etc.

22. Meditate. Each day get somewhere away from everyone else and close your eyes and think on something pleasant.

23. Go to the light. Many people who are experiencing grief have found that lighting helps their mood to improve. This may mean opening the curtains and doors or buying and installing more lighting inside your home.

34. Go to sleep. Most people need 8-10 hours of sleep per day to function well. Sleep defined as the unconscious replenishment of energy to the body, not just going to bed. If you are spending 8+ hours a night in bed but getting up unrested, you may need to see your doctor.

25. Avoid stress. There are certain variables in life that can't be avoided, but there are some that can. Stay away from unneeded situations that add or unduly distress you.

Chapter 8

A Summary of Customs & Practices

1. Introduction
2. Protestant Liturgical: Episcopal/Anglican/Lutheran
3. Protestant Non-Liturgical
4. Atheist
5. Baha'i
6. Buddhist
7. Catholic
8. Christian Science
9. Fraternal
10. Hindu
11. Humanist/Secular
12. Jehovah's Witness
13. Jewish
14. Mennonite/Amish
15. Mormon/Latter Day Saints
16. Moslem/Islamic
17. Native American/First Nations
18. Orthodox
19. Quaker
20. Scientology
21. Seventh Day Adventist
22. Sikh
23. Unification
24. Unitarian/Universalist
25. Veterans/Military
26. Zoroastrian

Introduction

Although funeral service is rapidly changing from past methodical rituals of most ceremonies being predictable and highly structured, tradition still holds a sacred and important role in how funerals are planned and carried out.

Oftentimes the survivors of a departed loved one may have very different ideas and wishes about how to memorialize the deceased, but at the same time want to incorporate or uphold certain religious or other traditions that may have been important to the deceased, to some member or part of the family, or to the next-of-kin who is planning the funeral themselves.

Photo by J. Sherritz

This chapter focuses on the rites, customs and traditions concerning death and practices of certain religions, churches and organizations belief systems in response to death and their individual ways of mitigating, approaching and carrying out the final rites of one of their own.

The description of each of the following rites is general since local customs and practices will differ on certain details in reference to local clergy, organizational representatives and community preferences.

The following types of ceremonial traditions of different major churches and other entities is by no means all-inclusive since there are literally hundreds of sects, subgroups and classes of the groups and organizations listed but is for your general use and information.

This chapter also provides information that can be referenced whenever you are going to attend a funeral or other ceremony or rite affiliated with or performed according to the traditions of a particular church, religion or belief, so that you will be somewhat prepared for what to expect.

Liturgical Protestant

A protestant church is any church that broke away from the Roman Catholic Church during the period of history known as the Reformation (a religious movement in the 1500s).

Liturgical is a prescribed order of worship that is more or less consistent regardless of location. Today in the United States, there are basically two protestant liturgical denominations: Episcopal and Lutheran, both of whose funeral customs are briefly described here.

Episcopal

As a traditional Christian liturgical church, the Episcopal Church is a part of the worldwide Anglican Communion, which separated from the Catholic tradition around 315 A.D.

It is strongly encouraged (but not required) that the funeral of a deceased Episcopalian be held in the Episcopal Church. Since it is liturgical, the funeral service will follow a prescribed order of worship which is found in the Book of Common Prayer.

Prior to or as part of the funeral, the celebration of the Holy Eucharist may be observed which provides the attendees with a chance to thank God and to pray for the soul of the deceased.

The sermon at the Episcopal funeral focuses on the church's beliefs concerning death, and there is no eulogy given during the service; singing of hymns is practiced by the congregation with the Resurrection of Jesus as the theme.

The funeral service will begin with the pall placed on the casket before entering the sanctuary, then a processional into the church with the crucifer, the priest or bishop, the pallbearers, the casket then the decedent's family.

Flowers are generally forbidden inside the sanctuary with the exception of the altar, but may be displayed in the vestibule (foyer outside the sanctuary).

The Episcopal funeral service concludes with the casket recession from the church with crucifer, bishop or priest, casket and family, with the pall removed once out of the sanctuary.

A committal service will usually be held at the cemetery after the funeral, which includes a scripture, prayer and the priest using sand or flower petals to make the sign of the cross on the closed casket.

Cremation is an accepted means of disposition, in which use of a memorial service instead of a funeral may occur.

Lutheran

Also a liturgical Christian church, the Lutheran Church was founded by protestant reformer Martin Luther in 1517 A.D.

In past days, the Lutheran funeral was usually held in the church, however, today it may be held at the funeral home or a location of the family's choosing. If the funeral is held in the church, the service will be highly structured and liturgical, but if held elsewhere, it will be more non-liturgical in order.

The use of the pall accompanies the service if held at the church, with viewing of the deceased taking place in the narthex prior to the start of the funeral. The pall is then placed over the closed casket immediately preceding the procession into the sanctuary, which is led by the cross bearer, the pastor, pallbearers, casket, then the family.

The funeral service may include communion if desired by the family. A recessional from the church will conclude the funeral with the funeral party returning to their automobiles for the trip to the committal service.

Flowers are permitted inside the Lutheran church and the use of cremation is discouraged but may be used.

Lutheran services held outside the church can be liturgical in nature but usually more closely resembles a non-liturgical funeral rite.

Since ground burial or entombment is the most preferred means of final disposition by Lutherans, a committal service is held at the final resting place which includes prayer, scripture reading and making the/sign of the cross on the casket with earth or flower petals.

Non-Liturgical Protestant

Most protestant churches today are non-liturgical, which means they have no set-in-stone, prescribed order of worship. Although these churches have some structure or suggested orders of service, they are merely suggestions and leave the actual form of service to the discretion of the pastor or minister in charge.

Churches that are considered or classified as non-liturgical include but are not limited to the following:

Apostolic	Assembly of God
Baptist	Bible
Charismatic	Church of God
Churches of Christ	Disciples of Christ
Methodist	Nazarene
Nondenominational	Pentecostal
Presbyterian	Wesleyan
United Church of Christ	

To Each His Own

Since the clergy determine in large part the order of service based upon their own preferences and the families wishes, there may be a fairly large variation in funerals for non-liturgical Protestants.

There may be little difference between a funeral held at the funeral home and one held at a protestant church. If a service is held in another facility such as a civic or community center, a lodge, auditorium or government building, the activities of the service may be dictated in full or in part by the type of facility where the service is held.

If a church or religious organization will not lead or participate in a service at a facility other than the church or funeral home, a separate service may be held before or after the religious service or at another time altogether.

Because of the less formal approach to the funeral service

by non-liturgical Protestants, usually the clergy and family will meet before services to discuss what the family's wishes are for the service with the clergy's guidance to determine the order and procedure for the service.

The visitation may be held at the church or funeral home where an open casket viewing is likely at either place. The casket may also be opened in the chapel or sanctuary before, during or after the service or closed at all for some of the time as the family may chose.

The family can also have a larger degree of freedom concerning any music selections they may want played- either live or recorded with consent of the funeral director if the service is held at the funeral home or with the clergy if held at the church.

Placement of flowers in the chapel/sanctuary is allowed in non-liturgical churches with advice concerning the arrangement and setting of the flowers from the church or funeral home based on which place services are held.

Any processional into the church or chapel at the beginning of the service will usually consist of the funeral director seating the family with the casket already placed at the front of the sanctuary or chapel. The recessional to end the service however may include the clergy, casket and pallbearers as well as the family exiting the sanctuary in prescribed order.

If the final disposition is some method other than burial or entombment, the committal service may be held at the end of the funeral with no processional to another site.

Regardless of form of disposition, the family and/or clergy will have great latitude in determining the content and order of any committal service, but it usually will include a prayer, reading and closing remarks, if desired.

Atheist

Atheism is the belief that God does not exist. The atheist inspired funeral or memorial service, therefore, will be void of any mention of God.

This service may be like other services that are religious or traditional in the sense of having an order of ceremony and being ritualistic but without reference to God or religiously inspired thinking.

The funeral for a departed atheist might include a eulogy of the deceased, favorite songs or poems and perhaps an invitation of those in attendance at the service an opportunity to share thoughts and experiences they had with the deceased during his/her lifetime. The rite for an atheist inspired service may be either a funeral (with casket/deceased present) or a memorial service with a burial/entombment, creation or other disposition.

With the exception of no acknowledgment of God or traditional religious thinking, the atheist funeral may very well resemble any other type of funeral rite with an officiant/speaker or speakers, music, flowers, pallbearers and a logically predetermined service order.

Baha'i

Baha'i is a religious faith started in present day Iran in 1863. It believes there is only one God and that He created the world for all mankind.

Baha'i is based on the ideas of unity and tolerance of all religions. It emphasizes worshipping God by doing good deeds and service to others without regard to race, nationality or other distinctions.

The Baha'i faith stipulates that a body should not be moved more than one hour's transport time from the place of death to place of burial/disposition. The deceased is to be buried not cremated (except in cases of contagious disease).

Since Baha'i believes embalming interferes with the natural process of decay, it is not usually done, but the Baha'i faith does not prohibit it either.

Another interesting point about Baha'i is that the believer may wish to be buried facing Qiblih- a place located about 10 miles north of Haifa, Israel.

Buddhist

Buddhism is one of the world's major religions. Founded in India in 500 B.C. by Buddha, Buddhism has been one of the dominant religious, social and cultural forces in Asia and the Far East for centuries.

Buddhists usually will have a funeral ceremony that in most Buddhist traditions consist of a eulogy, prayers and last between an hour and an hour and a half. Some Buddhist sects may have three separate services. A monk or Buddhist priest will usually lead the service. The casket is always open at the service and guests are expected to view the body.

Otherwise a guest is not expected to do anything other than to sit and then stand when others do so.

Cremation is the traditional form of disposition for Buddhists but burial is also accepted.

After the funeral, there will be a procession to the crematory or burial site and those guests at the funeral may attend the burial or cremation site if desired.

Catholic

The Roman Catholic Church is the largest Christian religion in the world with approximately one billion members worldwide and about 60 million in the U.S.

The funeral rites of the Catholic church are very traditional and follow a somewhat structured format. The church believes that all Catholics should be buried from the church with a funeral Mass. Although the appropriate place to conduct the service is at the Church, some Catholics will choose to have the service at the funeral home chapel or at graveside only.

A pre-service viewing normally takes place at the funeral home and a Rosary or Vigil Service can be held at the funeral home chapel or church.

The purpose of the Rosary (also can be called Vigil Service) is to provide people an opportunity to recite and share a series of prayers with the family and offer a time of reflection on the life of the deceased and upon the meaning of life, death and eternal life as well.

Since the Catholic funeral will normally take place at the church, there may be a procession from the funeral home to the church including the family, the deceased, the funeral home staff and others that may wish to participate.

Other times all parties attending the service all meet at the church separately.

The funeral or Mass of Christian Burial begins when the casket is moved into the narthex of the church. The casket will then be moved in procession down the main aisle of the church after the greeting, invocation and blessing of the casket by the celebrant (officiant in charge of the service) and placement of the pall (cloth covering) onto the casket. The procession into the sanctuary will include the celebrant, crucifer, altar attendants, casket, funeral director, pallbearers, family, and any congregational guests not already seated.

The Mass includes bible readings, sermon, eulogy and communion. The service will conclude with a Final Commendation, blessing of the casket and a recessional out of the church the same as going down at the start, with the pall removed from the casket once back in the narthex before exiting the church.

The casket is always closed in the Catholic Church with the only exception being a brief viewing before the service begins in the narthex of the church at the family's request and the celebrant's consent.

Flowers are also usually not displayed in the sanctuary of the Catholic Church however some individual churches now allow a few floral pieces at the front of the sanctuary near the altar area and the rest left in the narthex or vestibule. For very large Catholic funerals where many floral tributes have been sent, the majority of the flowers may be taken from the funeral home straight to the gravesite.

If the final disposition is burial or entombment at a cemetery, there will be a motor procession from the church to the place of disposition with a final committal service performed by the priest consisting of a scripture reading, invocation and presentation of the crucifix to the family. The priest and/or family may sprinkle the top of the casket with sand at the end of the committal service, and some Catholic families may also want to stay and witness the closing of the grave before departing.

Although previously forbidden by the Catholic Church through the centuries, the Church issued an instruction on cremation in 1963 allowing latitude for Catholics who requested to be cremated after death, so long as the choice for cremation did not come out of any anti-Christian motive.

The accepted procedure by the Catholic Church that includes cremation is for the deceased to be given a Mass at the Church as tradition dictates and for the cremation to follow the usual funeral Mass.

Since cremation is the exception to the Church's normal practice of Christian burial, the governing rule is for the Mass to take place before the cremation- ashes or cremated remains may not be brought into the church according to the universal church's general law, and that the cremated ashes be buried or entombed in a consecrated place. They are not to be left or scattered but must be given the same dignity as a Christian burial.

Christian Science

Also known as the Church of Christ, Scientist, Christian Science was founded in 1879 by Mary Baker Eddy in Boston, Mass.

Along with the King James Version of the Bible, the principle text is Science and Health with Key to the Scriptures, authored by Ms. Eddy in 1875.

The Christian Science movement has deep roots in Protestant Christianity and stresses spiritual healing of sickness.

A Christian Science funeral is usually very similar to the other protestant denominations. However, since the church has no clergy or ministers, the funeral will usually be officiated by a

Reader or Practitioner from the local Christian Science Church.

The Service itself may be held anywhere except the Christian Science Church, which is usually the funeral home or graveside (if burial is the final disposition).

The funeral will consist of readings from the text Science and Health with key to the Scriptures and from the Bible.

Since many of the details are at the family's discretion, flowers, music and different speakers may all be part of the service.

While it is possible to have the casket opened for a viewing at the Christian Science funeral it is traditional for it to be closed and is rarely opened.

The final disposition of the deceased is left up to the individual preference of the family with burial, entombment or cremation all possible.

Fraternal Organizations

If the decedent for which services are being held was a member of a fraternal organization, it is likely that a ceremony will be held in conjunction with the funeral or religious service or altogether separately for one of its members.

Such fraternal organizations may be one of, but not limited to, any of the following:

Benevolent and Protective Order of Elks
Fraternal Order of Eagles
Independent Order of Odd Fellows
Knights of Columbus
Knights of Pythias
Maccabbes
Masons
Modern Woodmen of America
The National Grange
Rebekah's
Royal Neighbors of America
Woodmen of the World

A Fraternal organization many times will hold its ceremony or portion thereof the day or evening before the funeral, immediately following the funeral service or if going to a cemetery or other site of final disposition, at that place.

It is usually the funeral director that coordinates any fraternal participation with the funeral itself, on the family's behalf.

Type of ceremony, activity and length of ritual varies depending on the fraternal organization involved.

Hindu

Unlike other religions, Hinduism has no founder and no exact doctrine or creed. The underlying theme is that God is within each being and object in the universe. It embraces different beliefs including the idea that Nirvana is the final stage reached after a series of births and rebirths.

Concerning death, Hinduism teaches that although the physical body dies, that the individual passes on to another lifetime.

Since cremation is the standard form of disposition for Hindus, the funeral may be held at the crematory. Married people are cremated with no expected time element involved, however most rituals take place within a day or two of the death (cremation will not happen until the governing authority issues the permit to cremate). Unmarried Hindus may be buried.

Regardless of disposition, there will be an open casket at the ceremony and guests will be expected to view (but not touch) the body.

Usually a priest or senior family member will officiate the ceremony and read from the mantras (priests only), which are special books for Hindu funerals. The ceremony usually just proceeds without a printed order to follow. Attendees may bring flowers but not food or donations.

Guests at the Hindu funeral may, but are not required to participate in the service. Guests may attend the cremation if they desire and also are not mandated to participate in the cremation ceremony.

Humanist/Secular

Humanism is the philosophy that man is the center of the universe. It is the viewpoint that emphasizes the importance of man whether religious or nonreligious.

Humanism developed in a more or less evolutionary form from the classical writings of Greeks and Romans and eventually abounded as a movement in Europe from the 1300s to 1500s, existing in some form or fashion until today.

A humanistic funeral will therefore be undergirded by the complete discretion of the person(s) making the arrangements. Although there may be mention of God and reference to religious ideas, the theme of the service will generally involve nonreligious music, poems, and message or eulogy. There also may be no mention of the afterlife since humanism is focused more on man's life and existence in this world.

Final disposition, like the funeral service content, will be left up to the family's discretion and individual wishes.

Jehovah's Witnesses

Founded as the watchtower Bible and Tract Society in 1879 by Charles Taze Russell, Jehovah's Witnesses are today a worldwide faith known for their loyalty and devotion to the Jehovah Witness cause of missionary work and referring to God only as Jehovah.

The Jehovah Witness funeral service will usually take place at a Kingdom Hall (local Jehovah witness church) or at the funeral home. The ceremony usually will last 20-30 minutes and will be led by a Congregation Elder who will speak from the Bible and the Sing Praises to Jehovah songbook.

There may or may not be an open casket viewing at the funeral depending upon the family's preference. There is usually a short graveside service following the main ceremony at the Kingdom Hall or funeral home and guests may attend at their own discretion. Sending of food and flowers are both appropriate and can both be done before the services.

Jewish

Judaism is a belief system of religious beliefs and rituals and a code of ethical behavior thought to date back to the 16th century B.C. Abraham is considered the founder of the Jewish faith, which also serves as the foundation of both Islam and Christianity.

Today there are four main religious sects within the Jewish faith, which includes Reformed, Reconstructionist, Conservative and Orthodox.

Although there are some differences and variations in the funeral customs among the four groups, here I want to focus on the similarities.

The Jewish funeral will usually last from 15 minutes to an hour and consists of intense grieving and mourning. The ceremony will typically be held at the temple or synagogue or possibly the funeral home. The family may gather at the place of the service 30 minutes to an hour before the ceremony.

It is never the Jewish custom to have an open casket at the funeral and embalming may not be done in a lot of cases due to the belief that the body should be left alone after death.

The funeral will usually be led by a rabbi, who delivers the eulogy, and assisted by a cantor, who sings. A family member and/or friend may give a eulogy if desired.

Although there are no standard books used in the ceremony, the rabbi leads the funeral and may make announcements. The guests at the Jewish funeral are expected to stand with the other mourners but only close friends and family members are expected to attend the committal service afterwards.

Those that do attend the Jewish graveside service are expected to participate in filling in the grave with a spade full of dirt.

Sending of flowers is not deemed appropriate (exception may be reformed Jewish), however contributions in memory of the decedent are customary to a charity or cause in which the deceased favored or may have had some involvement in. Sending food to the family's home after the funeral is appropriate as long as it is Kosher (in conformity with Jewish traditions).

Mennonite/Amish

The Mennonite Church is a group of very conservative evangelical Christians who settled in America in 1863. There are many groups within the Mennonite faith, which is associated with the Old Order Amish.

After death the Mennonite funeral will usually take place within 2-3 days. A visitation might be held at the funeral home, but also may take place at the family's home.

The funeral often happens at the church but could be held at the decedent's home. The funeral home could also be the setting for the service. There is often an open casket viewing at the visitation and the funeral. The pastor and a song leader or musician(s) will lead the service and different versions of the bible may be used for reading at the ceremony.

Flowers may be sent for the service so long as the deceased or the family does not belong to one of the more conservative sects, and food can also be sent to the family's home before or after the service.

Burial will take place after a procession to the cemetery in which attendance is usually optional and sometimes will only be held with family and sometimes close friends.

Mormon

Also known as the Church of Jesus Christ of Latter Day Saints, the Mormon faith was founded by Joseph Smith in the early part of the 1800s in New York State.

After several moves across the United States, the church eventually settled its headquarters in Utah under the leadership of Brigham Young and is still centered today in Salt Lake City, Utah with about 5-6 million members in the U.S. and Canada.

The Mormon funeral is usually very simple with the service being held within a week of the death. The funeral may be held at the funeral home or the Mormon tabernacle, but not at the Mormon temple. The visitation is usually held the evening before the funeral at the funeral home, the residence or the tabernacle (if the funeral will be there).

Although there are no full-time professional clergy in the Church of Latter Day Saints, the Bishop of the Ward (officer of the Church) usually conducts the service. It may last 1-1 1/2 hours and will have a prelude, prayer, eulogy, obituary, music, message and postlude. An open or closed casket at the funeral ceremony will be at the family's discretion and viewing is optional.

Both flowers and food may be sent but is not expected.

Although ground burial is the traditional method of disposition in the Mormon Church, other forms are permissible and left to the family's preference. For burial, the committal service is usually brief and open to guests, unless requested to be private.

Moslem/Islamic

The religion of Islam, which means "submission" to the will of God, has been in existence since around 600 B.C.

Muhammad is regarded as the prophet of Allah who received revelation from God that God himself is the one creator of mankind and demands loyalty and devotion from created man.

With over one billion Islams or Muslims worldwide, Islam is one of the fastest growing religions in the world.

The Islamic funeral usually lasts 30 minutes to an hour and takes place 48 to 72 hours after death.

The Muslim Church, which is called a Mosque, will provide a room within the building as the place for the funeral or it may be held at the funeral home.

The service is very simple and will be led by an inman, who will use a book referred to as the Quran. There is always a closed casket at the Islamic funeral and it is appropriate to send food and flowers to the home of the bereaved after the funeral.

After the service there will be an interment/committal service in which guests may attend. Janazah prayer recitation is the protocol at the graveside after which the deceased is buried. Muslims are never cremated.

Native American/First Nations

The native American/First Nations religion exists as a broad, generalized way of life rather than as a single intangible belief system.

These Native Americans or Indians are those in North America who consider themselves citizens of the United states and their own various nations as well.

Most Native Americans view death as the start of a new journey into the next world, and have strict rules about helping a deceased loved one successfully start this journey. This may include placing items into the casket with the deceased that the surviving relatives believe he or she may need to make the journey.

Since Native Americans do not believe the soul (or true Life) is terminated, they may still grieve the absence of the one who has died from this life. They may restrict their activities and abstain from consuming certain foods as a sacrifice for the decedent.

Orthodox

The Orthodox Church is a universal religion that evolved through a series of divisions, beginning with a separation from the Roman Catholic Church in 1054 A.D.

The Orthodox Church is usually called according to its geographical location or its nationality composition of its members, thus the terms Russian Orthodox, Eastern Orthodox, Greek Orthodox, etc. The Church believes in the separation of the body and soul at death. The funeral will happen within 2-3 days of passing.

Since the Orthodox usually have a traditional funeral service at the Church, the deceased will be embalmed with an open casket at the ceremony.

Oftentimes the family and pallbearers will meet at the funeral home and go in procession to the church where they will be met by the Priest, who will be assisted by a bishop and a deacon. The casket will be led down the aisle to the front where the service is conducted.

A service bulletin or program will be passed out to guests upon arrival at the church. The officiants will use a funeral text for conducting the service. The funeral will conclude in the church with a pass-by of the casket, and passersby will have a chance to stop and kiss the Icon (picture of Christ) at the casket. After exiting the church, the family then will have opportunity for a final viewing before the casket is closed.

The use of flowers is generally permitted but varies from church to church. It is acceptable to send food to the home of the bereaved either before or after the funeral.

There will be a procession to the place of disposition from the church, which is optional for guests to attend. The committal service consists of a short prayer followed by the priest or bishop placing soil on top of the casket in the shape of a cross.

Since cremation is objectionable in the Orthodox Church, disposition will usually consist of either ground burial or entombment.

<u>Quaker</u>

Also known as the Religious Society of Friends, Quakerism was founded in England in the 1600s by George Fox.

Known best for their humanitarian activities concerning peace, education, racial equality and public reform, Quakers believe in the saving power of God through His son Jesus Christ.

There are at least several opinions about life after death among Quakers since the Quaker faith is without creeds.

The Quaker funeral service is either programmed or unprogrammed, which will determine what happens during the service. Unprogrammed meetings are based upon silence while worshippers wait for the guidance of the spirit to lead them to speak or not.

In programmed meetings, singing hymns, prayers, Bible reading, a sermon, etc. are planned in advance. The worship is lead by a pastor and the meeting, programmed or not usually last about an hour.

The Quaker funeral usually takes place in the church or meetinghouse, or at the funeral home. Although rare, the service may take place in a private residence.

Rarely is there an open casket at a Quaker ceremony, however if there is, viewing the decedent is entirely optional.

The funeral is officiated by a pastor or one appointed by a Quaker Oversight Committee to lead. The bible and song hymnal are the books used and a program with an order of service and/or brief overview of Quaker customs may be explained.

Since silence is an important part of the customary Quaker ceremony, those present are not expected to participate in any special outward ritual.

The sending of food or flowers are both appropriate. The obituary may state if contributions or memorials are requested in lieu of flowers.

Quakers may be either buried or cremated and if cremated, the ashes are either buried or placed in a vault, but can also be scattered.

The Quaker graveside is usually only for close family members and is a short committal of the body to the ground.

Scientology

The Church of Scientology is a relatively new religion rooted in some ideas from both Buddhism and Hinduism.

Scientology worldwide is a nondenominational religious philosophy that is in search of self-knowledge and truth. The basic premise of scientology is that knowledge must be applied and put into use to be of value. Learning ideas and knowledge alone is not enough in order to be of help.

Funerals of the Scientology church are usually based on local customs and left up to the family and/or the leadership of the local Scientology church.

Seventh-Day Adventist

Formally organized and established in 1863, the Seventh Day Adventists are a Christian Denomination that came out of the religious revival of the mid 1800s, focused on the second coming of Christ. Adventists live in anticipation of Jesus' second coming and are best known for observing the Sabbath on Saturday, the seventh day.

Most Seventh Day Adventist funerals will take place within a week of the death. The service may be held at either the church or funeral home, with a viewing and an open casket. Sending flowers for the funeral is appropriate and sending food to the home of the bereaved is standard for after services.

The funeral will be conducted by a clergyman and maybe an associate or musician(s). The Bible is used by the clergy and the service on average lasts 30-45 minutes.

The preferred method of disposition is burial, which will take place after the funeral and a procession to the cemetery. The graveside consists of a prayer from the Clergy and a brief message of encouragement.

Sikh

This religion started in India in the late 15th Century based on the influence of Guru Nanak (1469-1539). As the first Sikh Guru, he taught in the existence of one creator and that all of creation is an extension of the creator.

Today there are over 20 million Sikhs worldwide.

Concerning death, the Sikh tradition includes the belief in the cycle of reincarnation and that the soul is everlasting.

Within 3 days (or as soon as lawfully permitted) the body of the deceased is always cremated.

Prior to the cremation there is a brief ceremony held, usually at the funeral home or crematory. This service consists of bible readings and singing songs that are appropriate for the occasion. There is also a post-cremation ceremony held at the Sikh temple. The service at the funeral home is about 45 minutes on average, whereas the temple service is about an hour. Since the cremation between services last several hours, only close family members remain for the cremation. If guests are invited they are not expected to participate in the cremation ceremony unless invited to do so.

Unification Church

Founded in Korea by Sun Myung Moon who later came to America in 1971, Unification is a religion that claims over 2 million members worldwide and is based on the ideas of Moon, who supposedly received divine revelation from Jesus in addition to what is written in the bible. The Divine Principle is the so called completed work of revelation that the Unification Church uses as its source of reference.

Unification funerals will closely resemble protestant ceremonies in format and usually include some reading from the Divine Principle and a service inclusive of the church's leadership.

Unitarian/Universalist

Created in 1961 through the merger of the American Unitarian Association and the Universalist Church of America, Unitarians believe in the conscience, experience and reason of man instead of strict adherence to creeds and dogmas.

Local Unitarian congregations maybe called a church, fellowship or society and operate autonomously.

Concerning death, Unitarian Universalists have no specific doctrine concerning the afterlife. The ritual marking one's death is termed a memorial service rather than a funeral, and it usually last 30 minutes to an hour and a half.

The memorial service will take place at the deceased family's discretion. Food and flowers can be sent directly to the bereaved's home upon hearing of the death.

The service usually takes place at the funeral home or church and there is rarely an open casket viewing.

The memorial ceremony is conducted by a minister who is

accompanied by a eulogist and a musician (organist), and the hymnal singing from the Living Tradition is used. Funerals have no set format and use no bible scripture or reading or poetry. The order of service may be printed in the service programs or posted at the front of the chapel.

The interment is optional for those guests who attend the memorial service. It consists of prayer recitation prior to the burial of the deceased.

Veterans/Military

Active Duty

If a decedent was on active duty in any branch of the United States Armed Forces, the U.S. Government will assist the family by providing through a Government contracting funeral home the cost for preparation, transportation to the location of the funeral and then to location of disposition or through reimbursement of expenses to the funeral home of the family's choice. The military will also include a flag and burial expenses up to a certain amount determined by the federal government.

In order to have a military funeral, the decedent's family must request it from the branch of service the deceased belonged to. This can be done through the funeral home who acts on the family's behalf.

The service can be a chapel/church funeral with committal at the site of burial or a graveside only (which is more common). If the graveside is the military portion of the service, a Chaplain of the Armed Forces Branch will conduct it. The military graveside will include but not be limited to the playing of Taps, folding and presentation of the flag, and a firing party to carry out a 21-gun salute.

Veteran

Funeral services for one who was honorably discharged from the armed forces is entitled to military involvement in the funeral process, but usually on a smaller scale. The activities of an honor guard for veterans will usually be held at the graveside only.

Depending upon the level of service or rank at time of discharge will determine the level of involvement in the service. The Department of Defense has issued an order that all honorably discharged deceased veterans receive a playing of Taps, folding and presentation of the flag, according to personal availability. In the event that no uniformed military representatives are present at the graveside service, the funeral home staff may substitute to perform the Taps and flag folding and presentation functions.

<u>Zoroastrian</u>

Zoroastrianism is a religion founded by the Persian prophet Zoroaster sometime around 600 B.C.

The Zoroastrians believe certain elements such as soil, water and fire as sacred and therefore must remain unpolluted.

This belief results in neither earth burial nor cremation of Zoroastrians since it would pollute the earth (burial) or fire (cremation).

There are several purification ceremonies that Zoroastrians conduct, including washing the body in sand and water and perhaps other substances as dictated by the religion.

The Zoroastrians believe that the righteous go directly to paradise upon death and the wicked are first purified in Hades and then are saved, according to Zoroaster's teachings.

SUMMARY OF CUSTOMS

	Service Inclusions	Viewing	Officiants
Protestant (Liturgical)	Pall/Eulogy/Sermon	Permitted	Bishop/Pastor
Protestant (Non-Liturgical)	Obituary/Eulogy/ Sermon	Permitted	Pastor
Atheist	Varies	Maybe	Service Leader
Baha'i	Baha'i Prayers	Rarely	Family Appointee
Buddhist	Readings/ Announcements	Yes	Monk Or Priest
Catholic	Pall/Reading/ Eulogy/Communion	No	Priest Or Father
Christian Science	Readings	Rarely	Reader/Practitione
Fraternal	Varies	Maybe	Varies
Hindu	Readings	Yes	Priest
Humanist	Varies	Permitted	Family Appointee
Jehovah's Witness	Reading/Songs	Maybe	Congregation Elde
Jewish	Eulogy/Songs	No	Rabbi
Mennonite Amish	Reading/Songs	Permitted	Pastor
Mormon	Message/Songs	Maybe	Bishop
Moslem	Readings	No	Iman
Native American	Varies	Yes	Spiritual Leader
Orthodox	Read Funeral Text	Yes	Priest/Bishop
Quaker	Speaking/Varies	Rarely	Church Appointee
Scientology	Varies	Varies	Leader
Seventh Day Adventist	Bible Reading	Yes	Clergyman
Sikh	Reading/Song	Maybe	Family Appointee
Unification	Varies	Permitted	Pastor
Unitarian	Varies	Rarely	Minister
Veteran/Military	Varies	Rarely	Varies
Zoroastrian	Varies	Permitted	Varies

AND PRACTICES

Music	Send Flowers	Send Food	Passby	Disposition
Yes	Yes	Yes	Restricted	Burial/Cremation
Yes	Yes	Yes	Yes	Any
Open	Yes	Yes	Maybe	Any
Possibly	Yes	Yes	Rarely	Burial
Possibly	Yes	No	Yes	Burial/Cremation
Yes	Yes	Yes	No	Burial/Cremation
Possibly	Yes	Yes	Rarely	Any
Possibly	Yes	Yes	Maybe	Any
No	Yes	No	Yes	Cremation
Possibly	Yes	Yes	Permitted	Any
Yes	Yes	Yes	Maybe	Burial
Yes	No	Restricted	No	Burial
Yes	Usually	Yes	Permitted	Burial
Yes	Yes	Yes	Permitted	Any
Possibly	Yes	Yes	No	Burial
Possibly	Maybe	Restricted	Usually	Burial
Yes	Varies	Yes	Yes	Burial
Yes	Yes	Yes	Rarely	Burial
Varies	Varies	Varies	Varies	Any
Yes	Yes	Yes	Permitted	Burial
Yes	Yes	Yes	Maybe	Cremation
Yes	Usually	Usually	Maybe	Any
Yes	Yes	Yes	No	Burial
Possibly	Yes	Yes	Rarely	Any
Varies	Yes	Yes	Varies	Entombment

Show me the manner in which a nation
or community cares for its dead
and I will measure with mathematical exactness
the tender mercies of its people,
their respect for the law of the land,
and their loyalty to high ideals.

William Gladstone,
Prime Minister of Great Britain
1809-1898

Photo courtesy of Resurrection Cemetery, Omaha Nebraska

Chapter 9

A Brief History (Where & Why)

1. Introduction
2. Definition And Overview
3. Funeral Homes And Directors
4. Clergy/Ministers/Officiants
5. Cemeteries/Graveyards/Tombs
6. Crematories
7. Mausoleums And Niches
8. Cryonics
9. Donation To Science
10. Sea Burial
11. Embalming And Refrigeration
12. Records And Information
13. Flowers
14. Shrouds And Garments
15. Caskets And Coffins
16. Outer Enclosures
17. Monuments And Grave Markers
18. Transportation
19. Ritual And Ceremony, The Funeral/The Wake

Introduction

As western society today continues its trend of changing ideas, changing economics, changing values, and overall changing culture, it is important to have some type of anchor, some kind of overview of where we have come from in order to make sense out of where we are going.

This chapter is devoted to giving you a brief yet descriptive historical account of where some of our present day practices concerning death and funeralization/memorialization started or came from either philosophically, literally, or both.

Having this basic knowledge of where and why will help you to understand the death-care industry and the customs that are almost universally embraced and consumed when death hits at home, and, help you to understand the choices and decisions you make when you do need to make final arrangements for a loved one.

Definition And Overview

The word Funeral is derived from the old Sanskir word of Northern India that means smoke.

Cremation is the act of destroying a corpse by fire. This intense heating process of producing a chemical change from human remains to ashes goes back to at least the ancient Babylonians. Burial is the event of placing one's body into the ground or earth. This dates back to the very beginning of time and was the first form of disposition.

Entombment is the process of placing the deceased into an above ground space known as a mausoleum crypt. The Egyptians built tombs for above ground placement in ancient times.

Burial at sea is as the phrase expresses, the casting into the ocean the bodies of those who died aboard ship. It started as a matter of necessity for sanitary reasons when a ship was far out at sea and days from land.

Donation is the bequeathal of a body to science for research or teaching purposes. This is not a new form of disposition, and the study of deceased corpses has been ongoing since man first discovered a need to study and learn about the human body.

To Know the Future, One Must Know the Past
Funeral Homes And Directors

The Funeral Director, also known in past days as mortician or undertaker, had become a service occupation in the United States by the mid 1800s, and by the start of the 20th century, was required to meet certain qualifications and training standards as established by law.

A professional mortician is one who has training and licensing as both a Funeral Director and an embalmer or a combination license. Some states allow licensing for either Funeral Director or embalmer separately for those who only wish to practice one but not the other.

Known before the turn of the 20th century as Funeral parlors, funeral homes did not become commonplace as such in the U.S. until around 1920. Before this time most of the services rendered by a Funeral Director were at the home of the deceased, or next-of-kin.

Because of the rural nature of society before and during this time, most deaths took place at home and the undertaker would be called to come out to the house, prepare the deceased for viewing and a ceremony at the home. Not until the tide turned toward rapid urbanization and the industrial revolution did people have a need or desire to go to another place for funeral services.

A good number of funeral homes in America started as or part of furniture stores - usually located in the downtown area of the community or city - due to the fact that the furniture dealers were also the ones to make and sell caskets. As time has progressed, the Funeral establishments and furniture stores have parted way in most places with each party specializing in its specific trade.

Clergy/Ministers/Officiants

Throughout history people in all societies have regarded the disposal of the dead as a solemn act desiring group involvement and accompanied by rites or ceremonies.

Since a large majority of western Funeral practices are rooted in Judeo-Christian Framework, even if the deceased or deceased's Family does not have strong church or religious ties it has been a long-held custom to involve a church pastor or minister of the Christian faith to speak or officiate at the Funeral service for the departed.

The belief in eternity and life after death constitutes a proper occasion to call upon a representative of the deceased's family's religious affiliation to act as a voice of comfort, hope, promise and helping lead survivors in carrying on their own lives after the loved one's departure.

Cemeteries/Graveyards/Tombs

Dating as far back as the stone-age, earth burial has been the dominant form of handling the dead all the way up to today.

Cemeteries, memorials parks, or memorial grounds as we know them were once called graveyards or known as burial grounds and first developed back around the 4th Century A.D. when Christianity emerged from its underground exile due to Roman persecution, to establish open air, or ground cemeteries.

Before this, Christians had buried their dead in underground tombs called catacombs, which consisted of tunnels and recesses under the earth.

The Romans original law forbade the burial of the dead within cities and the pagan practice was to bury the dead along the roads outside of the cities.

Early cemeteries were mostly within the walls of or vicinity of the local church. However as Christianity grew in popularity and statute among the masses, cemetery burial eventually became part of the community way of life.

Crematories

Although cremation has been used throughout world history by different nations and for different reasons, the cremation movement in America can be traced to the year 1876. It was on December 6th of this year that the first cremation in the United States took place at a private crematory built by Dr. Julius LeMoyne on his estate in Washington, Pennsylvania .

Baron Joseph Henry Louis Charles DePalm, who was a part of a cremation society founded in New York in 1874, offered his corpse to be used for America's First cremation. A widely publicized event, the DePalm cremation sparked a controversy and debate over cremation vs. traditional burial that would continue until 1896.

Mausoleums And Niches

The first mausoleums can be traced back to the ancient Egyptians who built above ground tombs or pyramids to place their rulers in. Many other peoples throughout history including Jews, Romans and Islams have also used tombs for disposition.

The term "mausoleum" comes from the mausolus structure that King of Caria built for his wife in Asia Minor around 1350 B.C.

Mausoleum disposition or entombment because popular in Europe by the 19th century. As a result, mausoleums also became fixtures in American cemeteries with crypts or tombs for corpse placement and later as cremation became more commonplace niches (place for cremated ashes) also.

Cryonics

A product of the union between American Business ingenuity and medical science, the concept of Cryonics is so new that little can be put into a historical context as of this writing.

This idea of placing a deceased human corpse into frozen storage to await future cures yet to be discovered can really only be discussed in a present tense (see Chapter 3 for a more thorough presentation).

Donation To Science

Body donation goes back to the early days of man when humans wanted to learn more about the body and would use corpses as a mode of study.

By the 1600s, mankind started making major strides into medical study of disease, helped in large part from the use of cadavers made available to physicians, anatomists and researchers.

Burial At Sea

As old as the history of sailing and ships, burial at sea had become a necessity procedure whenever a death took place during a voyage.

Because of the health concern to those on the ship while at sea, many times it could be days or even weeks before the vessel would dock again at dry land. If a death occurred, it became customary at the captain's discretion to place the corpse into a wooden box or other container and lower down to the water and let sink.

Sometimes rocks or other heavy objects may have been placed into, on top of or attached to the deceased's container to assure that it would descend to the ocean's bottom.

Embalming And Refrigeration

Used by the Egyptians as far back as 4000 B.C., embalming has been performed for many reasons using different techniques and methods.

Ancient Egypt believed that preserving a body or mummy was necessary for the soul's survival. The mummy of King Mer-en-re was discovered in his pyramid in 1880, almost perfectly preserved after 4,500 years.

Modern embalming began in the 1700s with fluid injection of the body's circulatory system.

Embalming was first used wide scale in the United States during the Civil War to preserve the war dead for sending home for burial.

Since the end of World War II, we have seen a great increase in the use and acceptance of embalming by the general public. Preservation by refrigeration is a much more recent phenomenon, replacing ice as the method used to retard decomposition when embalming is not used. Ice had previously been used for many different types of preserving activities dating back to the Chinese in 1000 B.C.

When modern mechanical refrigeration units were developed in the late 19th century, the idea of electric power has then added and by the 20th century, refrigeration units were being manufactured by industry for many different types of storage, including the preservation of the deceased until proper disposition.

Records And Information

Written records of death is one of the most interesting aspects that intrigues most everyone at some point in their lives.

Whether it is family tree research or interest in history or biographies of the famous, finding and getting death record information can be an adventure in itself.

Most states have either a long held requirement of death certificate filing on all deaths within its domain or at least some form of recorded information about a person's passing.

Because of varied forms and processes by different local, county and state governing agencies that deal with death information records, the best word of advise on getting historical data on death records is to start with the local vital statistics office, the public library, or the historical or genealogical society in the area you are researching.

Flowers

This tradition dates back to the days of ancient Greece, where the Greeks would send flowers as a token of remembrance to the family of the one passed away. These flowers were often woven into wreaths and were furnished by both relatives and friends of the deceased.

The beauty of fresh flowers has served as a comfort to the bereaved for many societies and generations since.

Shrouds And Garments

Different types of burial clothing were developed by different societies according to belief systems.

The Egyptians of course mummified or wrapped their dead in layers of oiled cloth for long-term preservation.

The Greeks would dress their dead in clothing socially accepted for their day and the Romans would dress the dead in white togas.

It has been customary in almost every culture since, to place some type of clothing or fabric-type covering over and or around the deceased.

Many times one's stature or function in life has dictated how he or she would be dressed at death. Chief, General, Solider, Peace Officer, King, etc.

Caskets And Coffins

Five thousand years before Christ the ancient Egyptians buried their dead in simple graves at the outer end of their early villages. Several thousand years later a high proportion of their energies was utilized toward the careful preservation and disposition of their dead.

Coming a long way through the many years, the early colonists in America plagued with sickness, disease, starvation and other trials undoubtedly buried their dead in the bare earth.

As the colonies progressed, the colonists in the new America, due to a large proportion of skilled craftsmen, started making coffins of wood, with the type of wood used revealing the economic status of the person buried.

Coffins of material other than wood made their first appearance in the first half of the 19th century. These burial coffins were being made of iron, stone, marble, cement, potter's clay as well as wood.

By the end of the 1800s the list also included burial cases made out of vulcanized rubber, aluminum, and cloth. This was made possible due to rapid industrial advances that allowed for mass production by large-scale manufacturers. The small coffin shop manned by skilled craftsman gave way to the new methods, but eventually became an ideal outlet for retail sale of the burial case products to the public.

The success of the metallic burial case began with the proposition that it preserved the body. This was a vex selling point when burial could not take place immediately, such as in colder climates where due to weather conditions the dead would have to be placed into vaults for the winter until the ground was thawed and dry enough for burial.

It was not until the 1890s that the term casket came to replace the term coffin as the descriptive term of burial case in popular culture.

The wood shops and craftsmen were replaced by the furniture store as the retail point of caskets/coffins to the public.

Although the wedge-shaped octagonal coffin no longer exists in America as such, the American "casket" has not been accepted in Europe as such.

Outer Enclosures

The concept of permanent protection of a decedent's body from ghouls and the elements has existed in various civilizations and cultures going back to ancient times.

As a result, the idea of a burial vault or outer burial container hasn't been an exclusive American burial practice, although the growth and development of the manufactured item the vault, and its popular usage is part of western taste in funeral service and burial today.

It was 1872 that Hartford, Connecticut resident Jacob Weidenmann first offered an affordable and durable covering for coffins and caskets. The term vault did not come into use as a popular term until the latter half of the 1870s.

Since Colonial times some type of container to enclose and protect both body and casket was in demand by those burying their dead.

As time progressed and experimentation increased, eventually concrete, metal and wood were the three types of "burial cases" made available to consumers.

One of the interesting features of outer containers was that they be burglar proof and were made accordingly. It was felt that the construction of these units include this variable as a key feature.

By the second decade of the 20th century the fear of grave robbing gradually diminished and the main function came to be protection of the casket and its contents.

And as a result of this/the wooden outer container couldn't fulfill the public's demand for a outer container that would provide enduring protection to the casket or a sacred body.

Monument And Grave Markers

With the establishment of the Roman burial customs in the early centuries after the death of Christ, the burial of the dead along the roads outside of cites led to certain decedent's burial places being honored by small monuments or stone tablets.

Later in time in early America, the concern to beautify the burial grounds of the dead developed into the practice of placing a small wooden cross into the ground on top of the grave. As society progressed in the 1800s, gravestones were made of the much more durable materials such as marble or limestone.

Not only were names and dates being inscribed on monuments but also designs, scrolls, insignias and sculptured artwork. The name of the game became memorization through prevailing idea of creating beauty and in the midst of even death, forging an environment that would present eye appeal to visitors.

Transportation

The death of a human being universally interrupts ordinary routines and calls for new modes of physical and emotional behavior.

One of the inescapable needs created by death in an organized society arises from the fact that the deceased must be removed from the place of death to other places for preparation and disposition[2].

The word "Funeral" is also derived from Funeralis, which in Latin means "torch-light procession."

Transportation's role in Funeral Services plays and has played a very colorful role in the funeralization process.

Since the funeral procession is the oldest of all processions of any kind, the need to move the deceased from point A to point B in ancient times usually took place on a hand-bier, which worked by placing the decedent upon a small wooden plan with hand and shoulder handles and walking the corpse to its burial place by six to twelve men depending on size and weight of the decedent.

With the establishment of cemeteries outside of cities, the hand-bier became impracticable due to distance and so a horse drawn vehicle became necessary.

These horse drawn hearses soon became a necessity as the world grew larger and more complex.

The use of carriages and coaches for making the journey to the grave was not a novelty and usually were leased from transportation companies for the exclusive purpose of transporting the dead.

Hearses with horses were the societal norm from 1850-1910 in the United States. Different styles were used, and until the Civil War hearses with black painted exteriors were the standard. After the war, some variation in color was incorporated.

By 1920 the automobile came to dominate funeral transportation and eventually replaced all other types of vehicles used in funeral service. It was also at this time that funeral homes offered other types of livery services in separate vehicles to include transporting the family and/or pallbearers in limousines and moving flowers or other memorial tokens to place of service and place of disposition.

Ritual And Ceremony

The Funeral:

Dealing with the concept of the funeral from a historical perspective in and of itself would require pages and pages of elaboration just to cover a broad overview of the history of the funeral.

What can be discussed briefly here is the influence that the past cultures and belief systems have on the funeral today.

Funeral services today in the western world are the product of the practices from the ancient Egyptians, Romans, Greeks and the early Christians just to name the major contributors.

Since the Middle Ages in Europe, the funeral ritual has been one practiced as a ceremony with from several to many participants and parties involved for the purpose of creating an event of value and significance to the survivors of the decedent and those attending the Funeral.

Christianity's influence has dominated the funeral's purpose through the centuries with the chapel or church setting and the graveside service. Having a minister or clergy member, hymns, prayer and Bible scripture reading has added much meaning and remembrance to the funeral for those of varying economic status.

The Wake:

This dates back to ancient times when people observed the custom of laying out the corpse after death until time for burial.

The old Jewish custom of watching or waking the dead was based on the idea that no one should be buried alive and therefore should be held for three days to watch the decedent for any signs of life.

The early Christmas would gather at the deceased repose to say prayers. The Greeks and Romans also would wait about three days before burying their dead and during the Middle Ages the wake was continued as an act of reverence and piety.

The practice of the wake has continued as part of the grieving process that allows survivors to confront and face the decedent's passing.

Chapter 10

Available Resources

1. Introduction
2. Books
3. Pamphlets/Periodicals
4. Other Publications
5. Computer Websites
6. Videos
7. Assistance Groups/Organizations
8. Consumer Information Contacts
9. Phone Numbers
10. Additional Helps
11. Memorial Donations List

Resources Available

Since there is an abundance of related information available that is relevant to the issues and subjects covered in this book, this chapter lists some of the names, titles, web pages and other materials and helps that are accessible in the marketplace for consumers to obtain.

Although these listing are not by any means comprehensive or all inclusive, these resources are good starting places in delving deeper into some of the text covered in the previous chapters of this book.

For further assistance in finding more information on a particular issue or subject, you may contact your local library, bookstore or funeral home/mortuary for advice and direction on getting more help.

Books

By Companion Press

1. The Journey Through Grief: Reflections On Healing. Dr. Alan Wolfelt

2. Understanding Grief, Helping Yourself Heal. Dr. Alan Wolfelt

3. Food For The Soul, A Best Of Bereavement Poetry Collection

By WBJ Press

4. What To Do When The Police Leave, A Guide To The First Days Of Traumatic Loss. Bill Jenkins

By Insight Books

5. The Gift Of Significance, Walking With People Through A Loss. Doug Manning

By The Funeral Service Education Foundation

6. Making Sense Out Of Suffering. An Insight Into The Mystery Of Suffering.

7. Flowers For The Ones You've Known- Unedited letters From Teens. Support Group For Teens In Book Form. Enid Samuel Traisman

8. When A Friend Dies-A Book For Teens About Grieving And Healing. Marily Gootman

9. Aarvy Aardvark Finds Hope. A Wonderful Story For Children And Families. Donna O'Toole

10. Children And Grief: Big Issues For Little Hearts. How To Book On Ways To Help Children And Adolescents Understand Their Pain And Grow Through Sorrow. By Johnette Hartnett.

11. The Empty Place, A Child's Guide Through Grief. Talks To Children About The Death Of A Brother Or Sister. By Roberta Ternes

12. Helping Children Cope With The Loss Of A Loved One- A Guide For Grownups. By William Koren

13. Losing Uncle Tom. Explains AIDS And Death To Children By Mary Kate Jordan

14. So Much To Think About When Someone You Care About Has Died. Activities For Children Who Are Bereaved. By Fred Rogers.

15. Talking About Death: A Dialogue Between Parent And Child. Book For Parents To Explain Death To Children. By Earl Grollman

16. Timothy Duck. Speaks To Children About Grieving And Their Feelings. By The Centering Corp.

17. When A Pet Dies. Helps Explain Death Of A Pet To Children By Fred Rogers

18. Our Children Live Forever In Our Hearts. A Keepsake Journal After The Loss Of a Child. By The Children's Mercy Hospital

19. Recovering From The Loss Of A Child. A Book For Bereaved Parents By Katherine Fair Donnelly

20. Recovering From The Loss Of A Parent. For The Adult Children Who've Lost A Parent. Kathrine Fair Donnelly

21. Recovering From The Loss Of A Sibling. Includes A Directory Of Support Groups And Organizations For Sibling Grief. Katherine Fair Donnelly

22. For Women Who Grieve, Embracing Life After The Death Of Your Partner. By Tangea Tansley

23. Going On: A Pathway Through Sorrow. About Helping Widowers Who Are Going Through Grief. By Jane Wood Shoemaker

24. How To Survive The Loss Of A Love. By Melba Colgrove

25. Living When A Loved One Has Died. By Earl Grollman

26. Widows Are Special. By Kathleen Peabody And Margaret Mooney

27. Life After Suicide-A Ray Of Hope For Those Left Behind. By E. Betsy Ross

28. No Time For Goodbyes. Suggestions For Survivors Grieving For Loved Ones 'Who Have Been Killed. By Janice Harris Lord

29. Different Losses Different Issues: what To Expect And How To Help. For Those Who've Lost A Sibling, Friend, or Relative as a result of Homicide. By Johnette Hartnett

30. I Know Just How You Feel. Book Of Sensitive Insights On Bereavement. By Erin Linn

31. Don't Take My Grief Away From Me. Takes Bereaved Through The Funeral And Its Aftermath. By Doug Manning

32. Handling The Holidays. Helpful Source For Those Dreading The Holidays. By Bruce Conley

33. Living With Grief After Sudden Loss. By Kenneth Doka

34. R.I.P.: The Complete Book Of Death And Dying. Reference Book On Issues About Death For Consumers. By Constance Jones.

By The National Funeral Directors Association

35. Helping Children Cope With Grief. By Dr. Alan Wolfelt

36. Recovering From The Loss Of Someone You Loved To AIDS By Katherine Fair Donnelly

37. The Class In Room 44- When A Classmate Dies. A Story For Children When A Classmate Dies. By Lynn Blackburn

38. For Those Who Live. Book For One Who Has Lost A Sibling To Death And A Parent To Grief. By Kathy LaTour

39. When Death Walks In. Book That Takes A Through Look At Facing Grief. By Mark Scravani

40. Challenge- A Mini Textbook To Help You Through The Emotions , Surprises And Devastation That Follows The Death Of Your Spouse. By Harris E. Adriance

41. For Crying Out Loud. Book On How To Work Through Grief. By Jean Jones

42. In Sickness And In Health. A Book That Provides Guidance And Suggestions To Help Others During Times Of Crisis. By Earl Grollman

43. Widow To Widow. By Phyllis R. Silverman

44. Good-Bye My Child. Book For Parents And Families Who Have Lost A Child. By Sara Rich And Margaret Pike.

45. When A Baby Dies. Practical Book For Families Who've Lost Perinatal or stillbirth Baby. By Sara Wheeler And Rana K. Limbo

46. How To Go On Living When Someone You Love Dies. By Therese A. Rando

47. Understanding Mourning. Discusses Overcoming Loss Of A Loved One And How To Work Through Grief. By Glen W. Davidson

48. Who Lives Happily Ever After? For Families Whose Child Has Died Violently/For Parents Who Do Not Get A Chance To Say Goodbye. By Sharon Turnbull

49. Purified By Fire: A History Of Cremation In America By Stephen Prothero; University of California Press

50. Celebrity Death Certificates. By Michael Steen; McFarland And Company, Inc.; Jefferson, North Carolina

51. Funerals Of The Famous. By Kates-Boylston Publications; Rockville, Md.

52. The Humanist Funeral Service. By Corliss Lamont; Prometheus Books, Buffalo, N.Y.

53. Parish Funerals: A Guide To The Order Of Christian Funerals By Michael Marchal; Liturgy Training publications, 1987, Chicago, Illinois

54. Dealing Creatively with Death: A Manual Of Death Education And Simple Burial. By Ernest Morgan; Celo Press, Burnsville, N.C., 1990.

55. In Memoriam: A Guide To Modern Funerals And Memorials, By Edward Searl, 1993; Skinner House Books, Boston, MA.

56. Final Celebrations: A Guide For Personal And Family Funeral Planning. By Kathleen Sublette; Pathfinder Publishing, Ventura, Ca.

57. What To Do When A Loved One Dies. By Eva Shaw, Dickens Press, Irvine, Ca.

58. Death Customs: An Antalytical Study Of Burial Rites. By Effie Bendam; Alfred A. Knopf, Inc., New York, N.Y.

59. It's Your Choice: The Practical Guide To Planning A Funeral. Thomas C. Nelson. American Association Of Retired Persons; Glenview, Illinois.

60. International Handbook Of Funeral Customs. By Kodo Matsunami; Greenwood Press, Westport Conn.

Periodicals And Pamphlets

1. Bereavement, A Magazine On Hope And Healing. By Companion Press, Fort Collins, Colorado

2. Journeys, A Newsletter To Help In Bereavement, By The Hospice Foundation Of America, Washington, D.C., 20009

3. National Funeral Directors Association, Milwaukee, Wisconsin. NFDA Learning Resources Center: Pamphlets Available On Funerals And Related Subjects.

Other Publications

By Companion Press

1. Healing Your Grieving Heart: 100 Practical Ideas. By Dr. Alan Wolfelt
2. Healing Your Traumatized Heart: 100 Practical Ideas Dr. Alan Wolfelt
3. Healing The Bereaved Child. Dr. Alan Wolfelt
4. Creating Meaningful Funeral Ceremonies: A Guide For Families. Dr. Alan Wolfelt
5. A Child's View Of Grief. By Dr. Alan Wolfelt

By The Funeral Service Education Foundation

6. Adult Children- How To Deal With The Grief Of A Surviving Parent (Booklet)
7. Caring And Coping When Your Loved One Dies
8. Going On: A Pathway Through Sorrow, Booklet For Men And Grief.
9. Holidays And Special Days, Coloring Book For Children About Grief Around The Holidays
10. It Means So Much To Know; Booklet For Families Whose Baby Has Died.
11. It's Not Your Fault: Coloring Book For Children On Their Feelings About Death.
12. Let The Choice Be Mine, Personal Guide To Planning Your Own Funeral (Workbook).
13. Should I Go To The Funeral. (Coloring Book), Explains What A Funeral Is To Children; The Importance Of Attending A Funeral.
14. What Is Cremation. (Coloring Book); Explains Cremation To Children

15. You Don't Have To Suffer. Inspirational And Practical Handbook that Points The Way Through Grief.

16. Will I Ever Stop Hurting. (Brochure).

17. Living When Your Spouse Has Died. (Brochure)

18. Suicide (Brochure).

19. Fire In My Heart, Ice In My Veins. A Journal For Teenagers Who've Experienced A Death, By Enid Samuel Traisman

20. Straight Talk About Death For Teenagers (How To Cope With Losing Someone You Love) By Earl Grollman

21. Holidays And Special Days, By Accord; (Coloring Book), Speaks To Children About Their Feelings About Death Around Holidays And Birthdays.

22. I Miss My Pet, By Accord; Coloring Book For Children Whose Pet Has Died.

23. Kolie And The Funeral, By Ralph Klicker; Coloring Book for Children Explaining the Death and Funeral of a Loved One.

24. Should I Go To The Funeral?, By Accord; Coloring Book Explaining What A Funeral Is And Its Importance To Children.

25. What Happens When Someone Dies, By Accord; Coloring Book Explaining Death To Children.

26. The Bereaved Parent, By Harriet Sarnoff-Schiff; Guide To Help After Loss Of A Child.

27. Dear Parents, By Centering Corporation; Thoughts And Advice For Bereaved Parents.

28. Empty Cradle, Broken Heart- Surviving The Death Of Your Baby, By Deborah Davis; A Guide For Parents Who've Lost An Infant Or Stillborn

29. For Bereaved Grandparents, By Margaret Gener; On How To Deal With The Death Of A Grandchild.

30. Adult Children...How To Deal With The Grief Of A Surviving Parent, By Grief Encounters.

31. Widow's Walk, By Jane Woods Shoemaker

32. Widowers...How They Grieve And What You Can Do To Help, By Grief Encounters.

33. After Suicide: A Unique Grief Process, By Eleanora Ross. For Surviving Family Of One Who Has Taken Their Own Life.

34. Suicide Of A Child, By Joy And Marvin Johnson And Adina Wrobleski; Booklet For Parents Of A Child Who Has Committed Suicide.

35. Being A Friend To Someone Who Is Grieving- What You Can Do And Say, By Grief Encounters; Booklet To Help You Help Others.

36. Death In The Workplace- Workers And Managers Dealing With Grief, By Grief Encounters; Booklet Gives Ideas For Dealing with The Loss Of A Co-Worker Or A Co-Worker's personal Loss.

37. Beyond Grief, By Carol Staudacher; A Complete Guide For Anyone Surviving The Death Of A Loved One.

38. Grieving The Death Of A Friend, By Harold Ivan Smith; Guide For Reader To Learn To Move Through The Grief Process.

39. Breaking The Silence: A Guide To Help Children With Complicated Grief- Suicide, AIDS, Violence And Abuse, By Linda Goldman

40. How Do We Tell The Children?, By Dan Schaefer And Christine Lyons; Step-By-Step Guide For Helping Children Ages Two To Teen Cope When Someone Dies.

41. After Suicide, By John H. Hewett, Westminster Press; Louisville, Kentucky

By The National Funeral Directors Association

42. Talking With Young Children About Death, By Fred Rogers, Illustrated Booklet.

Computer Websites

1. National Funeral Director Association: www.nfda.org

2. United States Federal Trade Commission: www.FTConsumer.gov

3. Directory Of Funeral Homes In the United States And Canada: www.funeralnet.com

4. Service Corporation International: www.sci-corp.com

5. United States Veterans Administration: www.va.gov

6. National Charities Information Bureau: www.give.org

7. United States Better Business Bureau (Business And Charity Reports): www.bbb.org

8. Non-Profit Organizations Database: www.guidestar.org

9. Cremation Information: www.cremation.com

10. Information About Cemetery Headstones: www.rootsweb.com/cemetery

11. Information About Protecting And Preserving Gravesites: www.savinggraves.com

12. Cemetery Records Information: www.internet.net

13. Resources Offered About Grief Support Products: www.griefresources.com

14. Database On Burial Information: www.FindA-Grave.com

15. Stewart Enterprises: www.stewartenterprises.com

16. Social Security Administration: www.ssa.gov

17. Alderwoods Group Funeral And Cemetery Company: www.alderwoods.com

18. American Cancer Society: www.cancer.org

19. Growth House (issues concerning hospice care, terminal illness, grief and bereavement): www.growthhouse.org

20. Death And Dying Grief Support: www.death-dying.com

21. GROWW.ORG (resource listings and secure chat rooms for the grieving): www.groww.org

22. Widow Net (Information and Support Resource For And By Widowers and Widows: www.fortnet.org/WidowNet/

23. The Compassionate Friends (Supports those who have experienced the death of a child): www.compassionate-friends.org

24. Center For Loss & Life Transition (Presents workshops and materials on the grieving process: www.centerforloss.com

25. Alive Alone (Helps Bereaved Parents Who Have Lost An Only Child or Their Children): www.alivealone.org

26. National SIDS (Sudden Infant Death Syndrome) And Infant Death Program Center: www.sids.org

27. SHARE Pregnancy & Infant Loss Support: www.nationalsharecoffee.com

28. Bereaved Parents USA (Nationwide Organization That Aids Parents And Their Families Who Are Grieving The Death Of A Child): www.bereavedparentsusa.org

29. Fernside Online (Online Resource For Grieving Children) www.fernside.org

30. Legacy.com (Website That Posts Obituary notices For Families That Chose This Service): www.Legacy.com

31. World Wide Flower Delivery (For Placing Flower Orders): www.flowersflowers.com

32. Monuments.com (Cemetery/memorial park/ memorializaion providers information): www.monuments.com

Videos

By The Funeral Service Education Foundation

1. How To Survive A Death In The Family

2. Ray Of Hope-Facing The Holidays (Shows How Bereaved Can Handle The Holidays And Other Days Of Remembrance)

3. Teen Grief- Climbing Back. Intimate Look At The Process Of Grieving As Experienced By Adolescents Ages 13-20.

4. Teen Grief-A Guide For Adults. Suggestions For Adults Supporting Teens In Grief.

5. Tenth Good Thing About Barney. For Children in First-Fifth Grade That Helps Them Understand Death.

7. The Tenth Good Thing About Barney (Aims MultiMedia); For Children Grades 1-5 Understand And Cope With The Death Of A Pet.

8. A Ray Of Hope: Facing The Holiday Following A Loss, By Film Ideas, Inc. J

9. The Courage To Grieve, The Courage To Grow, By Judy Tatelbaum

By The National Funeral Directors Association

10. Living Beyond The Shadow Of Death- A Therapeutic Video For Survivors Of Homicide.

11. Suddenly Someone You Love Is Gone

12. What About Me-Kids And Grief, By Film Ideas, Inc.

13. Finding Help When A Child Dies.

Assistance Groups/Organizations

1. The Living Bank
Organ And Tissue Donor Registry
Box 6725
Houston, Texas 77265
1-800-528-2971

2. Concerns Of Police Survivors
P.O. Box 3199
Camdenton, Mo. 65020
1-314-346-4911
To Help Family Members Of A Police Officer Killed In The Line Of Duty

3. Make-A-Wish Foundation
100 Charendon Avenue, Suite 2200
Phoenix, Arizona, 85013
602-279-9474
Works To Make The Wishes Of Children With Life Threatening Illnesses possible.

4. AIDS Project
3670 Wilshire Blvd., Suite 300
Los Angeles, CA. 90010
For those with a loved one who's died or dying from AIDS

5. National Organization For Victim Assistance
717 D. Street N.W.
Washington, D.C. 20004
Assist Those Who Have Been Crime Victims

6. National Victim's Resource Center
P.O. Box 6000
Rockville, MD. 20850
Crime victims Assistance

7. Medic Alert Foundation
P.O. Box 1009
Turlock, Ca. 95381
Information About Anatomical Gifts

8. United Network Of Organ Sharing
1100 Boulders Parkway, Suite 500
Richmond, Va. 23225
Information About Anatomical Gifts

9. DNA Connections
1-866-362-3623
www.dnaconnections.com
Offers Packages To Families For DNA Retrieval And Storage

10. Center of Loss and Life Transition
3735 Broken Bow Road
Fort Collins, Co. 80526
Prints information and education on dealing with and recovering from loss.

Consumer Information Contacts

1. American Cemetery Association
1895 Preston White Drive, Suite 220
Reston, Virginia 20191
800-645-7700
Largest Group In The U.S. Representing The Interests of Cemeteries And Memorial Parks

2. American Monument Association
30 Eden Alley, Suite 301
Columbus, Ohio 43215
614-461-5852
Represents The Interests Of Monument Sellers And Providers

3. Cemetery Consumer Service Council
P.O. Box 2028, Reston, VA 20195
703-391-8407
Helps resolve complaints between consumers and cemeteries

4. National Funeral Directors Association
11121 West Oklahoma Avenue
Milwaukee, Wisconsin 53227
414-541-2500
Largest Group Representing Funeral Directors In The U.S.

5. Continental Association of Funeral and Memorial Societies
20001 South Street NW, Suite 630
Washington, D.C. 20009
202-462-8888
Provides Consumer Information About Funerals

6. American Association Of Retired Persons
601 East Street
Washington, D.C. 20009

202-434-2260
Organization That Represents The Interests Of Older Americans

7. Association For Death Education And Counseling
342 North Main Street
West Hartford, Conn. 06117
860-586-7503
Consumer Information Related To Death

8. ThanaCap
1135 West Wells Street, Suite 600
Milwaukee, Wisconsin 53203
Consumer Information About Death And Dying

9. Pre-Arrangement Interment Association Of America
1133 15th Street N.W.
Washington, D.C. 20005
Help Provide Information About Pre-Arranged Burial

10. Cremation Association Of North America
111 East Wacker Drive
Chicago, Illinois 60601
Provide Information About Cremation

11. U.S. Federal Trade Commission
6th And Pennsylvania N.W.
Washington, D.C. 20580
1-877-FTC-HELP
Agency That Oversees The Funeral Industry For The National Government.

12. Funeral Consumers Alliance
1-802-482-3437/www.funerals.org
Can Help Locate A Funeral Or Memorial Society Near You.

Phone Numbers

1. Funeral Service Consumer Assistance Program

1-800-662-7666. Provides information and Acts As An Arbitrator In Problems Involving Funeral Homes and consumers.

2. Funeral Ethics Association

217-525-1520. Receives questions and concerns From Consumers About Services Rendered By A Funeral Home For Purposes Of Helping The Consumer Receive Satisfactory Solutions To Any Problems.

3. Concern For Dying

212-246-6962. Provides Information Related To Health Care And Dying.

4. National AIDS Hotline

1-800-877-3355. Non-Profit Organization To Help Those Who are or know someone dying from AIDS

5. Widowed Persons Service

202-872-4700. Offers Programs To The Newly Widowed.

6. Parents Without Partners

301-588-9354. National Organization Devoted To The Welfare Of Single Parents And Their Children.

7. Compassionate Friends

708-990-0010 Group Devoted To Helping Parents Whose Child Has Died.

8. Resolve Through Sharing

608-791-4747. International Program For Parents Who Have Lost A Baby During Or Shortly After Childbirth.

9. Social Security Administration

1-800-772-1213. Agency Of The United States Federal Government That Provides Any Survivor/Retirement Benefits For Those Eligible.

10. Department Of Veterans Affairs

1-800-827-1000/1-800-697-6947. Agency Of The United States Government That Handles Issues And Benefits For Honorably Discharged Veterans.

Additional Help

1. Funeral Service Education Foundation. Non Profit Organization dedicated to Advancing Public Knowledge and Understanding Through Education and Research. 13625 Bishop's Drive, Brookfield, Wisconsin 53005 (877-402-5900).
2. How To Recover From Grief, Provides Tools For Understanding Grief (Funeral Service Education Foundation).
3. Love Anew-Primer On Recovering From Spousal Grief (Funeral Service Education Foundation).
4. My Son...My Son, By Iris Bolton (Funeral Service Education Foundation). Based On Author's Own Experience. Helps Parents Cope With Suicide Of An Offspring.
5. For The Bereaved: The Road To Recovery (Funeral Service Education Foundation). Collection Of Thoughts On What To Expect And Do Following A Loss.
6. Loss During Pregnancy Or In The Newborn Period. (Funeral Service Education Foundation).
7. Recovering From The Loss Of A Loved One To AIDS, (Funeral Service Education Foundation).
8. Grief In The Workplace: 40 Hours Plus Overtime. By Johnette Hartnett (National Funeral Directors Association).
9. What Helped Me When My Loved One Died, By Earl Grollman (National Funeral Directors Association). A Collec-

tion of Feelings Expressed By People Who Have Lost a Loved One.

10. Beyond Sympathy, By Janice Harris Lord (National Funeral Directors Association). Offers Practical Suggestions And Examples On How To Help Others Who Are Hurting.

11. When Parents Die: A Guide For Adults, By Edward Myers (National Funeral Directors Association).

12. How I Feel, A Coloring Book For Grieving Children. Dr. Alan Wolfelt

13. A Scrapbook Of Memories. A Workbook For Grieving Children. Dr. Alan Wolfelt

14. Caring For Your Own Dead, By Lisa Carlson. (Upper Access Publishers, Hinesburg, VT.).

15. On Children And Death, By Elizabeth Kubler-Ross (Macmillan Publishing Company, New York, N.Y.).

16. Memorial Programs Service, National Cemetery Administration U.S. DEPARTMENT Of Veterans Affairs. 810 Vermont Avenue, N.W., Washington, D.C. 20420

Memorial Donations List

1. American Diabetes Association
P.O. Box 2680
North Canton, Ohio 44720
1-800-342-2383

2. American Cancer Society
P.O. Box 102454
Atlanta, Ga. 30368
1-800-ACS-2345

3. American Heart Association
7320 Greenville Avenue
Dallas, Texas 75231
1-800-527-6941

4. American Lung Association
P.O. Box 26460
Austin, Texas 78755
1-800-586-4872

5. Alzheimers Association
7610 North Stemmons Frwy, Suite 600
Dallas, Texas 75247
1-800-515-8201

6. Heart Disease Research Foundation
50 Court Street- 306A
Brooklyn, N.Y. 11201

7. Susan B. Komen Breast Cancer Foundation
National Headquarters
5005 LBJ Freeway, Suite 370
Dallas, Texas 75244
1-800-462-9273

8. American Sudden Infant Death Syndrome Institute
6065 Roswell Road, Suite 876
Atlanta, Ga. 30328
1-800-847-SIDS

9. American Kidney Fund
6110 Executive Blvd. Suite 1010
Rockville, Md. 20852

10. American Liver Foundation
2425 West Loop South, Suite 600
Houston, Texas 77027

11. Hospice Foundation Of America
777 17th Street Suite 401, Dept. S
Miami Beach, Florida 33139

12. American Foundation For AIDS Research
733 3rd Avenue, 12th Floor
New York, N.Y. 10017
212-682-7440

13. Leukemia Society Of America
2900 Eisenhower Ave., Suite 419
Alexandria, Va. 22314
703-960-1100.

14. Cystic Fibrosis Foundation
6931 Arlington Road, Bethesda, Maryland 20014
1-800-344-4823

15. March Of Dimes Birth Defects Association
1275 Mamaroneck Avenue
White Plains, N.Y. 10605
300-453-3816

Federal Trade Commission Funeral Trade Rule

Born Out Of the consumer rights movement of the 1970s, the Federal Trade Commission which functions as the United States Government's agency to maintain free and fair trade within the economy and protect consumers from unfair and deceptive practices, published the Funeral Rule originally in 1984 to require funeral homes to present accurate, timely information about prices, goods and services and communicate true and correct statements about what is or is not required by law concerning products and services offered for sale to the public.

The following is a reprint of complying with the Funeral Rule as presented for consumer use.

Part 453-Funeral Industry Practices Revised Rule

Section:
453.1 Definitions.
453.2 Price disclosures.
453.3 Misrepresentations.
453.4 Required purchase of funeral goods or funeral services.
453.5 Services provided without prior approval.
453.6 Retention of documents.
453.7 Comprehension of disclosures.
453.8 Declaration of intent.
453.9 State exemptions.

Authority: 15 U.S.C. 57a(a); 15 U.S.C. 46(9); 5 U.S.C. 552.

§ 453.1 Definitions

(a) Alternative container An "alternative container" is an unfinished wood box or other non-metal receptacle or enclosure, without ornamentation or a fixed interior lining, which is designed for the encasement of human remains and which is made of fiberboard, pressed-wood, composition materials (with or without an outside covering) or like materials.

(b) Cash advance item A "cash advance item" is any item of service or merchandise described to a purchaser as a "cash advance," "accommodation," "cash disbursement," or similar term. A cash advance item is also any item obtained from a third party and paid for by the funeral provider on the purchaser's behalf. Cash advance items may include, but are not limited to: cemetery or crematory services; pallbearers; public transportation; clergy honoraria; flowers; musicians or singers; nurses; obituary notices; gratuities and death certificates.

(c) Casket A "casket" is a rigid container which is designed for the encasement of human remains and which is usually constructed of wood, metal, fiberglass, plastic, or like material, and ornamented and lined with fabric.

(d) Commission "Commission" refers to the Federal Trade Commission.

(e) Cremation "Cremation" is a heating process which incinerates human remains.

(f) Crematory A "crematory" is any person, partnership or corporation that performs cremation and sells funeral goods.

(g) Direct cremation A "direct cremation" is a disposition of human remains by cremation, without formal viewing, visitation, or ceremony with the body present.

(h) Funeral goods "Funeral goods" are the goods which are sold or offered for sale directly to the public for use in connection with funeral services.

(i) Funeral provider A "funeral provider" is any person, partnership or corporation that sells or offers to sell funeral goods and funeral services to the public.

(j) Funeral services "Funeral services" are any services which may be used to: (1) care for and prepare deceased human bodies for burial, cremation or other final disposition; and (2) arrange, supervise or conduct the funeral ceremony or the final disposition of deceased human bodies.

(k) Immediate burial An "immediate burial" is a disposition of human remains by burial, without formal viewing, visitation, or ceremony with the body present, except for a graveside service.

(I) Memorial service A "memorial service" is a ceremony commemorating the deceased without the body present.

(m) Funeral ceremony A "funeral ceremony" is a service commemorating the deceased with the body present.

(n) Outer burial container An "outer burial container" is any container which is designed for placement in the grave around the casket including, but not limited to, containers commonly known as burial vaults, grave boxes, and grave liners.

(o) Person A "person" is any individual, partnership, corporation, association, government or governmental subdivision or agency, or other entity.

(p) Services of funeral director and staff The "services of funeral director and staff" are the basic services, not to be included in prices of other categories in § 453.2(b)(4), that are furnished by a funeral provider in arranging any funeral, such as conducting the arrangements conference, planning the funeral, obtaining necessary permits, and placing obituary notices.

§ 453.2 Price Disclosures

(a) Unfair or Deceptive Acts or Practices

In selling or offering to sell funeral goods or funeral services to the public, it is an unfair or deceptive act or practice for a funeral provider to fail to furnish accurate price information disclosing the cost to the purchaser for each of the specific funeral goods and funeral services used in connection with the disposition of deceased human bodies, including at least the price of embalming, transportation of remains, use of facilities, caskets, outer burial containers, immediate burials, or direct cremations, to persons inquiring about the purchase of funerals. Any funeral provider who complies with the preventive requirements in paragraph (b) of this section is not engaged in the unfair or deceptive acts or practices defined here.

(b) Preventive Requirements

To prevent these unfair or deceptive acts or practices, as well as the unfair or deceptive acts or practices defined in § 453.4(b)(1), funeral providers must:

(1) Telephone Price Disclosure

Tell persons who ask by telephone about the funeral provider's offerings or prices any accurate information from the price lists described in paragraphs (b)(2) through (4) of this section and any other readily available information that reasonably answers the question.

(2) Casket Price List

(i) Give a printed or typewritten price list to people who inquire in person about the offerings or prices of caskets or alternative containers. The funeral provider must offer the list upon beginning discussion of, but in any event before showing caskets. The list must contain at least the retail prices of all caskets and alternative containers offered which do not require special ordering, enough information to identify each, and the effective date for the price list. In lieu of a written list, other formats, such as notebooks, brochures, or charts may be used if they contain the same information as would the printed or typewritten list, and display it in a clear and conspicuous manner. Provided, however, that funeral providers do not have to make a casket price list available if the funeral providers place on the general price list, specified in paragraph (b)(4) of this section, the information required by this paragraph.

(ii) Place on the list, however produced, the name of the funeral provider's place of business and a caption describing the list as a "casket price list."

(3) Outer Burial Container Price List

(i) Give a printed or typewritten price list to persons who inquire in person about outer burial container offerings or prices. The funeral provider must offer the list upon beginning discussion of, but in any event before showing the containers. The list must contain at least the retail prices of all outer burial containers offered which do not require special ordering, enough information to identify each container, and the effective date for the prices listed. In lieu of a written list, the funeral provider may use other formats, such as notebooks, brochures, or charts, if they contain the same information as the printed or typewritten list, and display it in a clear and conspicuous manner. Provided, however, that funeral providers do not have to make an outer burial container price list available if the funeral providers place on the general price list, specified in paragraph (b)(4) of this section, the information required by this paragraph.

(ii) Place on the list, however produced, the name of the funeral provider's place of

business and a caption describing the list as an "outer burial container price list."

(4) General Price List

(i)

A. Give a printed or typewritten price list for retention to persons who inquire in person about the funeral goods, funeral services or prices of funeral goods or services offered by the funeral provider. The funeral provider must give the list upon beginning discussion of any of the following:

(1) the prices of funeral goods or funeral services;

(2) the overall type of funeral service or disposition; or

(3) specific funeral goods or funeral services offered by the funeral provider.

B. The requirement in paragraph (b)(4)(i)(A) of this section applies whether the discussion takes place in the funeral home or elsewhere. Provided, however, that when the deceased is removed for transportation to the funeral home, an in-person request at that time for authorization to embalm, required by § 453.5(a)(2), does not, by itself, trigger the requirement to offer the general price list if the provider in seeking prior embalming approval discloses that embalming is not required by law except in certain special cases, if any. Any other discussion during that time about prices or the selection of funeral goods or services triggers the requirement under paragraph (b)(4)(i)(A) of this section to give consumers a general price list.

C. The list required by paragraph (b)(4)(i)(A) of this section must contain at least the following information:

(1) The name, address, and telephone number of the funeral provider's place of business;

(2) A caption describing the list as a "general price list"; and

(3) The effective date for the price list;

(ii) Include on the price list, in any order, the retail prices (expressed either as the flat fee, or as the price per hour, mile or other unit of computation) and the other information specified below for at least each of the following items, if offered for sale:

A. Forwarding of remains to another funeral home, together with a list of the services provided for any quoted price;

B. Receiving remains from another funeral home, together with a list of the services provided for any quoted price;

C. The price range for the direct cremations offered by the funeral provider, together with:

(1) a separate price for a direct cremation where the purchaser provides the container;

(2) separate prices for each direct cremation offered including an alternative container; and

(3) a description of the services and container (where applicable), included in each price;

D. The price range for the immediate burials offered by the funeral provider, together with:

(1) a separate price for an immediate burial where the purchaser provides the casket;

(2) separate prices for each immediate burial offered including a casket or alternative container; and

(3) a description of the services and container (where applicable) included in that price;

E. Transfer of remains to funeral home;

F. Embalming;

G. Other preparation of the body;

H. Use of facilities and staff for viewing;

I. Use of facilities and staff for funeral ceremony;

J. Use of facilities and staff for memorial service;

K. Use of equipment and staff for graveside service;

L. Hearse; and

M. Limousine.

(iii) Include on the price list, in any order, the following information:

A. Either of the following:

(1) The price range for the caskets offered by the funeral provider, together with the statement: "A complete price list will be provided at the funeral home."; or

(2) The prices of individual caskets, disclosed in the manner specified by paragraph (b)(2)(i) of this section; and

B. Either of the following:

(1) The price range for the outer burial containers offered by the funeral provider, together with the statement: "A complete price list will be provided at the funeral home."; or

(2) The prices of individual outer burial containers, disclosed in the manner specified by paragraph (b)(3)(i) of this section; and

C. Either of the following:

(1) The price for the basic services of funeral director and staff, together with a list of the principal basic services provided for any quoted price and, if the charge cannot be declined by the purchaser, the statement:

"This fee for our basic services will be added to the total cost of the funeral arrangements you select. (This fee is already included in our charges for direct cremations, immediate burials, and forwarding or receiving remains.)" If the charge cannot be declined by the purchaser, the quoted price shall include all charges for the recovery of unallocated funeral provider overhead, and funeral providers may include in the required disclosure the phrase "and overhead" after the word "services";

or

(2) The following statement: "Please note that a fee of (specify dollar amount) for the use of our basic services is included in the price of our caskets. This same fee shall be added to the total cost of your funeral arrangements if you provide the casket. Our services include (specify)." The fee shall include all charges for the recovery of unallocated funeral provider overhead, and funeral providers may include in the required disclosure the phrase "and overhead" after the word "services." The statement must be placed on the general price list together with the casket price range, required by paragraph (b)(4)(iii)(A)(1) of this section, or together with the prices of individual caskets, required by (b)(4)(iii)(A)(2) of this section.

(iv) The services fee permitted by § 453.2(b)(4)(iii)(C)(1) or (C)(2) is the only funeral provider fee for services, facilities or unallocated overhead permitted by this part to be non-declinable, unless otherwise required by law.

(5) Statement of Funeral Goods and Services Selected

(i) Give an itemized written statement for retention to each person who arranges a funeral or other disposition of human remains, at the conclusion of the discussion of arrangements. The statement must list at least the following information:

A. The funeral goods and funeral services selected by that person and the prices to be paid for each of them;

B. Specifically itemized cash advance items. (These prices must be given to the extent then known or reasonably ascertainable. If the prices are not known or reasonably ascertainable, a good faith estimate shall be given and a written statement of the actual charges shall be provided before the final bill is paid.); and

C. The total cost of the goods and services selected.

(ii) The information required by this paragraph (b)(5) may be included on any contract, statement, or other document which the funeral provider would otherwise provide at the conclusion of discussion of arrangements.

(6) Other Pricing Methods

Funeral providers may give persons any other price information, in any other format, in addition to I that required by § 453.2(b)(2), (3), and (4) so long as the statement required by § 453.2(b)(5) is given when required by the rule.

§ 453.:1 Misrepresentations

(a) Embalming Provisions

(1) Deceptive Acts or Practices

In selling or offering to sell funeral goods or funeral services to the public, it is a deceptive act or practice for a funeral provider to:

(i) Represent that state or local law requires that a deceased person be embalmed when such is not the case;

(ii) Fail to disclose that embalming is not required by law except in certain special cases, if any.

(2) Preventive requirements

To prevent these deceptive acts or practices, as well as the unfair or deceptive acts or practices defined in §§ 453.4(b)(1) and 453.5(2), funeral providers must:

(i) Not represent that a deceased person is required to be embalmed for:

A. direct cremation;

B. immediate burial; or

C. a closed casket funeral without viewing or visitation when refrigeration is available and when state or local law does not require embalming; and

(ii) Place the following disclosure on the general price list, required by § 453.2(b)(4), in immediate conjunction with the price shown for embalming: "Except in certain special," cases, embalming is not required by law. Embalming may be necessary, however, if you select certain funeral arrangements, such as a funeral with viewing. If you do not want embalming, you usually have the right to choose an arrangement that does not require you to pay for it, such as direct cremation or immediate burial." The phrase "except in certain special cases" need not be included in this disclosure if state or local law in the area(s) where the provider does business does not require embalming under any circumstances.

(b) Casket for Cremation Provisions

(1) Deceptive Acts or Practices

In selling or offering to sell funeral goods or funeral services to the public, it is a deceptive act or practice for a funeral provider to:

(i) Represent that state or local law requires a casket for

direct cremations;

(ii) Represent that a casket is required for direct cremations.

(2) Preventive Requirements

To prevent these deceptive acts or practices, as well as the unfair or deceptive acts or practices defined in § 453.4(a)(1), funeral providers must place the following disclosure in immediate conjunction with the price range shown for direct cremations: "If you want to arrange a direct cremation, you can use an alternative container. Alternative containers encase the body and can be made of materials like fiberboard or composition materials (with or without an outside covering). The containers we provide are (specify containers)." This disclosure only has to be placed on the general price list if the funeral provider arranges direct cremations.

(c) Outer Burial Container Provisions

(1) Deceptive Acts or Practices

In selling or offering to sell funeral goods and funeral services to the public, it is a deceptive act or practice for a funeral provider to:

(i) Represent that state or local laws or regulations, or particular cemeteries, require outer burial containers when such is not the case;

(ii) Fail to disclose to persons arranging funerals that state law does not require the purchase of an outer burial container.

(2) Preventive Requirement

To prevent these deceptive acts or practices, funeral providers must place the following disclosure on the outer burial container price list, required by § 453.2(b)(3)(i), or, if the prices of outer burial containers are listed on the general price list, required by § 453.2(b)(4), in immediate conjunction with those prices: "In most areas of the country, state or local law does not require that you buy a container to surround the casket in the grave. However, many cemeteries require that you have such a container so that the grave will not sink in. Either a grave liner or a burial vault will satisfy these requirements."

The phrase "in most areas of the country" need not be included in this disclosure if state or local law in the area(s) where the provider does business does not require a container to surround the casket in the grave.

(d) General Provisions on Legal and Cemetery Requirements

(1) Deceptive Acts or Practices

In selling or offering to sell funeral goods or funeral services to the public, it is a deceptive act or practice for funeral providers to represent that federal, state, or local laws, or particular cemeteries or crematories, require the purchase of any funeral goods or funeral services when such is not the case.

(2) Preventive Requirements

To prevent these deceptive acts or practices, as well as the deceptive acts or practices identified in §§ 453.3(a)(1), 453.3(b)(1), and 453.3(c)(1), funeral providers must identify and briefly describe in writing on the statement of funeral goods and services selected (required by § 453.2(b)(5)) any legal, cemetery, or crematory requirement which the funeral provider represents to persons as compelling the purchase of funeral goods or funeral services for the funeral which that person is arranging.

(e) Provisions on Preservative and Protective Value Claims

In selling or offering to sell funeral goods or funeral services to the public, it is a deceptive act or practice for a funeral provider to:

(1) Represent that funeral goods or funeral services will delay the natural decomposition of human remains for a long-term or indefinite time;

(2) Represent that funeral goods have protective features

or will protect the body from gravesite substances, when such is not the case.

(f) Cash Advance Provisions

(1) Deceptive Acts or Practices

In selling or offering to sell funeral goods or funeral services to the public, it is a deceptive act or practice for a funeral provider to:

(i) Represent that the price charged for a cash advance item is the same as the cost to the funeral provider for the item when such is not the case;

(ii) Fail to disclose to persons arranging funerals that the price being charged for a cash advance item is not the same as the cost to the funeral provider for the item when such is the case.

(2) Preventive Requirements

To prevent these deceptive acts or practices, funeral providers must place the following sentence in the itemized statement of funeral goods and services selected, in immediate conjunction with the list of itemized cash advance items required by § 453.2(b)(5)(i)(B): "We charge you for our services in obtaining: (specify cash advance items)," if the funeral provider makes a charge upon, or receives and retains a rebate, commission or trade or volume discount upon a cash advance item.

§ 453.4 Required Purchase of Funeral Goods or Funeral Services.

(a) Casket for Cremation Provisions

(1) Unfair or Deceptive Acts or Practices

In selling or offering to sell funeral goods or funeral services to the public, it is an unfair or deceptive act or practice for a funeral provider, or a crematory, to require that a casket be purchased for direct cremation.

(2) Preventive Requirement

To prevent this unfair or deceptive act or practice, funeral providers must make an alternative container available for direct cremations, if they arrange direct cremations.

(b) <u>Other Required Purchases of Funeral Goods or Funeral Services</u>

(1) Unfair or Deceptive Acts or Practices

In selling or offering to sell funeral goods or funeral services, it is an unfair or deceptive act or practice for a funeral provider to:

(i) Condition the furnishing of any funeral good or funeral service to a person arranging a funeral upon the purchase of any other funeral good or funeral service, except as required by law or as otherwise permitted by this part;

(ii) Charge any fee as a condition to furnishing any funeral goods or funeral services to a person arranging a funeral, other than the fees for: (1) services of funeral director and staff, permitted by § 453.2(b)(4)(iii)(C); (2) other funeral services and funeral goods selected by the purchaser; and (3) other funeral goods or services required to be purchased, as explained on the itemized statement in accordance with § 453.3(d)(2).

(2) Preventive Requirements

(i) To prevent these unfair or deceptive acts or practices, funeral providers must:

A. Place the following disclosure in the general price list, immediately above the prices required by § 453.2(b)(4)(ii) and (iii): "The goods and services shown below are those we can provide to our customers. You may choose only the items you desire. If legal or other requirements mean you must buy any items you did not specifically ask for, we will explain the reason in writing on the statement we provide describing the funeral goods and services you selected." Provided, however, that if the charge for "services of funeral director and staff" cannot be declined by the purchaser, the statement shall include the sentence: "However, any funeral arrangements you select will include a charge for our basic services" between the second and third sentences of the statement specified above herein. The statement may include the phrase "and overhead" after the word "services" if the fee includes a charge for the recovery of unallocated funeral provider overhead;

B. Place the following disclosure in the statement of funeral goods and services selected, required by § 453.2(b)(5)(i): "Charges are only for those items that you selected or that are required. If we are required by law or by a cemetery or crematory to use any items, we will explain the reasons in writing below."

(ii) A funeral provider shall not violate this section by failing to comply with a request for a combination of goods or services which would be impossible, impractical, or excessively burdensome to provide.

§ 453.5 Services Provided Without Prior Approval

(a) Unfair or Deceptive Acts or Practices

In selling or offering to sell funeral goods or funeral services to the public, it is an unfair or deceptive act or practice for any provider to embalm a deceased human body for a fee unless:

(1) State or local law or regulation requires embalming in the particular circumstances regardless of any funeral choice which the family might make; or

(2) Prior approval for embalming (expressly so described) has been obtained from a family member or other authorized person; or

(3) The funeral provider is unable to contact a family member or other authorized person after exercising due diligence, has no reason to believe the family does not want embalming performed, and obtains subsequent approval for embalming already performed (expressly so described). In seeking approval, the funeral provider must disclose that a fee will be charged if

the family selects a funeral which requires embalming, such as a funeral with viewing, and that no fee will be charged if the family selects a service which does not require embalming, such as direct cremation or immediate burial.

(b) Preventive Requirement

To prevent these unfair or deceptive acts or practices, funeral providers must include on the itemized statement of funeral goods and services selected, required by § 453.2(b)(5), the statement: "If you selected a funeral that may require embalming, such as a funeral with viewing, you may have to pay for embalming. You do not have to pay for embalming you did not approve if you selected arrangements such as a direct cremation or immediate burial. If we charged for embalming, we will explain why below."

§ 453.6 Retention of Documents

To prevent the unfair or deceptive acts or practices specified in § 453.2 and § 453.3 of this rule, funeral providers must retain and make available for inspection by Commission officials true and accurate copies of the price lists specified in §§ 453.2(b)(2) through (4), as applicable, for at least one year after the date of their last distribution to customers, and a copy of each statement of funeral goods and services selected, as required by § 453.2(b)(5), for at least one year from the date of the arrangements conference.

§ 453.7 Comprehension of Disclosures

To prevent the unfair or deceptive acts or practices specified in § 453.2 through § 453.5, funeral providers must make all disclosures required by those sections in a clear and conspicuous manner. Providers shall not include in the casket, outer burial container, and general price lists, required by §§ 453.2(b)(2)-(4), any statement or information that alters or contradicts the information required by this Part to be included in those lists.

§ 453.8 Declaration of Intent

(a) Except as otherwise provided in § 453.2(a), it is a violation of this rule to engage in any unfair or deceptive acts or practices specified in this rule, or to fail to comply with any of the preventive requirements specified in this rule;

(b) The provisions of this rule are separate and severable from one another. If any provision is determined to be invalid, it is the Commission's intention that the remaining provisions shall continue in effect.

(c) This rule shall not apply to the business of insurance or to acts in the conduct thereof.

§ 453.9 State Exemptions

If, upon application to the Commission by an appropriate state agency, the Commission determines that:

(a) There is a state requirement in effect which applies to any transaction to which this rule applies; and

(b) That state requirement affords an overall level of protection to consumers which is as great as, or greater than, the protection afforded by this rule; then the Commission's rule will not be in effect in that state to the extent specified by the Commission in its determination, for as long as the State administers and enforces effectively the state requirement.

By direction of the Commission.

FUNERAL REGULATING BOARDS BY STATE

1. Alabama: Alabama Board Of Funeral Service
11 South Union Street, Suite 219
Montgomery, AI. 36104
334-242-4049
2. Alaska: Alaska Dept. Of Commerce,
Division Of Funeral Licensing,
P.O. Box 110806
Juneau, Alaska, 99811
907-465-2695
3. Arkansas: Arkansas Board of Embalmers/Funeral Directors
101 East Capitol Avenue 113
Little Rock, Arkansas, 72201
501-682-0574
4. Arizona: Arizona State Board Of Funeral Directors
1400 West Washington, Suite 230
Phoenix, Az. 85007
602-542-3095
5. California: Department Of Consumer Affairs
Cemetery And Funeral Bureau
400 R Street, Suite 340
Sacramento, Ca. 95814
916-332-7737
6. Colorado: Colorado State Funeral Service Board
7853 East Arapahoe Court, Suite 2100
Englewood, Co. 80112
303-694-4728
7. Connecticut: State Board Of Funeral Service Examiners
410 Capitol Avenue, MS #12
Hartford, Conn. 06134
860-509-7579
8. Delaware: State Board Of Funeral Service
861 Silver Lake Blvd. Suite 203
Dover, Delaware 19904 / 302-739-4522

9. Dist. Col.: D.C. Board Of Funeral Directors & Embalmers
941 North Capitol Street N.W., Suite 7200
Washington, D.C. 20002
202-442-4461

10. Florida: State Board of Funeral Directors & Embalmers
1940 N. Monroe Street, Suite 426
Tallahassee, Florida 32399
850-487-1395

11. Georgia: State Board Of Morticians
237 Coliseum Drive
Macon, Ga., 31217
478-207-1460

12. Hawaii: State Department Of Health Sanitation Branch
591 Ala Moana Blvd.
Honolulu, Hawaii 96813
808-586-8000

13. Idaho: Idaho Board Of Morticians
Bureau Of Occupational Licenses
1109 Main street, # 220
Boise, Idaho 83702
208-334-3945

14. Illinois: Department Of Professional Regulation
320 West Washington, 3rd Floor
Springfield, Ill 62786
217-782-8556

15. Indiana: Indiana Professional Licensing Agency
302 West Washington Street, Room E034
Indianapolis, Indiana 46204
317-232-7215

16. Iowa: Iowa Board Of Mortuary Science
321 East 12th Street
Des Moines, Iowa 50319
515-242-6385

17. Kansas: Kansas Board Of Mortuary Arts
700 S.W. Jackson, # 904

	Topeka, Kansas 66603
	785-296-3980
18. Kentucky:	Kent. Board of Embalmers & Funeral Directors
	7025 West Highway 22, # 7
	Crestwood, Ky 40014
	502-241-3918
19. Louisiana:	Board Of Funeral Directors And Embalmers
	3500 N. Causeway Blvd.
	Metarie, La. 70011
	504-838-5109
20. Maine:	Maine State Board Of Funeral Service
	State House Station 35
	Augusta, ME 04333
	207-624-8420
21. Maryland:	Maryland State Board Of Morticians
	4201 Patterson Ave. Room 315
	Baltimore, MD 21215
	410-764-4792
22. Mass.:	Mass. Board of Funeral Service Registration
	100 Cambridge Street
	Saltonstall Building Room 1406
	Boston, Ma. 02202
	617-727-4095
23. Michigan:	Michigan Board of Administrators in Mortuary Science; Funeral Licensing Division
	P.O.Box 30018
	Lansing, Mich. 48909
	517-241-9246
24. Minnesota:	State Board: Mortuary Science Unit
	121 E. Seventh Place
	St. Paul, MN 55164
	651-282-3829
25. Mississippi:	Mississippi Board Of Funeral Service
	7 Riverbend Place, Suite B
	Flowood, Miss. 39202 / 601-932-1973

26. Missouri: State Board Of Funeral Service
P.O. Box 423
Jefferson City, Mo. 65102
573-751-0813

27. Montana: Funeral Service Administration Office
P.O. Box 200513
Helena, Mt. 59620
406-444-5433

28. Nebraska: Board of Examiners In Funeral Directing And Embalming; Dept. of Healthand Human Services
P.O.Box 94986
Lincoln, Ne. 68509
402-471-2117

29. Nevada: State Board of Funeral Directors & Embalmers
4894 Lone Mountain Road
Las Vegas, NV, 89130
702-646-6860

30. N. Hamp.: Board of Registration of Funeral Directors & Embalmers
6 Hazen Drive
Concord, New Hampshire 03301
603-271-4648

31. New Jersey: Board Of Mortuary Science
P.O. Box 45009
Newark, N.J. 07101
973-504-6439

32. New Mex.: New Mexico State Board of Thanopractice
2055 South Pacheco Street Suite 400
Santa Fe, New Mexico 87504
305-476-7090

33. New York: State Department Of Health
Bureau Of Funeral Directing
Corning Tower, Empire State Plaza
Albany, N.Y. 12237

34. N. Car.: North Carolina Board Of Mortuary Science
P.O. Box 27368,
Raleigh, North Carolina 27611
919-733-9380

35. N. Dakota: Funeral Service Board
P.O. Box 633
Devil's Lake, N.D. 58301
701-662-2501

36. Ohio: Board Of Funeral Directors And Embalmers
77 South High Street
Columbus, Ohio 43266
614-466-4252

37. Oklahoma: Oklahoma Board Of Funeral Homes
4545 North Lincoln Blvd.
Oklahoma City, OK 73105
405-525-0158

38. Oregon: Oregon Funeral Service Board
800 N.E. Oregon Street, # 19
Portland, OR 97232
503-731-4040

39. Penn.: Board Of Funeral Directors And Embalmers
P.O. Box 2649
Harrisburg, Pa. 17105
717-783-3397

40. R. Island: Board Of Examiners In Funeral Directing
3 Capitol Hill Room 104
Providence, R.I. 02908
401-222-2827

41. S. Carolina: South Carolina State Board of Funeral Service
110 Crestview Drive
Columbia, S.C. 29211
803-896-4497

42. S. Dakota: State Board Of Funeral Service
135 East Illinois, Suite 214
Spearfish, S.D. 57783 / 605-642-1600

43. Tennessee: Board Of Funeral Embalmers & Directors
500 James Robertson Pkwy
Nashville, Tenn. 37243
615-741-2474

44. Texas: Texas Funeral Service Commission
510 South Congress, Suite 206
Austin, Texas 78704
512-936-2474

45. Utah: Department Of Commerce, Division of Occupational & Professional Licensing
P.O. Box 146741
Salt Lake City, Utah 84114
801-530-6396

46. Vermont: Office Of Professional Licensing
Board Of Funeral Service
109 State Street
Montpelier, VT. 05609
802-828-3228

47. Virginia: Board of Funeral Directors & Embalmers
6606 West Broad Street, 4th Floor
Richmond, Va. 23230
804-662-9907

48. Wash.: Washington Funeral & Cemetery Board
P.O. Box 9012
Olympia, Wa. 98507
360-586-3228

49. W. Virginia: Board Of Embalmers & Funeral Directors
179 Summers Street, Suite 305
Charleston, W.V. 25301
304-558-0302

50. Wisconsin: Funeral Directors Examining Board
Department of Regulation And Licensing
P.O. Box 8935
Madison, Wis. 53708
608-266-5439

51. Wyoming: Wyoming State Board Of Embalming
2020 Carey Ave. # 201
Cheyenne, W.Y. 82002
307-777-7788

52. Canada: Ontario Board Of Funeral Services
2810-777 Bay Street
Toronto Ontario, Canada M5G208

Cemetery Laws By State

The following grid chart shows the cemetery laws and regulations by state.

Although this is not comprehensive in relation to all laws and regulations, this chart gives the reader a general idea of what a particular state does in its regulatory power concerning cemetery law.

Since laws change frequently and since there has been no objective third party verification of the chart data, action should not be taken without researching current statutes as well as consulting with a attorney and/or cemetery professional familiar with the rules of the state in question.

A. Can a cemetery sell caskets and other funeral merchandise without an additional license.

B. Cemeteries are/are not allowed to sell grave markers monuments or burial vaults.

C. A Cemetery can/cannot own/operate a funeral home or mortuary.

D. Can the funeral home/mortuary be built on cemetery grounds.

E. Can the state levy a tax on undeveloped property- land not yet marked for designated burial spaces.

F. Can the state levy a tax on developed property-space that has been surveyed, designated and marked with grave spaces.

G. Can the state tax spaces where burials have taken place (graves).

H. Reclaiming Abandoned Spaces means that a cemetery may take back previously sold lots that have not been used.

I. Cancellation of a preneed contract means the state has a provision for the cancellation of a preneed contract in addition to the three-day period enforced by the Federal Trade Commission.

J. Sales License. Is a license required to sell cemetery products/services in that state.

K. Are cemetery sales people licensed as Real Estate agents.

L. Solicitation Restriction. Are there laws on who, where or how sales people can solicit.

M. Can Cemeteries sell funeral insurance without a funeral home license.

Chart: Cemetery Laws By State

	A		B		C
STATE	Sell Caskets & Funeral Merchandise	Sell Monuments	Sell Markers	Sell Vaults	Own & Operate Mortuary
1. Alabama	No	Yes	Yes	Yes	Yes
2. Alaska					
3. Arkansas	Yes	Yes	Yes	Yes	Yes
4. Arizona	Yes	Yes	Yes	Yes	Yes
5. California	Yes	Yes	Yes	Yes	Yes
6. Colorado	Yes	Yes	Yes	Yes	Yes
7. Conneticut	Yes	Yes	Yes	Yes	Yes
8. Delaware	Yes	Yes	Yes	Yes	
9. Dist. of Columbia	-	-	-	-	-
10.Florida	Yes	Yes	Yes	Yes	Yes
11.Georgia	Yes	Yes	Yes	Yes	Yes
12.Hawaii	No	Yes	Yes	Yes	Yes
13.Idaho	No	-	Yes	Yes	Yes
14.Illinois	Yes	Yes	Yes	Yes	Yes
15.Indiana	Yes	Yes	Yes	Yes	Yes
16.Iowa	Yes	Yes	Yes	Yes	Yes
17.Kansas	Yes	Yes	Yes	Yes	Yes
18.Kentucky	No	Yes	Yes	Yes	Yes
19.Louisiana	No	Yes	Yes	Yes	Yes
20.Maryland	Yes	Yes	Yes	Yes	No
21.Maine	No	No	Yes	No	
22.Minnesota	Yes	Yes	Yes	Yes	Yes
23.Montana	Yes	Yes	Yes	Yes	Yes
24.Mississippi	-	Yes	Yes	Yes	-
25.Missouri	-	-	-	-	Yes
26.Massachusetts	Yes	Yes	Yes	Yes	No
27.Michigan	Yes	Yes	Yes	Yes	No
28.Nebraska	Yes	Yes	Yes	Yes	Yes
29.Nevada	Yes	Yes	Yes	Yes	Yes
30.New Hamshire	Yes	Yes	Yes	Yes	Yes
31.New Jersey	No	No	No	No	No
32.New Mexico	Yes	Yes	Yes	Yes	Yes
33.New York	No	No	No	No	No
34.North Carolina	No	Yes	Yes	Yes	Yes
35.North Dakota	-	-	-	-	-
36.Ohio	No	Yes	Yes	Yes	No
37.Oklahoma	No	Yes	Yes	Yes	Yes
38.Oregon	Yes	Yes	Yes	Yes	Yes
39.Pennsylvania	Yes	Yes	Yes	Yes	Yes
40.Rhode Island	-	Yes	Yes	-	No
41. South Carolina	No	Yes	Yes	Yes	Yes
42.South Dakota	-	-	-	-	-
43.Tennessee	-	-	-	-	-
44.Texas	No	Yes	Yes	S/Note	Yes
45.Utah	No	Yes	Yes	Yes	Yes
46.Vermont	Yes	Yes	Yes	Yes	Yes
47.Virginia	No	Yes	Yes	Yes	Yes
48.Washington	No	Yes	Yes	Yes	Yes
49.West Virginia	Yes	Yes	Yes	Yes	Yes
50.Wisconsin	Yes	Yes	Yes	Yes	No
51.Wyoming	Yes	Yes	Yes	Yes	Yes

STATE	D On Cemetery Grounds	E Tax Undeveoped Property	F Tax Developed Property	G Tax Graves	H Reclaim Abandoned Spaces
1.Alabama	Yes	Yes	-	-	No
2.Alaska	-	-	-	-	-
3.Arkansas	Yes	Yes	Yes	-	No
4.Arizona	Yes	-	-	Yes	No
5.California	Yes	-	-	-	No
6.Colorado	Yes	-	-	-	No
7.Conneticut	No	No	No	No	Yes
8.Delaware	-	-	-	-	-
9.Dist. of Columbia	-	-	-	-	-
10.Florida	Yes	Yes	Yes	Yes	Yes
11.Georgia	Yes	-	-	-	Yes
12.Hawaii	Yes	Yes	-	-	No
13.Idaho	Yes	Yes	-	Yes	No
14.Illinois	Yes	-	-	-	Yes
15.Indiana	Yes	-	No	No	No
16.Iowa	Yes	-	-	-	Yes
17.Kansas	Yes	-	-	-	No
18.Kentucky	Yes	-	-	-	Yes
19.Louisiana	Yes	-	-	-	No
20.Maryland	-	Yes	Yes	Yes	No
21.Maine	-	No	No	No	Yes
22.Minnesota	Yes	Yes	No	No	Yes
23.Montana	Yes	Yes	-	-	No
24.Mississippi	-	-	-	-	-
25.Missouri	Yes	-	-	-	No
26.Massachusetts	-	No	No	No	Yes
27.Michigan	-	Yes	-	-	Yes
28.Nebraska	Yes	-	-	-	-
29.Nevada	Yes	No	No	No	Yes
30.New Hampshire	No	No	No	No	Yes
31.New Jersey	No	No	No	No	Yes
32.New Mexico	Yes	Yes	Yes	Yes	No
33.New York	No	-	-	-	Yes
34.NorthCarolina	No	Yes	Yes	No	No
35.NorthDakota	-	-	-	-	-
36.Ohio	-	Yes	Yes	-	No
37.Oklahoma	Yes	-	-	-	No
38.Oregon	Yes	Yes	No	No	Yes
39.Pennsylvania	Yes	-	-	-	No
40.Rhode Island	-	Yes	Yes	Yes	Yes
41.SouthCarolina	Yes	-	No	No	No
42.SouthDakota	-	-	-	-	-
43.Tennessee	-	-	-	-	-
44.Texas	Yes	Yes	Yes	No	No
45.Utah	Yes	Yes	Yes	-	Yes
46.Vermont	Yes	-	-	-	-
47.Virginia	Yes	Yes	Yes	Yes	No
48.Washington	Yes	Yes	-	-	Yes
49.WestVirginia	Yes	No	No	No	No
50.Wisconsin	-	-	-	-	Yes
51.Wyoming	Yes	Yes	Yes	-	No

STATE	I Cancel Preneed Contract	J Sales Personnel Licensed	K As Real Estate Agents	L Solicitation Restriction	M Sell Funeral Insurance
1.Alabama	Yes	No	No	No	Yes
2.Alaska	-	-	-	-	-
3.Arkansas	Yes	No	-	No	No
4.Arizona	-	Yes	-	Yes	Yes
5.California	Yes	Yes	No	No	Yes
6.Colorado	Yes	No	-	Yes	Yes
7.Connecticut	Yes	No	No	No	No
8.Delaware	-	-	-	No	No
9.Dist. of Columbia	-	-	-	-	-
10.Florida	Yes	Yes	No	No	No
11.Georgia	Yes	No	-	No	No
12.Hawaii	Yes	No	-	-	Yes
13.Idaho	Yes	Yes	No	No	Yes
14.Illinois	Yes	No	-	Yes	Yes
15.Indiana	Yes	No	-	Yes	Yes
16.Iowa	Yes	Yes	-	No	Yes
17.Kansas	Yes	No	No	Yes	N/A
18.Kentucky	Yes	No	No	No	Yes
19.Louisiana	No	No	-	No	Yes
20.Maryland	Yes	No	-	No	No
21.Maine	Yes	No	-	-	No
22.Minnesota	Yes	Yes	-	None	Yes
23.Montana	No	No	-	No	No
24.Mississippi	-	-	-	-	-
25.Missouri	Yes	No	No	No	Yes
26.Massachususetts	Yes	No	-	-	-
27.Michigan	Yes	No	-	Yes	Yes
28.Nebraska	-	Yes	N/A	Yes	Yes
29.Nevada	Yes	Yes	No	Yes	Yes
30.New Hampshire	Yes	No	-	No	Yes
31.New Jersey	No	Yes	No	No	No
32.New Mexico	Yes	-	-	Yes	N/A
33.New York	Yes	No	No	No	No
34.NorthCarolina	Yes	Yes	No	Yes	N/A
35.NorthDakota	-	-	-	-	-
36.Ohio	Yes	Yes	Yes	No	Yes
37.Oklahoma	No	No	-	No	Yes
38.Oregon	Yes	Yes	No	Yes	Yes
39.Pennsylvania	Yes	Yes	No	No	Yes
40.Rhode Island	Yes	No	-	No	No
41.South Carolina	No	No	-	Yes	No
42.South Dakota	-	No	-	Yes	-
43.Tennessee	-	-	-	-	N/A
44.Texas	No	No	Yes	Yes	Yes
45.Utah	Yes	Yes	No	No	No
46.Vermont	Yes	No	No	Yes	Yes
47.Virginia	Yes	No	No	No	–
48.Washington	Yes	No	No	Yes	No
49.West Virginia	No	No	-	No	Yes
50. Wisconsin	Yes	Yes	No	No	No
51.Wyoming	Yes	Yes	-	No	Yes

Summary Of Rules And Regulations
(Pertaining To Chart)

Alaska- No Licensing
District Of Columbia - No Licensing
Texas- Note: can only sell vaults at time of need, not before.

Governing Body Over Cemeteries
(By State)

1. Alabama: Alabama Department Of Insurance
201 Monroe Street, Suite 1700
Montgomery, Alabama 36104
334-241-4190

2. Alaska: None

3. Arizona: Arizona Department Of Real Estate
2910 North 44th Street Suite 100
Phoenix, Arizona 85018
602-468-1414

4. Arkansas: Arkansas Securities Department
201 E. Markham Street, Suite 300
Little Rock, Arkansas, 72201
501-324-9260

5. California: Department of Consumer Affairs
Cemetery And Funeral Bureau
400 R Street, Suite 3040
Sacramento, Calf. 95814
916-322-7737

6. Colorado: Colorado Division Of Insurance
1560 Broadway, Suite 850
Denver, Co. 80202
303-894-7475

7. Conneticut: Department of Public Health
P.O. Box 340308
Hartford, Conn. 06134 / 203-566-1039

8. Delaware: None
9. Dist. Col.: None
10. Florida: Department of Banking And Finance
Bureau of Funeral & Cemetery Service
101 E. Gaines St., Suite 636
Tallahassee, Fl. 32399
850-410-9843
11. Georgia: Georgia Secretary of State
Securities And Business Regulation Division
2 Martin Luther King Jr. Drive
West Tower, Suite 802
Atlanta, Ga. 30334
404-651-9420
12. Hawaii: State Department of Commerce & Consumer Affairs/Cemetery & Funeral Trust Program
P.O. Box 3469
Honolulu, Hawaii 96801
808-586-2694
13. Idaho: Department Of Finance Securities Bureau
P.O. Box 83720
Boise, Idaho 83720
208-332-8000
14. Illinois: Office Of Comptroller
Cemetery Care & Burial Trust
100 W. Randolph Street
Chicago, Ill. 60601
312-814-5921
15. Indiana: State Board Of Funeral & Cemetery Service
302 West Washington Street
Indianapolis, Indiana 46204
317-232-7215
16. Iowa: Iowa Securities Bureau, Regulated Industries Unit
304 Maple Street
Des Moines, Ia. 50319
515-281-4441

17. Kansas: Kansas Secretary Of State
120 SW 10th Avenue
Topeka, Kansas 66612
785-296-6187

18. Kentucky: Funeral & Cemetery Section:
Attorney General's Office
1024 Capitol Center Drive, Suite 200
Frankfurt, Ky. 40601
502-696-5389

19. Louisiana: Louisiana Cemetery Board
2901 Ridgelake Drive, Suite 101
Metarie, La. 70002
504-838-5289

20. Maine: Department Of Human Services
Division Of Health Engineering
State House St. # 10
Augusta, ME. 04333
207-287-5686

21. Maryland: Department of Labor,Licensing and Regulation
Attorney General's Office
500 North Calvert Street, Suite 406
Baltimore, MD. 21202
410-230-6143

22. Michigan: Department of Consumer & Industry Services
Cemetery Regulation
P.O. Box 30018
Lansing, Mich. 48909
517-241-9252

23. Minnesota: Assistant Attorney General-
Civil Enforcement & Consumer Services Division
1400 NCL Tower
St. Paul, MN 55101
651-296-1006

24. Mississippi: None

25. Mass.: None

26. Missouri: Missouri Division Of Professional Registration;
Office of Endowment Care
P.O. Box 1335
Jefferson City, Mo. 65102
573-751-0849
27. Montana: None
28. Nebraska: Nebraska Department of Insurance
941 O Street, Suite 400
Lincoln, NE. 68508
402-471-3580
29. Nevada: Board of Cemetery & Crematory Operators
4894 Lone Mountain Road, Suite 186
Las Vegas, NV 89130
702-646-6860
30. N. Hamp.: Bureau Of Vital Records
6 Hazen Drive
Concord, NH 03301
603-271-4505
31. N. Jersey: New Jersey Cemetery Board
P.O. Box 45036
Newark N.J. 07101
973-504-6553
32. N. Mexico: Financial Institutions Division,
Regulation And Licensing Department
725 Michael S. Drive
Santa Fe, NM 87504
505-827-7104
33. New York: New York Department Of State,
Division of Cemeteries
123 William Street
New York, N.Y. 10038
212-417-2322
34. N. Car.: North Carolina Cemetery Commission
1100 Navaho Drive, GL-2
Raleigh N.C. 27609 / 919-981-2536

35. N. Dakota: North Dakota Department of Health
600 East Blvd. Avenue
Bismark, N.D. 58505
701-328-2372

36. Ohio: Ohio Division Of Real Estate, Cemetery Section
77 South High Street
Columbus, Ohio 43266

37. Oklahoma: Oklahoma State Banking Department
4545 North Lincoln Blvd., Suite 164
Oklahoma City, OK. 73105
405-521-2782

38. Oregon: Oregon state Cemetery And Mortuary Board
800 Northeast Oregon Street, Suite 430
Portland, OR 97232
503-731-4040

39. Penn.: Penn. State Real Estate Commission
P.O. Box 2649
Harrisburg, PA 17105
717-783-3658

40. R. Island: None

41. S. Carolina: None

42. S. Dakota: None

43. Tennessee: Department of Commerce & Insurance
Burial Services
500 James Robertson Parkway, 2nd Floor
Nashville, Tenn. 37243
615-741-5062

44. Texas: Texas Department of Banking
1201 North Watson Road
Arlington, TX. 76006
817-640-4215

45. Utah: Dept. of Occupational & Professional Licensing
P.O. Box 146741
Salt Lake City, UT 84114
801-530-6511

46. Virginia: Cemetery Board Department of Professional
& Occupational Regulation
3600 West Broad Street,
Richmond, Va. 23230
804-367-2039

47. Vermont: None

48. Wash.: Dept. of Licensing, Funeral & Cemetery Unit
P.O. Box 9012
Olympia, WA. 98507
360-664-1528

49. W. Virginia: Attorney General's Consumer Protection Division
P.O. Box 1789
Charleston, WV. 25301
304-558-8986

50. Wisconsin: Wisconsin Division Of Board Services
P.O. Box 8935
Madison, WI 53708
608-266-5439

51. Wyoming: Wyoming Insurance Department
Herschler Building, 122 West 25th St.
Cheyenne, WY 82002
307-777-6884

Glossary

A

Aftercare- Any and all services provided by a funeral home and/or cemetery that occur after final disposition.

At Need- Arrangements that are made concerning a decedent at the time of need.

Air Seal-A type of burial vault that utilizes air pressure created by placing the dome of the vault onto the base of the vault.

Affinity-a relationship by kinship or other bond or purpose.

Acknowledgement Cards-note cards with accompanying mailing envelopes that are sent to friends and/or family members after services to thank them for providing help.

Alternative Container-a non-metal receptacle that is used for cremation, shipping or other means to encase human remains.

Air Tray-a transfer container consisting of a wooden tray and cardboard covering used for shipping caskets on commercial airlines.

Autopsy- a post mortem examination of a deceased human remains for the purpose of ascertaining the cause of death.

B

Burial Policy- a contract purchased for purpose of funds being paid to the beneficiary at the time of death to cover the funeral and/or burial expenses.

Bookmarks- Obituary that is cut out and laminated as a keepsake for family/friends of a decedent.

Bereavement- feelings/emotions felt by survivor of one who has passed away.

Bequest- a disposition by will of property.

Bereavement Fare- a discounted rate given by airlines to those flying to attend funeral services.

Burial Transit Permit- a legal document issued by a governmental agency authorizing transport and/or disposition of deceased.

Burial- earth or ground interment of deceased human remains.

C

Cremated Remains- the particles remaining after the cremation process. Usually a powdery substance of ashes.

Columbarium- a niche or space within a building or structure intended for the placement of cremated remains.

Cemetery Set Up- includes but not limited to the tent, chairs, placement carpet and lowering devise for accommodating a graveside or committal service.

Clergy- an ordained person in a sect or religion.

Catacombs-an underground cemetery.

Companion Marker- a cemetery grave monument made for two persons buried side by side (husband and wife).

Cash Advance- an item or items on a contract for purchasing funeral services that is obtained on the purchaser's behalf by the funeral home.

Cenotaph-a memorial marker or plaque that is erected to the memory of a dead person who is not buried on the site.

Committal Service- portion of funeral services that is held at the place of burial or final disposition of the deceased person.

Coach- a funeral vehicle that is used for transporting casketed remains. Formerly known as a hearse.

Coroner- a public officer whose chief duty is to investigate a death.

Cadaver-dead human body used for medical research or human anatomy.

Combination Unit- Alternative container made of particle board/cardboard tray used to comply with air shipment regulations.

Casket-container for deceased human remains made of wood, metal, or fiberglass in which deceased is placed in prior to disposition.

Coffin-an anthropoidal shaped case or receptacle for deceased human remains.

Casket Insert- a cardboard or fiberboard box for deceased that is placed inside a rental casket for viewing or service then can be removed with deceased and placed into cremation retort.

Cremation Container- an alternative container that is used for intended purpose of encasing a deceased human remains in for cremation.

Cremation- the irreversible process of reducing human remains to bone fragments through extreme heat and evaporation.

Cryonics-the controlled storage of a deceased human remains for an undefined period of time for the purpose of waiting for medical science to discover a cure to the disease causing death so that the cure when discovered can be applied to the remains.

Crypt- a burial space that is above ground or designed to be final resting place without an outer burial container.

Cemetery- grounds designated for purpose of burying deceased human remains. May be either public or private.

D

Disinterment- Removal of deceased remains after burial or disposition of deceased.

Death Notice- an announcement of the death of a person in a newspaper or other publication.

Discharge Papers- papers issued by the military branch of service providing that one has served in the armed forces.

Dedo- A photograph of the person(s) buried in a cemetery or other space imprinted upon the marker/headstone or monument.

Dummy Set-Up- the tent, chairs and other items used for a graveside or committal service at a cemetery or place of final disposition where the set up is not located directly at the burial space/niche, etc.

Donation To Science- a deceased human remains body that is given to a medical school or other institution for purpose(s) of research, medical education or harvesting of body organs or parts.

Death Certificate- a legal document filed with a governmental bureau that is the official record of death used for tracking vital statistics; a permanent legal record of the fact of the death of a person.

Direct Burial (Immediate Disposition)- the disposition of a deceased human remains without rites or ceremonies at the burial site or elsewhere.

E

Escorts- uniformed personnel either private or publicly hired for purpose of leading a funeral procession safely from place of service to place of disposition.

Exhumation- a legally ordered disinterment of a dead human body for purpose of investigating question(s) about the manner of death after burial has taken place.

Estate- all the personal and real property that was owned by a deceased person.

Eulogy- a message delivered by clergy or other person summarizing facts about the deceased life.

Embalmer- person licensed by a state board to chemically treat a dead human body for purposes of disinfection and preservation.

Epitaph- an inscription upon a marker or monument making a statement about the deceased person that is buried there.

Entombment- final disposition of a deceased human remains into a mausoleum or other above ground tomb.

F

Floral Tributes- Flowers that are ordered and sent to funeral home as a token of concern and sympathy for one who has passed away.

Full Couch Casket- casket in which the entire lid opens and closes as a whole (Head end and Foot end open and close as one).

Final Disposition- the end destination of dead human body such as a cemetery, crematory, burial at sea, etc.

Federal Trade Commission- Executive entity of the U.S.

Government that issues and enforces rules and regulations within the Department of Commerce.

First Call- Initial contact between the family of deceased and the funeral home concerning discussion of death and communication of family's wishes to funeral director.

Funeral Director- person licensed by a state to procure and carry out the disposition of deceased human remains.

Forwarding Funeral Home- mortuary that is in charge of sending/shipping human remains to the funeral home that will handle final disposition.

Food Register- a book that is given to the family to be used to record and track food containers brought to the family's house.

Funeral Service- a ritual or ceremony of remembrance held for friends and/or family of decedent with the decedent's remains present.

Forwarding Case- Shipment/transport of remains to another funeral home.

Flag Case- a permanent encasement for placing a folded flag into for display and safekeeping.

Funeral Home (Mortuary)- place where planning, viewing, visitation and services/merchandise are bought and procured for deceased human remains.

FTC- abbreviation for Federal Trade Commission.

G

Grave Service- agent or contractor of a cemetery that handles digging graves, setting up tent, chairs, etc. and then handles the take down and closing of the grave.

Grief Material- Literature consisting of books, papers, periodicals, tapes, videos or other media that addresses issues of dealing with and overcoming grief.

Graveside- a service that is held at the burial site of the deceased.

Grave Space-ground in a cemetery intended to be used for ground burial.

Grave Liner- a box, container or other enclosure that is placed around the casket to insulate it from surrounding dirt/ground.

H

Honorarium- a check or other payment that is given to a minister, musician or other participant as a gratuity for performing a service.

Half Couch Casket- Casket in which the lid is cut in half where the top can open in such a manner that deceased can be viewed from waist up with the half from waist down remaining closed.

I

Inquest - a judicial or official investigation, inquiry or examination regarding a death.

Insured Plan- a policy where benefits are payable to the funeral or beneficiary of a deceased person for funeral/burial expenses.

Inurnment- burial or entombment/innichement of cremated remains for final disposition.

Indigent Case- situation where the family of a decedent and decedent's estate cannot produce financial resources to cover burial expenses.

Internet Archive- obituary or death notice that is placed onto a computer generated program allowing it to be viewed on an Internet website.

Immediate Disposition (Direct Burial)- interment of deceased human remains without rites or ceremonies.

Interment- final disposition by ground burial.

K

Keepsake Box-a small enclosed receptacle used to keep personal effects and/or belongings of a deceased person.

L

Livery Items- transportation vehicles used in funeral service such as hearse/coach, limousine, flower van and other rolling stock.

Lowering Devise- Grave equipment that a casket or other container encasing remains is placed upon over the grave before burial.

Lead Car- automobile that the funeral director in charge of a service/ceremony drives in the course of conducting the service.

Lawn Crypt- preplaced chamber that is constructed of reinforced concrete either side by side or multi-depth.

M

Mortuary Law-local, state, or federal ordinances or statutes that governs the funeral industry.

Memorial Park- cemetery that does not have or allow the use of upright markers or monuments in all or some sectors.

Mortician- a state licensed funeral director and embalmer (usually possesses both or a dual license).

Medical Examiner- a public official whose main function is to investigate death when a physician is not in attendance or the law requires a review or inquest.

Memorial Service- a ceremony or formal ritual where the deceased body/remains is not present.

Minimum Service Fee- a charge levied by most funeral homes to cover the professional services of the funeral director and staff.

Music Card- a thank you/acknowledgement card to be given to a soloist, vocalist or other musician for performing at a funeral or memorial service.

Marker (Monument)- a structure made of marble, granite, bronze or other stone or metal placed at the burial place to commemorate one's life.

Mausoleum- a building with several crypts for entombment.

Mortuary- place of business used in the care, planning and

preparation for final disposition of human remains including but not limited to arranging and conducting funerals, sales of services and funeral merchandise and embalming.

N

Niche- place for putting cremated remains.

Notarization- the act of acknowledging and/or authenticating a document or instrument by a state authorized public servant for purposes of proving that the party(ies) who procured the document/instrument are genuine.

O

Obituary- a news item communicating the death of a person usually containing a biographical sketch.

Options- ability to make choices between different alternatives.

Opening & Closing- The process of making an interment that includes marking burial space, digging grave, lowering casket into ground, and filling the grave back with dirt.

Outer Burial Container- any durable container made for purpose of being placed around the casket in a grave.

Organ Donation- process where certain internal organs of a human body are harvested for the benefit of others who are in need of them.

P

Pre Need- before or prior to death or an imminent death.

Perpetual Care- endowment for the ongoing/future maintenance of a cemetery, memorial park or other burial grounds.

Postlude- music played at the close of a service, usually when family of deceased and others in attendance are walked out.

Prelude- music played at beginning of a service when family is walked in and seated.

Personalization- a method of creating a service, monument,

memento or other tangible or intangible remembrance unique to the deceased.

Postal Regulations- U.S. Government mailing rules/regulations procedures that must be followed in mailing cremated remains.

Personal Planning Guide- a booklet or folder issued by a funeral home or cemetery with information to be used in planning one's funeral and/or burial.

Processional- the orderly ritual at the beginning of a service where the Funeral Director or usher walks family into place of service and seats them.

Pallbearer- one who helps to carry the casket at a funeral.

Potter's Field- Section of a cemetery for the poor.

Prearrangement- a planned funeral that has been completed by an individual prior to death.

Predeveloped- designated areas or buildings within a cemetery that have been mapped and planned for future construction but are not completed.

R

Rubbing- the practice of using wax paper and a sponge to duplicate the surface inscription of a marker/headstone onto the paper.

Receiving Case- service where a funeral home receives a case from another funeral director for disposition.

Receiving Funeral Home- Funeral home that is recipient of case from another funeral home.

Retort- the chamber in a crematory that procures the cremation process.

Refrigeration- a cooling unit that is used to keep dead human remains that are not embalmed to inhibit and slow decomposition.

Restoration- the art of building, creating or constructing the viewable features of a deceased body to a more life-like appearance for viewing purposes.

Register Book/Memorial Book- a book used to record signatures of those who attended services and/or visitation for one being mourned.

Rental Casket- a casket that is used to have a service/ceremony for one who is to be cremated or in which final disposition is to take place using a more permanent receptacle.

Recessional- process of escorting those attending a funeral/memorial ceremony out of the chapel or place of service at the end of the ceremony.

S

Stateroom- a room or space inside a funeral home or mortuary where the deceased is placed for viewing and/or visitation for family and friends.

Support Benefits- items or services of value that are available to families that help them after disposition such as counseling, estate settlement, etc.

Selection Room- room or space in funeral home where merchandise such as caskets, urns, burial garments, etc. are displayed.

Sundry Items- Merchandise available for sale to families such as register book, service programs, acknowledgement cards, etc.

Space Flagging- the task of locating a grave that is to be dug for purpose of staking a marking flag in ground so that cemetery digging crew will know which grave to open.

Service Folders- Handouts/programs/bulletins that ushers at a funeral/memorial ceremony pass out to people attending the service.

State Board- commission/entity empowered by a state government to oversee and regulate an industry/profession such as funeral service.

Sexton- the superintendent of a cemetery or memorial park.

T

Trust Plan- a prearranged funeral contract that is not insured (the balance that is unpaid at the time of death is due).

Travel Protection Plan- a contract that is bought from a funeral provider calling for the provider to arrange and handle all aspects and details of one's death if death takes place away from home while traveling, in exchange for payment.

Tombstone- marker or monument marking a grave space in a cemetery

U

Utility Vehicle- a van, suburban automobile or other livery that is used for purpose of procuring some facet of services rendered.

Urn- a receptacle for placing cremated remains into such as bronze, metal, wood, porcelain, plastic, cardboard, etc.

Undertaker- outdated term for funeral director/embalmer or mortician.

Urn Vault- outer container of metal or concrete that a cremation urn is placed in when ground burial is desired.

V

Vault Installation- process of placing a burial vault of concrete or steel into an opened grave for casket to be placed in.

Viewing- act of seeing a deceased body that is laid out for identification purposes or for visitation or funeral ceremony.

Vital Statistics- Biographical information including but not limited to name, age, date of birth, death, birthplace, social security number, etc.

Visitation/wake- a time for a family to meet with one another and friends/visitors to talk and visit and share memories related to the decedent.

Vault- outer burial container made of steel or concrete that the casket is placed into for purpose of insulating it from surrounding elements.

W

Wake- see visitation

Z

Ziegler Case- a gasket sealed container that is used as an insert into a shipping container.

NOTES/BIBLIOGRAPHY

Chapter 1

1) SCI Annual Report, 2002

2) SCI Annual Report, 2002

3) American Funeral Director Magazine, June,2003, page 56.

4) Federal Trade Commission's: Funerals: A Consumer Guide, October 22, 2002, page 7.

5) He Says, She Says. Who Holds The Right To Disposition; October, 1998, The Director Magazine. T. Scott Gilligan with Kepley, Gilligan and Eyrich Law Firm, Cincinnati, Ohio

6) Growth Industry, Warren St. John, The New York Times as printed in the Sunday, September 28, 2003 Fort Worth Star Telegram.

7) Funerals: A Consumers Guide, FTC- Facts For Consumers, page 5 # 3, Cash Advances.

Chapter 2

1) Internal Revenue Service Code 501 (c) 13 covers entities exempt from income taxes which include cemetery companies owned and operated for benefit of its members or not operated for profit.

2) A Cemetery Should Be Forever, page 160 by John F. Llewellyn, Tropico Press 1998.

3) Ibid, page 267

4) Veterans Administration VA Form 40-1330, Marker/Headstone information.

5) American Cemetery Association (Lot Exchange program).

6) Mortuary Law, chapter 8, pages 49-53; T.S. Gilligan, Thomas Stueve, Cincinnati Foundation for Mortuary Education, 1995.

7) Ibid, p. 53

Chapter 3

1) A Cemetery Should Be Forever, page 65, by John Llewellyn, Tropico Press, 1998

2) Scattering Series Biodegradable Urns, Batesville Casket Company- Options Division, Batesville, Indiana

3) United Network For Organ Sharing, P.O. Box 28010, Richmond, Virginia 23228

4) DNA Connections, 1812 University Blvd., Tuscaloosa, Alabama, 35401

5) Minnesota Joins Florida, Michigan To Allow Bodies To Be Dissolved. American Funeral Director Magazine, September, 2003, pages 14, 16.

Chapter 4

1) Our Unspoken Language. Using Symbols To Create More Meaningful Memorials, Mike Fernandez, International Cemetery And Funeral Magazine, September, 1997, page 12.

Chapter 5

1) Preneed Bill Of Rights; National Funeral Directors Association, Milwaukee Wisconsin

Chapter 7

1) How To Go On Living When Someone You Love Dies, page 137. Therese A. Rando, PhD.

2) Restorative Art, J. Sheridan Mayer, page 20.

3) Grief Counseling And Therapy Handbook, J. William Worden.

Chapter 9

1) Refrigeration, World Book Encyclopedia, Volume 16, page 193.

2) The History Of American Funeral Directing, Chapter 9, page 233. Robert Habenstein and William H. Lamers.

Index

D

E

F

G

H

I

J

K

L

M

N

O

P

Q

R

S

T

U

V

W

Y

Z

Personal Planning Guide

TABLE OF CONTENTS

Introduction

The entire purpose of this book has been to give you information that will help you face and properly deal with one of life's most difficult yet inevitable responsibilities.

The last pages are therefore set forth for the recording of personal information for yourself, a spouse or other loved one either before death occurs or when the shock of one's passing does occur so that the data needed for obituaries, death certificates, service arrangements, etc. will be in place and therefore alleviate an additional burden of having to search, dig, or find information when needed.

It is suggested that you complete the following pages and put in a familiar place that is accessible to your designated next-of-kin and/or other person to handle your final arrangements.

Feel free to photocopy and use these pages for different family members as your status and situation- current or expected- may dictate.

Vital Statistics

Name: ____
First Middle Last Nickname

Date Of Birth: ______________ Birthplace: ______________________
Month/Day/Year City State Country

Sex: __Male __Female Race: ______________________

Marital Status: __Single __Married __Widowed __Divorced

Social Security/Govt. I.D. #: ______________________

Resident Address: ______________________________________
Street City State Zip

Mailing Address: ______________________________________
Designate City State Zip

Occupation: __________ Business/Industry: ______________

Education (Last Grade/Level Completed In School): __________

Veteran Of Armed Forces? __Yes __No Branch: _____

Father's Full Name: ______________________________________
First Middle Last

Mother's Full Name: ______________________________________
First Middle Maiden

Father's Date Of Birth: ______________ Birthplace: __________
Month/Day/Year

Mother's Date Of Birth: ______________ Birthplace: __________
Month/Day/Year

Spouse's Full Name: ______________________________________
First Middle Last

Spouse's Date Of Birth: ______________ Birthplace: __________
Month/Day/Year

Spouse's Social Security/ID# ______________________________

Vital Statistics Notes/Comments: ______________________

____

Date Of Marriage: ______________ Place: ______________________
Month/Date/Year City/State/Country

Married By: __________ Married Previously: __Yes __No
Name of Minister

Children

Name	Date of Birth	Place of Birth

1. ____
2. ____
3. ____
4. ____
5. ____

Medical History

Doctor's Name: ____________ Phone Number: ____________

Has Been Primary Care Doctor Since: ___ Other Doctor Y N

Conditions Treated For: Alzheimers Y N Cancer Y N

Circulation Problems Y N Diabeties Y N

Heart Y N Kidney Y N

Respritory Problems Y N Tumor(s) Y N

Other Problem(s)/Conditions: ____________

____

Any Allergies: Y N If Yes, Explain: ____________

____

Prescription Medications Taken: ____________

____

Any Non Prescription Medicines Taken on routine Basis: Y N

If Yes, Explain: ____________

____

Medical History Notes/Comments: ____________

____

____

____

____

Eulogy/Obituary Information

Name (As It Should Appear): ______________________________

Residence (City/Town/Province): ___________________________

Schools Attended: Name Place Year(s)

1. ____

2. ____

3. ____

4. ____

5. ____

School/Education/Academic Achievements,Awards,Citations,etc.:

____

____

School Activities, Clubs, etc.: ______________________________

____

Place of Employment: ______________________________
Company Name Location Years

Civic Activities: ______________________________

Awards/Citations: ______________________________

Name of Spouse (As It Should Appear): ____________________

Childrens Names:

1. ____________________ 2. ____________________

3. ____________________ 4. ____________________

5. ____________________ Others: ____________________

____

Clubs, Memberships, Other Activities: ____________________

____

Other Notable Achievements/Accomplishments: ______________

____

Prior Residence(s) (City/Town/Province): __________________

____

Previous Employment: ____
Company Location Years

Experiences To Share

Childhood: ____

____

Adolescence: ____

____

Adulthood: ____

____

Things I Have Enjoyed In Life: ______________________________

____

Favorite Hobbies/Pastimes: ______________________________

Proudest Family Moment: ______________________________

Favorite Song(s): ______________________________

Favorite Book(s): ______________________________

Favorite Movie(s): ______________________________

Favorite Quote/Saying: ______________________________

Fondest Memory: ______________________________

If I Could Live Life Over Again, I Would ______________________

Do More: ________________ Do Less: ________________

Special Stories or Experiences you would like shared by certain individuals:

Name: ________________ Story/Experience: ________________

Name: ________________ Story/Experience: ________________

Name: ________________ Story/Experience: ________________

Other Notes/Comments: ______________________________

____

____

Funeral/Memorial Service Instructions

Funeral Home/Mortuary Preferred: ______________________
Name

____
Street Address City State Phone #

Pre-Arranged With This Firm: __Y __N, If Yes, When: ______

Place Of Service Desired: ______________ Public/Private

Religious Preference: ________ Active Member: __Y __N

Name of Minister/Clergy/Celebrant/Other Desired: ________

Phone #: __________ Alternative Phone: ____________

Organizations(s) To Participate (Military/Fraternal/Lodge/Social/ Religious/Other): ______________________________

Other Individuals To Participate: ______________________
Name Phone #

______________ ______________________________
Duty To Perform; Name Phone Duty

Flag: __Y __N If Yes, Present Flag to: ____________

Rosary/Vigil Service: Yes No; Location: ______________

Officiant Desired: ____________________________________
Name Phone

Wake/Visitation Desired: Yes No Location: __________

Viewing Instructions (Open/Closed Casket, Public/Private): ____

____

Clothing Preference(Buy New or Current Wardrobe): ________

Description/Color: ____________________________________

Clothing Accessories (Tie/Scarf/Belt/Sweater/Vest/Shoes, etc.):

____

Jewelery To Wear (Eyeglasses, Pin(s), Watch, Rings): ________

____

Stay On/Return To: ____________________________________
Name Relationship

Casket Desired: ______________________________________
Name Exterior(Color/Material)

____
Interior (Color/Material)

Floral Preference: ____________________________________
Type/Color/Description/Number (Qty)

Items/Possessions To Display At Visitation: ______________

____

At Service/Ceremony: ______

Music (Background At Visitation/Wake): ______

Music For Service, Song Selections: ______

______

Reading For Service, Source: ______

______

Film/Slides/Video To Show: ______

Service Folders Preference: ______
Front Interior Back

Other Special Instructions Concerning Services: ______

______

Newspaper Notices: ______
Name of Publication City/State

______
Other Paper/Pub. City/St. Other Paper/Pub. City/St.

Memorial Donations:

______
Name of Organization Address City/State

______
Name Of Organization Address City/State

______
Name of Organization Address City/State

Names Of Active Pallbearers: ______
Name Phone #

______
Name Phone # Name Phone #

______
Name Phone # Name Phone #

______
Name Phone # Alternate Name Phone #

Desired Honorary Pallbearers:

______
Name Phone # Name Phone #

______
Name Phone # Name Phone #

Disposition of Flowers Received For Service: ______

______

Other Notes/Comments concerning Funeral/Memorial Services:

______

Additional Information

I am an Organ Donor: __Yes __No; If Yes, Name/Address/Phone # of Donee: ______

Institution: ______ Contact Name: ______

I Have A Living Will: __Yes __No; If Yes, Location: ______

I Have A Designated Power of Attorney: __Yes __No; If Yes, Name/Address/Phone#/Relationship: ______

Other Notes/Comments: ______

______

Final Disposition Instructions

Cemetery/Memorial Park/Final Resting Place Preferred:

______

Name Address City/State Phone

Pre-Arranged With Preferred Provider: __Yes __No

Final Disposition Preference: Ground Burial Lawn Crypt
Mausoleum Niche (Cremation)
Scattering(Crem.) Other (Desc.):

Description of Property (If Owned):

______

Space/Crypt Lot/Tier Block/Level Other Desc

Outer Burial Container Required: __Yes __No

Is Container Already Pre-selected: __Yes __No

Description Of Outer Container: ______

Material Color Emblem Inscription

Description of Permanent Memorial: __Bronze __Granite __Marble __Other (Describe): ______

Is Memorial Pre-Selected: __Yes __No

Placement Of Memorial: __Flat __Upright __Single __Companion

Memorial Inscription Instructions: ______

______

Name (As It Should Read On Memorial): ____________________

Other Inscription Information Desired: ____________________

Emblem(s) or Other Markings/Symbols Desired: ____________________

If Cremation, What Type of Cremains Container is desired:

__Urn __Keepsake Memorial __Other (Describe): ____________

Urn/Receptacle Description: ____________________

Additional Remarks/Special Instructions: ____________________

Family to witness Final Resting Place Closing: __Yes __No

Non-Family To witness: __Yes __No __Public __Private

Flowers/Other Articles to be placed on/at Grave/Final Resting Place:

__Yes __No Describe: ____________________

Family Members And Relatives To Contact

1. Name ____________ Relationship ____________
   Address ____________ Phone Number ____________
2. Name ____________ Relationship ____________
   Address ____________ Phone Number ____________
3. Name ____________ Relationship ____________
   Address ____________ Phone Number ____________
4. Name ____________ Relationship ____________
   Address ____________ Phone Number ____________
5. Name ____________ Relationship ____________
   Address ____________ Phone Number ____________

Friends And Others To Contact

1. Name ____________ Phone Number ____________
2. Name ____________ Phone Number ____________
3. Name ____________ Phone Number ____________

4. Name ____________________ Phone Number ______________
5. Name ____________________ Phone Number ______________
6. Name ____________________ Phone Number ______________
7. Name ____________________ Phone Number ______________
8. Name ____________________ Phone Number ______________
9. Name ____________________ Phone Number ______________

Other Contacts

Attorney	Address	Phone
Physician	Address	Phone
Accountant	Address	Phone
Minister	Address	Phone
Employer	Address	Phone
Executor/Executrix	Address	Phone

Organizations To Contact

1. Name ________________ Address ____________________
   Phone #________________ Contact Person ______________
2. Name ________________ Address ____________________
   Phone #________________ Contact Person ______________
3. Name ________________ Address ____________________
   Phone #________________ Contact Person ______________
4. Name ________________ Address ____________________
   Phone #________________ Contact Person ______________
5. Name ________________ Address ____________________
   Phone #________________ Contact Person ______________
6. Name ________________ Address ____________________
   Phone #________________ Contact Person ______________

Location Of Important Papers

Document	Dated	Location
Birth Certificate		
Marriage License		
Military Discharge		
Adoption Certificate		
Divorce Papers		
Graduation Diploma		
Degrees-College, Other		
Contractual Agreements		
Deeds/Titles		
Mortgages/Notes		
Stocks/Bonds		
Insurance Policies		
Last Will & Testament		
Anatomical Gift Papers		
Income Tax Return		
Bank, Other Accounts		
Purchase/Sale Agreements		
Title Abstracts		
Immigration Papers		
Baptismal Certificate		
Auto Registration		
Social Security Benefit Statement		
Other(s) (Describe):		

Financial Information

Status Of: ______________________
Your Name

As Of: ______________________
Month Day Year

Assets

Cash On Hand ______

Cash In Bank ______

Savings Account(s) ______

Amounts Owed You ______

Other Receivables ______

Furniture/Fixtures ______

Auto(s)/Vehicle(s) ______

Stocks/Bonds ______

Other Securities $ ______

Credit Union ______

Business Interests ______

Trust/Estates ______

Other Personal Property ______

House/Real Estate ______

Life Insurance Policy(ies) ______

401K/Retirement Accounts ______

Total Assets: ______

Liabilities

Utilities Payable ______

Credit Cards Payable ______

Mortgage Balance ______

Taxes Due ______

Other Payables ______

Bank Loans ______

Other Debts ______

Total Liabilities: ______

Total Assets

- Total Liabilities: ______

Total Equity/Liabilities: ______

Notes/Comments On Financial Information: ______

____

Valuable Assets Inventory

(Other than Real Estate)

	Article/ Item	Date Acquired	Purchase Price Or Market Value When Acquired	Location	Please Give To:
1.					
2.					
3.					
4.					
5.					
6.					
7.					
8.					
9.					
10.					

List Of Insurance Policies

	Company Name	Company Address	Company Phone #	Type of Policy	Policy Number	Amount	Beneficiary
1.							
2.							
3.							
4.							
5.							
6.							
7.							

Notes/Comments: ______________________________

____

List Of Bank/Other Accounts

	Account Issuer	Account Number	Type of Account	Issuer Address	Issuer Phone #
1.					
2.					
3.					
4.					
5.					
6.					
7.					

List Of Real Estate Holdings

	Property Description	Address	Location of Title
1.			
2.			
3.			
4.			
5.			
6.			
7.			
8.			
9.			

Notes/Comments: ______________________________

____

Estate Instructions

Special Instructions